Microsoft®
Publisher 2000
by Design

Luisa Simone

Microsoft Press

PUBLISHED BY
Microsoft Press
A Division of Microsoft Corporation
One Microsoft Way
Redmond, Washington 98052-6399

Library of Congress Cataloging-in-Publication Data
Simone, Luisa, 1955-
    Microsoft Publisher 2000 by Design / Luisa Simone.
      p. cm.
    Includes index.
    ISBN 1-57231-953-4
    1. Microsoft Publisher. 2. Desktop publishing. I. Title.
  Z253.532.M53S58 1999
  686.2'25445369--dc21   98-48181
                                                      CIP

Printed and bound in the United States of America.

1 2 3 4 5 6 7 8 9 WCWC   4 3 2 1 0 9

Distributed in Canada by Penguin Books Canada Limited.

A CIP catalogue record for this book is available from the British Library.

Microsoft Press books are available through booksellers and distributors worldwide. For further information about international editions, contact your local Microsoft Corporation office or contact Microsoft Press International directly at fax (425) 936-7329. Visit our Web site at mspress.microsoft.com.

TrueType fonts is a registered trademark of Apple Computer, Inc. Kodak is a registered trademark of Eastman Kodak Company. All rights reserved. ActiveX, Microsoft, Microsoft Press, the Microsoft Press logo, MSN, Picture It!, and Windows are either registered trademarks or trademarks of Microsoft Corporation in the United States and/or other countries.

The example companies, organizations, products, people, and events depicted herein are fictitious. No association with any real company, organization, product, person, or event is intended or should be inferred.

Acquisitions Editors: Kim Fryer, Christey Bahn
Project Editor: Anne Taussig
Editorial Assistant: Kristen Weatherby

To my husband, Bob Obrinsky, for his patience, encouragement, and love

Contents

Part 2 Design Projects

Acknowledgements

The book you hold in your hand—and indeed any book—is a collaborative work with many contributors. For this, the sixth edition of *Microsoft Publisher by Design,* I was pleased to work with a dedicated and professional group of editors and designers.

Sybil Ihrig of Helios Productions and Anne Taussig of Microsoft Press coordinated all of the disparate elements that make up this book and supervised all of the disparate people (located across the country) who worked on it. I have equal appreciation for their patience and their problem-solving skills.

I can only describe the technical editor, Greg Guntle, and copy editor, Kathy Borg-Todd, as an editorial safety net. Their attention to detail and thorough proofing of the manuscript have made this edition more accurate and readable than it would have been otherwise. Indispensable technical support was also provided by the Microsoft Publisher and Microsoft Office development teams. In particular, I'd like to thank Bill Linzbach, Mark Lium, and Nancy Jacobs.

I'm also grateful to the Microsoft Press management staff, Casey Doyle, Christey Bahn, and especially Kim Fryer, who provided invaluable assistance during the planning and production stages of this book. Finally, I owe long overdue thanks to Claudette Moore, who continues to be a source of encouragement and support in her role as my literary agent.

Introduction

From its inception, Microsoft Publisher has had one overriding goal: to provide powerful desktop publishing tools that are nevertheless easy to use. So it's no surprise that Microsoft Publisher 2000 provides a number of functions that, quite literally, automate the design process. For example, Publisher's wizards don't just create professional-looking publications; they modify the design in response to your input. As a result, Publisher's wizards can generate thousands of permutations of standard documents, like newsletters, flyers, brochures, and Web sites. Best of all, each wizard remains linked to the publication it creates. So you can change the design motif, switch to a new color scheme, or convert a printed publication into a Web document with just a few clicks of the mouse.

Publisher's Design Gallery is chock-full of ready-to-use page elements, such as mastheads, borders, pull quotes, and tables of contents. The objects in the Design Gallery are especially useful because they match the styles employed by the wizards.

As you gain publishing experience, you'll find that Publisher's tools can help you to create your own unique designs. The program can generate a wide variety of publications, including books, cards, posters, and mail merge documents. Task-specific tools produce complex objects quickly and easily. For example, the Table Frame Tool lets you enter and format tabular information in rows and columns. And you can use the WordArt Frame Tool to add curved or slanted effects to text.

Many of the objects you can create with Publisher have built-in intelligence. For example, the AutoFit command can enlarge or reduce the point size of text automatically in response to layout changes. And Publisher can synchronize key pieces of personal information (like your name and address). So if you change one instance of a Personal Information component, all similar components in the current publication are instantly updated with the new data. Publisher even helps you to coordinate the colors in a document with predefined color schemes. And because Publisher maintains a link between the objects in your publication and the color scheme itself, choosing a different scheme recolors all of the objects with new hues.

What's New in Publisher 2000

In response to user requests, Publisher 2000 can now generate process color separations. That means Publisher can convert computer based RGB colors into the cyan, magenta, yellow, and black (known as CMYK) ink colors necessary to print full color documents at a commercial printing service.

Publisher 2000 also supports the Pantone Solid and Pantone Process color libraries. Pantone Solid colors provide standardized formulas for premixed inks that are typically used to print spot color publications. The Pantone Process color library consists of a broad range of CMYK tints that can help you either to find the closest match to a Pantone Solid color or to choose colors for a process color document more consistently.

Prepress Tools

Many of Publisher's new functions help you to produce high quality, trouble-free output at a commercial printing service. If you are a novice desktop publisher and if your commercial printing service supports Publisher 2000 files in the native .pub format, you can safely ignore many of these advanced tools. The new Pack And Go Wizard can collect all of the necessary files that your commercial printing service will need to produce your publication.

If, however, you are an experienced desktop publisher and are using a commercial printing service that requires final PostScript output or if you are a commercial printer who receives Publisher files, you'll be grateful for the powerful new prepress functions. Publisher's commercial printing tools let you run a preflight check, where you can discover—and correct—potential printing problems.

Publisher 2000 can now create traps—whereby adjacent objects overlap slightly to avoid white gaps that sometimes appear between objects when the color plates don't align (or register) perfectly. And now when you import a picture, you have the option of inserting it or linking to it. A linked graphic is stored externally to the publication file, making it easier to access in order to adjust colors or change the resolution. Publisher can also embed fonts directly in a publication file. This solves the all-too-common problem of font substitution, which occurs when a commercial printing service bureau does not have the font you requested and uses a similar (but not identical) font in its place.

Microsoft Office Compliance

Though you may have purchased Publisher as a stand-alone product, chances are good that you actually received it as part of a version of Microsoft Office. Any-one familiar with the Microsoft Office suite of programs will feel immediately comfortable with Publisher 2000. That's because Publisher 2000 looks and works more like Office products than ever before.

For example, if you type an asterisk or a number followed by text followed by a line break, Publisher automatically converts the copy to a bulleted or num-bered list—just as it does in Microsoft Word. And Publisher's formatting toolbar contains a number of new shortcuts "borrowed" from Word and Excel.

Like other Office products, Publisher relies on new installation technology that helps you work more efficiently. When you install Publisher using the Typical installation, only the most frequently used functions are actually copied to your hard disk. If you subsequently access a feature that isn't fully installed, Publisher prompts you to insert the program disk in your CD drive to complete the instal-lation.

Publisher also takes advantage of Intellimenus—which are smart menus that simplify the program by displaying only the most recently or frequently used commands. You can fully expand an Intellimenu (by clicking the special arrows that appear at the bottom of the menu) to have Publisher display the previously hidden commands.

Finally, Publisher 2000 has a new function on the Help menu, called Detect And Repair. Use it if you suspect that the Publisher program has been corrupted. Once again, Publisher will prompt you to insert the installation disks in your CD drive in order to reinstall any code necessary to run properly.

Enhanced Web Publishing Tools

The majority of Publisher's specialized Web tools have not changed. You can still add interactive forms to a Web document, insert HTML code fragments (to add JavaScript or Dynamic HTML objects to your publication), and play sound files in the background.

In addition to generating .gif images, Publisher now preserves JPEG pictures that you insert into a Web document—providing higher quality display of full color pictures. And when you generate the final Web document, you have control over the HTML compatibility level. You can produce standard HTML documents that can be viewed with older Web browsers, or you can generate high-fidelity documents that are based on cascading style sheets and require newer browsers to be viewed properly.

Smarter Art

Publisher 2000 ships with the largest collection of images, sounds, and .gif animations yet. Luckily, the Clip Gallery Tool has been completely redesigned to provide smarter search functions that help you find just the right picture for your design. For example, you can now search for a file based on its content (using keyword searches) or based on its similarity to another clip. Just select a clip that you like and then search for other clips that share shapes and color or artistic style.

The Design Gallery also contains smarter-than-ever objects—called Accent Styles. Whenever you change one instance of an accent style, all instances of the design motif are automatically updated throughout the document. For example, if you change the colors in the Accent Box Masthead, the colors are automatically changed in the Accent Box Pull Quote and the Accent Box Sidebar as well.

Why This Book Is Easy to Use

This book is not a manual, but it does contain valuable reference material. The first part of the book, "Publisher 2000 Fundamentals," provides a guide to the features and tools that Publisher offers. Each chapter in this section focuses on a related group of tools. For example, Chapter 3, "Layout Tools," discusses the functions needed to build a cohesive page design, such as object positioning, grouping, alignment, and rotation. Whenever appropriate, these chapters also include technical information to help you understand how Publisher functions within the context of other computer based graphics applications. For example, Chapter 12, "Creating Documents for the World Wide Web," explains why and how Publisher's wide range of formatting options must be restricted to produce well behaved HTML documents for the Web.

The second part of the book, "Design Projects," illustrates essential desktop publishing concepts, teaches fundamental skills and elucidates the elements of good design. The sample projects have been developed to showcase Publisher's wide ranging capabilities and include Web documents, an advertisement, a newsletter, a flyer, and a three-fold brochure. If there is a faster or smarter way to accomplish a task in Publisher 2000, the design projects take advantage of it. Small businesses, families, nonprofit organizations, and individuals will find all of these projects inspiring—whether used as step by-step blueprints or as the starting point for original designs.

The projects give you the opportunity to put design theory into practice and illustrate, in a way that no description can, the synergy among Publisher's various functions. To show you how content drives design, each project contains text and pictures that reflect real-life business and personal situations, even though the companies, names, street addresses, telephone numbers, and Web and e-mail addresses contained in these sample publications are all fictitious. You can duplicate the design projects exactly as they appear in this edition. The sound file and all of the images used in the projects are part of Publisher's Clip Gallery. The full text for each project is provided in Appendix B. But if you don't want to retype the copy, you can download word processing files directly from the Microsoft Press Web site at http://mspress.microsoft.com/mspress/products/1426/.

Finally, Appendix A describes in detail the robust drawing tools offered by Microsoft Draw 98—a graphics program that ships with Publisher. Using Draw, you can create original art, modify existing pictures, and produce an even wider variety of WordArt effects.

A Graphical Approach to Explaining Application Features and Design Concepts

Even a cursory inspection reveals that *Microsoft Publisher 2000 by Design* is chock full of illustrations. This visual presentation of information not only is aesthetically appealing but also stresses the procedural nature of much of the book. For example, instead of simply telling you how to use a dialog box, this format *shows* you how to use a dialog box by annotating an illustration of the computer screen with numbered steps. You can use this book as a step-by-step instructional guide to Publisher's tools and functions. But it is also designed to be used as a reference book that explains computer graphics concepts and technology and as a design tutorial for a wide variety of publications.

Much of the ancillary information appears in a tip column in the left margin area of the page. This format allows the step-by-step instructions to proceed uninterrupted and lets you more easily find certain types of information by looking for these icons:

 Power tips give you the inside scoop on advanced functions in the program. Within the project chapters, power tips offer design advice.

 Troubleshooting tips answer frequently asked questions and warn you about potential problems.

Cross-references point you toward more information on a given topic.

 Toolbar shortcuts show you which buttons to click on Publisher's toolbars to invoke frequently used commands.

 Keyboard Shortcuts provide the keystroke equivalents for frequently used commands.

What You Need to Begin Using Publisher 2000

To use Microsoft Publisher 2000, you need to be running Microsoft Windows 95, Microsoft Windows 98, or Microsoft NT version 4.0 or later. The recommended hardware requirements include the following:

- 90 MHz Pentium processor (or faster)
- 16 MB of memory (32 MB for NT)
- Hard disk with 130 MB of free disk space for Publisher and 27 MB of free disk space for the clip art preview files
- VGA monitor
- Mouse
- A CD-ROM drive

Of course, your experience with Publisher will only be enhanced by better, faster, more powerful hardware. For example, a faster processor (such as a 450 MHz Pentium) will make Publisher more responsive, and a 256-color or 24-bit color monitor will provide a more accurate preview of the artwork in your publications. And if you plan to create large documents or if you've purchased the deluxe version of Publisher, you'll need lots of hard-disk space. For example, the deluxe version of Publisher requires 127 MB of free disk space for the clip art preview files. Finally, you'll also require a graphics-capable printer, though color output is optional. And you'll need a Twain 32-compliant scanner or digital camera if you want to capture original images directly within Publisher.

To get the most out of this book, you should also have a working knowledge of the Windows operating environment. The instructions assume that you understand how to locate files stored in folders on your hard disk and that you know the difference between clicking, dragging, double-clicking, and right-clicking the mouse buttons. If these concepts are not familiar, you should refer to your operating system's online help for more information.

A Desire to Experiment

I've said it before and it's still true: to become a competent designer, you need a little something more than hardware and software. You need a willingness to experiment. You can rely on wizards, the Design Gallery, and special effects such as BorderArt and WordArt to jump-start the design process and to serve as a source of visual inspiration, but Publisher's powerful tools ultimately let you develop your own design ideas. Luckily, the tools are so easy to use that the experimentation often feels more like play than work.

This book encourages you to exercise your creativity and develop confidence in your own aesthetic judgments. By the time you've finished reading this book, you'll look at the publications that surround you with new eyes—as designs that you too can create.

PART 1

Publisher 2000 Fundamentals

The Publisher 2000 Interface

Use the keyboard instead of the mouse. You can also operate Publisher using the keyboard. Shortcut keys are shown to the right of the command names on the menus that drop down from the menu bar.

Access shortcut menus. Right-clicking any object in the Publisher window invokes a shortcut menu containing commands that are specific to that element. For example, if you right-click a picture frame, the shortcut menu lets you insert an image file. Right-clicking a text frame instead brings up commands to change hyphenation options or run a spell check.

Microsoft Publisher 2000 is easy to use. When you master a few basic concepts and skills, you can create sophisticated and professional-looking publications. Taking a few minutes now to familiarize yourself with Publisher's interface and its unique approach to document creation will save you valuable time later and enable you to turn out products with a minimum of confusion and frustration.

A Quick Tour of Publisher's Interface

You interact with Publisher as you do with most Windows-based applications by using menu commands, toolbars, and dialog boxes. Publisher is Microsoft Office-compliant, which means that it shares many interface conventions with popular programs such as Microsoft Word and Microsoft Excel.

Menus and Toolbars

Menus and toolbars are actually quite similar because they both let you issue commands. But where menus use words to describe commands, toolbars use icons—or pictures—to represent the program's functions.

What is the meaning of the double arrow that appears below menu commands? The double arrow that appears at the bottom of a menu is a function of Publisher's Intellimenus. Intellimenus display the commands that you use frequently, and hide the commands that you don't use frequently. Holding the mouse over the arrow on an Intellimenu displays the hidden commands, as shown below.

 Turn Intellimenus off. To deactivate Intellimenus, open the Options dialog box (found on the Tools menu), click the General tab, and clear the check box for Menus Show Recently Used Commands First.

Think of the menu bar as the top level of an outline, with related commands appearing on a drop-down list under each title. Click a command to execute it.

The Standard toolbar contains frequently used functions, such as creating a file or Undo/Redo.

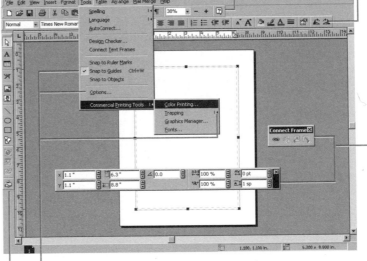

Formatting toolbars appear under the Standard toolbar. The buttons on the toolbar change depending on which tool or object is active.

Special function toolbars can float in the workspace.

Menu commands can be preceded by a check mark (which signifies that the command is currently active), followed by a triangle and bar (which open a submenu containing more choices), or followed by an ellipsis (which indicates a dialog box will open when you choose the command). A double arrow at the bottom of the menu indicates that there are hidden commands.

The Objects toolbar provides the tools to create and select objects, such as text or picture frames.

Why can't I find the dialog box options I need?

The options you want might be in distinct but related dialog boxes. Windows organizes these dialog boxes with tabs. Click a tab to bring it to the front of the stack and to reveal a new set of options.

Open dialog boxes with a double-click. You can quickly open many dialog boxes by double-clicking objects in your publication. For example, double-clicking an object boundary opens the Border Style dialog box.

Dialog Box Options

Whenever Publisher needs information from you to complete a command, it presents you with a window called a dialog box.

Click the Help icon to display the special Help cursor, then click an item in the dialog box for context-sensitive help.

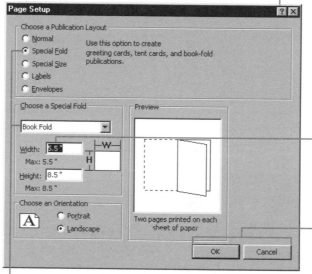

In some cases, you can type information directly into a text box.

You must select a command button in the dialog box to submit the information or cancel the operation. In some cases, you can call up additional options before returning to the main program.

You provide information by selecting radio buttons, check boxes (not shown), or items from drop-down list boxes.

Getting Feedback from Publisher's Interface

Publisher's tools are designed to provide valuable feedback on the currently selected object or operation. You can work more efficiently and more accurately if you learn to "read the screen."

Reset Tippages to reappear. Tippages are learning tools that appear on screen the first time you use a particular function, such as text frame linking or grouping. You can force Tippages to appear for features you have used previously by clicking the Reset Tips button found on the User Assistance tab in the Options dialog box (on the Tools menu).

The formatting toolbars display different functions depending on whether the currently selected object is a text frame, a picture frame, or a WordArt frame. For example, picture formatting options appear only when a picture frame is selected.

Menu commands that aren't available at the current time are displayed as gray embossed (rather than black) text.

Tippages and alert boxes are messages that pop up in response to specific situations.

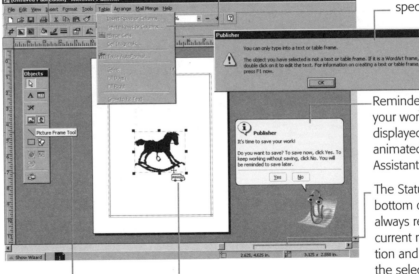

Reminders to save your work are displayed by the animated Office Assistant.

The Status bar at the bottom of the screen always reports the current mouse position and the size of the selected object.

ScreenTips appear whenever the mouse pointer is positioned over a screen element for a few seconds.

The pointer changes shape in response to the action you are performing. For example, the Move pointer (shown here) lets you reposition objects. Publisher also displays distinct pointers for editing text or selecting, drawing, cropping, and adjusting objects.

Customizing Publisher's Interface

Like other Microsoft Office products, Publisher offers configuration options to display or hide—and even animate—many elements of the interface. You can reconfigure the interface to suit your own work style.

Customize Interface Elements	
To take this action...	**Do this...**
Hide the Standard toolbar.	Choose Toolbars on the View menu. Clear the Standard command on the submenu.
Hide the formatting toolbars.	Choose Toolbars on the View menu. Clear Formatting on the submenu.
Float a toolbar.	Drag a docked toolbar's Move icon (the gray double bars at the left or top of the toolbar) to a new location in the workspace. You can move and change the shape of a floating toolbar.
Dock a toolbar.	Double-click a floating toolbar's title bar, or drag the toolbar to the top, bottom, left, or right edge of Publisher's window.
Hide the status bar.	Choose Toolbars on the View menu. Clear Status Bar on the submenu.
Switch from normal to large icons.	Choose Toolbars on the View menu and then choose Options on the submenu. Select Large Icons. Click OK.
Hide ScreenTips on toolbars or objects.	Choose Toolbars on the View menu and then choose Options on the submenu. Clear Show ScreenTips On Toolbars or Show ScreenTips On Objects. Click OK.
Show shortcut keys in ScreenTips.	Choose Toolbars on the View menu and then choose Options on the submenu. Select Show Shortcut Keys In ScreenTips. Click OK.
Animate menus as they open or close.	Choose Toolbars on the View menu and then choose Options on the submenu. Open the Menu Animations drop-down list and choose Random, Unfold, or Slide. Click OK.
Turn off Publisher's Helpful pointers.	Choose Options on the Tools menu. Click the User Assistance tab and then clear the Use Helpful Mouse Pointers check box.
Turn off Tippages.	Choose Options on the Tools menu. Click the User Assistance tab and then clear the Show Tippages check box.
Turn off Reminders.	Choose Options on the Tools menu. Click the User Assistance tab and then clear the Remind To Save Publication check box.

To invoke the Office Assistant, click the Help icon on the Standard toolbar.

To invoke the Office Assistant, press F1.

Access Publisher's electronic tutorials. Publisher contains tutorials that range from a general introduction to discussions of specific functions, such as layering and the background. To start a tutorial, open the Help menu, select Publisher Tutorials, and choose one of the available lessons.

Getting Answers from Publisher's Help System

Whenever you need help, Publisher displays the Office Assistant, which can be one of many available animated characters. The animated cartoon character allows you to type an English-language statement or question about your current problem.

Use Publisher Help

1 Select Microsoft Publisher Help on the Help menu. The Office Assistant appears.

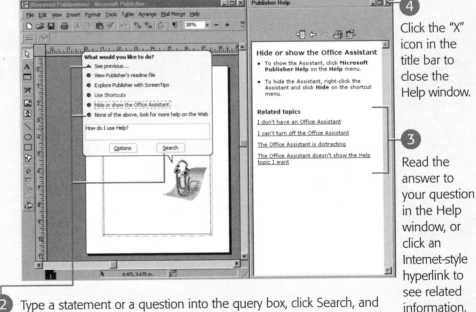

4 Click the "X" icon in the title bar to close the Help window.

3 Read the answer to your question in the Help window, or click an Internet-style hyperlink to see related information.

2 Type a statement or a question into the query box, click Search, and then click a topic in the Office Assistant box to open the Help window and display more specific information.

Visit Microsoft Publisher's Web Site. Clicking the Microsoft Publisher Web Site command on the Help menu invokes your Web browser and connects you to Publisher's World Wide Web site. Once you're online, you can learn about special offers, download free software and clipart, and access Microsoft's extensive help database.

What do I do if a Publisher tool isn't installed or isn't working properly? If you attempt to use a tool that isn't currently installed, Publisher displays an alert message and gives you the opportunity to install the feature. If you discover that a tool isn't working properly, select Detect And Repair on the Help menu to have Publisher automatically fix the problem, and if necessary, reinstall the tool.

Use Publisher Help *(continued)*

While the Help Window is open you can:

- Click the Show icon to display a Contents list, an Answer Wizard, or an Index that you can use in lieu of the Office Assistant.
- Click the Print icon to print the information displayed in the Help window.

You can control both the appearance and functions of the Office Assistant.

- If the Office Assistant is obscuring part of your document, drag the animation to a new location.
- To temporarily hide the animated character, choose Hide The Office Assistant on the Help menu (or right-click the animation and choose Hide on the shortcut menu).
- To determine how the Office Assistant behaves and the types of help it offers, right-click the animation and choose Options on the shortcut menu.
- To replace the default character, named Clipit, with one of seven different characters, right-click the animation and select Choose Assistant on the shortcut menu.

Reversing a Mistake with the Undo/Redo Commands

Don't worry if you click the wrong menu item, inadvertently resize a frame, or accidentally move an object while working on a design. You can easily correct these and many other common mistakes by issuing the Undo command on the Edit menu. You can even reverse the Undo action itself by issuing the Redo command on the Edit menu. Publisher can undo or redo the last 20 actions you performed.

Click the Undo button on the Standard toolbar to reverse the most recent action you performed.

Click the Redo button on the Standard toolbar to reverse the last Undo action you performed.

To undo your last action, press Ctrl-Z. To redo the last undo action, press Ctrl-Y.

But be warned. Some actions, such as choosing a new data source for a mail merge publication, can't be undone. You'll also find that once you've interrupted the Undo or Redo sequence, you can't continue to undo or redo previous actions.

The Undo command tells you exactly what operation it will reverse, in this case, a move.

The Redo command tells you exactly what operation it will reverse, in this case, filling an object with color.

The Building Blocks of Documents: Text, Pictures, Drawn Elements, and OLE Objects

Publisher treats words, pictures, and everything else in a document as objects. A document is simply a collection of different kinds of objects. Understanding object attributes and how objects behave and interact with one another is the key to working with Publisher. A Publisher document can contain four basic kinds of objects, as shown in the following table.

How does desktop publishing differ from word processing? Word processing documents are linear: one character leads to the next, lines of text are sequential, and pages follow each other in a predictable order. Desktop publishing documents are nonlinear. You use text and pictures as building blocks to construct a page design in any order you wish.

Microsoft Publisher is a desktop publishing application—not a word processing application. Although Publisher provides some word processing features (including a spelling checker and a find-and-replace feature), it isn't intended to function as a true word processing application.

Types of Objects in Microsoft Publisher		
Object Type	**Content**	**Description**
Text or Table	Words	Text that is typed directly into a Publisher document or imported from a word processing file
Picture	Any visual material imported from an external source	Scanned photographs, technical diagrams, clip-art images, pie charts, and other graphics
Drawn	Visual elements that you create in Publisher	Rules, decorative borders, and geometric shapes such as boxes, ovals, and polygons
OLE	Objects that are created by other programs	Any kind of computer-based data: cells from a spreadsheet, text from a word processor, pictures from a drawing application, or fields from a database

Components of Objects

In a Publisher document, each object consists of the content, the frame, and the formatting attributes.

Frames versus Content

Despite the very close relationship between a frame and the content it contains, you must learn to see a them as separate aspects of the same object.

Is a border the same as a frame? No. These two terms should not be used interchangeably. A frame is the rectangle that defines an object's boundary. A border is a formatting attribute, such as a 1-point black line, that can be applied to a frame. All objects have frames, but not all frames have borders.

You can think of the content of an object as its meaning. For example, the content of a picture object is the picture itself, and the content of a text object is the words. You can change the formatting attributes such as the size, shape, position, or color of an object without altering its content.

In your own home, picture frames contain pieces of art and allow you to position that art on the wall anywhere you please. Publisher's frames contain words, pictures, drawn elements, or other objects and allow you to size and position those objects on the publication page. The composition of frames on the page is called a layout.

Formatting Attributes

We often define objects by describing their properties or attributes. For example, a balloon can be red or blue, a chair can be straight-backed or cushioned, and a person can be tall or short. All objects in Publisher also have attributes, and you can alter the appearance of objects by changing their attributes. This alteration process is called formatting.

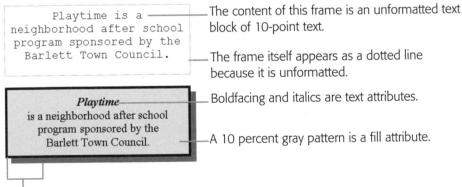

Playtime is a — The content of this frame is an unformatted text neighborhood after school block of 10-point text.

— The frame itself appears as a dotted line because it is unformatted.

Playtime— Boldfacing and italics are text attributes.

— A 10 percent gray pattern is a fill attribute.

A border and a shadow are frame attributes.

Instant frames. You can create a frame—or any Publisher object—by simply activating the appropriate tool and then clicking in the workspace. One word of warning: the frames you create in this way appear on the page in a standard size. You must then resize each frame.

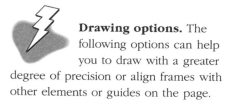 **Drawing options.** The following options can help you to draw with a greater degree of precision or align frames with other elements or guides on the page.

- Draw a frame starting from any corner.

- Press and hold the Ctrl key as you draw to create a frame from the center outward.

- Press and hold the Shift key as you draw to create perfectly symmetrical shapes, such as circles and squares.

 For more information on Publisher's drawing functions, see Chapter 9.

Creating a Frame

Before you can type text, import a picture, design WordArt, or insert an OLE element, you must draw the appropriate frame for that type of object.

Draw a Frame

1 Activate the toolbar tool that creates the kind of object you want. The pointer changes into a crossbar.

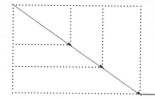

2 Position the crossbar on the page.

3 Press and hold the left mouse button while dragging the mouse diagonally. Drag the rectangle from one corner of the object to the opposite corner until the object is the size you want.

4 When the shape and size of the frame are to your liking, release the mouse button.

Identifying and Selecting an Object

Publisher helps you see where one object ends and another object begins by displaying a dotted line around each object. Before you can modify or format any object, you must select it. You can tell that an object has been selected because selection handles appear on the frame surrounding the object.

Why can't I see object boundaries on the screen? In all likelihood, you have hidden the object boundaries. To display them, open the View menu and choose the Show Boundaries And Guides command, or use the keyboard shortcut Ctrl-Shift-O.

Learn the difference between a multiple selection and a group. A multiple selection is a temporary group that's created when you select more than one object at a time. As soon as you cancel the selection of the elements, they are once again treated as individual objects. Publisher allows you to convert a multiple selection to a permanent group of objects that are "glued" together until you ungroup them. Grouped objects offer you flexibility because you can treat them like a single object while you design your publication.

For more information about working with grouped objects, see Chapter 3.

If an object has a border, such as the black rule surrounding the rectangle shown here, it exactly follows the object boundary and obscures it from view.

This dotted line represents an object boundary. Although you can see object boundaries on the screen, they never print.

Selection handles appear whenever you click an object.

Select an Object and Clear a Selection

1 If the pointer is not an arrow, click the Pointer Tool on the toolbar.

2 Click an object. Selection handles appear.

3 Click another object or any blank area of the screen to clear the selection.

Multiple Selections

Sometimes it is efficient to work with more than one object at a time, particularly when you want to move or delete them. Publisher lets you select several objects simultaneously in what is known as a multiple selection.

Every currently selected object in a multiple selection is displayed with gray (rather than the usual black) selection handles.

Every multiple selection displays a Group Objects icon, which you can click to group objects.

Mix and match selection tools. You can work more efficiently by using the various selection tools in combination. For example, if you want to select every element on a page but one, use the Select All command and then use the Shift key to clear the selection of a single object.

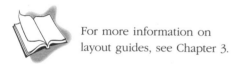

For more information on layout guides, see Chapter 3.

You can select more than one object in several ways, as explained in the following table.

Methods of Creating a Multiple Selection	
To select ...	**Do this...**
Every object on the page	Choose the Select All command on the Edit menu.
Objects that are not close to each other on the page, or to exclude objects from the current multiple selection	Press and hold the Shift key and use the pointer tool to click a series of objects.
Objects that are adjacent to one another on the page	Use the Pointer Tool to draw a special boundary—called a selection box or a marquee selection—around all the objects you want to select.

Previewing Your Layout with the WYSIWYG Screen

Publisher's *WYSIWYG* (What You See Is What You Get) display always attempts to show you how the final printed page will look. This on-screen preview provides instant feedback on your design decisions. You can enhance the appearance of Publisher's *WYSIWYG* display by hiding layout guides and special nonprinting characters (such as paragraph markers and spaces).

Make use of dialog box previews. Many of Publisher's dialog boxes contain a preview area that lets you see how the current settings will affect your publication. For the most part, dialog box previews are not *WYSIWYG*, but instead represent your design decisions with simple schematic drawings that are nevertheless accurate. Taking a few extra seconds to examine the preview can help you to discover and correct mistakes quickly—ultimately saving you time.

To toggle the display of special characters, press Ctrl-Shift-Y. Press Ctrl-Shift-O to toggle the display of boundaries and guides.

Click the Show Special Characters button on the Standard toolbar to display or hide non-printing characters.

A screen image with guides, boundaries, and special characters displayed can appear cluttered.

A screen image with guides, boundaries, and special characters hidden accurately represents the final printout.

Preview Your Document

1 Open the View menu.

2 Select Hide Special Characters and Hide Boundaries and Guides.

To redisplay special characters, object boundaries, and guides, click the Show Special Characters and Show Boundaries and Guides commands on the View menu.

Beginning Work on a Publication

Just like conventional paper documents, Publisher documents contain pages—albeit electronic ones. Instead of stacking and shuffling sheets of paper, however, you use Publisher's commands to manage and move around in your electronic documents.

For instructions on installing the Microsoft Publisher application, see the *Microsoft 2000 Publisher Companion*. For more information about shortcuts, see Windows Help.

Starting Publisher

Using the Windows Start button is the simplest way to open Publisher, but you can also double-click the program icon in the Microsoft Publisher folder or create a shortcut for Publisher on the Windows desktop

Open the Microsoft Publisher Application

1 Install Microsoft Publisher on your hard disk.

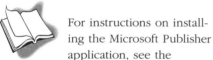 **2** Click the Windows Start button and open the Programs menu.

3 Click the icon for Microsoft Publisher. The Microsoft Publisher Catalog appears, allowing you to invoke a Wizard, start a new blank publication, or open an existing publication.

Circumvent the Catalog dialog box. You can bypass the Catalog dialog box when you start Publisher. Choose Options on the Tools menu. On the General tab, clear the Use Catalog At Startup check box. Publisher will start with a blank full page.

To start a new publication, press Ctrl-N.

To start a new publication, click the New icon.

Why can't I find a Templates button in the Catalog dialog box?
Publisher 2000 doesn't ship with templates and therefore won't automatically display a Templates button. The Templates button appears only if you have templates stored on your hard disk.

Starting a Publication from Scratch

Whenever you begin a new publication with a blank page, Publisher provides 11 predefined page layouts.

Begin Designing a New Publication

1 Start Publisher, or select New on the File menu. The Catalog appears.

2 If it is not already active, click the Blank Publications tab.

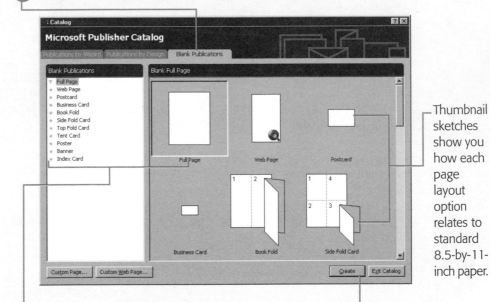

Thumbnail sketches show you how each page layout option relates to standard 8.5-by-11-inch paper.

3 Scroll through the thumbnail choices and select the page layout that matches the document you want to create. Alternatively, select a layout name from the list.

4 Click the Create button to proceed to Publisher's work area.

To access the Open
Publication dialog box,
press Ctrl-O.

To load an existing file,
click the Open icon.

**Open a publication
directly from the File
menu.** At the bottom of
the File menu you'll find a list of the last
four publications you worked on. Clicking a filename or typing the number that
precedes the filename, opens the file
immediately.

**Where do the shortcuts
in the Places bar point?**
The History folder lists the
publications you worked on recently. The
Personal folder is the default location
where Publisher stores documents. The
Desktop folder lists the shortcuts you
have placed on the Windows Desktop.
The Favorites folder lists shortcuts to files
or folders you use frequently. The Web
folder points to a location on your
Internet Service Provider's Web server.

Opening an Existing Publication

The Open Publication dialog box offers many functions to help you browse for files.

Open an Existing File

1 Select Open on the File menu, or click the Existing Files button in the
Catalog window. The Open Publication dialog box appears.

2 In the Look In drop-down list box, browse
the drives and individual folders to locate
the file you want.

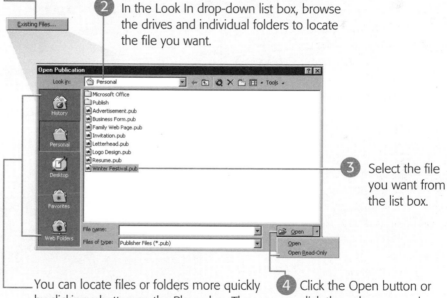

3 Select the file
you want from
the list box.

You can locate files or folders more quickly
by clicking a button on the Places bar. These
shortcuts can point to locations on your local
hard disk, a network, or the Web.

4 Click the Open button or
click the submenu and
choose Read-Only.

Why would I open a file as Read-Only? The Open Read-Only option displays a file on-screen but prevents you from saving the file with the same filename. This allows you to review a file and still safeguard it from any inadvertent changes.

Designating a default folder. Depending on the software installed on your system, Publisher attempts to store your documents in the Personal folder (found in the Windows folder) or the My Documents folder. You can work more efficiently by specifying a different startup directory for Publisher to use. Click Options on the Tools menu. In the File Locations list box select the type of file (either publications or pictures) for which you would like to change the default folder. Then click the Modify button. Use the Look In drop-down list box to locate and select a folder. Click OK, and then click Close.

Searching for a File

If you can't locate a file by browsing in the Open Publication dialog box, you can use the Find command to perform a sophisticated search.

Search for an Existing File

① In the Open Publication dialog box, select the Find command on the Tools menu. The Find dialog box appears.

② Choose And to narrow the search criteria, or choose Or to expand the search criteria.

③ Select a Property from the drop-down list.

④ Select a Condition from the drop-down list.

Click Delete to remove the currently selected search criteria, or click New Search to clear the contents of the list box.

⑤ In the Value text box, type a word or phrase to be matched.

⑥ Click the Add To List button.

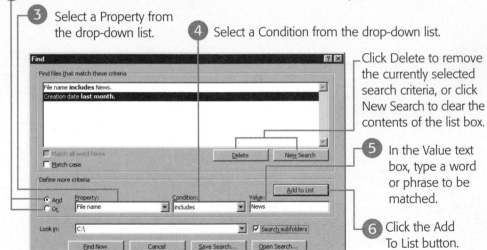

⑦ Repeat steps 2 through 6 to further modify the search criteria.

⑧ In the Look In drop-down list, specify the drive or folder you want to search. To have Publisher search subfolders, click the Search Subfolders check box.

⑨ Click Find Now to start the search. The results of your search appear in the Open Publication dialog box.

⑩ Select the name of the file you want to open, and click Open.

Why does Publisher display an alert message about embedded fonts when I attempt to open a file? Publisher 2000 has the ability to save (or embed) TrueType fonts as part of a publication file. If you open a file that contains an embedded font *and* you don't have the necessary font installed on your system, Publisher displays a dialog box that allows you to either display or install the embedded font.

For more information about embedding fonts, see Chapter 16.

Reuse search criteria. If you frequently search for the same type of file, use the Save Search button to preserve all of your search settings. For example, you can create a search routine to look for the newsletter file you created last month. To reuse search criteria that you've saved, click the Open Search button, and then choose the appropriate search routine from the list that appears.

Setting Up the Publication Page

The page layout determines the general size and orientation of your publication and affects how the pages are arranged at print time. The key to setting up a publication properly is understanding that paper size and Publisher's page size are not necessarily the same thing.

Paper size refers to the physical dimensions of the paper in your printer. Minimum and maximum paper sizes are determined by the capabilities of your printer.

Publisher's page size refers to the dimensions of your publication, which can be as small as 0.25 by 0.25 inch, or as large as 240 by 240 inches (that's 20 feet by 20 feet). Publisher assumes four possible relationships between page size and paper size:

- The page size can equal the paper size.

- The page size can be smaller than the paper size. In this case, the page size is the trim size of your document.

- Two or more pages can fit on a single sheet of paper. Publisher can even arrange the pages so that they can be folded to become a card or a book.

- A single page can be larger than a single sheet of paper. Publisher can print the page across several sheets of paper, as in a banner.

You choose a paper size in the Print Setup dialog box, which is described in Chapter 17.

How are the layouts in the Page Setup dialog box different from the layouts in the Catalog dialog box? The predefined layouts in the Catalog and the Page Setup dialog boxes are identical. However, the Page Setup dialog box offers advanced options that allow you to customize the size and orientation of your publication page.

Is the Normal setting synonymous with letter-sized paper? No. When you choose the Normal option, Publisher assumes that the page size and paper size are equal. If you have chosen a paper size other than 8.5-by-11 inches in the Print Setup dialog box, such as legal length (8.5-by-14 inches) or ledger size (11-by-17 inches), the Normal option in the Page Setup dialog box reflects the size of the chosen paper.

Creating a Publication Page Equal to the Paper Size

You will often want to create 8.5-by-11-inch pages on 8.5-by-11-inch pieces of paper, which is the standard size of paper used for business correspondence in the United States and is also the most common paper size for desktop printers.

Create a Page Size That Matches the Size of Your Paper

1 Choose Page Setup from the File menu, or click the Custom Page button on the Blank Publications tab in the Catalog dialog box. The Page Setup dialog box appears.

2 Select Normal.

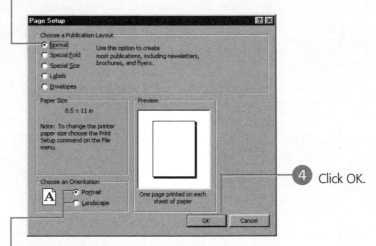

4 Click OK.

3 Select either Portrait (for a publication that is taller than it is wide) or Landscape (for a publication that is wider than it is tall).

For more information about Print Setup options, see Chapter 17.

Orientation of special-sized publications. When planning a special-sized publication, choose the Portrait or Landscape paper orientation carefully. When working with small publications such as business cards, the orientation determines how many copies you can fit on a single page. Larger publications are also affected. For example, the paper orientation determines the height of a banner: In Portrait mode banners are 11 inches tall, but in Landscape mode banners are only 8.5 inches tall.

Creating a Publication Page Not Equal to the Paper Size

Publisher allows you to create document pages that are larger or smaller than the paper installed in your printer.

Special-Sized Publications

Whether you are creating small documents, such as index cards and business cards, or oversized documents, such as banners and posters, Publisher always figures out the best way to position the page on the paper.

For small documents, Publisher centers a single page on the paper.

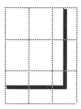

Publisher can print multiple copies of a small document on a single sheet of paper to avoid waste.

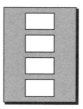

For oversized documents, Publisher prints your design across several sheets of paper.

Why won't Publisher allow me to change the width and height of a predefined publication size? When you choose a predefined publication size, Publisher displays dimensions in the Width and Height text boxes. These sizes, shown in the following list, are fixed. If you want to enter different values in the Width and Height text boxes, you must choose the Custom or Custom Banner option.

- Printer Sheet Size
- Index Card (5 x 3 in.)
- Business Card (3.5 x 2 in.)
- Poster (18 x 24 in.)
- Poster (24 x 36 in.)
- Banner (5 ft.)
- Banner (10 ft.)
- Banner (15 ft.)
- Post Card (5.5 x 4.25 in.)
- Post Card (5.85 x 4.13 in.)
- Post Card (3.94 x 5.83 in.)

Create a Document Larger or Smaller Than the Paper Size

1 Choose Page Setup from the File menu, or click the Custom Page button on the Blank Publications tab in the Catalog dialog box. The Page Setup dialog box appears.

2 Select the Special Size option.

3 Open the Choose A Publication Size drop-down list box, and select one of the predefined options. Alternatively, choose the Custom or Custom Banner option.

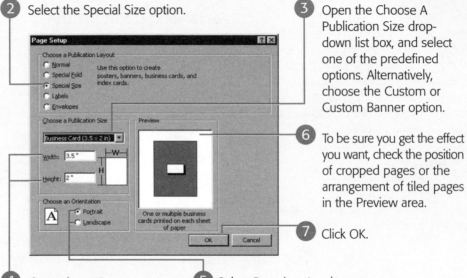

6 To be sure you get the effect you want, check the position of cropped pages or the arrangement of tiled pages in the Preview area.

7 Click OK.

4 If you chose Custom or Custom Banner, enter values from 0.25 inch through 20 feet into the Width and Height text boxes.

5 Select Portrait or Landscape.

Does Publisher contain a predefined page layout for a 3-fold brochure?

No. However, you can use a Wizard (accessed from the Catalog dialog box) to create a 3-fold brochure automatically. Alternatively, you can set up the page manually using Publisher's Layout Guides.

See Chapter 3 for a discussion of Layout Guides.

Folded Publications

Folded publications include books and cards. Although a folded document may seem simple to create, some pages might need to be printed out of order—or upside-down—for the publication to be ordered and oriented correctly after the paper is folded. The following illustrations show you the four predefined ways Publisher can arrange the individual pages on each sheet of paper. Each arrangement is called an imposition (the technical term for how multiple pages are placed on a single sheet of paper).

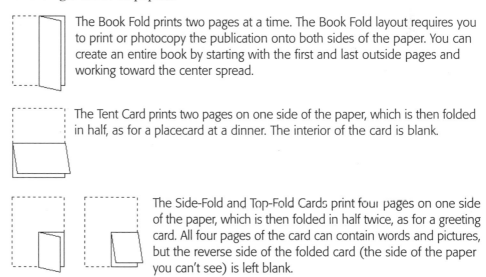

The Book Fold prints two pages at a time. The Book Fold layout requires you to print or photocopy the publication onto both sides of the paper. You can create an entire book by starting with the first and last outside pages and working toward the center spread.

The Tent Card prints two pages on one side of the paper, which is then folded in half, as for a placecard at a dinner. The interior of the card is blank.

The Side-Fold and Top-Fold Cards print four pages on one side of the paper, which is then folded in half twice, as for a greeting card. All four pages of the card can contain words and pictures, but the reverse side of the folded card (the side of the paper you can't see) is left blank.

Will my older printer be able to print the folded layouts? The Book Fold layout requires that pages print on both sides of the paper (duplex printing). If your printer can't do this, photocopy the pages back to back, and then fold, collate, and staple the pages into your book.

The Top-Fold and Side-Fold Card layout options require that two of the four pages be printed upside-down, and the Tent Card option requires that the second page be printed upside-down. Some older laser printers or dot matrix printers might have difficulty printing inverted text. To solve this problem, use Publisher's WordArt tool to create the text.

Create a Folded Document

1 Choose Page Setup from the File menu, or click the Custom Page button on the Blank Publications tab in the Catalog dialog box.

2 Select Special Fold.

3 Open the Choose A Special Fold drop-down list box and select one of the predefined layouts. Publisher computes the maximum page size and displays the values in the Width and Height text boxes.

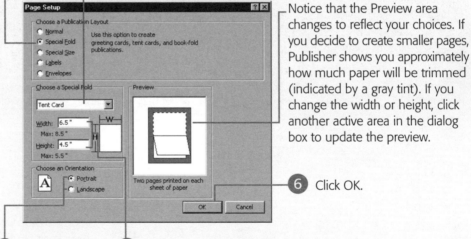

Notice that the Preview area changes to reflect your choices. If you decide to create smaller pages, Publisher shows you approximately how much paper will be trimmed (indicated by a gray tint). If you change the width or height, click another active area in the dialog box to update the preview.

6 Click OK.

4 Select Portrait or Landscape.

5 To change the page size, type smaller values in the Width and Height text boxes.

Printing options for envelopes. Publisher can use the choices you make in the Page Setup dialog box to determine the best way to print envelopes on your printer. Alternatively, you can specify the exact orientation and placement for envelopes on the Print tab of the Options dialog box (found on the Tools menu).

For more information about envelope printing options, see Chapter 17.

Creating Publications for Special-Sized Papers

Most of today's desktop printers can accommodate special-sized papers, such as pre-scored brochures or perforated business cards. Publisher provides Page Layout options for two of the most common specialty items—envelopes and adhesive labels.

Create an Envelope

1 Choose Page Setup from the File menu, or click the Custom Page button on the Blank Publications tab in the Catalog dialog box.

2 Select Envelopes.

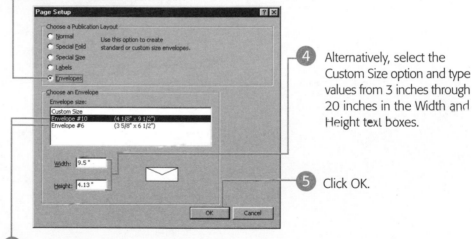

4 Alternatively, select the Custom Size option and type values from 3 inches through 20 inches in the Width and Height text boxes.

5 Click OK.

3 Choose one of the two standard envelope sizes.

How can I get different information to print on each label? When you choose a predefined label page layout, Publisher creates a page size equivalent to a single label. If you use normal text frames, the same information prints on every instance of the label. In order to print different information on each label you must use Publisher's Mail Merge and Print Merge functions.

For more information on Publisher's Mail Merge functions see Chapter 13. The Print Merge command is discussed in Chapter 17.

Create Labels

① Choose Page Setup from the File menu, or click the Custom Page button on the Blank Publications tab in the Catalog dialog box.

② Select Labels.

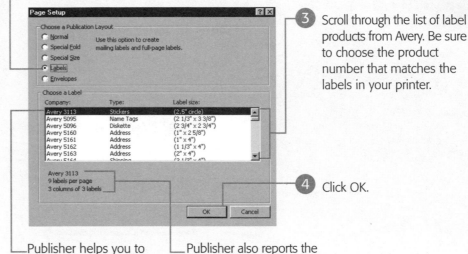

③ Scroll through the list of label products from Avery. Be sure to choose the product number that matches the labels in your printer.

④ Click OK.

Publisher helps you to identify the label product by providing information on each label, such as product number, purpose of the label, and the size of individual labels.

Publisher also reports the row and column arrangement of the labels and the total number of labels per sheet.

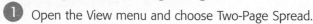
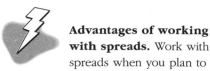

Advantages of working with spreads. Work with spreads when you plan to have rules or other elements print across facing pages, or when you want an overview of your design.

Changing Your View of Publication Pages

Publisher allows you to change your view of the pages in a document. You can view the pages in your document singly or by spreads. A spread mimics the layout of a book or magazine that is lying open in front of you, where two pages face each other.

You can also switch among various magnification levels. Viewing the page at a reduced size allows you to see an overview of your design. Zooming in on the page makes type legible and provides a higher degree of accuracy when creating or positioning frames.

View a Spread or a Single Page

1 Open the View menu and choose Two-Page Spread.

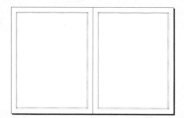

Now every time you turn a page, you see the two facing pages in the work area.

The left page is always an even-numbered page, and the right page is always an odd-numbered page.

2 To return to single-page view, clear the check mark in front of Two-Page Spread on the View menu.

Change the Magnification of a Page

1 On the Standard toolbar, click the arrow next to the Zoom drop-down list to display Publisher's predefined magnification choices.

2 Select a zoom level. Alternatively, highlight the contents of the Zoom box and type any number from 10 to 400 in one percent increments. Then press Enter.

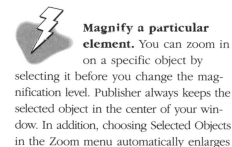

Magnify a particular element. You can zoom in on a specific object by selecting it before you change the magnification level. Publisher always keeps the selected object in the center of your window. In addition, choosing Selected Objects in the Zoom menu automatically enlarges the object to the edges of the window.

Toggle back and forth between actual size and the current magnification level by pressing the F9 key.

Use a menu to change zoom levels. You can also use menu commands to choose a magnification level. From the View menu, select Zoom. From the submenu, select one of the predefined magnification levels.

How do I insert pages into a spread? If you already have more than one page in your document and are working with a two-page spread, Publisher modifies the Insert Page dialog box slightly, allowing you to insert pages before the left page, after the right page, or between the pages of the spread. If you indicate that you want to insert an odd number of pages in the middle of a spread, Publisher asks with an alert box if you want to change the way the pages are paired.

To insert one new page after the current page, press Ctrl-Shift-N.

Change the Magnification of a Page *(continued)*

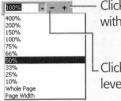

Click the plus sign to zoom in by one magnification level without opening the Zoom menu.

Click the minus sign to zoom out by one magnification level without opening the Zoom menu.

Inserting and Deleting Pages

You can add one page—or multiple pages—to your publication at any time during the design process. However, you can delete only one page or one spread at a time.

Add Pages to Your Document

1 Move to the page that falls before or after where you want to insert the new page.

2 Choose Page from the Insert menu.

3 Type the number of pages you want to add to the publication.

4 Indicate the location of the new pages.

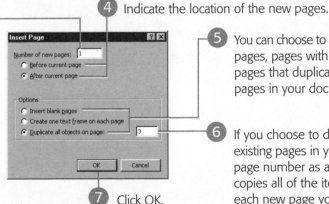

5 You can choose to insert completely empty pages, pages with a single text frame, or pages that duplicate one of the existing pages in your document.

6 If you choose to duplicate one of the existing pages in your document, enter a page number as a reference. Publisher copies all of the items on that page to each new page you add.

7 Click OK.

What happens to my text and pictures when I delete a page? When you delete a page, you also delete all the pictures and text frames on that page. The text itself will be deleted if the text frames are not linked to other frames. If links do exist, the text will reflow to other pages in the document.

For more information about linking text frames, see Chapter 4.

Access the Go To Page dialog box. Clicking the Go To Page command on the View menu opens a dialog box (shown below) where you can enter a specific page number.

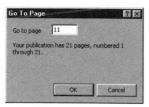

Press Ctrl-G to open the Go To Page dialog box.

Delete Pages from Your Document

① Check to make sure that the page you want to delete is the current one.

② Choose Delete Page from the Edit menu. If you are working in single-page view, Publisher deletes the page and renumbers the remaining pages.

③ If you are working with a two-page spread, Publisher asks whether you want to delete both pages, the left page only, or the right page only. Select the appropriate option.

④ Click OK.

Moving from Page to Page

You can move forward or backward through the pages of your document with a set of page controls at the bottom of the work area, as shown here.

Publisher displays an icon for each page in the publication and highlights the current page. To jump to a specific page in your publication, click the appropriate icon.

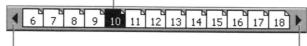

To display an icon for the previous page (or spread), click this arrow.

To display an icon for the next page (or spread), click this arrow.

How can I distinguish the background from the foreground? At times you might find it difficult to distinguish the background from the foreground. When they are empty, they look identical. Publisher identifies the background by replacing the page controls located at the lower-left corner of the window with a symbol that represents the background. When you have different backgrounds for the right and left pages, Publisher displays two background indicators, as shown below.

The Background and Foreground Relationship

Whenever you start a new design, Publisher automatically creates a blank background for your document. All the pages or spreads in a publication share the same background, so it is the ideal place on which to position elements that should appear on every page of the document. In contrast, the foreground contains text and design elements that are specific to an individual page.

The repetitive text and graphics that you place on the background, such as rules or a logo, show through the foreground overlay and appear on every page in your publication.

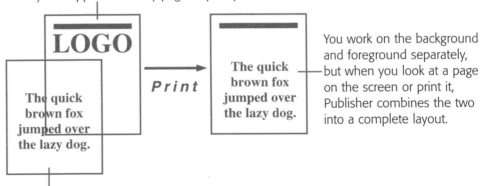

You work on the background and foreground separately, but when you look at a page on the screen or print it, Publisher combines the two into a complete layout.

Think of the foreground as a transparent surface on which you place the text and graphics for the current page. These elements float over the background as if they were on a clear overlay.

Moving Between the Background and Foreground

You work with the background and foreground in exactly the same way. You must draw text frames to add words and picture frames to add pictures. But you can't work on the background and foreground *simultaneously*. For example, when you are on the foreground you can't select background objects. However, you can use a special command to send objects from one layer to another.

To switch between the background and the foreground, press Ctrl-M.

Move to the Background or Foreground

1 Choose Go To Background on the View menu.

2 To return to the foreground, choose Go To Foreground on the View menu.

Send an Object to the Background or Foreground

1 Select the object you want to move to a different layer.

2 If you are on the foreground, choose Send To Background on the Arrange menu. Alternatively, if you are on the background, choose Send To Foreground on the Arrange menu.

Publisher displays an alert box informing you that the object has been moved.

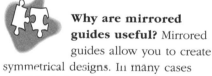

Why are mirrored guides useful? Mirrored guides allow you to create symmetrical designs. In many cases you'll find that symmetry makes documents more readable. For example, you can place page numbers on the outside edges of the page—meaning the extreme left and extreme right of a two-page spread—where they are easier to find. Mirrored guides also let you adjust the interior margins (called the gutters) for book layouts, creating a safety zone for staples or spiral binding.

Creating Different Backgrounds for Left and Right Pages

Publisher can create a left background page that is a reflection of the right background page. In order for this technique to work, you must first place frames on the right background page.

Use Mirrored Layout Guides

1 Choose Layout Guides from the Arrange menu.

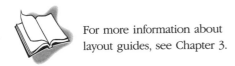

For more information about layout guides, see Chapter 3.

For more information about layout guides, see Chapter 3.

Use Mirrored Layout Guides *(continued)*

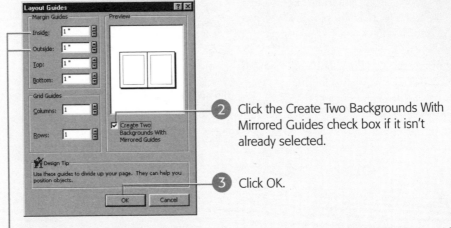

2 Click the Create Two Backgrounds With Mirrored Guides check box if it isn't already selected.

3 Click OK.

Notice that the names for the Margin Guides change from Left and Right to Inside and Outside—the appropriate labels for a mirrored layout.

Accommodating Unique Pages in a Multiple-Page Document

No matter how hard you strive for consistency, every publication contains a few unique pages. For example, title pages rarely contain page numbers or running heads. You can accommodate these pages by turning off the background.

What happens when I turn off the background?
When you turn off the background, all of the elements positioned on the background disappear from the current page. They have not been deleted; they are hidden from view and won't print. The background elements continue to appear on all the other pages in the document, including on any new pages that you insert.

Can I change the appearance of the page number? Yes, you can use any of Publisher's standard text formatting commands to change the attributes (such as font or point size) of a page number. Remember to highlight the page number (or the number sign) before you choose new formatting attributes.

For more information about text formatting attributes, see Chapter 6.

Turn Off the Background

1 Be sure that you are on the foreground of the page whose background you want to suppress.

2 From the View menu, choose Ignore Background.

3 If you are on a spread, the Ignore Background dialog box appears. Specify the left or right page and then click OK.

Adding Page Numbers

You can insert automatic page numbers on either the foreground or the background page. Publisher automatically adjusts the page numbering whenever you add or delete pages.

Insert Automatic Page Numbers

1 Select the Text Frame tool from the toolbar. Draw a text frame and position it where you want the page number to appear on the page.

2 Select Page Numbers from the Insert menu.

If you insert the page number on the foreground, Publisher displays the actual page number.

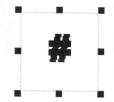

If you insert the page number on the background, Publisher displays a number sign. The number sign will be replaced by the correct page number on each foreground page.

Follow page numbering conventions. If you plan to bind your publication as a book, remember to design it so that right pages are always odd and left pages are always even. This means that you should always enter an odd number into the Start Publication With Page text box, because Publisher always begins multiple-page documents with a single right page.

 What kinds of file types can I create with Publisher 2000? Publisher 2000 can generate files that are compatible with a broad range of applications, including word processors and commercial printers. In addition, Publisher 2000 can save normal publication files, template files, and files that are compatible with Publisher 98.

 For more information about using and saving templates, see Chapter 14. For more information about Publisher's ability to import and save word processing formats, see Chapter 5.

Changing the Starting Page Number

Sometimes you might want to begin your publication with a page number other than 1. For example, your document might be a section of a long report or a chapter of a book.

Specify the Starting Page Number

1. Click Options on the Tools menu.

2. On the General tab, type the number you want to assign to the first page of your document in the Start Publication With Page text box. The starting page number must be between 1 and 16,766.

Saving a Document

After you have created or changed a document, you must save it on disk if you want to use it again. The way you save your document depends on whether you are working in a new document or one that has been saved previously. Publisher also lets you create automatic backups of your files or discard the changes you made since you last saved the file.

Save a New Document

1. Choose either Save or Save As from the File menu. In either case, the Save As dialog box appears.

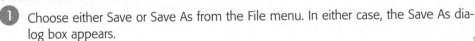

What happens when I save a Publisher 2000 document as a Publisher 98 document? The advanced formatting features that are specific to Publisher 2000 will either be dropped or modified in order to make the file compatible with Publisher 98. For example, embedded fonts are removed, CMYK and Pantone colors are converted to RGB values, and flipped graphics are returned to their original positions.

For a full list of Publisher 2000 features that are not supported, or only partially supported, by Publisher 98, see Publisher 2000's on-line Help.

How can I retrieve the backup file if my original file is lost or corrupted? If you choose the Save With Backup option in the Save As dialog box, Publisher saves an updated copy of the file each time you save the original publication. Publisher saves the backup file in the same directory as the original and adds the prefix "Backup of" to the original file name. To retrieve the backup, open it as an existing publication using the Open Publication dialog box.

Save a New Document *(continued)*

② Select a location for the file using the Save In drop-down list box and the files and folders list box.

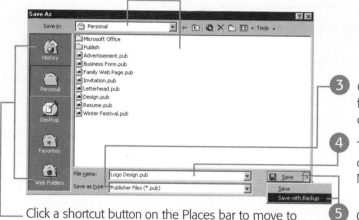

③ Choose a file type from the drop-down list.

④ Type the title of the document in the File Name text box.

—— Click a shortcut button on the Places bar to move to a location on your local hard disk, a network, or the Web. For example, the Favorites folder contains shortcuts to files or folders you use frequently.

⑤ Click Save. Or if you would like Publisher to automatically create backups, open the submenu and choose Save With Backup.

Save an Existing Document

① Choose Save on the File menu. Publisher saves the file under the current name by overwriting the previous version of the file stored on disk. Alternatively, choose Save As on the File menu. The Save As dialog box appears.

② Choose options and enter information, as described in the preceding procedure, Save a New Document.

To save your document, press Ctrl-S.

What is the difference between the Save and the Save As commands? The Save command stores the current file using the file name and options you selected when you first saved it. The Save As command allows you to type a new filename, designate a new folder, or choose different options.

Embed fonts for total fidelity. Normally a Publisher file contains instructions about font usage—not the actual fonts. This can cause problems when you send a publication file to another computer where the requested fonts are not available. Publisher 2000 can ensure that your designs are viewed and printed with the correct fonts by embedding TrueType fonts in the publication file.

For more information about embedding TrueType fonts, see Chapter 16.

Close a Document Without Saving Changes

1 Choose Close from the File menu.

2 When asked whether you want to save the changes, click No.

Using Autosave as a Reminder

The Autosave feature can remind you to save your publication. The Autosave alert appears on your screen at predetermined intervals. In the alert box, click Yes to save the current version of your publication. If you click No, you will return to the current document without saving the changes you have made. You can control whether the Autosave reminder is active or inactive.

Turn Autosave Reminder On or Off

1 Choose Options from the Tools menu, and then select the User Assistance tab.

2 Make sure that a check mark appears next to Remind To Save Publication.

3 In the Minutes Between Reminders text box, enter a value between 1 and 999 minutes.

4 Click OK.

5 To disable the Autosave Reminder, repeat step 1, and then clear the Remind To Save Publication check box.

6 Click OK.

Layout Tools

Professional art directors and designers use specialized tools, such as rulers, T-squares, and proportion wheels, to create neat and precise layouts. Microsoft Publisher 2000 provides these same tools in an electronic form that makes them easy to access and easy to use.

Rulers

Publisher's rulers lie along the left and top sides of the work area. You use these rulers to measure and position objects in relation to each other and in relation to the edges of your publication page. You can move the on-screen rulers, change the unit of measurement they display, reposition the zero point, and even mix different units of measurement in a single publication. You can choose to turn off the display of rulers and increase the size of your workspace in the bargain. To do so, open the View menu and clear Rulers. You can also right-click any portion of the work area to invoke a shortcut menu, shown below, from which you can activate or clear the rulers.

Clear the check mark in front of the Rulers command to turn the display of rulers off.

For more information on creating indents and tabs, see Chapter 6.

Why can't Publisher display points on the rulers? Publisher shows inches on the rulers because points are too small to be displayed clearly. However, if you choose points as the default unit of measurement, Publisher divides each inch into 24 equal segments of 3 points each, for a total of 72 per inch. In addition, the status line at the bottom of the work area uses points as the unit of measurement to report the size and position of objects.

A moveable box designates the intersection of the vertical and horizontal rulers.

The ruler displays finer increments as you zoom in on the page.

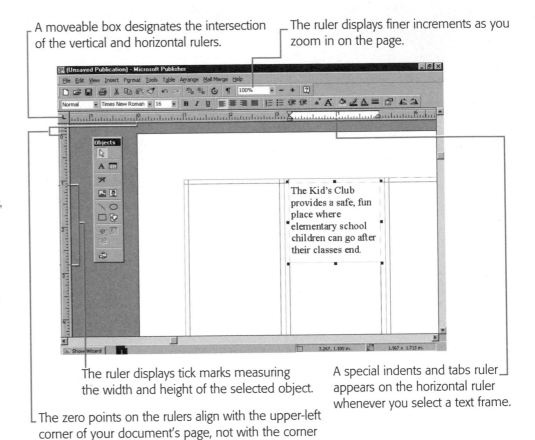

The ruler displays tick marks measuring the width and height of the selected object.

A special indents and tabs ruler appears on the horizontal ruler whenever you select a text frame.

The zero points on the rulers align with the upper-left corner of your document's page, not with the corner of the work area.

Why would I want to mix different units of measurement within a publication? Key elements of a design are often associated with a specific unit of measurement. For example, margins are typically specified in inches and paragraph indents are typically measured in picas.

 Use abbreviations to designate the unit of measurement. Use the following abbreviations whenever you override the default unit of measure in a dialog box.

- ✐ in or a double quote (") for inches
- ✐ cm for centimeters
- ✐ pi for picas
- ✐ pt for points

Change the Default Unit of Measurement

1 Choose Options from the Tools menu. The Options dialog box appears.

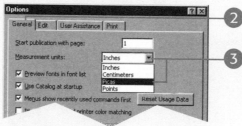

2 Select the General tab.

3 Open the Measurement Units drop-down list box and select a unit of measurement from the list.

4 Click OK.

Override the Default Unit of Measurement

1 Open any Publisher dialog box that requires numeric input, such as the Bullets And Indents dialog box shown here.

2 Highlight the measurement you want to change and type the numeric value followed by the abbreviation for your preferred unit of measurement.

3 Publisher automatically converts your entry to the default unit of measurement. If you enter 1 pi, for example, and the default unit of measurement is inches, Publisher displays 0.17" (or 1/6th of an inch).

Reposition the rulers and zero points simultaneously. You can save yourself a few mouse clicks by moving the rulers and the zero points in one operation. Simply place the pointer in the box where the two rulers intersect. When the pointer changes to a double-headed arrow, press and hold the Ctrl key and using the right mouse button, drag the rulers to the new location. The zero point now indicates the upper-left corner of an object, not of the page.

Reposition Both Zero Points

1 Position the pointer in the box where the rulers intersect at the upper-left corner of the work area. The pointer changes to a double-headed arrow.

2 Press and hold the Shift key, click the right mouse button, and drag the pointer to the new position on the document page next to the object you want to measure. The zero points on the rulers reflect this new location.

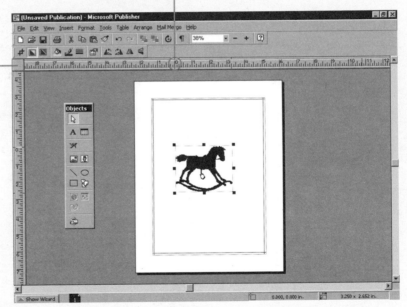

3 To return the zero points to their original positions, double-click the left mouse button on the box at the intersection of the vertical and horizontal rulers.

Set One Zero Point

 Position the pointer on the ruler that contains the zero point you want to move. Make sure that the pointer is positioned at the exact location where you want the zero point to appear.

2 When the double-headed arrow appears, press and hold the Shift key and click the right mouse button. The zero point moves to the new position.

3 To return the zero point to its original location, double-click the left mouse button on the box at the intersection of the vertical and horizontal rulers.

Zoom in before moving the rulers. If you move the rulers and then zoom in on a portion of the page, you'll find that Publisher can't reposition the rulers automatically. If you want to keep the rulers and the object you are measuring in sync, first zoom in on the object and then move the rulers.

For more information about Publisher's magnification tools, see Chapter 2.

Reposition One or Both Rulers

1 To reposition a single ruler, place the pointer on the vertical or the horizontal ruler. To reposition both rulers, place the pointer in the box where the two rulers intersect. The pointer changes to a double-headed arrow.

2 Using the left mouse button, drag the ruler to the new location. The ruler remains in its new position until you drag it back to its original location.

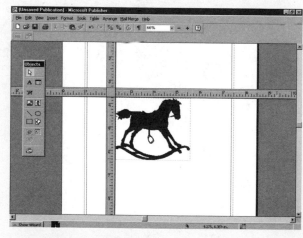

Use menu commands to create ruler guides. To create ruler guides using menu commands, select Ruler Guides on the Arrange menu. On the cascading menu, click either Add Horizontal Ruler Guide or Add Vertical Ruler Guide. When you create a ruler guide using the menu command, Publisher places a single guide in the center of your screen. You then must move the ruler guide to the desired location.

Why can't I see the ruler guides when I move to another page? Ruler guides are part of the page on which they are created. Normally, you create unique ruler guides for each page in a publication. If you want identical ruler guides to appear on all of the pages in your publication, you have two choices: you can create ruler guides on the background page, or you can use layout guides instead.

For more information on the background page, see chapter 2.

Ruler Guides

Instead of moving the rulers themselves, you can create ruler guides, which are more flexible than the rulers. You can create ruler guides interactively or by selecting menu options. And you can continue to adjust the position of ruler guides as you work.

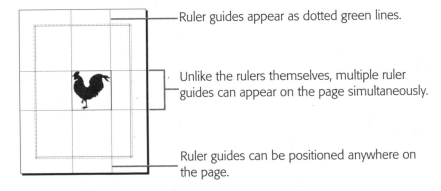

Ruler guides appear as dotted green lines.

Unlike the rulers themselves, multiple ruler guides can appear on the page simultaneously.

Ruler guides can be positioned anywhere on the page.

Drag a Guide from the Ruler

1 Pressing and holding the Shift key, position the pointer over either the horizontal or vertical ruler. The pointer changes to the Adjust pointer.

2 Press the left mouse button and drag a ruler guide to any position on the page.

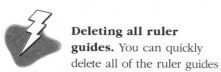

Deleting all ruler guides. You can quickly delete all of the ruler guides on a page. Choose the Ruler Guides command on the Arrange menu. On the submenu select Clear All Ruler Guides.

Move and Delete Individual Ruler Guides

1. While pressing and holding the Shift key, position the pointer over the ruler guide you want to move or delete. The pointer changes to the Adjust pointer.

2. Drag the ruler guide to a new location on the page or delete it by dragging it entirely off the page or back to the ruler with which it is parallel.

Layout Guides

Layout guides are visual guidelines that appear on every page of your electronic document but never on the printed output. They function purely as an internal tool that helps you position objects accurately and maintain a consistent look from page to page.

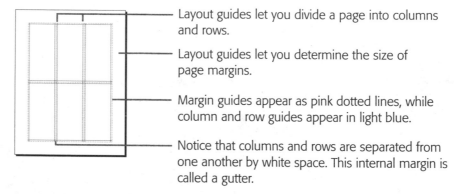

Layout guides let you divide a page into columns and rows.

Layout guides let you determine the size of page margins.

Margin guides appear as pink dotted lines, while column and row guides appear in light blue.

Notice that columns and rows are separated from one another by white space. This internal margin is called a gutter.

Colors indicate guide status. When you move an object, Publisher confirms that the object boundary has correctly aligned with the guide by displaying the overlap between the guide and the object boundary in reverse video. That means the pink margin guides turn bright green, the light blue layout guides turn orange, and the green ruler guides turn red.

 Why can't I find my layout guides? Layout guides (and ruler guides) are obscured by opaque objects, such as text or picture objects with solid or tinted backgrounds. If you want to see the layout guides at all times, you must make any opaque objects transparent. Select the object, and then press Ctrl-T.

Create Margins, Columns, and Rows on Every Page

① Choose Layout Guides from the Arrange menu.

② Set the margin guides by entering values in these text boxes.

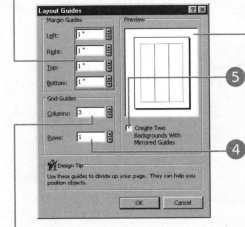

Look at the Preview area to confirm the results of your choices.

⑤ If you want to reflect the guides onto a left-hand page, turn on the Create Two Backgrounds With Mirrored Guides check box.

④ Change the number of row guides by entering any number from 1 through 256 in the text box labeled Rows.

③ Change the number of column guides by entering any number from 1 through 256 in the text box labeled Columns.

⑥ Click OK.

Customizing the Position of Layout Guides

When you first create layout guides, Publisher divides the page into columns of equal width and rows of equal height. Your page design, however, may require irregularly sized columns and rows.

Create a drawing grid. You can create a precise drawing grid with layout guides to help you develop detailed designs, charts, or diagrams. For example, you could create the electronic equivalent of 0.25-inch graph paper by dividing an 8.5-by-11-inch sheet of paper into 34 columns and 44 rows, without margins. If you choose to use Publisher's layout guides as drawing paper, draw objects to align with the pink margin guides, which represent the precise page divisions. The blue guides include a safety margin (or gutter allowance) of 0.10-inch.

Hide ruler and layout guides. Turning off the display of ruler guides, layout guides, and object boundaries gives you an accurate screen preview of the printed page. To hide the guides, choose Hide Boundaries And Guides on the View menu. To display guides and object boundaries, choose Show Boundaries And Guides on the View menu.

To switch between hiding and showing boundaries and guides, press Ctrl-Shift-O.

Move Column and Row Guides to New Custom Positions

1 Create the appropriate number of column and row guides by following the preceding procedure titled "Create Margins, Columns, and Rows on Every Page."

2 Go to the background page. The background page displays the column and row guides.

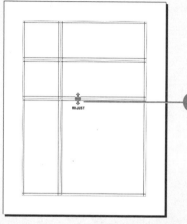

3 While pressing and holding the Shift key, position the pointer over a column or row guide you want to move. The pointer changes to the adjust pointer.

4 Drag the column or row guide to a new location.

5 Go to the foreground page. The new custom arrangement of columns and rows appears on every page.

Using Publisher's Snap To Functions

You can create and position objects purely by eye using Publisher's rulers and guides, but you'll produce tighter layouts if you take advantage of Publisher's Snap To functions. When the Snap To function is in effect, Publisher forces any frame you draw, move, or resize to align with the closest ruler mark, guideline, or object. Objects already placed on a page don't move, but new objects you add

Return column and row guides to standard positions. After you have created custom positions for column and row guides, you can easily return to a standard layout with evenly spaced columns and rows. Select Layout Guides on the Arrange menu to open the Layout Guides dialog box. Two new check boxes appear in this dialog box, allowing you to Reset Even Spacing for columns and rows. Turn on one or both of the check boxes. When you click OK, Publisher moves the column and row guides to standard positions.

 Use Snap To Ruler Marks to position guides. When Snap To Ruler Marks is turned on, everything you move—including ruler guides and layout guides—snaps into precise alignment with the ruler. This can help you create accurate layouts.

are affected by the Snap To functions. The pointer also snaps to the ruler marks or guides as you move it around the publication page.

Publisher's Snap To functions work at all magnification levels and allow you to position objects accurately even when you are working in a zoomed-out view of the document, such as Full Page view.

Turn Snap To Functions On and Off

1 Open the Tools menu.

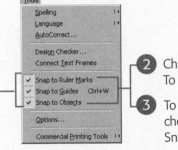

2 Choose Snap To Ruler Marks, Snap To Guides, or Snap To Objects.

3 To toggle these commands off (and remove the check mark), open the Tools menu and select a Snap To command that has a check mark next to it.

Snap To functions are invoked with a toggle command.
A check mark indicates that the command is active.
All three Snap To functions can be active at the same time.

Object Groups

Every time you select two or more objects, you automatically create a temporary group, or multiple selection. Publisher always gives you the option of converting a multiple selection into a permanent group. You can think of a group as a collection of objects that are "glued" together. A true group gives you layout and design flexibility because you can do the following:

Why don't objects snap to the ruler guides when Snap To Ruler Marks is turned on? Ruler guides are pulled down from the rulers, but once created they function like layout guides. In order to have ruler guides exert a magnetic pull, turn on the Snap To Guides command in the Tools menu.

To toggle Snap To Guides on or off, press Ctrl-W.

Use the Group/Ungroup command. You can also choose Group Objects or Ungroup Objects on the Arrange menu.

To group or ungroup objects, press Ctrl-Shift-G.

ⓔ Copy, move, rotate, resize, or delete a group as though it were a single object.

ⓔ Subselect any element within the group to change its formatting attributes.

ⓔ Select all the elements in a group to apply new formatting attributes uniformly to all elements.

ⓔ Type or import text into text objects within the group and link text frames.

ⓔ Group groups. You can create 16 levels of groups within groups.

Even when you clear a group, the elements remain together until you ungroup them.

In a multiple selection, selection handles (in gray instead of black) surround each object.

A Group button appears at the bottom right of the selection box containing two or more objects. Click the Group button to "lock" the two parts of the icon (and the multiple selected objects) together.

A single set of selection handles surrounds the whole group. Individual object boundaries, however, are maintained.

You can subselect objects within a group. A pink outline (or another color if the object background is colored) appears around a subselected object within a group.

Clicking the locked Group button again ungroups the objects and returns them to a multiple selection.

Why won't objects align with each other even when I have Snap To Objects turned on? Snap To Objects might not work as you expect for two reasons:

@ You didn't move the objects close enough to one another. The objects must be within 0.125 (1/8) inch of each other for Snap To Objects to work properly.

@ You've turned on Snap To Ruler Marks or Snap To Guides. These snap modes can interfere with Snap To Objects. It's best to toggle them off before using Snap To Objects.

For more information on multiple selections, see Chapter 1.

For more information on the Size and Position dialog box, see "Resizing Objects" later in this chapter.

Moving Objects

Publisher makes it easy to move individual objects, a multiple selection, or a group of objects on the same page or from page to page. You can also move an object up and down or left and right in small increments by using the Nudge command.

Move a Single Object, a Multiple Selection, or a Group

1 Select the object or objects you want to move.

2 Position the pointer along the edge of an object. The pointer changes to the Move pointer.

3 Drag the object or objects to the new position and release the mouse button.

The Martin Krump Trio

While you move a single object, a multiple selection, or a group, Publisher displays the object boundary of each individual object. This can help you to position both multiple selections and grouped objects more precisely in relation to other objects on the page.

Move an Object or Group Using the Size And Position Dialog Box

1 Select the object or group you want to move.

2 Choose Size And Position on the Format menu.

3 In the Position area enter new coordinates for the Horizontal and Vertical values.

4 Click OK. Publisher positions the upper-left corner of the object or group at the coordinates you specified.

Move objects in a perfectly straight line. You can move an object, a multiple selection, or a group in a perfectly straight line by pressing and holding the Shift key as you drag the mouse. Publisher constrains your movements to either vertical or horizontal movement.

What is the difference between the page and the scratch area?

Publisher indicates page boundaries with a solid black border and a drop shadow. Only objects on the page will print. The scratch area refers to the gray area outside the page. It is a temporary holding area for objects. Objects in the scratch area will be saved along with the publication file, but they will not print.

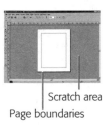

Scratch area

Page boundaries

Move an Object or Group Using the Floating Toolbar

1. Select the object or group you want to move.

2. On the Format menu, select Size And Position.

3. In the Size And Position dialog box, click the Show Toolbar button. A toolbar with size and positioning options appears.

4. Enter a new value in the X text box to change the horizontal position, or enter a new value in the Y text box to change the vertical position.

5. Publisher accepts the new value and moves the object or group when you press the Tab key, or press the Enter key, or click anywhere else on screen. The toolbar will remain open until you click the Close button.

Move Objects from Page to Page

1. Select the object or objects you want to move.

2. Drag the selected object(s) completely off the page onto the scratch area.

3. Use the page controls to turn to any other page in your document.

4. Drag the object(s) from the scratch area onto the current page.

Move and copy objects simultaneously. Instead of copying, pasting, and then moving an object to a new location, you can position a duplicate in a new location. First select the object, objects, or group you want to duplicate. While pressing and holding the Ctrl key, drag the object to a new location on the page, to the scratch area, or to another application that supports drag-and-drop editing. Publisher leaves the original object in its previous position and draws a copy of the object in the new location.

To move the selected object 1 pixel at a time (or by whatever amount you specified in the Nudge By text box), press and hold the Alt key and press any of the arrow keys on your keyboard.

What is the smallest amount that I can nudge an object? If you clear the Nudge By text box, Publisher moves an object by 1 pixel increments. But be warned—a pixel represents a different distance depending on the resolution of your screen and the current magnification level. For the smallest possible nudge, zoom in to 100-percent view or higher.

Nudge an Object into Place

① Select the object or objects you want to move.

② Select Nudge on the Arrange menu. The Nudge dialog box appears.

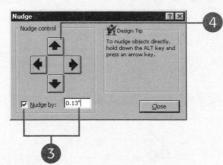

④ Click the appropriate Nudge Control arrow to move the selected object up, down, left, or right. If you didn't specify a value in the Nudge By text box, Publisher moves the object 1 pixel at a time.

If you want to specify the increments by which the object moves, turn on the Nudge By check box and either accept the value Publisher suggests or type a new value from 0.01 through 2 inches in the text box.

Resizing Objects

Often you must reduce or enlarge the size of individual elements to create a balanced, visually pleasing layout. Publisher allows you to resize an object using numerical values or interactively using selection handles. Depending upon the handle you select, you can resize only the height, only the width, or both the height and the width simultaneously. When you resize an object, it is often important to maintain the object's proportions, as the following example shows.

Resizing an object from its center. Pressing and holding the Ctrl key as you move a selection handle enlarges or reduces an object from its center. Use this technique to help keep objects in a complex layout properly aligned.

Can I maintain the aspect ratio of text frames, table frames, drawn shapes, and Design Gallery objects when I resize them? Yes, you can maintain the aspect of these objects, but you must press and hold the Shift key as you drag the corner selection handle. If you neglect to hold the Shift key, you will resize the height and the width simultaneously but disproportionately.

The relationship between an object's width and its height is called its aspect ratio.

If you don't maintain an object's aspect ratio (its original proportions) the object becomes distorted when you resize it.

Using a corner selection handle to resize a picture changes its width and height by the same percentage. This maintains the original aspect ratio.

Resize an Object Using Selection Handles

1 Select the object.

Grab a selection handle on either side of an object to change only its width.

Grab a selection handle at the top or bottom of an object to change only its height.

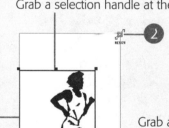

2 Position the pointer on a selection handle. The pointer changes to the Resize pointer.

Grab a selection handle at one of the four corners of an object to change its height and width simultaneously. If the selected object is a picture or a WordArt or Clip Art object, using the corner handle to resize the object automatically maintains the aspect ratio.

3 Drag the handle until the object is the size you want.

Resize by percentages. You can use the Scale Picture or Scale Object command on the Format menu to resize a WordArt, OLE, or picture object an exact percentage of its original size. But you can't use this command on a text object, table, or drawn shape.

For more information about the Scale Picture and Scale Object dialog boxes, see Chapter 10.

If the floating toolbar is displayed you can change the selected object's size by entering new values into the Width and Height text boxes, as shown below.

Width

Height

For more information on the floating toolbar, see "Move an Object or Group Using the Floating Toolbar," earlier in this chapter.

Resize an Object or Group Numerically

1 Select the object or group you want to resize.

2 Select Size And Position from the Format menu.

3 Enter values in the Height and Width text boxes.

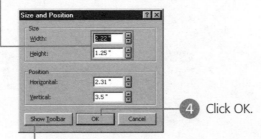

4 Click OK.

Alternatively, you can click Show Toolbar to open a floating toolbar containing size and position options where you can enter new sizing information. The toolbar will remain open until you close it.

Layering Objects

In a complex design, objects frequently overlap. The sequence in which objects overlap is called the stacking order. Though layering works identically on the foreground and background pages, Publisher treats objects on the foreground and background as two separate stacks. Objects on the background always appear below objects on the foreground.

By default, Publisher always stacks objects in the order you create them, but you can change the stacking order at any time.

Can I change the stacking order of grouped objects? You can change the stacking order of grouped objects only in relation to other objects on the page. Publisher moves the whole group of objects up or down in the stacking order. But within the group, the objects maintain their order relative to one another. If you want to change the stacking order within a group, you must ungroup the objects.

Can I change the stacking order of objects on the background with objects on the foreground? No. You can change the stacking order of background objects only relative to other background objects. And you can change the stacking order of foreground objects only relative to other foreground objects. If you want to change the stacking order of objects on the background with objects on the foreground, you must select the background object and use the Send To Foreground command.

For more information on relationships between backgrounds and foregrounds, see Chapter 2.

The picture frame was drawn first, so it is positioned at the bottom of the stack.

The text frame was drawn next and is positioned in the middle of the stack.

The circle was drawn last and is positioned at the top of the stack.

Selecting and Seeing Stacked Objects

Sometimes it is difficult to understand the stacking order and especially difficult to select objects lower in the stack. The following illustrations explain how to identify and select objects in a stack.

A large opaque object hides any smaller objects and guides layered beneath it in the stack. Clicking selects only the topmost object.

You can select all of the objects in the stack by drawing a selection box around the elements. Then press Shift+click to clear the selection of the topmost object.

To see and select only the objects lower in the stack, you can make the topmost object transparent by selecting it and using the Ctrl-T shortcut keys.

To bring an object to the top of a stack, press F6. To send an object to the bottom of a stack, press Shift-F6.

The Bring To Front and Send To Back icons, shown below, let you quickly change the stacking order of selected objects.

Rearrange the Stacking Order

1 Select an individual object, multiple objects, or a group.

2 Choose one of the four layering commands from the Arrange menu.

Send To Back moves the object to the bottom of the stack.

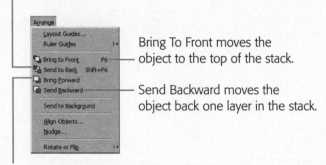

Bring To Front moves the object to the top of the stack.

Send Backward moves the object back one layer in the stack.

Bring Forward moves the object up one layer in the stack.

Rotating and Flipping Objects

You can add visual interest to a page design, or simply make elements fit together better, by rotating objects. You can experiment with the orientation of an object by dragging a selection handle. You can also rotate objects by specifying an exact numerical value in the Rotate Objects dialog box or the floating toolbar. You can even use shortcut keys and toolbar buttons to rotate objects by a standard amount.

Publisher also lets you flip pictures, drawn shapes, WordArt elements, and OLE objects. Flipping an object inverts it vertically (top-to-bottom) or horizontally (left to right). It creates a mirror image that isn't the same as rotating the object 180 degrees. Publisher cannot flip text objects or tables.

Rotate in 15-degree increments. You can rotate objects in 15-degree increments by pressing and holding the Ctrl and Alt keys as you rotate an object.

To open the Custom Rotate dialog box, click the icon of the same name.

To rotate objects clockwise in 5-degree increments, press Ctrl-Alt-RIGHT ARROW. To rotate objects counterclockwise in 5-degree increments, press Ctrl-Alt-LEFT ARROW.

Rotate an Object Using a Selection Handle

1 Select the object you want to rotate.

2 While pressing and holding the Alt key, position the pointer over a selection handle. The pointer changes to the Rotate pointer.

3 Continue to press the Alt key and drag the pointer in a circular path to rotate the object by the desired amount.

The Martin Krump Trio — Publisher displays an outline of the object to help you position it.

Specify the Rotation Angle

1 Select the object you want to rotate.

2 Open the Arrange menu and select the Rotate Or Flip command. From the submenu, select Custom Rotate. The Custom Rotate dialog box appears.

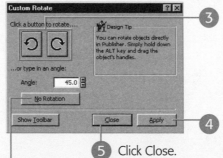

3 Click either the clockwise or counter-clockwise rotation button as many times as necessary to rotate the object in increments of 5 degrees. Or type a rotation value between 0 and 359 degrees in 0.1-degree increments in the Angle text box.

4 Click Apply to see the effects of the rotation without closing the dialog box.

5 Click Close.

Click here to remove the rotation from the currently selected object.

Rotate an Object Using the Formatting Toolbar

① Select the object you want to rotate.

② Open the Arrange menu and select Rotate Or Flip. On the submenu select Custom Rotate.

③ In the Custom Rotate dialog box, click the Show Toolbar button. A floating toolbar (the Formatting toolbar) appears.

④ Enter a new value between 0 and 359 degrees in 0.1-degree increments into the Rotation text box. Then press the Tab key, press the Enter key, or click anywhere else on screen to accept the new value and rotate the object.

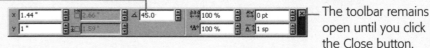

The toolbar remains open until you click the Close button.

Icons on the formatting toolbar let you rotate or flip the selected object easily.

Click here to rotate an object 90 degrees to the left (counter-clockwise).

Click here to flip an object vertically (top to bottom).

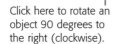

Click here to rotate an object 90 degrees to the right (clockwise).

Click here to flip an object horizontally (left to right).

Rotate or Flip an Object by a Standard Amount

① Select the object you want to rotate.

② Open the Arrange menu and select the Rotate Or Flip command.

③ On the submenu, choose one of the following commands:

❧ Rotate Left turns an object counterclockwise by 90 degrees.

❧ Rotate Right turns an object clockwise by 90 degrees.

❧ Flip Vertically inverts a drawn object, bottom to top.

❧ Flip Horizontally inverts a drawn object left to right.

Center an object on the page. The Align Objects dialog box doesn't contain an explicit command to center an object on the page, but you can do that. Choose the Centers option for both the Left To Right and the Top To Bottom alignments and select Align Along Margins. Making these three selections for a group of objects stacks the objects concentrically in the middle of the page.

Aligning Objects

To align objects with each other or with the page margins, use the Align Objects command.

Align Objects

(1) Select the objects you want to align by drawing a selection box around them or by Shift+clicking each object.

(2) Choose Align Objects on the Arrange menu. The Align Objects dialog box appears.

(3) In the Align Objects dialog box, select the options you want for Left To Right alignment and Top To Bottom alignment. Publisher aligns the selected objects in the direction that you choose.

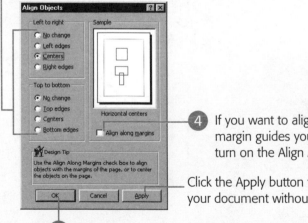

(4) If you want to align the objects along the margin guides you specified for your publication, turn on the Align Along Margins check box.

Click the Apply button to align objects in your document without closing this dialog box.

(5) When the Sample area displays the arrangement you want (such as the horizontally centered option shown here), click OK.

To quickly cut, copy, and paste objects or text, click the appropriate icons on the Standard toolbar.

Use shortcut menus. If you right-click an object or highlighted text, the shortcut menu that pops up contains all the Clipboard commands.

Why can't I cut or delete a text frame? When a text frame contains text, the Del key, the Backspace key, and the Cut command on the Edit menu affect only the text—not the frame. If the text frame is empty, however, the Del or Backspace key deletes the frame. If you want to remove a text frame that contains text, choose Delete Object on the Edit menu or press Shift-Del.

The Clipboard

You can temporarily store text, numbers, and pictures on the Windows Clipboard. You can then paste any of these elements within the same publication, in different publications, or in different Windows-based applications.

Copy, Cut, or Delete an Object or Text

1 Select an object or highlight text.

2 From the Edit menu choose one of the following Clipboard commands.

Select Cut to remove the object or text from the current publication and place it on the Clipboard.

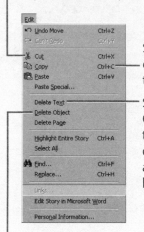

Select Copy to place a duplicate of the object or text on the Clipboard. The original text or object remains in the publication.

Select Delete Text to remove text from the publication. Only the highlighted words or paragraphs are deleted; the text frame itself remains in the publication. No copy of the text is placed on the Clipboard. This command appears on the Edit menu only if you have highlighted text.

Select Delete Object to remove the object from the publication. No copy is placed on the Clipboard.

All Clipboard operations have shortcut keys.

- Ctrl-C copies objects.
- Ctrl-X cuts objects.
- Ctrl-V pastes objects.
- Del or Backspace deletes objects.

Can I paste text into an existing text frame? Yes. Select the text frame before you choose the Paste command from the Edit menu. Publisher inserts the text from the Clipboard at the location of the Text Insertion pointer.

For information about the background and fore-ground, see Chapter 2.

Paste an Object or Text from the Clipboard

① With no object selected, choose Paste on the Edit menu. Depending on the magnification level, Publisher places the object in approximately the original position or in the center of the window. If you are pasting text, Publisher creates a text frame.

② You can continue to paste instances of the object or text into your document, because a copy remains on the Clipboard until you cut or copy something else.

The Design Checker

Before you print your document or publish it to the Internet, you should look for potential layout problems. The Design Checker automates this process.

Check Your Design for Errors

① From the Tools menu, choose Design Checker. The Design Checker dialog box appears.

② To check every page in your publication, select All. To check a specified range of pages, select Pages and type the starting and ending pages in the From and To text boxes.

④ Click Options to display a dialog box where you can choose to have Publisher look for all possible problems in a document, or for one or more specific errors.

③ To check the background as well as the foreground, click the check box at the bottom of the dialog box.

Look for errors in Web documents. When you use the Design Checker to troubleshoot Web documents, Publisher looks for problems specific to Internet publishing, such as pages that can't be reached by hyperlink or images that take a long time to download.

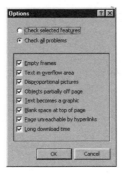

For more information about creating Web documents, see Chapter 12.

Check Your Design for Errors *(continued)*

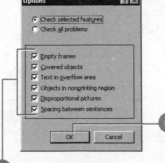

6 Click OK to close each dialog box. Publisher begins checking the layout.

5 Choose the type of errors you want to find.

7 If Publisher finds a problem, it describes the problem in a dialog box and suggests ways to fix it. As shown here, the Design Checker has found an empty text frame and suggests deleting it. Click the button that corresponds to the action you want to take.

  @ You can take Publisher's suggestions and fix each problem before you continue with the design check. Publisher also allows you to ignore the current instance or all instances of the problem.

  @ If you don't understand how to fix the problem, click the Explain button. Publisher provides instructions for analyzing the problem and helping you fix it.

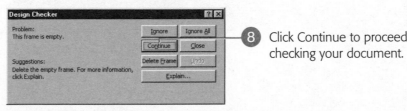

8 Click Continue to proceed checking your document.

9 When Publisher finishes checking the layout (or if Publisher finds no problems), an alert box appears advising you that the design check is complete.

Text Frames

One of the most basic rules in Microsoft Publisher 2000 is that you can't type or manipulate text unless the text is inside a frame. Text frames allow you to position blocks of text on the page.

How can I display text that is hidden in the overflow area? As the following illustration shows, Publisher preserves all of the text you have typed or inserted. It hides the text from view by storing it in the overflow area. To display text in the overflow area, either enlarge the text frame or connect it to an empty text frame.

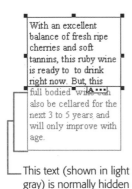

This text (shown in light gray) is normally hidden in the overflow area.

Autofit Mode Versus Text Overflow Mode

Publisher's autofitting function can automatically adjust the size of text to fit a frame.

With an excellent balance of fresh ripe cherries and soft tannins, this ruby wine is ready to drink right now. But, this full bodied wine can also be cellared for the next 3 to 5 years and will only improve with age.

With an excellent balance of fresh ripe cherries and soft tannins, this ruby wine is ready to drink right now. But, this full bodied wine can also be cellared for the next 3 to 5 years and will only improve with age.

The Best Fit autofitting option enlarges or reduces the size of the text to fill the text frame.

The Shrink Text On Overflow autofitting option reduces the size of the text to make it fit in the text frame. It doesn't enlarge the size of the text.

When autofitting is turned off, Publisher stores any text that can't fit into the text frame in the overflow area. In overflow mode, changing the size or shape of a text frame doesn't change the size of the text; it changes only the amount of text displayed.

For information on creating frames, see Chapter 1.

Why can't I see the text flow buttons on a text frame? The Text In Overflow, Go To Previous Frame, and Go To Next Frame buttons appear only when the text frame is selected.

Why can't I see the Connect Frames toolbar? There are three possibilities:

- You may not have a text frame selected. The Connect Frames toolbar appears on the screen only when a text frame is active.

- You may have docked the toolbar at the bottom of the work area. To float the toolbar, double-click the Move icon (the gray double bars at the left of the toolbar).

- You may have closed the toolbar (by clicking the "X" icon in the upper-right corner). Reopen the toolbar by choosing Text Frame Connecting on the Toolbars submenu of the View menu.

> With an excellent balance of fresh ripe cherries and soft tannins, this ruby wine is ready to to drink right

Enlarging or shrinking the text frame changes the amount of text it can contain.

> With an excellent balance of fresh ripe cherries and soft tannins, this ruby wine is ready to to drink right now. But, this full bodied wine can also be cellared for the next 3 to 5 years and will

Changing the shape of a text frame (short and wide versus tall and skinny) changes how the text flows within the frame.

> With an excellent balance of fresh ripe cherries and soft tannins, this ruby wine is ready to to drink right now. But,

Text Flow Between Text Frames

You can control the way the stories flow in your publications by connecting, disconnecting, and deleting text frames or by using the Autoflow option. By using the Connect Frames toolbar, you can link and unlink frames that are adjacent to each other on the same page, or that fall on different pages. Special text frame buttons appear whenever there is text in the overflow area, or when two or more text frames are linked in a chain.

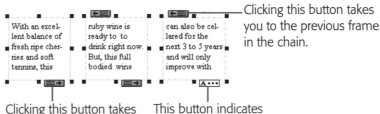

Clicking this button takes you to the previous frame in the chain.

Clicking this button takes you to the next frame in a chain of connected frames.

This button indicates that text is in the overflow area.

Draw multiple text frames. After you draw a text frame, the crosshair pointer normally reverts to the arrow pointer. You can keep the crosshair pointer active and continue to draw text frames by Ctrl-clicking the Text Frame Tool on the toolbar. After you've drawn a series of text frames, select another tool on the toolbar to return to normal selection mode.

Connecting text frames on noncontiguous pages. If you need to turn to another page, position the pointer over the page control. The Pitcher pointer becomes the standard pointer. Go to the page that contains the next text frame you want added to the chain. When you move the pointer over a text frame, the tilted pitcher reappears.

Connect Text Frames

① Using the Text Frame Tool, create any number of text frames on the same page or on different pages in your publication.

② Select the text frame that will be the first in the chain. This frame can be empty, or it can contain text. The Connect Frames toolbar appears.

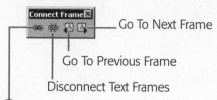

Go To Next Frame

Go To Previous Frame

Disconnect Text Frames

③ Select the Connect Text Frames tool. The pointer changes into an upright pitcher, indicating that the pointer isn't positioned over an empty text frame.

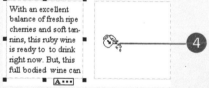

④ Position the pitcher over an empty text frame. The upright pitcher tilts, indicating that Publisher can now flow text.

⑤ Click the empty text frame. If the overflow area of the first frame contains any text, it flows into the newly connected text frame.

Disconnect a Text Frame

① Select the text frame that immediately precedes the point at which you want to break a chain of text frames.

② Click the Disconnect Text Frames button. The text from the disconnected text frame and all subsequent frames in the chain flows into the overflow area for the selected frame.

What happens to the text when I delete a text frame from a chain of frames? You delete only the frame. The text itself flows into the remaining text frames in the chain.

What happens when I delete text frames along with a page? If you delete a page that contains unconnected text frames, Publisher deletes the frames and their text along with the page. If you delete a page that contains connected text frames, however, Publisher deletes only the text frames with the page. The text itself flows into the remaining connected frames in the chain or into the overflow area for the previous text frame.

Inserting text into a text frame from an externally stored file is covered in Chapter 5.

What happens if I click No in the Autoflow dialog box? If you click No when presented with the first Autoflow dialog box, Publisher places all the remaining text in the overflow area. You can then create and connect frames manually.

Delete a Text Frame from a Chain

① Select the frame you want to delete.

② Choose Delete Object from the Edit menu, or press the Shift-Del shortcut keys.

Flowing Text Automatically

Publisher's Autoflow function is available only when you insert a text file. If the story is too long for the selected text frame or text frame chain, a dialog box asks whether you want to use the Autoflow feature.

Flow Text Automatically

① Select an unlinked text frame or the first frame in a linked chain and insert a text file. The following dialog box appears.

② Click Yes to have Publisher flow text into frames that already exist in your publication. The following dialog box appears.

Publisher displays this dialog box for each preexisting text frame regardless of whether the frames are connected.

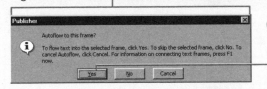

③ Click Yes to have Publisher automatically connect a frame during the autoflow process or click No if you want Publisher to skip to the next frame. If you still have text remaining, Publisher prompts you to create text frames.

Flow Text Automatically (continued)

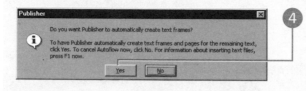

4 Click Yes if you want Publisher to create pages and connected text frames to accommodate the entire text file. The formatting of the new text frames will match that of the text frame you started with.

For more information about formatting a frame with a border or a shadow, see Chapter 9. For more information about fills, see Chapter 15.

Text margins affect how text wraps around artwork. The text frame margins you create affect how text appears next to the art in your publication. If you create narrow margins—or none at all—in your text frames, the body copy prints very near the edge of the picture frame, as shown here.

If you create wide margins in your text frames, your layout is more open because the pictures have a wide berth, as shown below.

Formatting a Text Frame

You can change the appearance of a text frame with formatting attributes. You can add a border, choose a fill, or create a shadow for a text frame. Certain crucial formatting attributes—specifically margins, columns, continued notices, and text wrap—help you to control the flow of text within a text frame.

Text Frame Margins

Publisher defines margins for all four sides of a text frame using whatever unit of measurement you select in the Options dialog box. If you select inches as the unit of measurement, the default text frame margin is 0.04 inches.

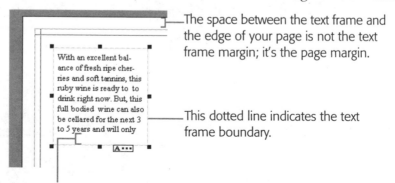

The space between the text frame and the edge of your page is not the text frame margin; it's the page margin.

This dotted line indicates the text frame boundary.

The text frame margin is the space between the actual type and the text frame.

To access the Text Frames Properties dialog box, click its icon on the Formatting toolbar.

Change the Text Frame Margins

① Select the text frame whose margins you want to set.

② From the Format menu, choose Text Frame Properties. The Text Frame Properties dialog box appears.

③ Enter any value between 0 and 16 inches for the text frame margins into the Left, Right, Top, and Bottom text boxes.

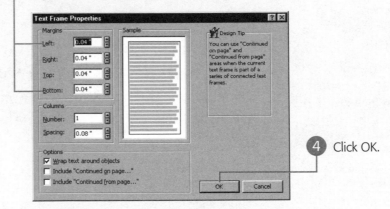

④ Click OK.

Multiple Columns Within a Text Frame

In addition to margins, the Text Frame Properties dialog box lets you set up your text in columns. Columns automatically adjust the alignment and flow of your text.

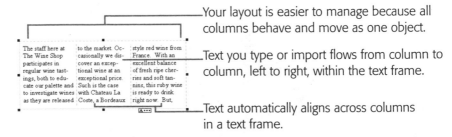

Your layout is easier to manage because all columns behave and move as one object.

Text you type or import flows from column to column, left to right, within the text frame.

Text automatically aligns across columns in a text frame.

Forcing a column break. If you want text to appear in the next column (even if it has not yet filled the current column), press Ctrl-Shift-Enter to force a column break. If you want text to appear in the next linked text frame (even if it has not yet filled the current frame), press Ctrl-Enter.

Format the Text Frame as Two or More Columns

① Select the text frame.

② Choose Text Frame Properties on the Format menu.

③ Enter any value from 1 through 63 to indicate the number of columns you want for your text.

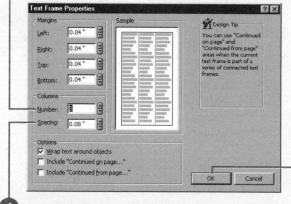

⑤ If the preview of your layout that appears in the Sample area is acceptable, click OK.

④ Specify the space between your columns by typing a value from 0 through 16 inches in the Spacing text box.

Wrapping Text Around Other Elements

You can create a more integrated design by wrapping text around another element, such as a picture, WordArt, a table, an OLE object, or even another text frame.

Turn On Text Wrap

① Select a text frame.

② Open the Text Frame Properties dialog box.

③ Select Wrap Text Around Objects and click OK.

Changing the text style of all Continued notices within a document.

When Publisher creates Continued notices, it also defines two separate text styles, called Continued-From Text and Continued-On Text. You can change the formatting of all the Continued notices in your document by editing these text styles.

For more information about editing text styles, see Chapter 6.

Can I change the contents of the Continued notices? Yes, but you must edit each Continued notice individually using Publisher's standard text editing features—there is no way to change the automatic wording globally.

Automated Continued Notices

A good text layout makes it easy for the reader to follow a story from page to page, in part by including elements such as Publisher's automated continued notices.

Insert a Continued Notice

① Select the text frame in which you want to add a Continued notice.

② Open the Format menu and choose Text Frame Properties.

③ Select the Include "Continued On Page" and/or the Include "Continued From Page" check boxes.

④ Click OK. Publisher automatically applies a standard format to Continued notices as shown below.

The "Continued From Page" notice appears at the upper-left corner of the text frame.

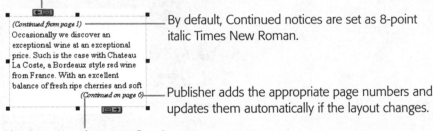

(Continued from page 1)
Occasionally we discover an exceptional wine at an exceptional price. Such is the case with Chateau La Coste, a Bordeaux style red wine from France. With an excellent balance of fresh ripe cherries and soft
(Continued on page 6)

By default, Continued notices are set as 8-point italic Times New Roman.

Publisher adds the appropriate page numbers and updates them automatically if the layout changes.

The "Continued On Page" notice appears at the lower-right corner of the text frame.

Inserting and Editing Text

Microsoft Publisher 2000 allows you to insert text by typing directly into a text frame or by importing a word processing file. Publisher's text editing tools give you the power to fine-tune the content of your publications. Specialized text features, such as the ability to add symbols or typographic characters, give your publications a professional typeset look.

For more information on Publisher's text frames, see Chapter 4.

Publisher's Text Editing Modes

Publisher requires you to type into a text frame. If you begin typing without first creating a text frame, one of two things happens.

- If the page is totally blank, Publisher automatically creates a text frame that fills the page. The text you type appears in this text frame.

- If the page contains other objects, Publisher displays an alert box informing you that you can type only into a text frame. You must then create or select a text frame.

Typing directly into a text frame is the most efficient way to add small amounts of text, such as headlines or captions, to your publication. Even when you decide to import text, you'll find that it's often necessary to edit the text to make it work with your design. Publisher lets you type and edit text in several different ways, and it offers options to help you select and alter text more easily. You can switch between the different editing functions described in the following table.

What is the difference between Highlight Entire Story and Select All on the Edit menu? The Highlight Entire Story command on the Edit menu selects all the text in a story, even if the text is placed in multiple text frames across different pages. However, it doesn't select the text frames. Select All on the Edit menu selects all the *objects* on the current page or spread, including text frames, pictures, OLE objects, and drawn shapes.

Ctrl-A highlights all of the text in a story.

For more information about the Windows Clipboard, see Chapter 3.

What happens if I drop or paste text outside a text frame? If you drop or paste text outside a text frame, Publisher automatically creates a new text frame to hold the copy.

Methods of Typing and Editing Text	
Method	**Directions for Use**
Insertion mode	Create or select a text frame and begin typing. Publisher adds the new text at the location of the insertion point. You can reposition the insertion point anywhere in a text block using the arrow keys or the mouse.
Replacement mode	Highlight the text you want to replace and begin typing. Publisher replaces the highlighted text with new text you type.
Drag-and-drop editing	Highlight the text you want to move and drag it to a new location. Press and hold the Ctrl key as you drag to create a copy of the highlighted text.
Windows Clipboard	Use the Cut or Copy commands to place highlighted text on the Clipboard. Position the text insertion point in a text frame before using the Paste command.
Microsoft Word	Select a text frame and choose Edit Story In Microsoft Word from the Edit menu, or right-click the text frame and select Edit Story In Microsoft Word from the Change Text submenu. To take advantage of this feature, you must be using Publisher 97 or later and Word 6 or later.

Enable Text Editing Assistance

1 On the Tools menu, select Options. The Options dialog box appears.

2 Select the Edit tab.

3 Select Drag-And-Drop Text Editing.

4 Activate the option When Selecting, Automatically Select Entire Word. Now, when you select across more than one word, Publisher automatically selects entire words.

5 Click OK.

What are the advantages of using Microsoft Word as my text editor? You can utilize Word's robust editing tools, such as the grammar checker. In addition, you can edit a nonlinear design (with text placed in multiple text frames on different pages) in a linear and logical fashion because Word presents the text as a normal word processing document.

 Can I import a Microsoft WordPad file into a text frame? Yes. WordPad is compatible with Microsoft Write, so choose the Microsoft Write format when you import the file.

 Can I import text from a word processing program that isn't directly compatible with Publisher? Yes, but you must save the text in one of two generic file formats that Publisher supports. The Rich Text Format (RTF) contains formatting information that Publisher preserves. The Plain Text format is a universal file type that you can export from word processors, databases, and spreadsheets. Publisher accepts Plain Text and Plain Text (DOS). Because Plain Text files contain no formatting information, Publisher applies its default Normal style.

Inserting a Text File

You should create longer blocks of text, such as stories, articles, or reports in a word processing program, and then import the files into your Publisher document. When you import a file from one of the following applications, Publisher usually retains any text formatting you've used, such as font and point size, italics and boldface, paragraph indents, customized line spacing, and defined text styles.

- ❧ Microsoft Word versions 2, 6, and 97 through 2000
- ❧ Microsoft Works versions 3 and 4
- ❧ WordPerfect versions 5 and 6
- ❧ Microsoft Write
- ❧ Microsoft Publisher, all versions
- ❧ Microsoft Excel

Import a Text File Created in a Word Processing Application

1 Select the frame into which you want to import text.

2 Open the Insert menu and choose Text File. The Insert Text file dialog box appears.

The Find File dialog box is covered in Chapter 2.

Structure Excel files for optimum import. Publisher imports individual worksheets within a spreadsheet file, and individual named ranges within the worksheet. Provided that you've structured the spreadsheet properly, this feature allows you to extract only the data you need from a larger Excel file. Although you select an empty text frame to import an Excel worksheet, Publisher always creates a new table containing the data.

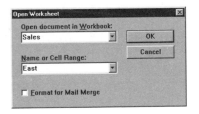

Import a Text File Created in a Word Processing Application *(continued)*

③ Open the drop-down list box to select a file type.

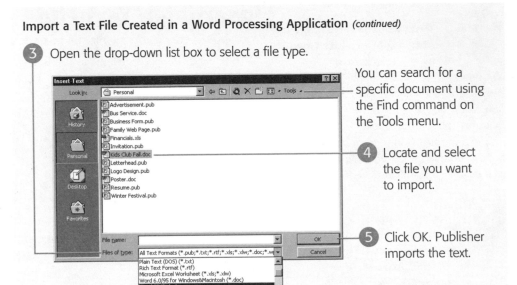

You can search for a specific document using the Find command on the Tools menu.

④ Locate and select the file you want to import.

⑤ Click OK. Publisher imports the text.

Finding and Replacing Text

Using the Find command, you can locate specific words or phrases anywhere in your document. With the Replace command, you can simultaneously find text and change it. The Replace command is particularly helpful when you edit long documents. For example, if you discover that you misspelled a client's name in your marketing materials, you can search for each occurrence of the incorrect spelling and replace it with the correct spelling.

Press Ctrl-F to access the Find dialog box.

Refine the search criteria. You can help Publisher find the exact instance of the word or phrase for which you are searching. Click Match Whole Word Only to find the text only where it appears as a whole word and ignore where it is part of another, longer word. For example, if you search for the whole word "dent," Publisher doesn't highlight "accident," "correspondent," or "dentist." Click Match Case if you want to find the text only if it uses the same capitalization (for example, all uppercase) as the word in the Find What text box.

Find Text

① Click the I-beam pointer anywhere in a text frame to set the insertion point. It's best to start at the beginning or end of a story.

② On the Edit menu, choose Find. The Find dialog box appears.

③ Type the text you want to find in the Find What text box.

④ Refine the search criteria by selecting Match Whole Word Only or Match Case.

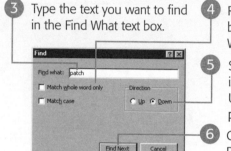

⑤ Select Down if you want to search from the insertion point to the end of the story. Select Up if you want to search from the insertion point to the beginning of the story.

⑥ Click Find Next to begin the search. When Publisher finds the text, it highlights it. To search for the next occurrence of the word or phrase, click Find Next again.

⑦ Click Cancel to return to the story.

Replace Text

① Click the I-beam at the beginning or end of a text frame to set the insertion point.

② On the Edit menu, choose Replace. The Replace dialog box appears.

Choose a magnification level before using the Find or Replace functions. Although Publisher highlights each instance of the text you are searching for, it doesn't magnify it. So before you open the Find or Replace dialog boxes, switch to a magnification level that allows you to easily read the words on screen.

Searching for misspelled words. Publisher can search for a word even if you're not sure of the spelling. Simply substitute a question mark character (?) for each letter you are unsure of. For example, you could type "p?tch" to search for "patch" or "pitch."

Press Ctrl-H to access the Replace dialog box.

Replace Text *(continued)*

3 Type the text you want to find in the Find What text box.

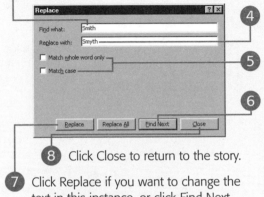

4 Type the new text in the Replace With text box.

5 Refine the search criteria by selecting Match Whole Word Only or Match Case.

6 Click Find Next to find the next occurrence of the text that you want to replace. Publisher highlights the text if it finds it. Alternatively, click Replace All to replace every occurrence of the text automatically.

8 Click Close to return to the story.

7 Click Replace if you want to change the text in this instance, or click Find Next to leave the document unchanged and search for the next occurrence of the text.

Finding and Replacing Special Characters

In addition to searching for standard letters and punctuation marks, you can use the Find command to search for special characters, such as tabs and spaces. You can use the Replace command to insert such characters into your text.

The codes in the following table show some of the most common special characters you'll want to find or replace. You type the codes into the Find What and Replace With text boxes, just as you would normal text.

Use Find and Replace to convert typewriter-style characters to typeset characters. Many of the rules that you learned in typing class don't apply when you are using a desktop publishing program. For example, two spaces after a period is good typing style, but the spaces will look too wide when the document is typeset.

Instead of manually scrolling through a long document to remove characters like extra spaces or unnecessary tabs, you can use the Replace command to search for and delete them.

For more information on optional and nonbreaking hyphens, see the "Hyphenation Options" section later in this chapter.

Viewing special characters on-screen. Publisher can display special characters as part of a text block. This is purely a convenience feature that can help you keep track of tabs and end-of-paragraph markers. To display special characters, select Show Special Characters from the View menu. To preview your text as it will print, select Hide Special Characters from the View menu.

Commonly Used Special Character Codes	
Type This Code	**To Find or Replace...**
Spacebar	A space.
^^	A caret.
^?	A question mark.
^-	An optional hyphen.
^~	A nonbreaking hyphen.
^m	The contents of the Find What text box plus the contents of the Replace With text box. For example, if the Find What text box contains the word *leap* and the Replace With text box contains the command ^*ing*, Publisher creates the word *leaping* every time it finds *leap*.
^n	A line break.
^p	The end of a paragraph.
^s	A nonbreaking space.
^t	A tab.
^w	Any blank space between characters, including spaces and tabs.

Working With Publisher's Spell Check Features

On the simplest level, Publisher's spelling checker catches misspellings in your documents. On a more advanced level, a number of customization options let you choose exactly how the spell checker works.

To toggle the display of special characters on and off, press Ctrl-Shift-Y.

Click the Show Special Characters button on the Standard toolbar to toggle the display of non-printing characters on and off.

Exclude words from the spell check. You can use the Set Language command to exclude technical or unusual words from the normal spell check. First select the word or paragraph you don't want to spell check. In the Mark Selected Text As box (found in the Language dialog box), select the (no proofing) option.

Configuring the Spell Checker

Publisher lets you determine the language, the kinds of mistakes the Spell Checker looks for, and whether it flags mistakes as you type. You can designate unusual, technical, or all uppercase words as exceptions to normal spelling rules.

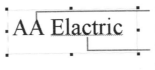

You can prevent Publisher from flagging an unusual capitalization as a misspelling.

You can have Publisher flag possible errors with red underlining.

Choose a Language

1 Select a text frame or highlight text.

2 On the Tools menu, select Language. On the submenu, select Set Language. The Language dialog box appears.

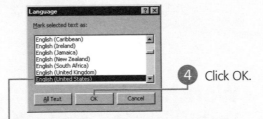

4 Click OK.

3 Select one of the 94 languages and language variations from the list. Optionally, click the All Text button, which assigns the language to all text in the entire publication.

Now when Publisher checks your English-language document, it will ignore any text designated as a foreign language.

Turn off the display of wavy red underlining. If you find Publisher's method of alerting you to possible spelling errors distracting, you can turn off the display of wavy red underlining. On the Tools menu, select Spelling. From the submenu, select Hide Spelling Errors. This command is available only if you have selected Check Spelling As You Type in the Spelling Options dialog box.

Set Spelling Options

① On the Tools menu, select Spelling. On the submenu, click Spelling Options. The Spelling Options dialog box appears.

② Select the options you would like to activate.

Check Spelling As You Type instantly corrects misspellings listed in the AutoCorrect dialog box and marks possible errors with a wavy red underline.

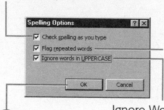

Flag Repeated Words marks double words with a wavy red underline. The red underline appears instantly only if you have also selected Check Spelling As You Type. If you have cleared Check Spelling As You Type, the underlining appears during a normal spell check.

③ Click OK.

Ignore Words In Uppercase omits words containing only capital letters from the spell check.

Add and Delete Words From Publisher's AutoCorrect List

1 On the Tools menu, select AutoCorrect. The AutoCorrect dialog box appears.

2 Select the AutoCorrect tab.

3 Select the types of mistakes you would like Publisher to correct.

Click here to change two consecutive uppercase letters to an uppercase and lowercase letter.

Click here to automatically capitalize words that start a sentence (following a period and a space).

Click here to capitalize days of the week.

Click here to correct reversed capitalization, such as mONEY.

Click here to replace text listed in the left column with text listed in the right column.

5 Type the correct word or phrase in the With text box. Alternatively, select an existing word or phrase from the With list and modify it.

6 If you are entering a new word or phrase, click Add. If you are changing an existing word or phrase, click Replace. If you are removing an existing word or phrase, click Delete.

7 Repeat steps 4, 5, and 6 for any additional words or phrases.

8 Click OK.

4 Type the incorrect word or phrase in the Replace text box. Alternatively, select an existing word or phrase from the Replace list and modify it.

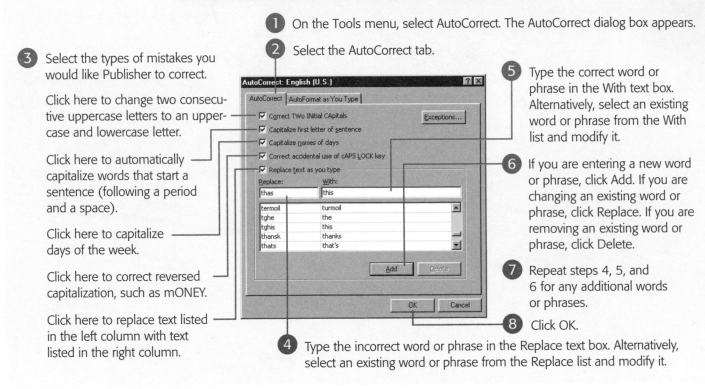

Exempt specific words and phrases from automatic capitalization. There are always exceptions to rules. If you click the Exceptions button in the AutoCorrect dialog box, you can view a list of abbreviations. Publisher doesn't capitalize words that follow the abbreviations in this list. As shown below, you add or delete entries from the list. Click the Initial Caps tab to create your own list of words with unusual capitalization that should be exempt from automatic correction.

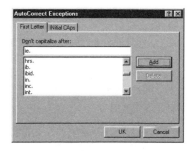

Where can I purchase a foreign-language dictionary? To purchase a foreign language dictionary contact Alki Software, the maker of Proofing Tools for Microsoft Office, at 800-669-9673 or *www.alki.com.*

Checking Spelling

Publisher's default dictionary can spell check English-language documents. If you have installed a foreign-language dictionary, Publisher can check the spelling of foreign-language words.

Check the Spelling in a Publication

1 Select a text frame.

2 Choose Spelling on the Tools menu. Select Check Spelling from the submenu. One of three things happens:

 ❧ If Publisher finds no questionable words, it returns you to the document.

 ❧ If Publisher finds no questionable words and the Check All Stories check box is clear, Publisher asks whether you want to check the rest of your publication. (Clicking Yes automatically activates Check All Stories.)

 ❧ If Publisher finds a word not in its dictionary or a word with a capitalization error, it displays the Check Spelling dialog box.

Press F7 to open the Check Spelling dialog box.

Add new words to the dictionary. The Spell Checker treats unusual or technical words as possible misspellings. You can prevent the Spell Checker from seeing those words as errors. Make sure that the word is correctly entered into the Change To text box. Then click the Add button to permanently enter the word in Publisher's dictionary.

Check the Spelling in a Publication *(continued)*

Publisher shows the misspelled word in the Not In Dictionary text box and also highlights it in your publication.

If the word has a capitalization error, Publisher displays it in the Error In Capitalization text box, which replaces the Not In Dictionary text box.

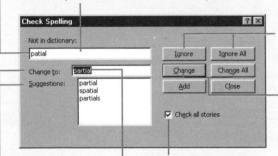

Click Ignore to leave the word alone. Or click Ignore All to ignore every instance of the word throughout the story.

④ If you agree with Publisher's spelling of the word, or if you selected or typed the correct word, click the Change button to replace the incorrect spelling with the correct spelling in the document. If you click the Change All button, Publisher searches for and replaces every instance of the misspelled word.

Publisher shows its best guess for the correct spelling or capitalization in the Change To text box. Other possible spellings appear in the Suggestions list box.

To check all of the stories in your document, click Check All Stories.

③ If Publisher's best guess on the spelling is not the word you intended, select one of the words from the Suggestions list or type the correct spelling directly into the Change To text box.

Check the spelling of specific words or phrases. You can check the spelling of a single word or a selected text block by highlighting it before you choose the Check Spelling command. If Publisher doesn't find the word in its dictionary, it presents the usual Check Spelling dialog box. When Publisher finishes checking the spelling of the word you highlighted, it offers you the opportunity to check the spelling in the rest of the story.

Alternatively, position the text pointer over a word that Publisher has flagged as a possible error and press the right mouse button. A list of alternative spellings displays on the shortcut menu, as shown below.

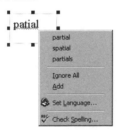

What are alternate or extended characters? The letters and symbols that don't appear on your keyboard are called alternate or extended characters.

Special Typographic Characters

The standard computer keyboard contains typewriter-style characters. You can make your publications look more professional by substituting or inserting true typographic characters instead. Publisher can automatically create commonly used typographic characters in response to standard keystrokes, as shown below.

Publisher's Automatic Typographic Characters		
To create ...	You type...	Publisher substitutes...
Curly opening and closing double quotes	""	" "
Curly opening and closing single quotes	'	' '
Em dash	--	—
En dash	space- (between any two characters)	–
Copyright, trademark, and registered symbols	(c) (tm) (r)	© ™ ®
Ellipsis	...	…
A bullet list	*space (your text) Enter	• (your text)
A numbered list	1. space (your text) Enter	1. (your text) 2. (your text)

You can specify which typographic characters Publisher inserts by configuring options in the AutoCorrect dialog box. In addition, you can use the Symbol dialog box to insert alternate or extended characters into your document.

Choose AutoFormat Options

① Choose AutoCorrect from the Tools menu. The AutoCorrect dialog box appears.

Click this check box to substitute straight typewriter-style quotes with curly quotes. Clear the check box in order to type straight typewriter-style quotes.

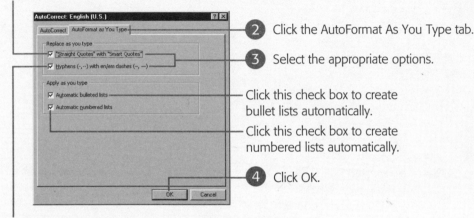

② Click the AutoFormat As You Type tab.

③ Select the appropriate options.

Click this check box to create bullet lists automatically.

Click this check box to create numbered lists automatically.

④ Click OK.

Click this check box to substitute hyphens with en and em dashes. Clear this option to type hyphens in all instances.

Insert a Symbol

① Click the insertion point where you want to insert the symbol.

② Choose Symbol on the Insert menu. The Symbol dialog box appears.

Use the AutoCorrect function to insert typographic characters.

You can customize the AutoCorrect function to substitute typographic characters for standard typewriter-style characters. On the AutoCorrect tab of the AutoCorrect dialog box, make sure that Replace Text As You Type is active. In the Replace text box, enter a combination of standard characters you will use to designate a typographic character. Choose a unique combination of standard letters, numbers, and punctuation that won't ever appear in normal text. In the With text box, enter the typographic character. As an example, you could use the combination of Y$ to automatically create the typographic character for Japanese currency, yen (¥).

You can enter the typographic character into the With text box in one of two ways. You can press Num Lock and then enter the code directly using the number keypad. For example, the code for the yen symbol is Alt-0165. Alternatively, you can use the Windows Character Map utility to place the typographic character on the Clipboard. Then use the Ctrl-V keyboard shortcut to paste the typographic character into the With text box in the AutoCorrect dialog box.

Insert a Symbol *(continued)*

3 Open the Font drop-down list box and choose a typeface.

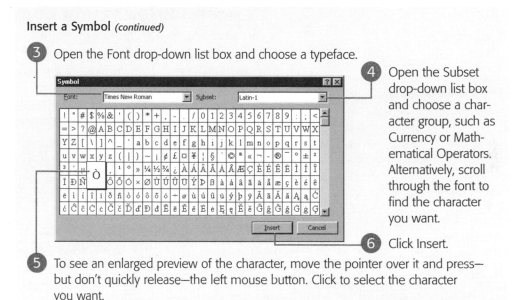

4 Open the Subset drop-down list box and choose a character group, such as Currency or Mathematical Operators. Alternatively, scroll through the font to find the character you want.

6 Click Insert.

5 To see an enlarged preview of the character, move the pointer over it and press—but don't quickly release—the left mouse button. Click to select the character you want.

Inserting and Updating Information Automatically

There are specific types of information that Publisher can insert into your document automatically. They are called information components and include the date, the time, and personal information such as your name and address.

Information components look like standard text frames, but you can distinguish between the two by placing the pointer over an element until a ScreenTip appears.

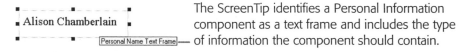

The ScreenTip identifies a Personal Information component as a text frame and includes the type of information the component should contain.

How do I edit the Logo Personal Information component? The Logo Personal Information component is actually a Smart Object that consists of a picture and one or more text frames. Click the Wizard button located on the lower right corner of the Smart Object to invoke the Logo Creation Wizard. When you use the Wizard, you can change the design, insert a new picture, or type new text.

To learn more about synchronization, the Logo Creation Wizard, and Smart Objects, see Chapter 14.

Personal Information Components

Personal Information components function like the fields in a database, because Publisher can update the information they contain automatically. Your address, for example, often appears in multiple locations within a publication. If you change the text in a single address information component, Publisher instantly propagates the change to all other address information components throughout the document. You can turn this feature—which is known as synchronization—on and off for each Personal Information component in a publication.

Because we often wear different hats, Publisher provides four personal information sets.

- Primary Business
- Secondary Business
- Other Organization
- Home/Family

Each set contains eight components.

- Name
- Job or Position Title
- Organization Name
- Address
- Tag Line Or Motto
- Phone/Fax/E-mail
- Logo
- Color Scheme (for print and Web documents)

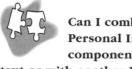

Can I combine a Personal Information component with normal text or with another Personal Information component in the same text frame? No. Each Personal Information component must remain in a separate text frame.

Can I change the appearance of a Personal Information component using Publisher's standard layout and formatting tools? Yes. You can use any of Publisher's tools to change the object's appearance. You can resize the frame, reposition the element on the page, and change the font, point size, text color, fill color, and border of the frame.

Create a Personal Information Set

1 On the Edit menu, choose Personal Information. The Personal Information dialog box appears.

2 Choose one of the four Personal Information sets. You can have only one Personal Information set associated with a publication.

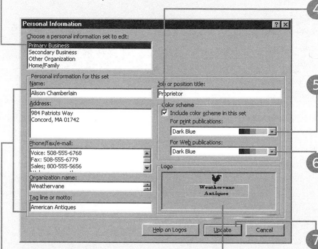

4 Click this check box to associate a color scheme with the Personal Information set.

5 Open the drop-down list and choose a color scheme to be used for print documents.

6 Open the drop-down list and choose a color scheme to be used for Web documents.

7 Click Update.

If you have inserted a Logo component into your document, it appears in this window.

3 Enter your name, address, telephone numbers, e-mail address, company name, title, and a descriptive phrase into the appropriate text boxes.

Update a Personal Information component for future publications.

If you want to change a Personal Information component for all subsequently created documents, you should make the change in the Personal Information dialog box (accessed from the Edit menu). When you click the Update button, all instances of the Personal Information component in the current document change. All Personal Information components you insert into future documents will also contain the updated information.

Alternatively, you can select the Update Personal Information When Saving check box on the User Assistance tab of the Options dialog box (accessed from the Tools menu). This feature allows you to edit Personal Information components in your document, and automatically updates the contents of the Personal Information dialog box whenever you save the document.

Insert a Personal Information Component

① On the Insert menu, select Personal Information.

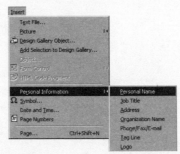

② From the submenu, choose the type of Personal Information component you want to insert. Publisher creates a new Personal Information component in a separate text frame.

Update a Personal Information Component for the Current Document

① Select the Personal Information component you want to change.

② Highlight the text, and then use Publisher's standard editing tools to change the copy.

③ Click outside of the frame. If the document contains other instances of this Personal Information component, Publisher automatically updates them with the new text.

④ Save the publication. The changes are saved in the current Personal Information set. Publisher uses the new information when creating the Personal Information component in this document.

Delete or Clear a Personal Information Component

① Select the Personal Information component you want to delete or clear.

Delete or Clear a Personal Information Component *(continued)*

2 To remove the Personal Information component without changing its information, select the Delete Object command from the Edit menu or from the shortcut menu.

3 To clear the text from a Personal Information component, highlight all of the text and press the Delete or Backspace key. Publisher deletes the text from this Personal Information component and from all synchronized components in the document. In the future, when you insert this Personal Information component in this document, it will be blank.

Turn synchronization on. Even after you have disabled synchronization, you can turn it back on. Open the Options dialog box from the Tools menu. On the Editing And User Assistance tab, click the button labeled Click To Reset Wizard Synchronizing.

Turn Off Synchronization

1 Insert or select a Personal Information component.

2 Use Publisher's standard editing tools to highlight and change the text.

3 Click outside of the frame. If the document contains other instances of this personal information component, Publisher automatically updates them with the new text.

4 Select Undo Propagate Personal Information on the Edit menu.

Date and Time

Publisher always gets the current date and time from your computer's internal clock. You can insert the date and time separately or as a single element. You can also decide whether to insert the information as a standard text element or as an updateable field.

Insert the Date and/or Time

1 Create or select a text frame. If the text frame contains text, position the insertion point where you want to insert the date and/or time.

2 On the Insert menu, select Date And Time. The Date And Time dialog box appears.

Insert the Date and/or Time *(continued)*

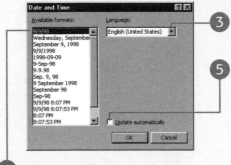

3 Open the drop-down list and choose a language.

5 Select Update Automatically if you would like Publisher to revise the date and time whenever you subsequently open or print the publication. Clear this check box if you would like the current date and time to be preserved as a static text element.

4 Scroll through the list and select one of 17 date/time formats.

6 Click OK.

Why do automatic and optional hyphens appear and disappear?
Whenever you change the text by editing or reformatting and whenever you change the layout by resizing or moving frames, Publisher recomputes the hyphenation. Words that move into the hyphenation zone are hyphenated to accommodate the changes. Words formerly hyphenated that move out of the hyphenation zone are closed up again.

Hyphenation Options

You can smooth ragged margins by using hyphens to break words that fall at the ends of lines. Publisher offers several different hyphenation options:

 @ Automatically hyphenate every story in your publication.

 @ Turn off hyphenation for a selected story or for all the stories in a publication.

 @ Approve each of Publisher's suggested hyphens.

 @ Insert optional hyphens that will appear only if the word falls at the end of a line.

 @ Insert nonbreaking hyphens or nonbreaking spaces for words that you don't want to break between two lines.

When automatic hyphenation is active, Publisher breaks and repositions words based on a number of factors, as shown in the following illustration.

Controlling the number of hyphens in your story or publication.

You can find the Hyphenation Zone setting on the Edit tab in the Options dialog box or in the Hyphenation dialog box. In either case, you should increase the hyphenation zone to hyphenate fewer words and decrease the hyphenation zone to hyphenate more words.

A wider text frame produces longer lines and fewer hyphens.

> The staff here at The Wine Shop participates in regular wine tastings, both to educate our palette and to investigate wines as they are released to the market. Occasionally we discover an exceptional wine at an exceptional price. Such is the case with Chateau La Coste, a Bordeaux style red wine from France. With an ex-

Long words that fall in the hyphenation zone are divided between syllables as determined by Publisher's default dictionary.

One-syllable words that are too long to fit are pushed to the next line.

A narrow text frame produces shorter lines and more hyphens.

> The staff here at The Wine Shop participates in regular wine tastings, both to educate our palette and to investigate wines as they are released to the market. Occasionally we discover an exceptional wine at an exceptional price. Such is the case with

The hyphenation zone defines a region in which Publisher looks for words to hyphenate. The default value is 0.25 inch.

Automatically Hyphenate Every Story in your Publication

1. On the Tools menu, choose Options, and then select the Edit tab.
2. Select Automatically Hyphenate In New Text Frames.
3. Enter a value from 0 through 10 inches in the Hyphenation Zone text box.
4. Click OK to accept the hyphenation settings.

Customize Hyphenation for a Single Story

1. Select the text frame that contains the story whose hyphenation you want to modify.
2. On the Tools menu, choose Language. From the submenu, select Hyphenation. The Hyphenation dialog box appears.
3. Select the appropriate options.

Press Ctrl-Shift-H to open the Hyphenation dialog box.

Hyphenation in justified text. If the text you're hyphenating is justified (aligned on both the left and right margins), increasing the hyphenation zone leaves more spaces between words, creating unpleasant gaps between the words in your text. Decrease the hyphenation zone setting to hyphenate more words and give your text a smoother appearance.

Customize Hyphenation for a Single Story *(continued)*

Clear this check box to deactivate automatic hyphenation for this story, or click this check box to activate automatic hyphenation for this story.

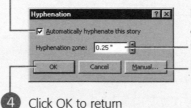

If you have selected automatic hyphenation, enter a value between 0 and 10 inches in 0.01-inch increments in the Hyphenation Zone text box.

Click the Manual button to review the hyphens that Publisher suggests. You can choose a different hyphenation point if another is defined in Publisher's dictionary.

4 Click OK to return to your document.

Hyphenate Words Manually

1 Position the insertion point between the two characters where you want Publisher to break the word.

2 Press Ctrl-hyphen.

bi⌐cycle

If Show Special Characters is activated, Publisher displays a modified hyphen that looks bent.

Viewing optional hyphens. Hyphens that you enter manually are normally printed and displayed only when they fall at the end of a line. If you want to see all of these optional hyphens on screen, choose the Show Special Characters command on the View menu.

Why would I want to insert a nonbreaking hyphen or a nonbreaking space between two words? It's grammatically incorrect to break compound words or hyphenated names when they fall at the end of a line. It is also good editorial practice to keep words or characters together that wouldn't be clearly understood if broken onto separate lines.

Insert a Nonbreaking Hyphen

1 Position the insertion point between two characters or two words.

2 Delete all spaces between the words.

3 Press Ctrl-Alt-hyphen.

Binet⊤Simon·scale

If Show Special Characters is activated, a nonbreaking hyphen is displayed as a larger-than-standard hyphen.

Insert a Nonbreaking Space

1 Position the insertion point between two characters or two words.

2 Delete all spaces between the words.

3 Press Ctrl-Alt-space.

Fra⸰Angelico

If Show Special Characters is activated, a nonbreaking space is displayed as a small circle.

Text Formats

The fonts and formatting attributes that you apply to the text in a document can enhance your message and make your publications easier to read. Microsoft Publisher 2000 provides tools for formatting text on a character level, on a paragraph level, and globally. You can also combine paragraph-level and character-level formats.

Why doesn't the formatting change for words I've already typed? To make changes to a few words in a larger block of copy, you must first select the text. If you change the formatting attributes without selecting the text, you change only the attributes of the next text you type.

As part of a federally funded sweat equity project, Lewis Balthazar, a senior designer here at Broadside Associates, recently helped restore a small 6-story apartment building. Coincidentally, the building is located in *Shorehaven*, the part of town where Balthazar himself grew up.

Balthazar was involved in every aspect of design and construction. He pored over engineering reports and researched turn-of-the century construction techniques to ensure the structural integrity of the building. He

Character-level formats, such as a drop cap or italicized text, can be applied to selected letters within a larger block of text.

Paragraph-level formats include attributes such as indents and alignment options.

In order to use text formatting attributes consistently throughout a publication, you should save them as text styles. Making formatting changes to a text style updates the entire document.

Character Formatting

You can use any of several different methods to reformat individual words in a paragraph or individual letters within a word. You can select a feature from the text toolbar, select options in the Font dialog box, or use Publisher's character spacing and drop cap options to create special effects.

You can display a simple list of font names, rather than an actual preview of each font, in the Font drop-down list on the Formatting toolbar and in the Font dialog box. Doing so enables you to fit more font names into the drop-down list box. To disable the preview, choose Options from the Tools menu. On the General tab, clear the Preview Fonts In Font List check box.

Automatically format entire words. In most cases, you want to apply the same formatting to all of the letters in a word. For example, you wouldn't want to have the last letter in an italicized word print as regular text. You can have Publisher automatically apply formatting changes to the whole word, regardless of whether the whole word is selected. Open the Options dialog box from the Tools menu. Click the Edit tab and make sure a check appears next to When Formatting, Automatically Format Entire Word.

The Formatting Toolbar

Whenever you create or select a text frame, tools for formatting text appear on the Formatting toolbar. Although it provides access to only a portion of Publisher's text formatting options, it is often the fastest way to change the appearance of text.

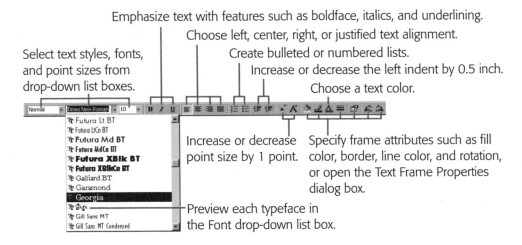

Emphasize text with features such as boldface, italics, and underlining.

Choose left, center, right, or justified text alignment.

Create bulleted or numbered lists.

Increase or decrease the left indent by 0.5 inch.

Choose a text color.

Select text styles, fonts, and point sizes from drop-down list boxes.

Increase or decrease point size by 1 point.

Specify frame attributes such as fill color, border, line color, and rotation, or open the Text Frame Properties dialog box.

Preview each typeface in the Font drop-down list box.

Format Text Using the Formatting Toolbar

1 Select a text frame. If the frame contains text, select the text you want to format.

2 Select an option from a drop-down list box or click a formatting button.

When would I apply a font effect to text? Most of the Effects options in the Font dialog box have legitimate typographic functions. For example, Superscript, Subscript, Small Caps, and All Caps are traditionally used for footnotes, equations, and time references. Other effects, such as Outline, Emboss, Engrave, and Shadow, are purely decorative and can be used to create special effects that are similar to those found in WordArt.

For more information on WordArt, see Chapter 8.

Change the size of text by changing the size of its frame. You can resize text simply by dragging the text frame's selection handle, provided that you have turned on Publisher's automatic copyfitting options for the text frame. With a text frame selected, choose AutoFit Text on the Format menu. Select either Best Fit or Shrink Text On Overflow from the submenu.

For more information on AutoFit Text, see Chapter 4.

The Font Dialog Box

A wider range of text formatting options is available from the Font command on the Format menu.

Change the Character Formatting of Text

1 Select a text frame. If the frame contains text, select the text you want to format.

2 On the Format menu, choose Font. The Font dialog box appears.

3 Select the options you want.

Choose a typeface from the Font drop-down list box.

To change the emphasis of your text, open the Font Style drop-down list box and choose Regular, Italic, Bold, or Bold Italic.

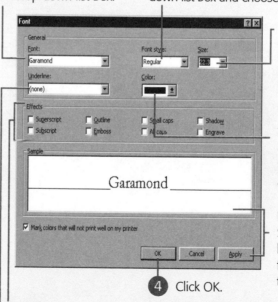

Open the Size drop-down list box and select one of the available sizes, or select the size displayed in the text box and type any value between 0.5 and 999.9.

To change the color of your text, open the Color drop-down list box and click one of the available colors.

Preview your changes in the Sample box, or click the Apply button to see how the new formatting affects the selected text in your document.

4 Click OK.

Click one or more check boxes to add effects to your text.

Choose one of 18 underlining styles from the Underline drop-down list.

What is the difference between automatic and manual kerning? Certain well-known letter combinations, such as "TO" and "AV," always appear a little too loose. At normal point sizes (typically 12 points or less), the standard spacing for these and other troublesome letter pairs is often acceptable. The awkward inter-character spaces become noticeable only at larger point sizes. When you activate Automatic Kerning, Publisher adjusts the letter spacing for specific letter pairs. You can specify a point size at which automatic kerning kicks in, but you can't specify which letter pairs are kerned, and you can't control the amount of kerning. Manual kerning gives you total control. You can kern any two letters at any point size. You can move letters closer together or further apart. And you can specify the exact amount of space to add or remove between the letter pair.

Character Spacing

You can adjust the spacing of individual characters to fine-tune the legibility of text (especially critical at very small or very large point sizes) and to turn plain text into dramatic graphic elements. Publisher can alter the spacing of the characters themselves by expanding or condensing a font's width. In addition, you can control the spacing between letters using Publisher's kerning and tracking functions. These controls are available in a dialog box or a floating toolbar.

The visible gap between these letters is an optical illusion caused by the shape of the letters.

You can compensate with automatic or manual kerning—a process that moves letter pairs closer together.

As part of a federally funded sweat equity project, Lewis Balthazar, a senior designer here at Broadside Associates, recently helped restore a small 6-story apartment building. Coincidentally, the building is located in *Shorehaven*, the part of town where Balthazar himself grew up.

Balthazar was involved in every aspect of design and construction. He pored over engineering reports and researched turn-of-the century construction techniques to ensure the

Tracking is applied to larger blocks of text.

As part of a federally funded sweat equity project, Lewis Balthazar, a senior designer here at Broadside Associates, recently helped restore a small 6-story apartment building. Coincidentally, the building is located in *Shorehaven*, the part of town where Balthazar himself grew up.

Balthazar was involved in every aspect of design and construction. He pored over

Tracking changes of just a few percentage points can dramatically change the amount of text that fits into a text frame.

Specifying the kerning point size to speed up performance. Publisher kerns letter pairs at point sizes greater than or equal to any point size you specify in the Character Spacing dialog box. Clearing the Kerning check box disables automatic kerning and speeds up Publisher's performance. Typing a size smaller than 14 points can seriously degrade Publisher's performance.

Why doesn't the value in the Character Spacing dialog box match the value I typed? In all likelihood, you entered a value with one too many decimal places. Publisher always rounds the number you type for Tracking, Scaling, and Kerning to the nearest 0.1 percent increment. If, for example, you entered a value of 99.99 percent into the Tracking text box, Publisher would round up to 100 percent. Likewise, if you entered a value of 3.22 points into the Kerning text box, Publisher would round down to 3.2 points.

Change Character Spacing Using the Dialog Box

① Select the text you want to change. If you are manually kerning two letters, place the text insertion point between them.

② On the Format menu, choose Character Spacing. The Character Spacing dialog box appears.

③ Apply character spacing attributes, as explained in the following illustration.

To reduce the width of selected text, enter a percentage from 0.1 percent through 99.9 percent in 0.1 percent increments. To increase the width of selected text, enter a percentage from 100.1 percent through 600 percent in 0.1 percent increments.

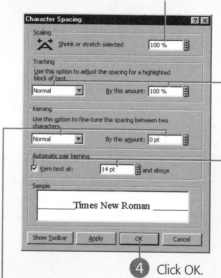

Choose one of the spacing options. To adjust the tracking using preset values, open this drop-down list and choose Normal, Tight, Very Tight, Loose, or Very Loose. Alternatively, choose the Custom option and enter a value from 0.1 percent through 600 percent (in 0.1 percent increments) in the By This Amount text box.

Click this check box to turn Automatic Pair Kerning on. Enter a point size from 0.5 through 999.9 points in 0.1-point increments. Publisher automatically kerns any text formatted with this or a larger point size.

④ Click OK.

To adjust the kerning for selected characters, open the drop-down list and choose Expand or Condense. Then enter a value from 0 through 600 points in 0.1-point increments into the By This Amount text box. To revert to the standard letterspacing for the selected characters, open the drop-down list box and select Normal.

What is the difference between the Character Spacing dialog box and the Formatting toolbar? The Character Spacing dialog box provides more explanation and more explicit options than the Measurement toolbar. For example, a drop-down list in the Character Spacing dialog box offers preset tracking values. Moreover, you can choose to apply kerning values in one of two modes—Expand or Condense. In contrast, the Measurement toolbar requires you to enter a specific value for tracking or kerning. A low percentage value tightens tracking; condensed kerning requires you to enter a minus sign before the number.

Change Character Spacing Using the Formatting Toolbar

① Select the text you want to change. If you are manually kerning two letters, place the text insertion point between them.

② On the Format menu, choose Character Spacing. The Character Spacing dialog box appears.

③ Click the Show Toolbar button. The Formatting toolbar appears.

④ Enter the appropriate value for each option.

Enter a scaling value from 0.1 through 600 percent.

Enter a kerning value from -600 through 600 points.

| x | 2.13 " | | 4.38 " | | A | 0.0 | | | 100 % | | A↔ | 0 pt | | ✕ |
| y | 2.2 " | | 5.11 " | | | | | | 0.4 % | | | 1 sp | | |

Enter a tracking value from 0.1 through 600 percent.

Enter a line spacing value from 0.25 through 124 spaces (or from 3 through 1488 points).

Drop Caps

Drop caps (jargon for dropped capital letters) and initial caps are common design devices, often used to indicate the beginning of a new text unit, such as a chapter. Publisher provides a gallery of preformatted designs for both drop caps and initial caps. You can also create your own unique effects and apply them to a single initial letter, multiple letters, or an entire word.

A s part of a federally funded sweat equity project, Lewis Balthazar, a senior designer here at Broadside Associates, recently helped restore a small 6-story apartment building. Coincidentally, the building is located in *Shorehaven*, the part of

First letters that share a baseline with the first line of text are called initial caps.

A s part of a federally funded sweat equity project, Lewis Balthazar, a senior designer here at Broadside Associates, recently helped restore a small 6-story apartment building. Coincidentally, the building is located in *Shorehaven*, the part of town where Balthazar himself

First letters that hang below the first line of text are called drop caps.

Can I change or remove drop or initial caps? Yes. Select a paragraph that already contains a drop cap or an initial cap and choose the Change Drop Cap command on the Format menu. In the Drop Cap dialog box, you can choose a different preformatted style, select custom options, or return the drop cap letter to normal by clicking the first style (none) in the gallery or by clicking the Remove button.

Insert a Preformatted Drop Cap or Initial Cap

① Select the paragraph where you want to add a drop cap or an initial cap.

② Open the Format menu and choose Drop Cap. The Drop Cap dialog box appears.

③ Click the Drop Cap tab.

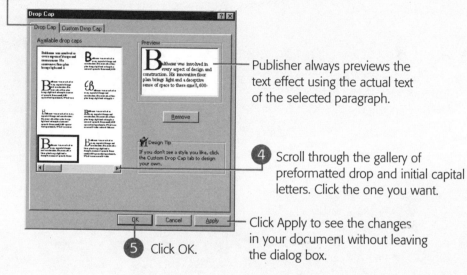

Publisher always previews the text effect using the actual text of the selected paragraph.

④ Scroll through the gallery of preformatted drop and initial capital letters. Click the one you want.

Click Apply to see the changes in your document without leaving the dialog box.

⑤ Click OK.

Create a Custom Drop Cap, Initial Cap, or Lead Word

1 Select the paragraph where you want to add a custom drop cap, initial cap, or lead word.

2 On the Format menu, choose Drop Cap.

3 Click the Custom Drop Cap tab.

4 Choose a Dropped cap, an Up (initial) cap, or a custom (Lines) position. If you choose the Lines option, you must enter a value from 0 through 3.

5 Enter a value from 2 through 32 in the Size Of Letters text box. The size of a drop cap is always relative to the height of the remaining text in the paragraph. For example, a size of 4 produces a drop cap 4 lines tall.

6 If you want to apply the effect to multiple letters or an entire word, enter a value between 1 and 15 in the Number Of Letters text box.

7 Open the Font drop-down list box and choose a typeface. Alternatively, you can pick up the current font from the selected paragraph by clicking Use Current Font.

8 Open the Font Style drop-down list box and choose an emphasis. Alternatively, you can pick up the current emphasis from the selected paragraph by clicking Use Current Font Style.

9 Open the Color drop-down list box and choose an available color. Alternatively, you can pick up the current font color from the selected paragraph by clicking Use Current Color.

10 Click OK. Publisher includes your customized drop cap or initial cap in the gallery, located on the Drop Cap tab. It is available in this publication only.

Do the math when creating paragraph indents. You should pay special attention to the values for the Left and First Line indents. Publisher's Indents And Lists dialog box (available from the Format menu) adds these values to one another to produce the final indented effect for the paragraph.

Formatting a paragraph with a left indent of 0.5 inch and a first line indent of 0.5 inch creates a cumulative effect: the first line indent now measures 1 inch from the margin, as shown in the following illustration.

> As part of a federally funded sweat equity project, Lewis Balthazar, a senior designer here at Broadside Associates, recently helped restore a small 6-story apartment building. Coincidentally, the building

Using a negative number (such as -0.25 inch) for the first line indent creates a hanging indent, where the first line of text hangs to the left of the remaining text, as shown in the following illustration.

> As part of a federally funded sweat equity project, Lewis Balthazar, a senior designer here at Broadside Associates, recently helped restore a small 6-story apartment building. Coincidentally, the building is located in *Shore-*

Paragraph Formatting

Publisher defines a paragraph as any amount of text followed by a carriage return, so the formatting applied to paragraphs in Publisher can be as short as one character or as long as the whole publication. You can also apply paragraph formats to text in a table cell.

Indents and Lists

Publisher's Indents And Lists dialog box offers numerous preset options to create the most commonly used paragraph formats (shown in the following illustration). In addition, you can create custom paragraph styles.

> As part of a federally funded sweat equity project, Lewis Balthazar, a senior designer here at Broadside Associates, recently helped restore a small 6-story apartment building. Coincidentally, the building is located in *Shorehaven*, the part of town where Balthazar himself grew up.
>
> Balthazar was involved in every aspect of design and construction. He pored over engineering reports and researched turn-of-the century con-

This is a flush left paragraph with no indent. Blank lines usually separate individual paragraphs. This is a typical format for business correspondence. Notice that the right margin is irregular, or ragged.

> As part of a federally funded sweat equity project, Lewis Balthazar, a senior designer here at Broadside Associates, recently helped restore a small 6-story apartment building. Coincidentally, the building is located in *Shorehaven*, the part of town where Balthazar himself grew up.
>
> Balthazar was involved in every aspect of design and construction. He pored over engineering reports and researched turn-of-the century construction techniques to ensure the

Newspapers and magazines typically indent the first lines of second and subsequent paragraphs. The paragraph is justified so that text is flush with both the left and right margins.

> 1. Lewis Balthazar is a senior designer at Broadside Associates.
> 2. He recently helped restore a small 6-story apartment building.
> 3. The building is located in *Shorehaven*, the part of town where Balthazar himself grew up.
> 4. Balthazar was involved in every aspect of design and construction.
> 5. He pored over engineering reports and researched turn-of-the-century construction techniques to

Publisher considers each of these numbered items to be a new paragraph because each is followed by a carriage return. Numbered lists often use a hanging indent to offset the numeral from the rest of the text.

Customize the Paragraph Indents

1. Click in the paragraph you want to format. If you want to format more than one paragraph at a time, select them all.

2. Choose Indents And Lists from the Format menu. The Indents And Lists dialog box appears.

To assign any of Publisher's standard alignment options to the currently selected paragraph or paragraphs, click the Left, Right, Center, or Justified buttons on the Formatting toolbar.

To adjust the indent of a selected paragraph by 0.5 inch, click the Increase Indent and Decrease Indent buttons on the Formatting toolbar.

Customize the Paragraph Indents *(continued)*

3 Click the Normal option.

4 The Left and Right text boxes specify the distance between the left and right edges of the text and the frame margins. Enter a value from 0 through 22 inches.

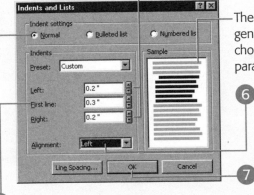

The Sample area shows generally how your choices affect the selected paragraph or paragraphs.

6 Choose one of four alignment options in the drop-down list box.

7 Click OK.

5 The First Line text box specifies how the first line is indented from the left indent setting. You can choose either a negative (hanging) indent or a positive (normal paragraph) indent. Enter a value from −22 through 22 inches.

Choose a Preset Indent

1 Click in the paragraph you want to format. If you want to format more than one paragraph at a time, select them all.

2 On the Format menu, choose Indents And Lists.

3 In the Indents And Lists dialog box, click the Normal option.

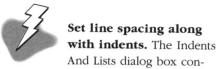

Set line spacing along with indents. The Indents And Lists dialog box contains a button to open the Line Spacing dialog box where you can control the amount of space between lines of text.

You can assign the most recently used bullet to selected text by clicking the Bullets button on the Formatting toolbar. To remove a bullet from selected text, click the button again.

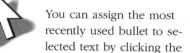

Choose a Preset Indent *(continued)*

④ Open the Preset drop-down list box to choose one of five presets:

  ❧ Original: makes no changes to the existing indents.

  ❧ Flush Left: assigns indents of zero and aligns the text with the left margin.

  ❧ 1st Line Indent: creates a 0.5-inch indent for the first line only and aligns the text with the left margin.

  ❧ Hanging Indent: indents every line *after* the first by 0.5 inch and aligns the text with the left margin.

  ❧ Quotation: indents text by 1 inch on both the left and right and justifies the text.

⑤ Click OK.

Bulleted Lists

Bulleted lists draw attention to the important points in your publication and create visual interest by breaking up dense blocks of text. You can add bullets to your text manually, but it's faster to have Publisher create a bulleted list for you.

Format Several Paragraphs as a Bulleted List

① Select the paragraphs you want to include in the bulleted list. Remember that a paragraph can consist of a character, a single word, or a sentence.

② Choose Indents And Lists from the Format menu. The Indents And Lists dialog box appears.

③ Click Bulleted List. The Bullet Type area displays.

The New Bullet dialog box is identical to the Symbol dialog box found on the Insert menu. See Chapter 5.

Better bullets. You can insert decorative bullets into your text by choosing a font like Wingdings in the New Bullet dialog box.

Take advantage of accurate previews. Although the sample area shows only broad shaded lines for text (referred to as greeked text), it is an accurate preview. Use it to make sure that the carryover lines align under the first character of the first line. In order for this to occur, the indent you specify in the Indent List By text box must be equal to the amount of space required for the bullet plus the white space between the bullet and the text.

Format Several Paragraphs as a Bulleted List *(continued)*

4 Either choose one of the six bullets displayed, or click New Bullet to bring up the New Bullet dialog box, where you can choose a new bullet from any font installed on your system.

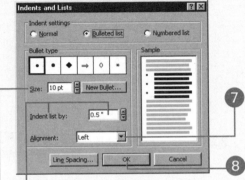

7 Open the Alignment drop-down list box and choose Left, Center, Right, or Justified alignment.

8 Click OK.

6 Enter a value between 0 and 22 inches in the Indent List By text box to indent all of the subsequent, or carryover, lines in the paragraph to the specified measurement. To effectively turn this feature off, enter a value of 0.

5 Change the bullet size by entering any value from 0.5 to 999.9 points in the text box.

Numbered Lists

Numbered lists enumerate a series of items or give sequential instructions. When you use the numbered list format, every new paragraph automatically begins with the next higher number or letter in the series.

Set Up a Numbered List

1 Select the paragraphs you want to include in the numbered list.

2 Choose Indents And Lists on the Format menu to display the Indents And Lists dialog box.

3 Choose the Numbered List option. The Number area appears.

Change the appearance of numbered lists. You can create distinctive formats for your lists by choosing among the 8 options in the Separator drop-down list box. These include a period, dashes, a colon, and an assortment of separators, as shown below.

1

2.

3)

4|

5:

(6)

[7]

-8-

Set Up a Numbered List *(continued)*

4 Open the Format drop-down list box and choose one of three options: numbers, lowercase letters, or uppercase letters.

5 To specify how you want the numbers separated from the text, open the Separator drop-down list box and choose one of the eight options.

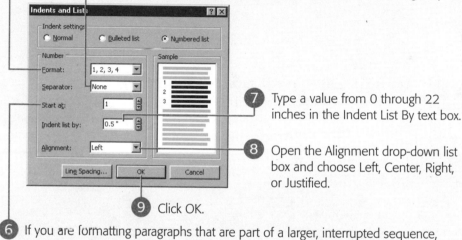

7 Type a value from 0 through 22 inches in the Indent List By text box.

8 Open the Alignment drop-down list box and choose Left, Center, Right, or Justified.

9 Click OK.

6 If you are formatting paragraphs that are part of a larger, interrupted sequence, type the number or letter that should begin the current sequence.

Vertical Alignment

Vertical alignment options let you position text at the top, bottom, or center of a text frame. You can apply Publisher's vertical alignment options to a single text frame, to a text frame containing multiple columns, to connected text frames, and to cells in a table.

Align Text Vertically

1 Select a text frame.

2 On the Format menu, choose Align Text Vertically.

3 On the submenu, choose one of the three vertical alignment options: Top, Center, or Bottom.

Now whenever you resize the height of the text frame, Publisher repositions the text to maintain the vertical alignment option you've chosen.

The line spacing changes automatically according to the text point size. Publisher's default single line spacing (1 sp) is set at 120 percent of point size. As an example, for 10-point type, the 1 space setting inserts 12 points from baseline to baseline. The advantage of this arrangement is that the line spacing changes automatically when the point size changes. For example, if you decide to format your text at 12 instead of 10 points, the line spacing of 1 space automatically increases to 14.4 points.

Line Spacing

Publisher uses a measurement called line spacing, or leading, to determine the amount of space between the bottom, or baseline, of the characters in one line of text and the baseline of the next line, as illustrated below. To give you even more control over the appearance of your text, you can add extra spacing before and after paragraphs, separately from leading.

As part of a federally funded sweat equity project, Lewis Balthazar, a senior designer here at Broadside Associates, recently helped restore a small 6-story apartment building. Coincidentally, the building is located in *Shorehaven*, the part of town where Balthazar himself grew up.

As part of a federally funded sweat equity project, Lewis Balthazar, a senior designer here at Broadside Associates, recently helped restore a small 6-story apartment building. Coincidentally, the building is located in *Shorehaven*, the part of town where Balthazar himself grew up.

Increasing the leading of a text block can improve legibility or create a special effect.

Decreasing the leading (even by a small increment such as 0.5 point, which is only 1/144 inch) can help you to fit more text on a page.

For more information on the floating toolbar, see "Character Spacing" earlier in this chapter.

Using points as the unit of measurement. By default, Publisher uses a relative unit of measurement (line spaces) to add space between lines of text. You have much more control over line spacing if you instead use an absolute unit of measure, such as points. To change the line spacing using points, enter a value from 3 through 1488 points in 0.01-point increments in the Between Lines text box in the Line Spacing dialog box. Remember to add the "pt" abbreviation to specify points.

Add the appropriate spacing between paragraphs. Pressing the Enter key to add space between paragraphs creates a full blank line space, which can disrupt the text flow. Use the Line Spacing dialog box to add small amounts of white space before or after paragraphs to separate them without disrupting text flow.

Change the Line Spacing

1 Click anywhere in a paragraph or select the paragraphs you want to reformat.

2 On the Format menu, choose Line Spacing. The Line Spacing dialog box appears.

3 Enter a new value from 0.25 through 124 spaces (sp) in increments of hundredths of a line space.

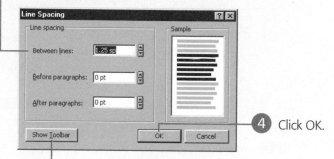

4 Click OK.

Click here to display a floating toolbar that lets you alter line spacing interactively.

Specify Extra Leading Before and After Paragraphs

1 Click anywhere in a paragraph, or select the paragraphs you want to change.

2 On the Format menu, choose Line Spacing.

3 In the Line Spacing dialog box, enter any value from 0 through 1488 points (pt) in the Before Paragraphs and After Paragraphs text boxes.

4 Click OK.

Tabs

Tabs are useful if you want to align several items in column-and-row format or space several words evenly across a wide column. By default, Publisher places tab stops at 0.5-inch intervals. Use the Tabs dialog box to alter those settings.

When to avoid tabs. You should never use the Tabs command to indent the first line of a paragraph. If you subsequently modify your design, you'll have to manually edit each paragraph. Use the Indents And Lists dialog box instead. It lets you modify indents globally.

Consider using the Table Frame Tool to format rows and columns. The Table Frame Tool, which can format text into rows and columns, is often easier to use than the Tabs command. Adding or deleting text from a table doesn't alter the row and column alignment. However, adding or deleting tabbed text can misalign text elements.

For more information about Publisher's Table Frame Tool, see Chapter 7.

Set and Delete Tabs in the Tabs Dialog Box

1 Click in any paragraph, or select the paragraphs in which you want to set tabs.

2 From the Format menu, choose Tabs. The Tabs dialog box appears.

3 To add a tab stop, type the measurement of the distance between the left margin of the text frame and the alignment position of the tab and then click the Set button. When you click the Set button, the new tab setting is included in the Tab Stop Position list box.

5 Select one of the four alignment options: Left, Center, Right, or Decimal.

6 To select a leader character (which fills the space between the point at which you press the Tab key and the tab stop), select one of these options.

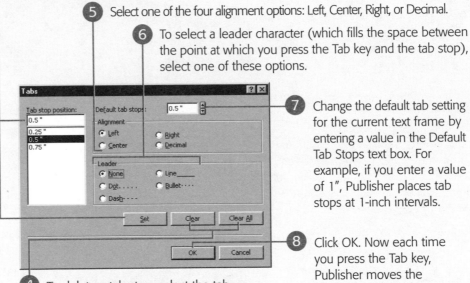

7 Change the default tab setting for the current text frame by entering a value in the Default Tab Stops text box. For example, if you enter a value of 1", Publisher places tab stops at 1-inch intervals.

8 Click OK. Now each time you press the Tab key, Publisher moves the insertion point (and any text to the right of the insertion point) to the next tab stop.

4 To delete a tab stop, select the tab from the Tab Stop Position list box and then click Clear. Click Clear All to remove all the tabs that have been set for the selected paragraphs.

Identify tab markers.
Publisher always identifies the alignment associated with a tab marker.

Left aligned tab   Center aligned tab

Right aligned tab   Decimal aligned tab

Which is a better tab format for aligning numbers, right or decimal? Both the Right and the Decimal alignment options in the Tabs dialog box work well for numerical data provided that all of the values have the same number of decimal places, such as currency. If, however, you are attempting to align values that don't contain the same number of decimal places, choose Decimal alignment. Doing so creates true columns of numbers where single digits, tens, hundreds, and thousands are properly aligned.

Can I use the indents and tabs ruler to change the alignment of a tab stop? No, but you can double-click a tab marker on the indents and tabs ruler. Double-click the tab marker whose alignment you want to change. The Tabs dialog box, in which you can specify the alignment and a leader character, appears.

Indents and Tabs Ruler

Every time you create or select a text object, a special ruler appears on the horizontal ruler. You can set or modify indent and tab positions by clicking and dragging icons that appear on this ruler.

Set Indents on the Ruler

1 Click in the paragraph or select the paragraphs in which you want to adjust indents. The indents and tabs ruler appears.

2 Drag any of the triangles to a new position on the ruler.

The upper left triangle controls the first line indent.

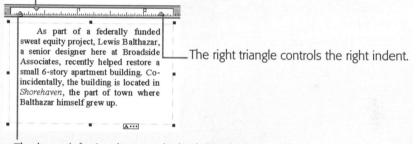

The right triangle controls the right indent.

The lower left triangle controls the left indent.

Set and Delete Tabs on the Ruler

1 Click in the paragraph or select the paragraphs in which you want to set tab stops.

2 Click the indents and tabs ruler where you want to place the tab stop. A tab marker, which looks like a 90-degree angle, appears on the ruler.

The default tab is left aligned and appears as a 90-degree angle.

To move a tab stop, drag the tab marker to a new location on the ruler.

3 To remove a tab stop, drag the tab marker off the ruler.

Why don't the keyboard shortcuts to change the font and the point size have an immediate effect? When you use the keyboard shortcut Ctrl-Shift-F to change the font, Publisher highlights the contents of the Font drop-down list. You must use the Up and Down arrow keys to change the font name, and then hit the Enter key to apply the new font to the selected text.

When you use the keyboard shortcut Ctrl-Shift-P to change the point size, Publisher highlights the contents of the Point Size drop-down list. You must use the Up and Down arrow keys to choose a new point size, and then hit the Enter key to apply the new size to the selected text.

To boldface, italicize, or underline highlighted text, click the appropriate button on the Formatting toolbar. To remove any of these attributes, click the button a second time.

Formatting Shortcuts

You can use keyboard shortcuts to quickly change the format of both individual characters and paragraphs. It's efficient to use keyboard shortcuts to format text, because you don't have to remove your hands from the keyboard. For example, if you type Ctrl-I, all of the subsequent text you type is in italics. You can also use keyboard shortcuts to select text and then reformat it.

The same keyboard shortcuts allow you to remove formatting attributes as well. For example, if you select a boldface word and then press Ctrl-B, the text returns to the normal (or Roman) weight. You can even use keyboard shortcuts to select text or to copy formatting from one object to another. The following table summarizes the most frequently used formatting shortcuts.

Character Format Shortcuts	
Keyboard Shortcut	**Effect**
Ctrl-B	Applies boldface
Ctrl-I	Applies italic
Ctrl-U	Applies underline
Ctrl-Shift-K	Changes to small caps
Ctrl-=	Changes to subscript
Ctrl-Shift-=	Changes to superscript
Ctrl-Spacebar	Returns to the style's default formatting
Ctrl-Shift-F	Changes font
Ctrl-Shift-P	Changes point size
Ctrl-]	Increases font size by 1.0 point
Ctrl-[	Decreases font size by 1.0 point
Ctrl-Shift-}	Increases kerning of selected letters by 0.25 point
Ctrl-Shift-{	Decreases kerning of selected letters by 0.25 point

Paragraph Format Shortcuts

Keyboard Shortcut	Attribute
Ctrl-Shift-S	Changes text style
Ctrl-Q	Returns paragraph to current text style
Ctrl-E	Centers paragraph
Ctrl-J	Justifies paragraph
Ctrl-L	Left aligns paragraph
Ctrl-R	Right aligns paragraph
Ctrl-1	Applies single line space
Ctrl-2	Applies double line space
Ctrl-5	Applies line space of 1.5 lines
Ctrl-0 (zero)	Removes line space before paragraph
Shift-Enter	Creates a new line without beginning a new paragraph

Selecting and Formatting Shortcuts

Keyboard Shortcut	Attribute
Shift-Arrow key	Selects text
Shift-End key	Selects text from insertion point to end of line
Shift-Home key	Selects text from insertion point to beginning of line
Ctrl-Shift-C	Copies text formatting
Ctrl-Shift-V	Pastes text formatting

Can I use a text style on one word in my document? You can't apply a text style to single words in a sentence or to particular characters within a text string. Using the Text Styles command always changes the entire paragraph.

Naming your text styles. You can use up to 32 characters for the text style name, so make the name as descriptive as possible. For example, *Headline 32pt* tells you a lot more than *Heading01*.

Text Styles

When you want to apply the same formatting options to many paragraphs in your document, you can save a lot of time by creating a text style. A text style is a combination of formats that you name, save, and reuse. You can apply both character-level formats (such as font, point size, italics, and color) and paragraph-level formats (such as indents, alignment, line spacing, tabs, and bullets) with a single mouse click. In addition, text styles guarantee consistency throughout a long document.

Creating and Applying Text Styles

You can create text styles in one of two ways:

@ By example. If you aren't sure how to format a particular paragraph, experiment with sample text. After you've created a good-looking paragraph, you can create a text style based on it.

@ From scratch. If you know how to define the features of your paragraph, you can create a text style from scratch in the Text Styles dialog box. You don't need to select a paragraph before you start.

Once you've created a text style, you can apply it to any of the paragraphs in your document.

Create a Text Style by Example

1 Format the paragraph.

2 Click inside the paragraph.

3 Click in the Style drop-down text box to select its contents. The Style drop-down list is located on the left end of the Formatting toolbar.

4 Replace the existing style name by typing a new style name and then press Enter. The Create Style By Example dialog box appears.

5 In the Create Style By Example dialog box, click OK to create the new text style.

Copy formatting from one object to another.
Publisher gives you four ways to copy formatting attributes or text styles from one object to another.

- ❦ Format Painter: Select the text block whose style you want to copy. Click the Format Painter icon on the Standard toolbar and then select the text you want to reformat. Alternatively, click a blank area in the text frame to reformat all of the text in the frame.

- ❦ Right drag: Using the right mouse button, drag one text object over another text object. Then click the Apply Formatting Here command on the shortcut menu

- ❦ Keyboard shortcuts: To copy formats, press Ctrl-Shift-C. To paste formats, press Ctrl-Shift-V.

- ❦ Format menu: Highlight the text whose style you want to copy. On the Format menu, select Pick Up Formatting. Highlight the text you want to format. On the Format menu, select Apply Formatting.

Create a Text Style from Scratch

1 On the Format menu, choose Text Style. The Text Style dialog box appears.

2 In the Click To area, choose Create A New Style. The Create New Style dialog box appears.

3 In the Enter New Style Name text box, type a new name.

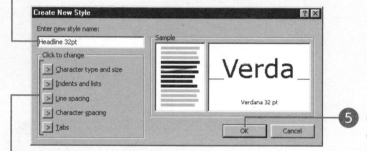

5 Click OK to create the style.

4 Select one of these five options Publisher presents you with the standard text and paragraph formatting dialog boxes.

6 Repeat steps 2 through 5 to create additional text styles.

7 Click Close in the Text Style dialog box.

Apply Text Styles

1 Click in the paragraph or select the paragraphs in which you want the style to apply.

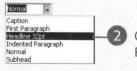

2 Open the Style drop-down list box on the Formatting toolbar and select a style name.

Can I return a paragraph to the previously defined text style? Yes. After you select the paragraph and change its formatting, open the Style drop-down list box and click the name of the style you want to reapply. In the Change Or Apply Style dialog box that appears, click the Return The Selection To The Original Formatting Of The Style? option. Click OK.

Managing text styles. The Text Styles dialog box lets you organize text styles for greater efficiency. You can do the following:

© Delete styles you no longer use.

© Rename styles so that related styles are grouped together on the Style drop-down list box. Because Publisher arranges style names alphabetically, styles such as Table Text and Table Titles appear next to each other.

Modify Existing Text Styles

Even after you have created a style and applied it to your text, you can still modify it. When you modify an existing text style, every paragraph in the document associated with that style is instantly updated. You can modify an existing style by example or by using the Text Styles dialog box.

Modify Existing Text Styles by Example

1 Select the paragraph whose style you want to change.

2 Change the formatting to your satisfaction.

3 Open the Style drop-down list box. Click the style that is currently assigned to the paragraph. The Change Or Apply Style dialog box appears.

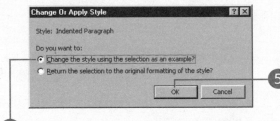

5 Click OK. Publisher reformats all paragraphs that use this style.

4 Click the first option to modify the style based on the currently selected paragraph.

Modify Existing Text Styles Using the Text Style Dialog Box

1 On the Format menu, choose Text Style. The Text Style dialog box appears.

2 In the Choose A Style list box, select the name of the style you want to modify.

3 In the Click To area, select Change This Style. The Change Style Dialog box appears.

4 Use the option buttons—Character Type And Size, Indents And Lists, Line Spacing, Character Spacing, and Tabs—to access the standard text formatting dialog boxes.

How does Publisher handle text styles when I insert a text file into a publication? If the text file you insert doesn't contain formatting information, Publisher assigns the Normal text style, which is defined as Times New Roman, 10 points, left-aligned. If the text file you insert does contain formatting information, and if Publisher can read the word processing file in its native format, Publisher tries to duplicate the formatting, including any defined text styles.

Modify Existing Text Styles Using the Text Style Dialog Box *(continued)*

⑤ When you have modified the text formatting options to your satisfaction, click OK to accept the changes, or click Cancel to return to the previous dialog box.

⑥ Click Close in the Text Style dialog box to return to your document.

Importing Styles from Other Documents

You can get more value from the styles you've created for one Publisher publication by using them in other Publisher documents. You can also import and use styles you've created in your word processing application if Publisher can read the word processing format in its native form.

Import a Text Style

① Open the Format menu and choose Text Style.

② In the Text Style dialog box, choose Import New Styles. The Import Styles dialog box appears.

③ Open the Files Of Type drop-down list box and select any file type Publisher supports. The default is Publisher's format.

④ Use the Look In drop-down list box and the Files list box to locate and select the file that contains the styles you want to import.

Import styles from a word processing file to reconcile duplicate text style names. If you create text styles in a Publisher document and subsequently insert a word processing file that includes duplicate text style names with different formatting attributes, you produce a conflict. Publisher doesn't reconcile this conflict well, often producing text with the right style name but the wrong formatting attributes.

There is a solution. Before you insert the text itself, use the Import New Styles button to bring the style names from the word processing document into your Publisher document. When you explicitly import the style names, Publisher alerts you to the conflict and allows you either to keep the current definition of the text style or to accept the new definition from the word processing file.

Import a Text Style *(continued)*

5️⃣ Click OK. Publisher compares the style names in the current publication with the styles you are importing. If Publisher discovers a duplicate style name, an alert box appears.

6️⃣ Click Yes in the alert box to maintain the style as it exists in the current publication. Click No to import the new style. The Text Style dialog box reappears.

The Text Style dialog box now contains the names of additional text styles imported from the document you selected in step 3.

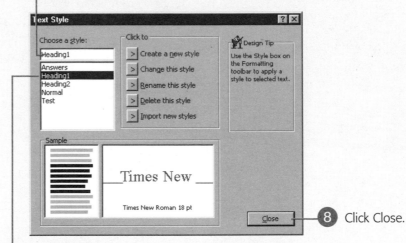

8️⃣ Click Close.

7️⃣ You can select a style name and use the options in the Click To area to change, rename, or delete the style.

Table Frame Tool

When you are dealing with lots of small, interrelated pieces of information, a table is often the best way to organize your text. You can change the size and shape of a table and easily rearrange the information it contains. Tables are very flexible and can be used to create entire documents, such as a price sheet, a résumé, or a business form. As tables of contents, indexes, schedules, or reply coupons, they also can serve as partial-page elements within a larger design.

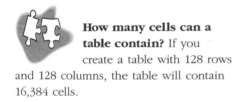

How many cells can a table contain? If you create a table with 128 rows and 128 columns, the table will contain 16,384 cells.

Table Components: Rows, Columns, and Cells

A single table can contain as many as 128 rows, 128 columns, and thousands of individual cells. You can control the table structure with functions built into the table's borders and with commands on the Table menu. Whenever you select a table, Microsoft Publisher 2000 displays special row and column buttons in addition to the standard object selection handles. Use them to highlight portions of the table—or the entire table—efficiently.

For more information about creating frames, see Chapter 1.

Create a Table

① Click the Table Frame Tool and draw a table frame. The Create Table dialog box appears.

② Enter a value from 1 through 128 in the Number Of Rows text box.

③ Enter a value from 1 through 128 in the Number Of Columns text box.

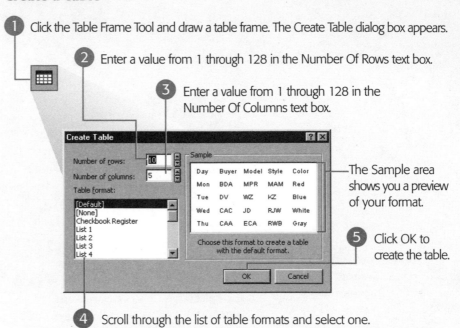

The Sample area shows you a preview of your format.

⑤ Click OK to create the table.

④ Scroll through the list of table formats and select one.

Quick ways of selecting cell contents. The Highlight Text command (on the Edit menu) selects all text within the current cell.

Select a Table, Rows, Columns, a Single Cell, or a Group of Adjacent Cells

① Click anywhere within the table's boundaries to select it. The row and column buttons appear along the top and left side of the table.

To select any rectangular combination of adjacent cells, columns, or rows, first select a single cell. Drag the pointer over adjacent cells to select them, or Shift-click another cell to automatically select everything between it and the originally selected cell.

To select an empty cell, click inside it. The insertion point appears. If the cell contains text, drag the I-beam pointer to select all or part of the contents of a cell.

How can I tell where one cell ends and another cell begins?
A table normally displays gridlines showing the boundaries between individual cells. The gridlines appear on-screen to help you arrange elements, but they never print. If the gridlines don't appear on-screen, choose Show Boundaries And Guides on the View menu. If you want to print lines between the columns and rows in a table, you must assign borders to the gridlines.

For more information about Publisher's text editing features, see Chapter 5.

Why does Publisher insert all of my imported text into a single table cell? When you use the Text File command on the Insert menu to import text into a table, Publisher places the entire file into the current cell. In most cases, this isn't useful. If you want to preserve tabular material, don't use the Text File command—use the Clipboard as explained in "Importing a Table or Part of a Table from an External Source" later in this chapter.

Select a Table, Rows, Columns, a Single Cell, or a Group of Adjacent Cells *(continued)*

To select the contents of the entire table, click the table selector in the upper left corner of the frame.

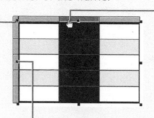

To select an entire column in a table, position the pointer over the gray column selector at the top of the column. Click when the pointer changes to the Hand pointer.

To select an entire row in a table, position the pointer over the gray row selector directly to the left of the row. Click when the pointer changes to the Hand pointer.

Entering Text in a Table

When you first create a table, the upper-left cell contains the insertion point, indicating that the cell is active. Text can be entered only in the active cell, but you can make any cell active by clicking it with the I-beam pointer. You can use any of the text editing commands, as if you were working in an ordinary text frame, to perform these tasks:

- Type normally.

- Import text from an external word processing file into the current cell.

- Cut, copy, and paste text via the Windows Clipboard.

- Move and copy text using the Drag-And-Drop feature.

- Fine-tune your copy with the Check Spelling, AutoCorrect, Find, and Replace commands.

- You can also use special table commands to copy text into every cell in a selected range.

Moving from Cell to Cell

Special key combinations help you navigate from cell to cell in a table, as explained in the following table:

How to Move Between and Within Table Cells	
To move ...	**Press ...**
To the next cell in a table	Tab
To the preceding cell	Shift-Tab
Forward one character (or to the next cell if there is no more text)	RIGHT ARROW
Backward one character (or to the previous cell if there is no more text)	LEFT ARROW
Up one line or cell	UP ARROW
Down one line or cell	DOWN ARROW
To the next tab stop within a cell	Ctrl-Tab

When should I lock the table size? If the table *must* fit into a tight layout, turn off the Grow To Fit Text command to guarantee that the table won't interfere with other elements on the page. Be warned—unlike text frames, table cells don't alert you when the overflow area contains text. Therefore, you should try to lock a table's size only when you are satisfied with the content and formatting of your table. Otherwise, you could inadvertently print a publication that contains hidden table text in the overflow area.

For more information about table sizing, see "Resizing Tables and Table Components" later in this chapter.

Controlling How Text Behaves in Table Cells

Cells within a table automatically expand vertically to accommodate the text you type. To maintain alignment, Publisher increases the height (but not the width) of every cell in the current row.

To lock the table size and prevent Publisher from increasing row height, clear the Grow To Fit Text command on the Table menu. Any text that doesn't fit into its cell is placed in the overflow area. You can't link tables or table cells. To make overflow text visible again, try these techniques:

@ Reduce the point size to fit more text into the current cell.

@ Edit the text to shorten your copy.

@ Make the cell larger by resizing the entire table, the column, or the row.

@ Unlock the table size by selecting the Grow To Fit Text command.

Inserting Identical Text in Cells

You can add the same piece of information to every cell in a selected range, which is useful when you need to repeat an identifying code or part number, as in tables for catalogs or price sheets.

Repeat Text in a Range of Cells

Product	Contents	Item	Price
Lettuce, Apollo	2 gr.	#220-	$1.95
Lettuce, Bibb	2 gr.		$1.25
Lettuce, Brunia	3 gr.		$1.85
Lettuce, Oak Leaf	2 gr.		$1.75

1 Type the text you want to repeat in a cell.

2 Highlight the cell that contains the text, as well as the cells where you want to repeat the text.

3 Open the Table menu. Choose Fill Down to repeat the text in the selected area below the original cell or choose Fill Right to repeat the text in the selected area to the right of the original cell.

Convert tabbed text into tables. Select a table before pasting tabbed text into a Publisher document. Publisher pastes each tabbed item into a separate cell.

Why does the text I just imported into my table look so strange? When you import an external table or part of an external table, Publisher preserves its original formatting—which may be inconsistent with your existing table design.

Importing a Table or Part of a Table from an External Source

Taking advantage of the Clipboard allows you to import a table or part of a table that you've created in another application, such as Microsoft Excel, Microsoft Word, or Microsoft Works. You can either add the external table to an existing Publisher table, or you can create a completely new Publisher table from the external data. Publisher maintains the column and row structure by placing each table item in its own cell.

Import a Table or Part of a Table into an Existing Publisher Table

1 Open the application and then the file that contains the table you want to import.

2 Highlight the cells you want to copy.

Why did my original table data disappear when I pasted new data into the table? In all likelihood you instructed Publisher to increase the size of the selection area in order to paste all of the data on the Clipboard into the table. When you do so, Publisher imports data into as many adjacent cells as necessary to maintain the original row and column structure. Rather than inserting new cells, Publisher overwrites the contents of existing cells. To avoid losing important information by inadvertently pasting new data over old, be sure you've added the correct number of empty rows and columns to your table.

Import Excel worksheets. Publisher allows you to directly import a table in the Excel Worksheet format using the Text File comand on the Insert menu.

For more information about inserting text, see Chapter 5.

Import a Table or Part of a Table into an Existing Publisher Table *(continued)*

③ Choose Copy on the Edit menu (or press Ctrl-C) to place the cells on the Clipboard.

④ Open the Publisher document that contains the table you want to edit.

⑤ Select the table. If you know how many cells the information on the Clipboard will occupy, highlight them. If not, select the first cell in which you want to insert information.

⑥ Choose Paste from the Edit menu (or press Ctrl-V) to add the data on the Clipboard to your Publisher table. If the amount of data on the Clipboard is too great to fit into the selection, the following dialog box appears.

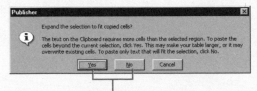

Click No to have Publisher truncate the data to fill only the highlighted cell or cells, or click Yes to have Publisher increase the size of the selection area and paste all of the data on the Clipboard into the table. If your table does not contain enough cells to hold the new data, Publisher adds sufficient rows and/or columns.

Create a New Publisher Table from an External Table

① Open the application and then the file that contains the table you want to import.

② Highlight the cells you want to copy.

③ Choose Copy on the Edit menu (or press Ctrl-C) to place the cells on the Clipboard.

④ Open your Publisher document.

⑤ Open the Edit menu and choose Paste or Paste Special. If you choose Paste, Publisher pastes the table into your publication as a new object and preserves the formatting of the original table. If you choose Paste Special, the following dialog box appears.

Can I use the Paste Special command to insert data from the Clipboard into an existing Publisher table? Yes. In order to insert data from the Clipboard into an existing table using the Paste Special command, found on the Edit menu, you must select specific options within the Paste Special dialog box. Choose the Paste option and in the As list box select either Table Cells With Cell Formatting or Table Cells Without Cell Formatting. Don't choose the Formatted Text option, because it pastes all of the data on the Clipboard into a single cell in your table. None of the other options in the Paste Special dialog box paste the information into an existing table; each generates a new table.

Using the Paste Special command in this way isn't recommended. It offers no benefits over the Paste command and it requires several extra mouse clicks.

Can I create rows and columns of any size?
You can easily increase the size of rows and columns in a table. The only limit is the size of your page. Columns can't be smaller than 0.13 inch and rows can't be smaller than 0.24 inch, or the point size of the text they contain.

Create a New Publisher Table from an External Table *(continued)*

6 Select Paste.

7 Select New Table.

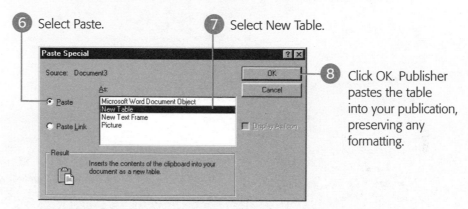

8 Click OK. Publisher pastes the table into your publication, preserving any formatting.

Resizing Tables and Table Components

Publisher offers you several different ways to change the size of a table. You can resize an entire table, resize individual rows and columns, and insert or delete rows and columns. You can even merge or divide cells to accommodate special information such as a table heading or minimum/maximum values.

When you resize an entire table, Publisher changes the dimensions of all the rows and columns equally. To make specific changes to the height of a row or the width of a column, use the Adjust pointer.

Resize an Entire Table

1 Select the table you want to resize.

2 Position the pointer over one of the selection handles until the Resize pointer appears.

For more information about resizing objects in Publisher, see Chapter 3.

Change row or column size while maintaining the overall size of a table.

Using the Adjust pointer to resize rows and columns increases or decreases the size of the entire table. To resize a row or a column without changing the overall size of the table, press and hold the Shift key as you drag the Adjust pointer. Notice that if you increase the size of a row or column, the adjacent row or column decreases by the same amount. If you decrease a row or column, the adjacent row or column increases by the same amount.

Resize an Entire Table *(continued)*

Product	Contents	Item	Price
Lettuce, Apollo	2 gr.	#220-	$1.95
Lettuce, Bibb	2 gr.		$1.25
Lettuce, Brunia	3 gr.		$1.85
Lettuce, Oak Leaf	2 gr.		$1.75

3 Drag the handle to a new location, either inside the table to decrease its size or outside the table to increase its size.

Resize Individual Rows and Columns

1 Select the table.

2 If you want to resize more than one row or column simultaneously, highlight the rows or columns by Shift-clicking the row or column selectors or by dragging the pointer across the row or column selectors.

3 Position the pointer on the gridline between two row or column selectors. The pointer changes to the Adjust pointer. Drag the Adjust pointer to a new position.

Product	Contents	Item	Price
Lettuce, Apollo	2 gr.	#220-	$1.95
Lettuce, Bibb	2 gr.		$1.25
Lettuce, Brunia	3 gr.		$1.85
Lettuce, Oak Leaf	2 gr.		$1.75

Notice that Publisher always shows you the new sizes of the rows or columns by displaying a dotted line. In this illustration, one column is being resized.

Insertion limits for table rows and columns. The number of rows and columns you can insert on a given page depends on the size of the cells in the row or column that contains the insertion point. The smaller the cells, the more rows or columns you can insert.

Insert rows quickly. The fastest way to insert rows into a table is to press the Tab key when you reach the last cell in the table. Publisher adds a new row and also advances the insertion point.

Why can't I use the Del or Backspace key to remove a table from my document? Tables are like collections of miniature text frames. The Del and Backspace keys delete only text within a table cell—not the table itself, just as they delete text from inside text frames, not the frames themselves. To remove a table from your document, select the table and then select the Delete Object command from the Edit menu (or from the shortcut menu that appears when you right-click the table).

Insert Rows or Columns

1 Select the table and click a cell adjacent to where you want a new row or column to appear.

2 Open the Table menu and choose Insert Rows Or Columns. The Insert dialog box appears.

3 Select Rows or Columns.

4 Type the number of rows or columns you want to insert.

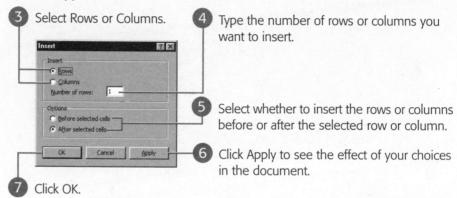

5 Select whether to insert the rows or columns before or after the selected row or column.

6 Click Apply to see the effect of your choices in the document.

7 Click OK.

Delete Rows or Columns

1 Select the table.

2 Select the rows or columns you want to delete. Alternatively, select one or more cells in the rows or columns you want to delete.

3 Choose Delete Rows Or Columns From the Table menu. The Delete dialog box appears.

4 Select Current Rows or Current Columns.

5 Click Apply to preview the effect in your document.

6 Click OK.

Can I merge cells vertically as well as horizontally? Yes, Publisher can merge two or more adjacent cells, regardless of whether the cells are arranged horizontally (in rows) or vertically (in columns).

Merge Cells in a Row

① Select the table and then select the cells you want to merge.

Ordering Information			
Product	**Contents**	**Item**	**Price**
Lettuce, Apollo	2 gr.	#220-01	$1.95
Lettuce, Bibb	2 gr.	#220-02	$1.25
Lettuce, Brunia	3 gr.		
Lettuce, Oak Leaf	2 gr.		

Ordering Information			
Product	**Contents**	**Item**	**Price**
Lettuce, Apollo	2 gr.	#220-01	$1.95
Lettuce, Bibb	2 gr.	#220-02	$1.25
Lettuce, Brunia	3 gr.	#220-03	$1.85
Lettuce, Oak Leaf	2 gr.	#220-04	$1.75

② Open the Table menu and choose Merge Cells. Publisher creates one large cell.

Split a Merged Cell

① Select the merged cell.

② Open the Table menu and choose Split Cells. The merged cell is split according to the existing row and column structure.

Insert Cell Diagonals

① Select a cell, a range of cells, a column, or a row where you want to insert diagonal divisions.

② Choose Cell Diagonals on the Table menu.

Why would I split a cell diagonally? You can often save space in a table by combining two columns of information into a single column that is split diagonally. This technique works well only when the two pieces of information are clearly related. For example, a scientific table might include minimum and maximum values. Likewise, a catalog might contain prices for both individual and quantity purchases.

Insert Cell Diagonals *(continued)*

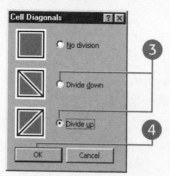

3 Select Divide Down to split the cells diagonally from the upper left to lower right corner. Or select Divide Up to split the cells diagonally from the lower left to the upper right corner.

4 Click OK.

Publisher divides the cells diagonally. You can now enter discrete information into each half of the divided cells.

Remove Cell Diagonals

1 Select the cell, range of cells, column, or row from which you want to remove diagonal divisions.

2 Choose Cell Diagonals on the Table menu.

3 In the Cell Diagonals dialog box, select No Division.

4 Click OK.

Formatting Tables and Table Components

You can change the appearance of a table by assigning both standard attributes (such as text styles or borders) and specialized formatting attributes (such as AutoFormat), as described in the following table. Note which formats can be applied to selected rows and columns or to individually selected cells.

Methods of Formatting Tables

Formatting Attribute	Description	Table Element(s)
AutoFormat	AutoFormat provides a collection of predefined table styles that include attributes such as borders, fill colors, tints and shades, patterns, and text alignment. Except for the Default option, you can't redefine the AutoFormat table styles. Nor can you create your own table formats and save them as AutoFormat options.	Publisher applies the AutoFormat style you choose to the entire table.
Text formats	You can apply any of Publisher's text formats, including character-level formats, paragraph-level formats, and text styles, to text in a table.	You can format text in the entire table or in selected rows, columns, or cells.
Cell margins (the amount of space between the text and the boundaries of each cell)	You can specify different values for the left, right, top, and bottom margins.	You can adjust cell margins for the entire table or for selected rows, columns, or cells.
Line Borders	You can choose a predefined border or create a customized border.	You can assign borders to the entire table or to selected rows, columns, or cells.
BorderArt	You can choose a decorative BorderArt frame.	You can assign BorderArt only to the perimeter of the table.
Shadow	You can add a gray drop shadow to the table.	You can assign a shadow only to the perimeter of the table.
Fill Color	You can fill tables with colors, tints, shades, gradients, and patterns.	You can choose fills for the entire table or for selected rows, columns, or cells. However, you can achieve the full transition of a gradient (from the Base Color to Color 2) only when you apply the gradient to the entire table.

Select an AutoFormat Style

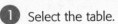 Select the table.

2️⃣ Choose Table AutoFormat on the Table menu. The Auto Format dialog box appears.

Why doesn't the type-face change when I use AutoFormat? AutoFormat changes font styles, such as boldface and italic, but it does not change the typeface used in a table. You must change the typeface using the Format toolbar or the Font command on the Format menu.

Copy formatting from one table to another.

You can quickly copy formatting attributes, such as fill color, border style, shadow, and table cell margins, from one table to another. Select the entire table that contains the formatting you want to duplicate. Click the Format Painter icon on the Standard toolbar and then highlight all of the cells in the table to which you want to copy the formatting.

Alternatively, you can right-drag the table whose formatting you want to copy on top of the table you wish to format. Select Apply Formatting Here from the shortcut menu that appears.

For more information on templates, see Chapter 14.

Select an AutoFormat Style (*continued*)

③ Select one of the 23 table formats.

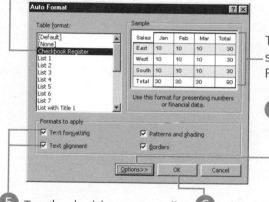

The Sample area is updated as you select and clear options in the Formats To Apply area.

④ If you want to apply only certain attributes to a table, click Options. The Auto Format dialog box expands, revealing the Formats To Apply area.

⑤ Turn the check boxes on or off to customize the formatting.

⑥ Click OK.

Change Frame Attributes and Cell Margins for the Default Table Format

① Select the Table Frame Tool but don't create a table.

② Select the formatting attributes you want for the fill color, border style, shadow, and table cell margins.

③ If you don't want to create a table at this time, select another tool. If you do want to create a table, draw a table frame.

④ Choose the Default table format in the Create Table dialog box, which appears.

⑤ Click OK to create a table with the new default format.

⑥ Save the document to disk as a publication file or as a template. Publisher applies the new default settings whenever you create a table in this document or in documents based on it.

For more information about text formats, see Chapter 6. For more information about borders and BorderArt, see Chapter 9. For more information about Fills, see Chapter 15.

To open the Table Cell Properties dialog box, click its button on the Format toolbar.

Adjust Cell Margins

1 Select all or some of the cells in the table.

2 Choose Table Cell Properties on the Format menu. The Table Cell Properties dialog box appears.

3 Enter any value from 0 through 16 inches for the Left, Right, Top, and Bottom margins.

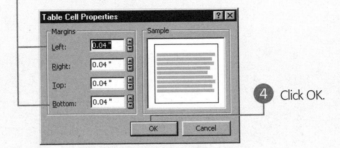

4 Click OK.

WordArt Frame Tool

With Microsoft Publisher 2000's WordArt Frame Tool you can enhance the appearance of text by creating special effects that aren't available with ordinary text objects. You can combine and control these effects to create a wide variety of display-type designs, ranging from sophisticated logos to whimsical headlines. You can create WordArt objects using either the WordArt tool found on Publisher's Object toolbar or the WordArt tool found in Microsoft Draw 2000.

Entering Text into WordArt Frames

WordArt frames are similar—but not identical—to Publisher's normal text frames. One difference is that you must first draw a WordArt frame and then use a special dialog box to enter text.

For more information about Microsoft Draw, see Appendix A.

For more information about drawing a frame, see Chapter 1.

Enter Text into a WordArt Frame

 Click the WordArt Frame Tool (shown in the following illustration) and draw a frame. The WordArt menu bar and toolbar replace Publisher's menu bar and toolbar. The WordArt dialog box appears.

How is entering text into a WordArt frame different from entering text into a normal text frame?

When you work with a WordArt frame, you must enter your text manually in the special dialog box provided. Many of the automated functions associated with ordinary text aren't available. For example, you must manually break a multiple-line text block by pressing the Enter key, because text lines don't automatically wrap to fit the frame. In addition, you can't use a spelling checker on a WordArt object. You can't insert text from a word processing file into a WordArt frame, and the normal commands found on the Edit menu to cut, copy, and paste text are unavailable. (However, the shortcut keys for cut, copy, and paste still work.)

Can I choose a different font when I insert a symbol into WordArt?

No. The Insert Symbol dialog box always displays the font selected on the WordArt toolbar. You can't mix fonts within a WordArt frame.

Enter Text Into a WordArt Frame *(continued)*

② Type your display copy here.

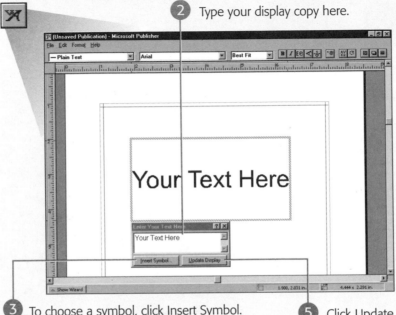

③ To choose a symbol, click Insert Symbol. The Insert Symbol dialog box appears.

⑤ Click Update Display to see the effects of your changes.

④ Select the character you want from the map and then click OK.

⑥ After you have completed the WordArt design to your satisfaction, click anywhere outside the WordArt frame to return to your publication.

Why can't I see all of the fonts installed on my system when I open the font drop-down list box? WordArt uses only TrueType fonts, so only TrueType fonts appear in WordArt's font drop-down list. Fixed-size fonts or Adobe Type 1 fonts aren't accessible from WordArt.

Why does Publisher try to resize the WordArt frame when I specify a large point size for my text? If you choose a point size that is too large for the current dimensions of the WordArt frame, Publisher displays an alert box asking if you want to enlarge the WordArt frame. Click Yes to enlarge the frame. If you click No, you must either make the text smaller by choosing a smaller point size or resize the WordArt frame manually.

Choosing a Font and Point Size for WordArt

Publisher automatically installs numerous TrueType fonts on your computer system, which you can use to format WordArt elements. WordArt can also use TrueType fonts installed with other software applications.

You can apply only one font and one size to all of the text in each WordArt frame. If you need to use a second font or mix type of different sizes, create a second WordArt frame for the text. You can assign a specific point size to WordArt text, or you can use WordArt's powerful Best Fit option, which generates the best type size to fit your frame.

Select a Font and Size for WordArt Text

1 If the WordArt Frame Tool and dialog box aren't active, double-click the WordArt object to activate them.

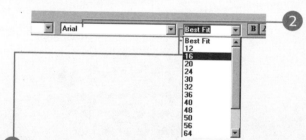

2 Open the Font drop-down list box from the toolbar and select a font name.

3 Specify a size for the text by using one of the following three procedures.

  ✒ Open the Font Size drop-down list box and select a numeric value from the list.

  ✒ Highlight the contents of the Font Size drop-down list box, type a size between 6 and 500 points in 1-point increments, and then press Enter.

  ✒ Select Best Fit to make the WordArt frame function like a picture frame. The text shrinks or grows to fit the frame whenever you resize the frame.

Shape and edit WordArt text to fit your design.
To create successful WordArt designs, you must choose the most appropriate shape for your text—or edit your text so that it works with a particular shape. For example, to make a successful design for the button shown below, you must enter the words out of order (Kellerman, 1999, For Congress) and separate each phrase by pressing the Enter key.

Some WordArt shapes don't work well with long phrases. In the next example, the Inflate shape distorts letters of Broadside Associates. Shortening the phrase to a single word, or breaking it into two lines (shown here), avoids a cramped look.

Text Shaping Options

The single most powerful aspect of WordArt is its ability to manipulate the outlines of a font. The following illustrations demonstrate a few of the shapes you can create with WordArt.

 — Run text along a wavy path.

Create arched or circular text.

Squeeze and slant text.

Change the Shape of Text

1 Click the Shape drop-down list box at the far left of the WordArt toolbar.

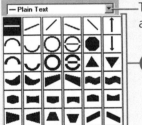

The name of the current shape appears in the drop-down list box.

2 Click one of the 36 available shapes.

Customizing the Text Shape with Special Effects

You can fine-tune any of the WordArt shapes by clicking the Special Effects button on the WordArt toolbar and changing the settings in the Special Effects dialog box. This dialog box presents you with various effects, which can include rotation, arc angle, and slider (or strength) values, depending on the shape you chose for your text.

How is the rotation effect in WordArt different from Publisher's object rotation feature? When you use the WordArt rotation effect, text is rotated *within* the frame. In addition, the WordArt rotation effect can simulate three-dimensional rotations for certain shapes, such as the Wave 1 shape shown here.

Publisher's object rotation feature, on the other hand, rotates an entire object—frame and all—and always rotates an object in two-dimensional space.

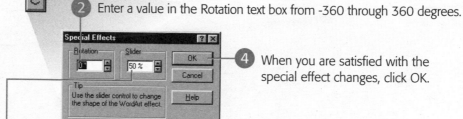

Change the Rotation and Angle of a Shape

1 Click the Special Effects button. If your WordArt follows a straight line or fills a shape, the following dialog box appears.

2 Enter a value in the Rotation text box from -360 through 360 degrees.

4 When you are satisfied with the special effect changes, click OK.

3 Enter a value from 0 through 100 percent in the Slider text box. The slider effect decreases or increases the intensity of a shape effect. Changing the value makes the angles of individual letters more or less acute, or flattens or exaggerates the arc of a curve.

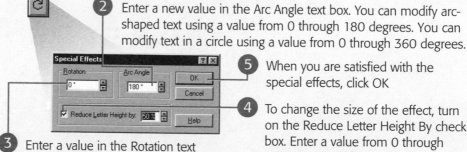

Change the Rotation and Curve of Arced or Circular WordArt Text

1 Click the Special Effects button. If your WordArt text follows an arc or a circle, the following dialog box appears.

2 Enter a new value in the Arc Angle text box. You can modify arc-shaped text using a value from 0 through 180 degrees. You can modify text in a circle using a value from 0 through 360 degrees.

5 When you are satisfied with the special effects, click OK

4 To change the size of the effect, turn on the Reduce Letter Height By check box. Enter a value from 0 through 100 percent in the text box.

3 Enter a value in the Rotation text box from -360 through 360 degrees.

You can toggle WordArt effects on and off. Publisher applies each effect on the WordArt toolbar to the WordArt object when you click the button. To remove the effect, click the button a second time.

Letterspacing (also known as Character Spacing) and the uses for tracking and kerning are explained in Chapter 6.

Formatting Options: Toolbar Button Effects

When the WordArt toolbar is displayed, you can change the overall appearance of your text by clicking the appropriate toolbar button. The effects can range from standard font styles that add emphasis to zany transformations, as illustrated in the table below.

Click this button...	To create this effect...	Sample text
B	Boldface text.	**Broadside**
I	Italic text.	*Broadside*
Ee	Uppercase and lowercase letters of the same height.	BROADSIDE
A	Vertically stacked (top to bottom) text.	BROADSIDE
A	Words that stretch both vertically and horizontally to fill the boundaries of the WordArt frame.	Broadside

Letterspacing and Alignment Controls

There are times when the success of a special effect depends entirely on small details such as letterspacing and alignment. Publisher gives you two controls to fine-tune these attributes.

Tap the power of letterspacing. Letterspacing is a powerful formatting feature that can help you fit text into a shape or along a path. Increasing the letterspacing can help you to avoid crashing letters when you are wrapping text around a circle or arc. Decreasing the letterspacing can help you add artistic effects, such as overlapping letters, to a logo design.

What is the difference between the Stretch button and the Stretch Justify alignment option? The Stretch button stretches letters both horizontally and vertically to fill the boundaries of the WordArt frame. The Stretch Justify option stretches letters only horizontally.

Modify Letterspacing

① Click the Spacing Between Characters button. The Spacing Between Characters dialog box appears.

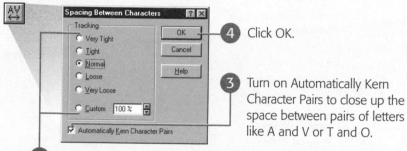

④ Click OK.

③ Turn on Automatically Kern Character Pairs to close up the space between pairs of letters like A and V or T and O.

② Select one of the five preset options, or select Custom and type any value from 0 through 500 percent in the text box. A Custom value of 100 percent is the same as Normal letterspacing.

Align Letters in a WordArt Frame

① Click the Alignment button to open a menu of six options.

② Select one of the following alignment options:

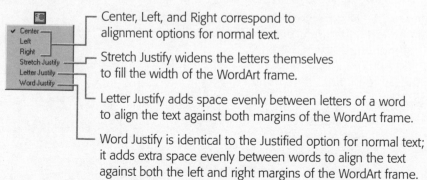

Center, Left, and Right correspond to alignment options for normal text.

Stretch Justify widens the letters themselves to fill the width of the WordArt frame.

Letter Justify adds space evenly between letters of a word to align the text against both margins of the WordArt frame.

Word Justify is identical to the Justified option for normal text; it adds extra space evenly between words to align the text against both the left and right margins of the WordArt frame.

WordArt Frame Tool

Why can't I see a fill pattern? In order to see a fill pattern, you must choose different colors for the foreground and background. Although the terminology is identical, the foreground and background colors you choose in the Shading dialog box are not in any way related to the foreground and background pages in your document.

Fill a WordArt object with a standard scheme color, custom color, tint, or shade. To fill a WordArt object with a standard scheme color, custom color, tint, or shade, you must exit WordArt (by clicking outside the WordArt frame), select the WordArt frame, and then choose the Recolor Object command from the Format menu.

The WordArt Object appears in the new color in the Publisher document on-screen and at print time. However, if you double-click the WordArt object in order to edit it, the screen display reverts to the original (incorrect) color until you exit WordArt again.

Alternatively, you can use the WordArt tool found in Draw, which offers much more robust formatting features than Publisher's WordArt Frame tool.

Color, Fill Pattern, Shadow, and Letter Outline Options

You can create dramatic and playful WordArt text designs using color, fill pattern, shadow, and letter outline options. You might find these WordArt options especially useful for short text blocks printed at large sizes, such as store signage.

You can assign colors and fill patterns to WordArt text.

You can alter the color and thickness of each letter's outline (border) without affecting its fill color.

You can apply three-dimensional shadows to all letters in the WordArt frame.

Shade WordArt Text by Choosing a Color and Fill Pattern

① Click the Shading button. The Shading dialog box appears.

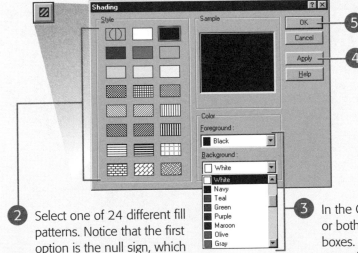

⑤ Click OK.

④ Click Apply to see the effect of your choices in your publication without closing the dialog box.

② Select one of 24 different fill patterns. Notice that the first option is the null sign, which produces transparent letters.

③ In the Color area, open one or both of the drop-down list boxes. Then choose a foreground or background color, or both, from Publisher's standard palette of 35 colors.

The Recolor Object command is explained in Chapter 10. For more information about tints and shades, see Chapter 15. To learn about the WordArt tool in Draw, see Appendix A.

 Is there a difference between the shadow and outline effects applied to WordArt and the same effects applied to ordinary text? Yes. The WordArt Frame tool gives you more formatting options. For example, Publisher's Font dialog box lets you apply a simple gray dropshadow to the individual letters in a normal text frame. In contrast, the WordArt Frame tool lets you choose from seven different shadow effects and 35 colors. And only the WordArt tool lets you change the thickness and color of the letter's outline independently of its fill color and pattern.

 Why does the shadow appear around the WordArt frame instead of the individual letters? You have selected the WordArt frame by singleclicking the object. Double-click to run WordArt, where you can edit the text and apply shadows to individual letters.

Change the Letter Outlines

1 Click the Border button. The Border dialog box appears.

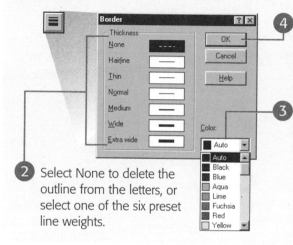

4 Click OK.

2 Select None to delete the outline from the letters, or select one of the six preset line weights.

3 Open the Color drop-down list box and select a color. If you choose Auto, Publisher matches the outline to the solid fill color you selected. If you selected foreground and background fill colors in the Shading dialog box, the Auto outline is matched to the darker of the two.

Create a Shadow

1 Click the Shadow button. The Shadow dialog box appears.

2 Choose a shadow option. The No Shadow option on the far left removes shadows from WordArt text.

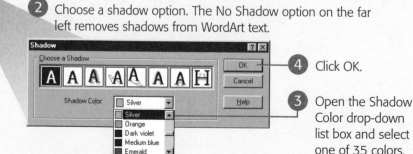

4 Click OK.

3 Open the Shadow Color drop-down list box and select one of 35 colors.

Running WordArt in a separate window. If you choose Microsoft WordArt Object from the Edit menu and then select Open, the WordArt functions appear in a separate window instead of on a toolbar, as shown below. Which method you choose is purely a matter of preference and has no impact on performance.

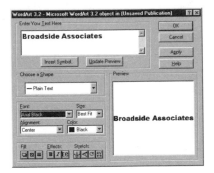

For more information on Publisher's layout tools, see Chapter 3. Text wrap options, the cropping tool, and frame margins are discussed in Chapter 10. Frame shadows and borders are discussed in Chapter 9. Color and fill effects are discussed in Chapter 15.

Editing Options

You can open the WordArt toolbar and Enter Your Text Here dialog box in a very direct manner—simply double-click an existing WordArt object. You can also use the Edit menu to access the WordArt functions.

Edit WordArt Text and Formatting

1 Select a WordArt frame.

2 Open the Edit menu and select Microsoft WordArt Object.

3 Choose Edit on the cascading menu. The Enter Your Text Here dialog box and the WordArt toolbar appear. The toolbar displays the current formatting attributes for the selected object.

4 Type new text and/or choose new formatting options.

5 Click anywhere outside the WordArt frame to accept the changes and return to your publication.

Formatting WordArt Frames

Publisher makes a distinction between a WordArt frame and WordArt text. You must use WordArt's internal functions to create, edit, and format the text that composes the WordArt effect. However, when you single-click a WordArt object, Publisher treats the object (and more specifically the frame) very much like a picture. You can format a WordArt frame in the following ways:

@ Alter a frame's size, position, and rotation using standard layout tools.

@ Format a frame with a shadow, a border, a fill color, or a fill effect.

@ Wrap text around a frame or around the WordArt letters.

@ Crop a WordArt element to hide portions of the design.

@ Specify frame margins.

Drawing Tools and Formatting Options

You can draw a wide variety of shapes with Publisher 2000's four drawing tools. Use the Line, Oval, Rectangle, and Custom Shapes tools to draw basic shapes. These elements work well as backgrounds and borders for your designs.

In addition, you can combine several simple objects into more complex shapes, as shown in the following illustration. Publisher's layout tools let you group objects together, rotate and flip objects, align objects automatically, and control how objects overlap.

For more information about Publisher's layout tools, such as stacking, grouping, rotating, and aligning, see Chapter 3.

The international prohibition sign was created by grouping two objects (a line and a circle).

This simple airplane is composed of three shapes: an oval, a chevron, and a triangle. Notice how the shapes have been rotated to add a sense of movement to the plane.

The benefits of formatting frames. You can apply all of Publisher's formatting options to text, picture, table, and WordArt frames. By applying formatting directly to a frame, you make the formats integral to the object, which in turn makes the combination easy to manage. When you move a text frame that has a BorderArt format, for example, the decorative border moves with the text automatically.

 For more information about color and fill effects, see Chapter 15.

 For more information about creating objects, see Chapter 1. For more information about Publisher's layout tools, see Chapter 3.

You can also change the appearance of drawn objects and frames by choosing formatting options, such as border or line styles, fill colors and fill effects, and drop shadows. The following illustration provides an overview of Publisher's formatting options.

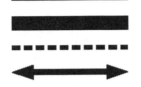

Borders and lines range in width from 0.25 to 127 points. You can also format lines with dash-and-dot patterns and arrowheads. You can also use 10 different arrowhead types to format lines.

You can use fill options, such as solid colors, tints and shades of a color, repeating patterns, and (as shown here) gradients.

Add drop shadows to any shape or frame to create a three-dimensional effect.

BorderArt designs range in width from 4 to 250 points and come in more than 160 patterns, from simple dots to zany cartoons.

Lines, Rectangles, Ovals, and Custom Shapes

Using Publisher's drawing tools is easy— just select a tool and then click and drag the Crossbar pointer in the workspace to create a basic shape. You can alter the outline of many of the objects created with the Custom Shapes tool, thanks to special Adjust handles that appear along the perimeter of the object.

You can increase the accuracy of your drawings by pressing special keys as you create shapes. The Shift key enables you to draw symmetrical objects and

Use Publisher's layout tools to draw with precision. Remember that Publisher's powerful layout tools can help you draw objects more precisely.

@ Turn on the appropriate Snap To function to have the Crosshair jump to the nearest ruler mark, guideline, or existing object.

@ Draw a shape at an arbitrary size, and then use the Size And Position dialog box to specify exact dimensions.

@ Read the Status line at the bottom of the screen to measure an object interactively as you draw it.

the Ctrl key allows you to draw an object from its center outward. You can use the Shift key and the Ctrl key together to combine these effects, as demonstrated in the following illustration:

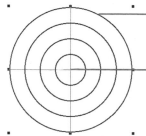

This series of perfectly round and concentric circles was drawn while pressing and holding the Ctrl and Shift keys simultaneously.

Each circle was started from the same center (the coordinates where the guidelines intersect).

Draw a Shape

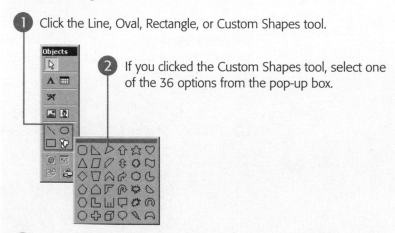

① Click the Line, Oval, Rectangle, or Custom Shapes tool.

② If you clicked the Custom Shapes tool, select one of the 36 options from the pop-up box.

③ Position the Crossbar pointer where you want the first corner of the object to begin.

④ Click and drag the pointer until you are satisfied with the size and shape of the object. Release the mouse button.

Can I create a free-form shape with Publisher's drawing tools? No. Publisher lets you resize drawn shapes and it lets you adjust the outline of a Custom Shape. But Publisher isn't a drawing application. It doesn't let you draw and connect curves or erase portions of a shape to create a free-form shape. If you want to draw a free-form shape, you must use Microsoft Draw or another drawing application.

For more information about Microsoft Draw, see Appendix A.

Alter the Outline of a Shape

1 Position the pointer over the Adjust handle. The Adjust pointer appears.

2 Drag the Adjust handle to change the shape of the object.

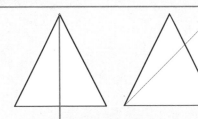

The arrows on the Adjust pointer tell you in which directions you can drag the handle to alter the shape.

The Adjust handle, which looks like a gray diamond, appears at a vertex when you draw or select certain custom shapes.

Create a Straight Line, Perfect Square, True Circle, or Proportional Shape Using the Shift Key

1 Select the drawing tool you want to use.

2 Press and hold the Shift key.

3 Click and drag the Crossbar pointer to draw the object. Because you are pressing and holding the Shift key, the tools perform in the following ways:

- ✎ The Line Tool draws only horizontal, vertical, or 45-degree diagonal lines.

- ✎ The Rectangle Tool draws only perfect squares.

- ✎ The Oval Tool draws only perfect circles.

- ✎ The Custom Shapes Tool draws the selected object only in its original proportions.

4 Release the mouse button before you release the Shift key.

Other uses for the Shift and Ctrl keys. You can use the Shift and Ctrl keys alone or in combination when you create, resize, or move text frames, picture frames, WordArt frames, and drawn shapes.

Use the Shift key to make any of the frames you draw of equal width and height, and use the Ctrl key to begin drawing any frame from its center.

You can also use the Shift key to constrain the movement of an object to the horizontal or vertical axis. That is, if you want to realign an object in only one direction, you can move the object either up and down or side to side.

Finally, if you press and hold the Ctrl key as you move an object, you will create a duplicate of the object, leaving the original object in its original location.

Center an Object Using the Ctrl Key

1 Click the tool you want to use.

2 Press and hold the Ctrl key.

3 Position the Crossbar pointer where you want the object's center to be. Click and drag the pointer to draw the object.

4 Release the mouse button before you release the Ctrl key.

Formatting Lines

You can change the appearance of lines by specifying a thickness and a color. You can also format a line with dash and dot patterns or by adding arrowheads to the right end, the left end, or both ends of the line.

Format Lines

1 Draw or select a line to format.

2 Click the Line/Border Style button on the Formatting toolbar or the Line/Border Style command on the Format menu. Point to More Styles on the submenu that appears.

To quickly format a line with arrowheads, line weights, or a dash style, click the appropriate button on the Formatting toolbar. When you click the Line/Border Style button or the Dash Style button, a submenu appears from which you can choose an option.

Control the size of the arrowhead. The thickness of a line determines the size of the arrowhead. To increase the size of the arrowhead, make the line thicker.

Draw arrows with the Custom Shapes tool. You can create a wide variety of arrows by choosing one of the four arrow shapes in the Custom Shapes pop-up box. Unlike arrows created with the Line tool, these shapes include curves and arrowheads and can be modified using the Adjust handles.

Adjust handles

Format Lines *(continued)*

3 Select one of the six preset line weights or type a value from 0.25 through 127 points into the text box.

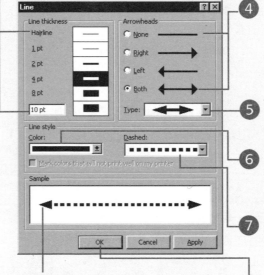

4 If you want to apply an arrowhead to the line, select one of the three options to specify the arrowhead's direction, or select None to remove an arrowhead from a line.

5 Choose one of the 10 arrowhead types from the drop-down list box.

6 Open the Color drop-down list box and choose one of the available colors, tints, or shades.

7 Open the Dashed drop-down list box and choose one of the 11 dash or dot styles.

Preview the current line settings in the Sample area, or preview the actual line within your publication by clicking the Apply button.

8 Click OK.

Does the frame size expand when I apply a border? Publisher draws the border inside the frame; the outside dimensions of the frame remain the same. This means that if you create a small text frame and then format it with a wide border, you might cover text within the text frame. To solve this problem, you can reduce the width of the border or enlarge the text frame.

Borders and BorderArt

You can add borders to a wide range of elements within a Publisher document, including drawn shapes and text, table, picture, or WordArt frames. You also can create a border for an individual cell or a range of cells in a table. You can even insert rules between columns of text in a text frame.

When you select a box, a frame, or cells within a table, the Border Style dialog box gives you the ability to format each side of the object with different line widths or colors. When you select a drawn object that isn't rectangular, such as a circle or a triangle, Publisher applies the border to the irregular shape of the object.

If you want more than a simple border around an object, consider BorderArt, a collection of over 160 designs that includes geometric patterns, symbolic icons, and miniature illustrations. You can customize a BorderArt border by changing its size and color. You can even create your own BorderArt patterns based on imported clip art or other picture files.

Apply a Line Border to a Rectangle or a Frame

1 Select the rectangle or frame you want to format.

2 Click the Line/Border Style button on the Formatting toolbar or select the Line/Border Style command on the Format menu. Select More Styles on the submenu that appears.

Drawing Tools

To format the perimeter of an object with a border, click the Line/Border Style button on the Format menu. Choose one of the four preformatted line weights (Hairline, 1 point, 2 points, or 4 points) on the submenu that appears.

Apply a Line Border to a Rectangle or a Frame *(continued)*

3 If it is not already selected, choose the Line Border tab.

4 Click the Box button to apply the same border to all four sides of a frame. Alternatively, in the Select A Side area, choose the top, bottom, left, or right edge of the rectangle or frame. The selected side is indicated by two triangles pointing to it. You can choose any combination of sides by pressing the Shift key and clicking the desired sides. In this example, one set of triangles points to the top of the frame.

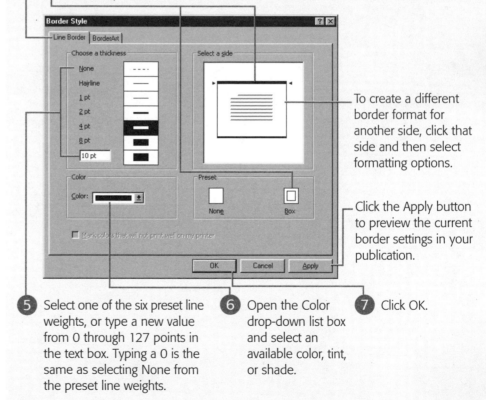

To create a different border format for another side, click that side and then select formatting options.

Click the Apply button to preview the current border settings in your publication.

5 Select one of the six preset line weights, or type a new value from 0 through 127 points in the text box. Typing a 0 is the same as selecting None from the preset line weights.

6 Open the Color drop-down list box and select an available color, tint, or shade.

7 Click OK.

Why can't I create interior rules for a text or table frame? You can create interior rules in a text frame only when the text frame contains multiple columns of text. Open the Text Frame Properties dialog box, and increase the number of text columns to two or more.

You can create interior rules in a table frame for only those cells that are selected.

For more information about text frames, see Chapter 4. For more information about table cells, see Chapter 7.

Apply different borders to the perimeter and interior of a text or table frame. You can develop endless combinations of borders for text and table objects by using the Select A Side feature of the Border Style dialog box. You can even apply custom borders to a range of cells within a table. The two tables shown below are structurally identical, but they appear different because of the way in which the perimeter and the interior grid have been formatted.

Apply a Line Border to the Interior Divisions of a Text or Table Frame

1 Select a text frame that contains two or more columns of text or select all (or a portion of) the cells in a table frame.

2 Click the Line/Border Style button on the Formatting toolbar or select the Line/Border Style command on the Format menu. Select More Styles on the submenu that appears.

3 If it isn't already selected, choose the Line Border tab.

4 Click the Grid button to apply the same border to both the interior divisions and the perimeter of the frame. Alternatively, if you select a text frame, choose the vertical column division in the Select A Side Area. If you select cells in a table, choose the vertical column division or the horizontal row division. The selected side is indicated by two triangles pointing to it.

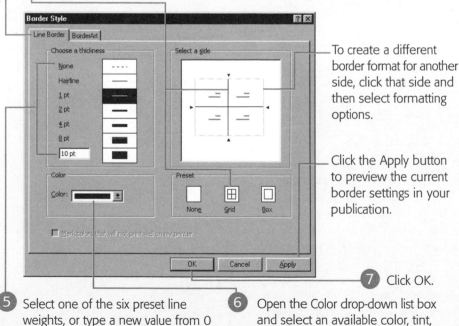

To create a different border format for another side, click that side and then select formatting options.

Click the Apply button to preview the current border settings in your publication.

7 Click OK.

5 Select one of the six preset line weights, or type a new value from 0 through 127 points in the text box.

6 Open the Color drop-down list box and select an available color, tint, or shade.

Can I apply a border to only a portion of an oval or a custom shape?

When you select a drawn object that isn't rectangular, such as a circle or a triangle, the border is applied to the irregular shape of the object. You can't apply different formats to individual sides of these objects.

 Can I apply Border Art to an oval, a custom shape, or table cells?

No. BorderArt can't follow the curved or irregular outlines of ovals and custom shapes. You can apply only standard line borders to ovals and custom shapes. You'll also find that you can't apply BorderArt to the interior cell divisions of a table. You can apply BorderArt only to the rectangular perimeter (or frame) of a table.

Apply a Line Border to an Oval or a Custom Shape

1 Select the oval or custom shape you want to format.

2 Click the Line/Border Style button on the Formatting toolbar, or select the Line/Border Style command on the Format menu and choose More Styles. The Border dialog box opens.

3 Select one of the six preset line weights, or type a new value from 0 through 127 points in the text box.

4 Open the Color drop-down list box and select an available color, tint, or shade.

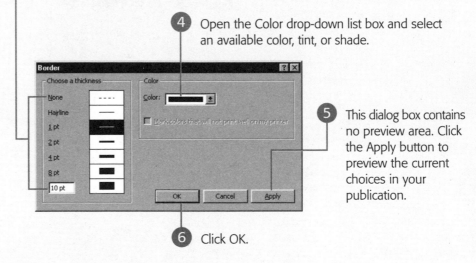

5 This dialog box contains no preview area. Click the Apply button to preview the current choices in your publication.

6 Click OK.

Add BorderArt to a Frame or a Rectangle

1 Select the frame or rectangle to which you want to add BorderArt.

2 Click the Line/Border Style button on the Formatting toolbar or select the Line/Border Style command on the Format menu. Select More Styles from the submenu. The Border Style dialog box appears.

Add BorderArt to a Frame or a Rectangle *(continued)*

3 Select the BorderArt tab. ——————

4 Scroll through the list of available designs and then select the BorderArt style you want. ——

5 Accept Publisher's recommended point size, or clear the Use Default Size check box and type a new value from 4 through 250 points in the Border Size text box. ————

Turn on this check box to restore the BorderArt pattern to its original color. ————

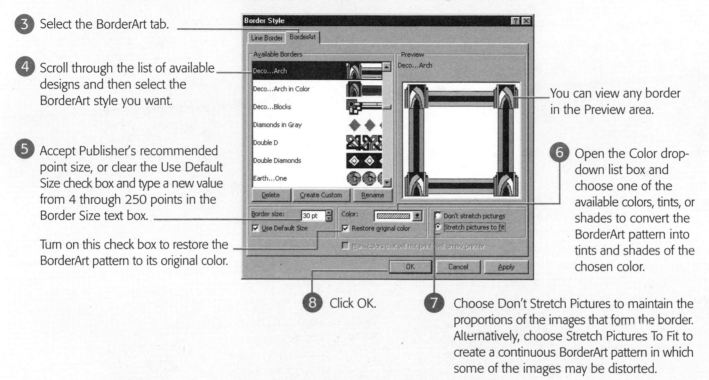

You can view any border in the Preview area.

6 Open the Color drop-down list box and choose one of the available colors, tints, or shades to convert the BorderArt pattern into tints and shades of the chosen color.

8 Click OK.

7 Choose Don't Stretch Pictures to maintain the proportions of the images that form the border. Alternatively, choose Stretch Pictures To Fit to create a continuous BorderArt pattern in which some of the images may be distorted.

Create Custom BorderArt

1 Select the frame or rectangle to which you want to add BorderArt.

2 Click the Line/Border Style button on the Formatting toolbar or the Line/Border Style command on the Format menu and select More Styles from the submenu. The Border Style dialog box appears.

3 Select the BorderArt tab.

For more information about the Microsoft Clip Gallery and picture import functions, see Chapter 10.

 Manage BorderArt Patterns. Whenever you select a BorderArt pattern in the Available Borders list box, two buttons become available. Click Delete to remove the currently selected BorderArt pattern from the list. Click Rename to change the name of the currently selected BorderArt pattern. Because BorderArt patterns appear in alphabetical order, you can use the Rename function to move a favorite BorderArt pattern from the bottom of the list to the top. Just choose a new name that begins with the letter A. For example, you can rename Vine to A-Vine.

Create Custom BorderArt *(continued)*

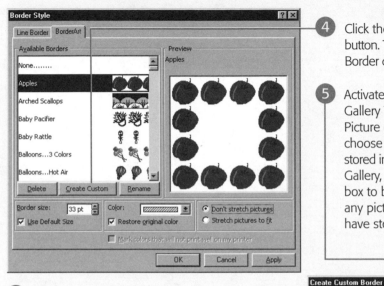

④ Click the Create Custom button. The Create Custom Border dialog box appears.

⑤ Activate the Use Clip Gallery To Choose The Picture check box to choose from the images stored in the Microsoft Clip Gallery, or clear this check box to be able to choose any picture file that you have stored on disk.

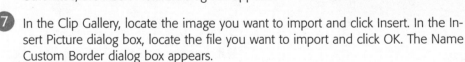

⑥ Click Choose Picture to use a picture file—in any graphic file format that Publisher supports—as a BorderArt pattern. If you activated the Use Clip Gallery To Choose The Picture check box, the Microsoft Clip Gallery 4.0 dialog box appears. Otherwise, the Insert Picture dialog box appears.

⑦ In the Clip Gallery, locate the image you want to import and click Insert. In the Insert Picture dialog box, locate the file you want to import and click OK. The Name Custom Border dialog box appears.

Create decorative lines and bullets using BorderArt. You can use BorderArt to produce decorative lines and bullets. To make a decorative line, first select a box that you have formatted with BorderArt. Then resize the box by either dragging the bottom selection handle until it overlaps the top selection handle, or by dragging the right selection handle until it overlaps the left selection handle.

To create a decorative bullet, first select a box that you have formatted with BorderArt. Then resize the box by dragging a corner selection handle until it overlaps the selection handle diagonally opposite.

Create Custom BorderArt *(continued)*

⑧ Replace the numerical designation used by the Microsoft Clip Gallery with a descriptive name.

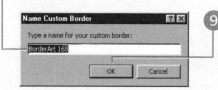

⑨ Click OK to add the custom border. Publisher adds the new BorderArt pattern to the Available Borders list box. You can apply the custom border to any frames or boxes you create in the future.

Removing Borders and BorderArt from Objects

Publisher offers several different ways to remove borders or BorderArt from an object, as the table below explains. Your choices will vary depending upon the type of object you're working with.

Remove Borders and BorderArt from an Object		
To remove…	**From…**	**Do This…**
The entire border	A frame, drawn shape, cell, or range of cells.	In the Border Style dialog box, select the Line Border Tab. In the Preset area, click None.
A portion of a line border	A frame, rectangle, cell, or range of cells.	In the Border Style dialog box, select the side of the object from which you want to remove the border. Then click None in the Choose a Thickness area.
A BorderArt border	A rectangle or frame.	In the Border Style dialog box, select the BorderArt tab. Select None from the Available Borders list box.

To remove the perimeter border or a BorderArt pattern from any selected frame, or any selected range of table cells, click the Line/Border Style icon on the formatting toolbar and choose None from the submenu.

 Can I apply shadows to individual letters? You can apply shadows to individual letters, but you can't do it using the Shadow command. Instead, you must select the text and choose the Shadow effect in the Font dialog box. Alternatively, you can create a WordArt element. The Shadow effect in the WordArt module allows you to choose both the placement and color of the shadow.

 For more information about text formatting, see Chapter 6. For more information about WordArt, see Chapter 8.

Shadows

You can create the illusion of depth for frames, lines, and drawn objects by adding a drop shadow behind them. Publisher always colors a shadow with a tint of the border (or BorderArt) color. For example, if you have assigned a solid blue border to a text frame, the drop shadow appears as a lighter tint of blue.

The Martin Krump Trio

Regardless of the size of the frame or shape, the drop shadow falls behind and to the lower right of the original object.

Publisher mimics the outline of the original object. Boxes and frames have rectangular shadows, while oval and custom shapes have irregular shadows.

Add or Remove a Shadow

1 Select the frame, line, or drawn object.

2 Select Shadow on the Format menu. Publisher adds a shadow to the object.

3 Shadow is a toggle command. To remove a shadow, click the Shadow command again.

Picture and Clip Media Tools

Microsoft Publisher 2000 can import a wide variety of computer-based media—not just pictures—into your documents. For example, you can incorporate sounds and motion clips into electronic documents that you plan to publish on the World Wide Web. Pictures, however, remain the primary way to enhance both electronic and paper-based documents. The first step toward mastering Publisher's picture tools is learning to distinguish between different graphics types.

Categories of Graphics

Graphics file formats can be grouped into two overall categories: bitmapped (or raster) images and vector (or draw-type) images. Take a look at the following table, which compares the two file formats. As you can see, there are pros and cons to using each kind of image.

Comparison of Bitmapped and Vector Images		
Image Attribute	**Bitmapped Image**	**Vector Image**
How the image data is stored and interpreted by the computer.	The image data is a collection of picture elements, or pixels. The information in the image file specifies the location, or map, of each pixel.	The image data is a series of drawing instructions.
Overall output quality.	High, provided that the image contains the appropriate number of pixels (referred to as resolution) for your final output device.	Always high. An image always prints at the highest resolution of the output device.

Comparison of Bitmapped and Vector Images *(continued)*		
Image Attribute	**Bitmapped Image**	**Vector Image**
Enlargement capability.	Poor. When enlarged in Publisher, the individual pixels of a bitmap picture create a jagged staircase pattern, known as aliasing. The lines of the image don't look smooth.	High. You can scale the image or change its proportions without reducing quality.
Color capability.	Images contain a specific number of potential colors: 1 color (black-and-white), 16 colors, 256 colors or shades of gray, or 16.7 million colors.	All color information is stored as a series of instructions, which can generate black-and-white, grayscale, or full color (16.7 million colors) pictures.
Appropriate content.	Scanned photographs and realistic illustrations.	Line drawings, illustrations, charts, and technical diagrams.
File size.	Bitmapped images can require a great deal of storage space. As the resolution and the number of potential colors increase, file size grows dramatically. For example, at the standard resolution used for the Internet (72 pixels per inch, or ppi), a color image measuring 640 x 480 pixels requires 900 KB of storage space. At the appropriate resolution for a color desktop printer (113 ppi), a full color, full page image requires nearly 3.5 MB of storage space.	Drawing indications and color information are stored as a series of instructions. This results in efficient file sizes that don't require a great deal of storage space.

The following images illustrate some of the differences between bitmapped and vector images.

The computer sees this bitmapped circle as a series of black-and-white dots.

Enlarging a bitmapped image also enlarges the individual dots, which creates a jagged pattern (aliasing).

The computer sees this vector circle as a series of drawing instructions for radius, line thickness, and fill pattern.

You can enlarge or reduce a vector image without degrading quality.

A Special Case:
The Encapsulated PostScript Format

The Encapsulated PostScript (EPS) format is a graphics file format that can contain both vector and bitmapped images. The information for both of these image types is stored in Adobe's PostScript printer language. In fact, EPS is a subset of the commands used to control a PostScript printer.

When Publisher displays an EPS file on-screen, it shows you a picture of the graphic only if a bitmapped image of the picture, called a TIFF (Tagged Image File Format) header, is included in the file. The TIFF header contains a low-resolution representation of the image to help you position the picture. If no header is included, the EPS file appears as a simple box with an identifying file name and the name of the program that created the image. The size of this bounding box indicates the dimensions of the EPS picture.

The low resolution screen display of an EPS image makes it unsuitable for Web publications. Furthermore, if you print a publication containing an EPS image on a non-PostScript printer, only the screen image will be printed. That means you will either see a low resolution preview bitmap or a plain box in your printed document, as shown below.

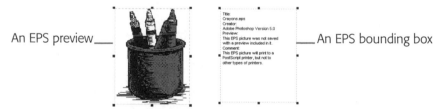

An EPS preview ___   ___ An EPS bounding box

Title:
Crayons.eps
Creator:
Adobe Photoshop Version 5.0
Preview:
This EPS picture was not saved
with a preview included in it.
Comment:
This EPS picture will print to a
PostScript printer, but not to
other types of printers.

Importing Pictures

You can easily import many different types of pictures into your publications, giving you a lot of design flexibility. The following table lists the many graphics file formats that Publisher can import. Pay attention to the Comments column for information about each format's performance in Publisher.

You may already have access to additional graphics file formats.
Publisher can take advantage of many graphics file filters that have been installed on your system by other Microsoft products. The exact choices that appear in the Insert Picture dialog box vary, but here are a few formats that you might be able to access:

- Enhanced Metafiles (EMF)
- Microsoft Picture It! (MIX)
- Targa (TGA)
- AutoCAD Format 2D (DXF)
- HP Graphics Language (HGL)

Types of Graphics Files That Publisher Imports

Format Name	Image Type	Filename Extension	Comments
Windows Bitmaps	Bitmapped	BMP	Best suited for black-and-white, 16-color, and 256-color images.
CorelDraw	Vector	CDR	Can include bitmapped data as well, but rarely does.
Computer Graphics Metafile	Vector	CGM	Many older third-party clip art libraries are in this format.
Macintosh PICT	Bitmapped, vector	PCT	Can include bitmapped data, vector data, or both.
Micrografx Designer/Draw	Vector	DRW	Can include bitmapped data as well, but rarely does.
Encapsulated PostScript	Bitmapped, vector	EPS	Can contain bitmapped data, vector data, or both. Must be printed to a PostScript device. EPS images aren't suitable for Internet publications. Can contain named spot colors, CMYK colors, or RGB colors.
CompuServe Graphics Interchange Format	Bitmapped	GIF	Can contain a maximum of 256 colors. A popular graphics file format for the Internet. GIF files can contain transparent areas and multiple images, which, when viewed sequentially, create animation effects.
Joint Photographic Experts Group	Bitmapped	JPG	This highly compressed file format is ideal for high resolution images, stored in what are called JPEG files. A popular graphics file format for the Internet.

For more information about RGB, CMYK, or spot colors, see Chapter 15.

Types of Graphics Files That Publisher Imports *(continued)*			
Format Name	Image Type	Filename Extension	Comments
Kodak Photo CD	Bitmapped	PCD	Images stored at highest resolution can be too large for Publisher to save; lower resolutions take up less disk space and print faster.
PC Paintbrush	Bitmapped	PCX	Best suited for black-and-white, 16-color, and 256-color images.
Portable Network Graphics	Bitmapped	PNG	Can contain either 256 colors or 16.7 million colors. A popular graphics file format for the Internet. PNG files can contain transparent areas.
Tagged Image File Format	Bitmapped	TIF	TIFF compression options are ideal for high resolution images. Can contain CMYK or RGB colors.
Windows Metafile	Vector	WMF	Can include bitmapped data as well, but rarely does.
WordPerfect Graphics	Vector	WPG	Offers compatibility with WordPerfect.

It's best not to draw a picture frame when importing bitmapped images. Importing a picture without first drawing a picture frame is especially useful when working with bitmapped images. It guarantees that you don't inadvertently resize and therefore degrade the picture. If you want to resize a bitmap picture, use the cropping tool instead.

Picture Import Methods

Before you import a picture into your publication, you should decide whether you need to draw a picture frame. If you want to import a picture at its original size, don't draw a picture frame first. Publisher will create a picture frame to fit the image.

Alternatively, you can create a picture frame prior to importing an image. This method works best if you want to fit a picture into a predetermined layout.

In either case, Publisher always maintains the picture's original aspect ratio—the proportional relationship between the width and height of the image.

Draw multiple picture frames. Normally after you draw a picture frame, the crosshair pointer reverts to the arrow pointer. You can keep the crosshair pointer active and continue to draw picture frames by Ctrl-clicking the Picture Frame Tool. Select another tool on the toolbar to return to normal selection mode.

A quick way to access the Insert Picture dialog box. You can access the Insert Picture dialog box quickly by double-clicking a picture frame. If the image that you double-click contains a picture from the Microsoft Clip Art collection, Publisher displays the Insert Clip Art dialog box.

The Find File command is described in Chapter 2. For more information about linking to externally stored pictures, see Chapter 16.

Import a Picture into Your Publication

1. If you want Publisher to size the imported image to fit into a predetermined layout, choose the Picture Frame Tool (shown below) and draw a picture frame. Alternatively, you can select an existing picture frame. If you want to import a picture in its original size, begin this procedure with step 2.

2. Open the Insert menu and choose Picture. On the submenu, select From File. The Insert Picture dialog box appears.

3. Open the Files Of Type drop-down list box and choose the format of the file you want to import. All the files of your chosen format appear in the main list box.

4. Locate and select the picture file you want using the shortcut buttons, the Look In drop-down list box, and the File Name list box.

5. Click Insert to embed the image. Alternatively, open the drop-down menu and click Link To File to create a link to the externally stored graphic.

If you have difficulty locating the file, click the Tools button and the Find command to search for it.

Other picture import methods. You can import pictures into Publisher using two other methods:

@ Use the drag-and-drop method to import pictures from Windows Explorer or from a draw or paint application that supports Windows drag-and-drop functions.

@ Paste a picture from the Windows clipboard. The clipboard converts files to a standard file format that all Windows-based applications can use.

Printing hidden pictures. If you hide the pictures on your screen to speed performance and then print the document, Publisher asks whether you want to print the pictures or suppress them. Click Yes to print the pictures; click No to print the document with blank spaces where the pictures should be. Publisher prints a dotted outline to indicate where a hidden picture would normally appear on the page. Suppressing pictures can greatly decrease the time required to print a proof of your publication.

Imported Picture Display Options

You might notice performance degradation as the number of pictures in a publication increases. It takes a fair amount of processing power to update the display of graphics. You can speed Publisher's performance by reducing the quality of the picture display.

Control the Display of Pictures

1 On the View menu, choose Picture Display. The Picture Display dialog box appears.

2 Select an option. The choice that you make in this dialog box affects the display of pictures on-screen.

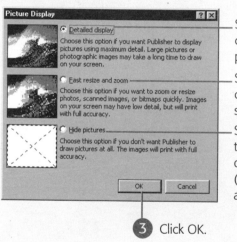

Selecting Detailed Display might slow down Publisher's performance if the publication contains complex graphics.

Selecting Fast Resize And Zoom displays low resolution images but speeds performance.

Selecting Hide Pictures gives Publisher the largest performance boost, but all of the pictures in your document (including WordArt and OLE objects) appear as crossed-out frames.

3 Click OK.

Available sound and motion clip formats. Publisher can import any digital sound or motion clip format supported by the Windows Media Player. If you have the proper hardware and the necessary drivers installed on your computer system, you should be able to import files in the following multimedia formats:

@ WAV sound files

@ MIDI sound files

@ RMI sound files

@ AVI video files

@ GIF animation files

Using Clip Art and Clip Media

The CD-ROM version of Publisher includes more than 15,000 drawings and photographs, upwards of 500 animated GIF files, and more than 100 sound files. You can store and manage these files—and other media files stored on your system—using Microsoft Clip Gallery 5.0, as long as the file formats are ones that Publisher recognizes. You can use the Clip Gallery to organize vector pictures, bitmapped images, digital sound files, and motion clips. Specifically, you can do the following with Clip Gallery:

@ Search for a picture or clip file based on criteria such as keywords or color and shape.

@ Insert a picture or clip file into a Publisher document.

@ Group media files by category.

@ Assign a descriptive phrase to a media file.

Importing a Clip File

During installation, Publisher installs thumbnail sketches (miniature previews) of all the clip art contained on the CD-ROM onto your hard disk. This means you can search and preview the entire clip art collection of images, even if you don't have the compact disc in the CD drive. To actually insert artwork stored on the CD into your publication, however, you must have the compact disc in the CD drive.

You can display the Insert Clip Art window's opening screen, which shows all of the categories, by pressing Alt-Home. Press Ctrl-LEFT ARROW to move to the previous screen. Press Ctrl-RIGHT ARROW to move to the next screen. Press Ctrl-Shift-< to reduce the size of the Insert Clip Art window. Press Ctrl-Shift-> to restore the size of the Insert Clip Art window.

Drag-and-drop pictures from the Clip Gallery.
You can also insert pictures by dragging an image from the Insert Clip Art window directly into a publication. You can even drag a picture into a waiting picture frame. When you drag a picture, Publisher automatically collapses the Insert Clip Art window to allow you to see the publication page. After you've dropped the picture into place, Publisher restores the Insert Clip Art window.

Import a File from the Clip Gallery

① If you want Publisher to size the clip art image to fit into a predetermined layout, choose the Clip Gallery Tool and draw a picture frame. If you want to import a clip art image at its original size, open the Insert menu, select Picture, and choose Clip Art on the submenu. The Microsoft Clip Gallery 5.0 window appears.

② Select the Pictures tab to import drawings or photographs, click the Sounds tab to import sound files, or click the Motion Clips tab to import animation and video files.

Click the standard Windows icons to copy and paste a selected picture or multimedia file.

Click this icon to reduce the size of the Clip Gallery window. If the window is reduced, this icon is replaced by an icon to restore the window to its original size.

③ Scroll through the list box and select a category icon. Alternatively, enter one or more keywords in the Search For Clips text box and then press Enter. The results of your selection or search appear in the list box.

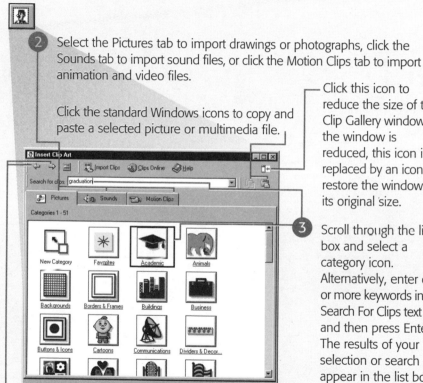

Use the arrows to display the previous or next screen.

Preview files. You can preview the currently selected thumbnail in the Insert Clip Art window. The shortcut menu always contains a preview icon, shown below, which, when clicked, allows you to view pictures at an enlarged size or play sound and motion clips.

Preview picture clip   Play multimedia clip

Use the Insert menu to import or create multimedia files. You can insert sound files and motion clips into a document using standard Object Linking and Embedding (OLE) functions. Click the Object command on the Insert menu. In the Insert Object dialog box, select Create From File to establish a link to an existing sound file or motion clip. Alternatively, you can select Create New to invoke an OLE application where you can record or edit a WAV sound, MIDI sequence, or AVI video.

For more information about OLE, see Chapter 11.

Import a File from the Clip Gallery *(continued)*

Click the All Categories icon to return to the Clip Gallery's opening screen.

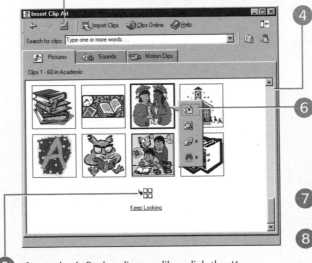

④ Use the scroll bar to move through the thumbnail previews.

⑥ Select the file you want to import. On the pop-up menu, click the first icon to insert the clip into your publication.

⑦ Repeat steps 2 through 6 to insert additional clips.

⑧ Click the Close icon to close the Insert Clip Art window.

⑤ If you don't find a clip you like, click the Keep Looking icon at the bottom of the screen to view additional thumbnails.

Search for a Clip by Example

① In the Insert Clip Art window, select a thumbnail as an example of the kind of picture, sound clip, or motion clip you want to find.

Why is the Artistic Style or Color And Shape button unavailable?

These buttons are unavailable when Publisher can't search for a particular characteristic. For example, Publisher can't search for similar colors and shapes if the selected file is a sound clip.

For more information about the Clip Properties dialog box, see "Manage an Individual Clip File" later in this chapter.

Press Alt-I to open the Add Clip To Clip Gallery dialog box.

Search for a Clip by Example *(continued)*

2 On the pop-up menu, select the Binocular icon.

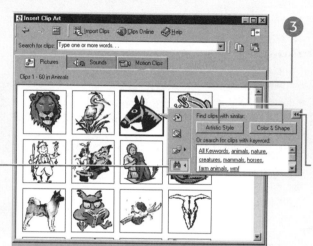

3 On the pane, click one of the two buttons to search for clips that have a similar artistic style or a similar color and shape. Alternatively, click one of the keywords in the scroll box.

Click the double arrows to hide the pane.

4 Select a clip that matches your search criteria, or continue to look for a clip using one of the following methods:

- Enter a keyword or multiple keywords into the Search For Clips text box.
- Click the Keep Looking icon at the bottom of the list box.
- Select another clip and repeat steps 2 and 3 to search for a clip by example.

Building a Library of Clips

You can add vector images, bitmapped pictures, sounds, or motion clips to the Clip Gallery at any time. Publisher makes it easy for you to add files from a variety of sources, including your local hard disk, removable disks, and networked drives. A special version of Clip Gallery, called Clip Gallery Live, is maintained

Add more than one file to the Clip Gallery at a time. If you purchase a Microsoft Clip Gallery package, you can install all the clip files along with keywords, categories, and previews in one step. In the Import Clips dialog box, open the Files Of Type drop-down list box, and select Clip Gallery Catalogs.

Even if you are not installing a Microsoft Clip Gallery package, you can still add multiple files. In the Files list box, press and hold the Shift key or the Ctrl key while clicking file names.

Assign properties to multiple files. If you are importing more than one file, the Clip Properties dialog box offers additional options. Click Mark All Clips With The Same Properties to assign the clips the same keywords, categories, and description in one step. Alternatively, click the Skip This Clip button to bypass the current file and proceed to the next file you selected.

For more information about the Clip Properties dialog box, see "Manage an Individual Clip File" later in this chapter.

on the World Wide Web. If you have an Internet Service Provider, such as the Microsoft Network, and browsing software, such as Microsoft Internet Explorer, you can download additional clips from Clip Gallery Live.

Add One or More Files to the Clip Gallery

1 Select the Clip Gallery tool and draw a picture frame, or choose Clip Art from the Picture submenu (opened from the Insert menu). The Insert Clip Art dialog box appears.

2 Click the Import Clips button. The Add Clip To Clip Gallery dialog box appears, which allows you to search local and networked drives for clip files.

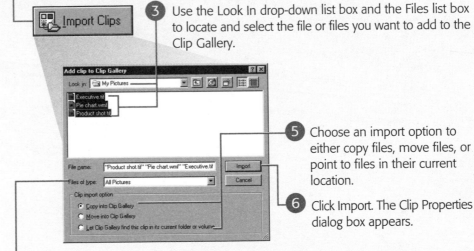

3 Use the Look In drop-down list box and the Files list box to locate and select the file or files you want to add to the Clip Gallery.

5 Choose an import option to either copy files, move files, or point to files in their current location.

6 Click Import. The Clip Properties dialog box appears.

4 Open the Files Of Type drop-down list box and choose a general category, such as All Pictures, All Sounds, or All Motion Clips. Alternatively, select All Files to see all of the files available for import.

7 In the Clip Properties dialog box, enter or modify the Description, Categories, or Keywords associated with the clip.

Use Clip Gallery Live on the World Wide Web

1 In Publisher, select Clip Art from the Picture submenu (opened from the Insert menu). The Insert Clip Art window appears.

2 Click the Clips Online button, shown below. Publisher asks if you want to connect to the Internet. Click OK. Publisher then loads your Web browser and locates the Clip Gallery Live Web page.

3 If this is the first time you are using Clip Gallery Live, read the licensing agreement and click the Accept button.

9 Click the Download hyperlink to copy the file to your hard disk and automatically add a thumbnail or icon of the file to the Clip Gallery. The thumbnail is assigned to the Downloaded Clips category along with its keyword information.

4 Click one of the four tabs representing the clip types: Clip Art, Pictures, Sounds, or Motion.

5 Type a keyword in the Search text box and then click Go. Alternatively, open the Browse drop-down list box and choose a category.

8 Click the Selection Basket to view and confirm your choices.

6 Use the Previous and More arrows to move through the thumbnail sketches in the Preview area.

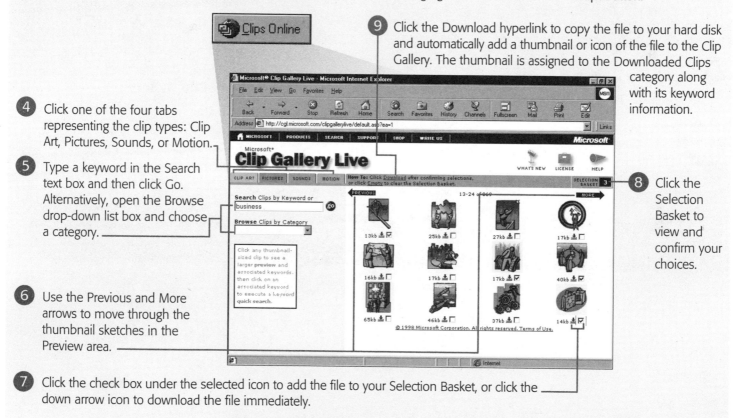

7 Click the check box under the selected icon to add the file to your Selection Basket, or click the down arrow icon to download the file immediately.

10 Close your Web browser and disconnect from your Internet provider.

Paste clips into the Clip Gallery. If you have copied a picture, sound, or motion file to the Windows Clipboard, you can insert it directly into the Clip Gallery. Simply select the category where you want to copy the file and then click the Paste icon within the Clip Gallery window. Alternatively, you can right-click a Category icon and then select Paste Clips from the shortcut menu.

Press Alt-C to invoke Clip Gallery Live.

Maintaining the Clip Gallery

Whenever you add a vector image, bitmapped image, sound, or motion clip to the Clip Gallery, a new thumbnail sketch is added to the already extensive collection of thumbnail sketches that Publisher creates during installation. The Clip Gallery continues to show you the same thumbnail sketch even when you have moved, modified, or deleted the actual file from your disk. In addition, you'll find the Clip Gallery to be more useful if you create your own categories and assign your own keywords to your file. Luckily, functions within the Clip Gallery let you manage both individual clips and entire categories.

Compress or Restore the Contents of the Clip Gallery

1. Select Clip Art from the Picture submenu (opened from the Insert menu). The Insert Clip Art window appears.

2. Right-click any clip or any category icon. On the shortcut menu that appears, select Recover.

3. Click Compact to recover any unused space in the Clip Gallery database.

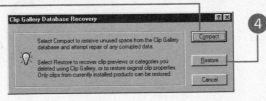

4. Click Restore to return the Clip Gallery to its original state and reinstall any clips, categories, or keywords you may have deleted.

5. In the Clip Gallery Restore dialog box, click Restore Categories, Restore Clips, or Restore Properties. In the confirmation dialog box that appears, click OK.

Use categories to create a personal clip collection.

The existing categories in the Clip Gallery are based on the content of an image. However, you can organize images based on any criteria, such as an illustration style you particularly like, images you use frequently, or pictures that are suitable for a particular project. Publisher provides an empty category called Favorites for exactly this purpose. But you can create your own categories also. For example, a category called "Company Logos" would allow you to access quickly all the variations of your company logo stored on your hard disk.

To add a clip to a category, click the Favorites icon on the pop-up menu, as shown below.

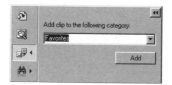

Manage Existing Categories Within the Clip Gallery

1 Select Clip Art from the Picture submenu (opened from the Insert menu). The Insert Clip Art window appears.

2 Right-click a category icon.

3 Select a command from the shortcut menu that appears.

Select Open In New Window to create another instance of the Clip Gallery. All of the Clip Gallery's functions are available to you in the new window.

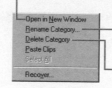

Select Rename Category to open the Rename Category dialog box, where you can type a new name for the selected category.

Select Delete Category and then click Yes or No in the confirmation dialog box that appears.

Create a New Category

1 Select Clip Art from the Picture submenu (opened from the Insert menu). The Insert Clip Art dialog box appears.

2 If necessary, click the All Categories button at the top of the dialog box (or press Alt+Home) to view the category icons.

3 Click the New Category icon. The New Category dialog box appears.

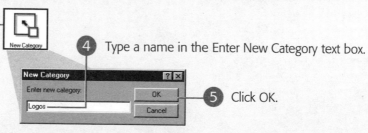

4 Type a name in the Enter New Category text box.

5 Click OK.

Use the Refresh button to update the location of the clip file. If you are attempting to refresh the clip properties of an externally stored file and if Publisher can't find the externally stored file, the Cannot Locate Clip dialog box appears (as shown below). Click Update Location to browse your computer for the current location of the source file. Alternatively, click the Remove This Clip button to delete the thumbnail from the Clip Gallery.

Delete unwanted Clip Gallery images. Publisher automatically copies hundreds of clip art images to your hard disk during installation. You can conserve disk space by deleting from your hard disk any clip art images you don't use.

Manage an Individual Clip File

1 Select Clip Art from the Picture submenu (opened from the Insert menu). The Insert Clip Art dialog box appears.

2 Locate the thumbnail sketch that you want to manage.

3 Right-click the thumbnail and select Clip Properties from the shortcut menu. The Clip Properties dialog box appears.

4 Click the Description tab.

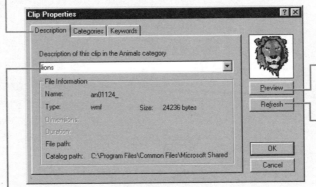

Click the Preview or Play button to see (or hear) the actual clip file.

To automatically update the clip properties, click the Refresh button.

5 Type a name for the clip; it will appear below the thumbnail in the Clip Gallery.

Can I delete clip files from my disk from within the Clip Gallery?
No. You must delete a file by using Windows Explorer or by dragging a file icon to the Windows Recycle Bin. Be sure to update the Clip Gallery after you delete files from your disk.

Delete an individual thumbnail. If you know which files have been deleted from your hard disk, you can delete individual thumbnails from the Clip Gallery. Open the Clip Gallery and then right-click the thumbnail you want to remove. Select Delete from the shortcut menu.

Use ScreenTips to enter keywords consistently.
As you type a new keyword into the New Keyword dialog box, ScreenTips appear with keywords that are similar to the word you are typing. If for example you type "Executive," a ScreenTip with the keyword "Executives" appears. For consistency's sake and to improve the accuracy of your searches, type an exact match for the existing keyword.

Manage an Individual Clip File *(continued)*

6 Click the Categories tab.

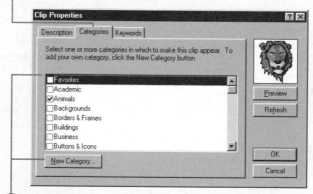

7 Select one or more categories in the list box, or click the New Category button and enter a new category name in the dialog box that appears.

8 Click the Keywords tab.

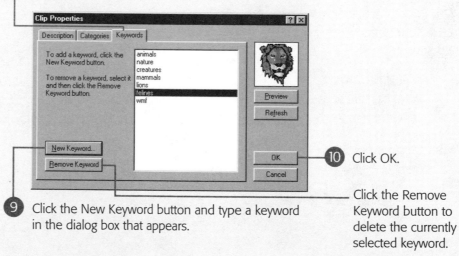

9 Click the New Keyword button and type a keyword in the dialog box that appears.

10 Click OK.

Click the Remove Keyword button to delete the currently selected keyword.

For more information about bitmapped picture formats, see "Categories of Graphics" earlier in this chapter.

What does the Out Of Memory error message mean? Standard bitmapped file formats, such as TIFF and JPEG, use compression routines to shrink the size of a scanned image and save disk space. When Publisher incorporates a TWAIN picture (or inserts any bitmapped image), it converts the picture to an uncompressed format. This uncompressed form might require more memory than your computer has available. Instead of importing the picture, create a link to the externally stored file. Alternatively, you can rescan the image at a lower resolution or with fewer colors.

What is the difference between picture resolution and output resolution? Picture resolution, or scanning resolution, is measured in pixels per inch (ppi), where each pixel can be a different color. Output resolution, or the printer's hardware capability, is measured in dots per inch (dpi).

Image Acquisition Functions in Publisher

Microsoft Publisher supports the TWAIN32 image acquisition interface. If your hardware uses a TWAIN32 driver, you can directly access a scanner or digital camera from within your Publisher document. Scanners and digital cameras produce bitmapped images. To a large extent, the quality of a bitmapped image is determined by its resolution. So it is important for you to understand how digital cameras and scanners address the issue of picture resolution.

Digital cameras produce pictures at predetermined image resolutions that are typically identified by the total number of pixels in the picture. (Image resolution is expressed as the number of horizontal pixels multiplied by the number of vertical pixels.) For example, consumer-oriented digital cameras generate pictures at 640 x 480 pixels or 1024 x 768 pixels. These resolutions are suitable for screen display (when publishing on the Internet) and for comparatively low resolution output devices, such as black-and-white or color desktop printers.

In comparison, desktop scanners generate images at the size and resolution you choose. As a result, image resolution is specified as the number of dots—or pixels—per inch (dpi or ppi) and can range from 300 to 1200 dpi or ppi (or higher). When creating an image with a scanner, you will want to produce the smallest possible file size without degrading image quality to unacceptable levels. To accomplish this, you should scan a picture with the colors and resolution required by the final output device. For example, you shouldn't create a full color scanned image if you are printing to a black-and-white device. Nor should you scan a picture at 300 dpi if you intend to display it on a monitor with a resolution of 72 dpi. Unfortunately, there are no hard and fast rules concerning scanning parameters. The following table lists the most efficient scanning resolutions for standard output devices.

Computing grayscale and color photograph resolution for printed output. The tonal variation in a grayscale or color photograph is printed using a cluster of dots called a halftone cell. Halftone resolution is measured in lines per inch (lpi). Ask your service bureau for the proper lpi setting for a given document. Then, for best output results, scan your photographs at a ppi value that is 1.5 times the lpi value. Note the following scanning recommendations:

- For 52 lpi, scan at 80 ppi.
- For 75 lpi, scan at 113 ppi.
- For 90 lpi, scan at 135 ppi.
- For 120 lpi, scan at 180 ppi.
- For 133 lpi, scan at 200 ppi.

Why doesn't the From Scanner Or Camera command appear on the Insert Picture submenu? If the From Scanner Or Camera command doesn't appear or if your scanner doesn't appear in the Sources list box, your scanner might not support the TWAIN32 interface. If that is the case, you must create the scanned photograph outside Publisher, save it in a file, and then use the Picture command on the Insert menu to incorporate it into your publication.

Appropriate Scanning Resolutions for Standard Output Devices			
Hardware Device	Hardware Resolution	Black-and-White Scan	Grayscale or Color Scan
Laser printer	300 dpi	300 ppi	80 ppi
Laser printer	600 dpi	600 ppi	113 ppi
Inkjet printer	720 dpi	720 ppi	135 ppi
High resolution desktop printer or service bureau imagesetter	1200 dpi	800 ppi	180 ppi
Service bureau imagesetter	2400 dpi	800 ppi	200 ppi
Monitor	72 dpi	Not applicable; for best results scan black-and-white drawings as grayscale artwork.	72 ppi

Acquiring a Picture While Working in Your Publication

Before you can create a scanned image, you must establish a link between Publisher and the image acquisition hardware. Unless you switch from one device to another, you should perform this operation only once.

Link Publisher to Your Digital Camera or Scanner

1. On the Insert menu, choose Picture. On the submenu, select From Scanner or Camera.
2. On the next submenu, choose Select Device. The Select Source dialog box appears.
3. In the Sources list box, choose the device (either a scanner or a digital camera) that you wish to use.
4. Click Select.

Picture and Clip Media Tools

Why do the control options for my scanner or digital camera differ from the instructions here?

Although the TWAIN32 interface is an industry standard, the actual options you see will vary depending on your particular hardware and software setup. In some cases, manufacturers use different terminology to describe identical functions. Whereas one manufacturer might employ a scaling function to size images, another might require you to specify explicit values for width and height.

More fundamentally, the TWAIN32 interface was designed to handle all sorts of input devices, including scanners, video frame grabbers, and digital cameras. The options that appear (or do not appear) in the control panel reflect the capabilities of the device. For example, the interface for a digital camera typically provides commands for viewing and downloading photos you previously snapped. You will not find commands to change the size or resolution of an image, because digital cameras produce pictures at a predetermined resolution.

 For more information about aspect ratio, see Chapter 3.

Acquire a Scanned Image

① If you want Publisher to size the image to fit into a predetermined layout, choose the Picture Frame tool and draw a frame, or select an existing picture frame. If you want Publisher to automatically create a frame for the scanned image, begin this procedure with step 2.

② On the Insert menu, choose Picture. On the Picture submenu, select From Scanner Or Camera.

③ Select Acquire Image on the next submenu. The control window appears for your scanner or digital camera.

④ Use the software provided with your scanner or digital camera to:

- Preview the image.

- Specify the size, resolution, and number of colors.

- Adjust brightness and contrast.

⑤ When you click OK (or the corresponding command, such as Final or Scan) to create the image, Publisher inserts the image into your document and, if necessary, resizes the picture frame you drew or selected in order to maintain the picture's original aspect ratio.

Modifying the Size and Appearance of Your Image

Whether you use commercial clip art, create original drawings, or scan personal photographs, you can use Publisher's tools to modify the pictures in a publication. The standard layout tools allow you to change a picture's size, position, or rotation. In addition, specialized picture editing tools let you emphasize a portion of a graphic, integrate images with text, and alter the colors of imported artwork.

How does the Scale Picture command differ from the Size And Position command? The Scale Picture command allows you to resize an image or Clip Gallery object by specifying a percentage of the picture's original size. You can easily maintain the correct aspect ratio by entering identical values in the width and height text boxes. The Size And Position dialog box requires you to enter explicit values for the picture's width and height. This approach makes it all too easy to size a picture disproportionately—distorting the aspect ratio. The good news is that Publisher always keeps track of an imported picture's original size. So even if you distort a picture using the Size And Position command, you can correct the error by using the Scale Picture command.

 Can I use the Scale Object command to resize WordArt objects? Yes. Because WordArt is inserted into a publication as an OLE object, you can use the Scale Object command to alter its size. However, because the WordArt object is generated within Publisher, the size you specify in the Scale object dialog box becomes the "original size." You therefore can't revert to the WordArt object's previous size by using the Original Size check box in the Scale Object dialog box.

Scaling a Picture

The Scale Picture or Scale Object command gives you precise controls that enable you to easily maintain the aspect ratio (the original proportions) of the picture.

Resize an Image Using Scale Picture or Scale Object

1 Select the picture, Clip Gallery object, or OLE object that you want to resize.

2 Choose Scale Picture on the Format menu. If you are working with an OLE object, choose Scale Object on the Format menu. The Scale Picture or Scale Object dialog box appears.

3 To maintain the picture's aspect ratio, enter equal percentage values for the height and width.

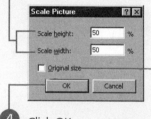

Select the Original Size check box to return the height and width to 100 percent.

4 Click OK.

Featuring a Section of Your Image

You can hide portions of a picture by using Publisher's Crop Picture tool. Think of the picture frame as a window with a window shade. Using the Crop Picture tool is like pulling down the window shade. Although the view doesn't change, you can see more of the landscape (or the picture) when the window shade is up and less when it is down. Cropping is not the same as resizing, which enlarges or shrinks the entire picture.

Crop all sides or opposite sides of your picture equally. To crop all four sides of a picture equally, press and hold the Ctrl key as you drag a corner selection handle. To crop opposite sides of a picture equally, press and hold the Ctrl key as you drag any selection handle except a corner handle.

Cropping letters and words. The Crop Picture tool can also be used with WordArt frames. You can create special effects, abstract patterns, or logos by trimming outer portions of the letters in a WordArt frame.

Crop a Picture

1 Select the picture, Clip Gallery object, or OLE object you want to crop.

2 Click the Crop Picture button on the Formatting toolbar (shown below). Alternatively, choose Crop Picture or Crop Object on the Format menu.

3 Place the pointer over any selection handle so that it changes into the Crop pointer.

4 Using the Crop pointer, drag a selection handle inward until only the portion of the picture that you want visible appears. Repeat this step with as many selection handles as necessary to achieve the effect you want.

5 If you want to restore the cropped portions of the picture, use the Crop pointer to drag a selection handle outward until all of the original picture appears in the frame.

6 When you have finished trimming a picture, deactivate the Crop Picture tool by clicking the Crop Picture button on the Formatting toolbar again, or by selecting the Crop Picture or Crop Object command on the Format menu again.

For more information on text frame properties, see Chapter 4.

Turn off text wrapping.
You can create interesting design effects by turning off text wrapping. To have an object (such as the picture shown below) print on top of text, select the text frame and turn off Wrap Text Around Objects in the Text Frame Properties dialog box. This technique works well for headlines or logos.

To have text print over another object, select the text frame and bring it to the front of the stack. In order for this technique to work, the text frame must be transparent (so that you can see the object beneath it) and the text itself must contrast with the background object (so that the copy remains legible).

Text Wrapping

One of the best ways to show the relationship between the various elements in a design is to wrap the text around other objects. You can wrap text around frames regardless of whether the frame contains a picture, WordArt, text, a table, or an OLE object. In order for text wrapping to work properly, two conditions must be met, as shown in the following illustration.

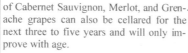

Occasionally we discover an exceptional wine at an exceptional price. Such is the case with Chateau La Coste, a Bordeaux-style red wine from France. With an excellent balance of fresh ripe cherries and soft tannins, this ruby wine is ready to drink right now. But, this full-bodied mix of Cabernet Sauvignon, Merlot, and Grenache grapes can also be cellared for the next three to five years and will only improve with age.

Wrap Text Around Objects must be selected in the Text Frame Properties dialog box.

The text frame must be positioned at the bottom of the stack. The object the text wraps around (such as the picture shown here) must lie on top of the text object.

By default, Publisher wraps text around the rectangular frame of an object. But if you are working with a picture or WordArt object, you can sometimes create a more interesting and tighter text wrap by flowing the text around the outline of the actual image rather than around the rectangular frame.

Wrap Text Around a Frame

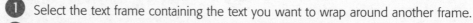

① Select the text frame containing the text you want to wrap around another frame.

② In the Text Frame Properties dialog box, confirm that Wrap Text Around Objects is selected. Click OK to close the dialog box.

Wrapping text around drawn objects. You can wrap text around closed geometric or irregular shapes that you create with Publisher's drawing tools. If you want to wrap text around a drawn object, you must deal with these inherent restrictions:

ℰ Text will not wrap around a transparent drawn shape. You must fill the shape with a color, tint, shade, pattern, or gradient to wrap text.

ℰ You cannot control the shape of the irregular wrap around a drawn object. The wrap always follows the outline of the drawn shape closely. A star shape, for example, creates a zigzag wrap.

ℰ You cannot wrap text around a line or an arrow created with the Line tool. If you want to wrap text around an arrow, create the arrow using the Custom Shapes tool.

Wrap Text Around a Frame *(continued)*

③ Select the picture or WordArt frame that you want to flow text around and then click the Bring To Front button on the Standard toolbar.

The Crop Picture tool appears on the Formatting toolbar when the Wrap Text To Frame button is selected.

④ If it is not already selected, click the Wrap Text To Frame button on the Formatting toolbar.

> Occasionally we discover an exceptional wine at an exceptional price. Such is the case with Chateau La Coste, a Bordeaux-style red wine from France. With an excellent balance of fresh ripe cherries and soft tannins, this ruby wine is ready to drink right now. But, this full-bodied mix of Cabernet Sauvignon, Merlot, and Grenache grapes can also be cellared for the next three to five years and will only improve with age.

The text wraps around the frame.

Wrap Text Around the Outline of a Picture or WordArt Design

① Select the text frame containing the text you want to wrap around another frame.

② In the Text Frame Properties dialog box, confirm that Wrap Text Around Objects is selected.

③ Select the picture or WordArt frame that you want to flow text around and then click the Bring To Front button on the Standard toolbar.

Access text wrapping options through the Picture Frame Properties or the Object Frame Properties dialog box. You can also access text wrapping options by using either the Picture Frame Properties or Object Frame Properties dialog box. You can open this dialog box using the icon on the Formatting toolbar or the command on the Format menu.

- Select Entire Frame to wrap text around the rectangular picture or WordArt frame.

- Select Picture Only to wrap text around the outline of the image.

Wrap Text Around the Outline of a Picture or WordArt Design *(continued)*

The Edit Irregular Wrap button appears on the Formatting toolbar when the Wrap Text To Picture button is selected.

④ Select the Wrap Text To Picture button on the Formatting toolbar.

Occasionally we discover an exceptional wine at an exceptional price. Such is the case with Chateau La Coste, a Bordeaux-style red wine from France. With an excellent balance of fresh ripe cherries and soft tannins this ruby wine is ready to drink right now. But, this full-bodied mix of Cabernet Sauvignon, Merlot, and Grenache grapes can also be cellared for the next three to five years and will only im-

Publisher wraps text around the image outline.

⑤ If you want to change back to the default setting and wrap text around the picture frame, click the Wrap Text To Frame button.

Fine-Tuning the Text Wrap

When you wrap text around a picture or a WordArt design, Publisher maintains a nonprinting boundary between the image or frame and the text. You can change that boundary to wrap text more tightly around the image. You can even create a special boundary shape (such as a triangle or a free-form shape) that the text will flow around.

You can modify the text wrapping boundary by moving the existing Adjust handles, or by adding or deleting Adjust handles. Adding handles allows you to follow the outline of an image more precisely. Deleting handles simplifies the boundary, smoothes the text wrap and makes individual handles easier to grab.

Controlling how text wraps around an image.

The distance between text and the picture or WordArt design it wraps around is affected by the following elements:

- The text wrapping boundary, which you can reshape using the Edit Irregular Wrap tool.

- The picture frame margins, which are controlled in the Object Properties dialog box or the Picture Crop tool.

- The margins you set in the text frame, which are controlled in the Text Frame Properties dialog box.

Adjust an Irregular Text Wrapping Boundary

1 Select the picture or WordArt object you want to fine-tune and click the Wrap Text To Picture button on the Formatting toolbar.

2 Click the Edit Irregular Wrap button on the Formatting toolbar (as shown below), or choose Edit Irregular Wrap on the Format menu.

3 Position the pointer over one of the control handles that appears along the dotted boundary line. The pointer changes to the Adjust pointer.

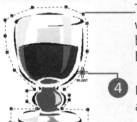

The Adjust handles are located at the vertices of the text wrapping boundary. As the shape of the boundary line becomes more complex or irregular, the number of Adjust handles increases.

4 Drag the Adjust handle to change the shape of the boundary around the image.

5 Release the mouse button. Publisher rewraps the text around the adjusted boundary.

Add and Delete Adjust Handles in an Irregular Text Wrapping Boundary

1 Select the picture or WordArt design whose boundary you want to adjust. Click the Wrap Text To Picture button on the Formatting toolbar.

2 Click the Edit Irregular Wrap button.

3 To add a control handle, position the pointer along the text wrapping boundary where you want a new handle. Press and hold the Ctrl key to turn the pointer into the Add pointer, and then click the left mouse button.

4 To delete a control handle, position the Adjust pointer over a handle you don't need. Press and hold the Ctrl key to turn the pointer into the Delete pointer, and then click the left mouse button.

For more information about adding graphic accents such as borders, BorderArt, or shadows to a frame, see Chapter 9.

Why can't I find individual text boxes for the left, right, top, and bottom margins in the Picture or Object Frame Properties dialog box? You have created an irregular text wrap boundary for the selected picture or WordArt element. To adjust the margin for the entire perimeter of the image, enter a value from 0 through 16 inches in the Outside text box. This will insert a uniform amount of space outside the image, but within the text wrap boundary.

Create margins with the Crop Picture tool. You can create a picture frame margin by using the Crop Picture tool. Select a handle and pull the picture frame out until all of the image is revealed. As you continue to pull the picture frame, Publisher adds white space between the image and the frame—generating a custom margin.

Adjusting Picture Frame Margins

You can create white space between a picture and the frame surrounding it to add a decorative touch to a picture or to add breathing room between a picture and an elaborate border.

The picture becomes smaller if you increase the margins.

The picture becomes larger if you decrease the margins.

The margin (and background) can be filled with a color, tint, shade, pattern, or gradient.

Adjust Picture Frame Margins

1 Select the picture or WordArt frame.

2 Choose the Picture Frame Properties or Object Frame Properties tool from the Formatting toolbar or the corresponding commands on the Format menu. The Picture Frame Properties dialog box appears.

3 Enter values from 0 through 16 inches in the Left, Right, Top, and Bottom text boxes.

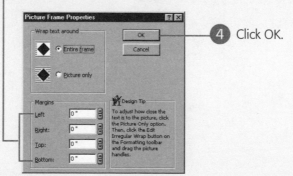

4 Click OK.

For a fuller discussion about color choices in Publisher, see Chapter 15.

Why can't I change the color of an Encapsulated PostScript picture?
Publisher merely passes an Encapsulated PostScript (EPS) file through to a PostScript printer. As a result, Publisher can't access the actual picture data. Therefore, you cannot recolor an EPS picture. To change the colors in an EPS file, use a drawing program that can edit EPS images, such as CorelDRAW, Adobe Illustrator, or Macromedia Freehand.

Can I change the color of individual elements in a picture? No. Publisher's ability to recolor pictures or WordArt elements is limited. The Recolor Picture (or Recolor Object) command can distinguish black from all other colors. It can leave black elements as black. However, it changes all other colors contained in a picture to shades or tints of a single color. To recolor individual elements in a picture, you must use a graphics (drawing or paint) application.

Color Options for Imported Pictures and WordArt

With a single command, Publisher allows you to change all of the colors in an imported picture. You might want to adjust a color scheme for artistic reasons, or for technical reasons related to the capability of your output device. For example, you could recolor a multicolored picture to shades of gray if you are planning to output your publication to a black-and-white printer. You can also circumvent the 35-color limit of the WordArt module by using the Recolor command to fill a WordArt object with a custom color, tint, or shade.

Recolor a Picture or WordArt Object

① Select the picture or WordArt object you want to recolor.

② Choose Recolor Picture or Recolor Object on the Format menu. The Recolor Picture or Recolor Object dialog box appears.

③ Open the Color drop-down menu and choose an available color, tint, or shade.

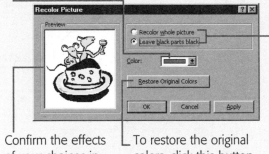

Confirm the effects of your choices in the Preview area.

To restore the original colors, click this button.

④ Click Recolor Whole Picture to apply the new color to all elements within the picture. Alternatively, click Leave Black Parts Black to recolor only non-black (and non-white) portions of the image.

⑤ Click Apply to preview the recolored picture in the actual document.

⑥ Click OK.

Working with OLE

Y ou can easily establish connections between Microsoft Publisher files and files created and stored in other applications by using a process called Object Linking and Embedding (OLE). The OLE process allows you to embed objects from other applications into your Publisher documents. You can also embed only a portion of a file as an OLE object. For example, you might need only the summary information from a large spreadsheet.

The two functions of OLE—linking and embedding—are related but exhibit important differences, which are described in the following table.

Functions of OLE		
	Linking Files	**Embedding Files**
Process description	You connect an OLE frame in Publisher to a file (or portion of a file) created with an external application. The file is stored on your hard disk or a network drive.	You store a copy of a file (or portion of a file) in an OLE frame in Publisher. Or you create an object while working in Publisher by using another application.
Access	After you establish the link, you can still access the file from the originating application as well as from Publisher.	Because the file object is stored internally in Publisher, only Publisher has access to the object.
Advantages	You can use the same file in more than one publication. You can access files created or revised by other people on a network. Other people on a network can access and update the external files linked to your publication without accessing your publication directly.	You can create and edit objects in Publisher because you have direct access to all of the source application's functions. No one other than you can access the OLE object embedded in your Publisher document.
Object behavior	You determine whether the links in a publication are updated automatically or manually on a case-by-case basis. Double-clicking a linked object starts the source application.	Double-clicking an embedded object starts the source application.

When can I take advantage of OLE? You can take advantage of OLE only if the other Windows-based applications on your computer support it. To see a list of OLE-compliant programs, open the Insert menu and choose Object. In the Insert Object dialog box, scroll through the Object Type list to see all of the source programs currently installed on your system.

Switch between Open Editing and In-Place Editing. You can make changes to an OLE object using Open Editing (in a separate window) instead of the default In-Place Editing (which is integrated into Publisher's window). Select the OLE object. On the Edit menu, select the command that identifies the application you used to create the object. On the cascading menu, choose the Open command.

Creating an OLE Object

The current version of the OLE specification supports two editing modes, depending on the source application. When you create a new OLE object, the source application appears on-screen in one of the following ways:

◎ An application or utility using the Open Editing mode appears in a separate window. Microsoft Clip Gallery, which is discussed in Chapter 10, is a good example of an application that uses Open Editing.

◎ An application or utility using In-Place Editing becomes part of the Publisher work area. Toolbars, menus, and dialog boxes appear for you to use. WordArt, discussed in Chapter 8, is a good example of a utility that uses In-Place Editing.

Create an OLE Object While Working in Publisher

1 Open the Insert menu and choose Object. The Insert Object dialog box appears. Publisher scans your system and lists all the applications that support OLE as source programs.

2 Choose the type of object you want to incorporate into the publication.

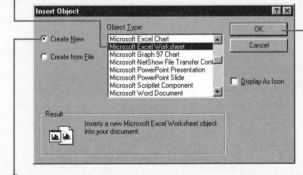

4 Click OK. The source utility or application appears.

3 Select Create New.

Why do certain OLE object types generate an error message when I attempt to insert them into a document? The OLE specification continues to evolve. Supersets of OLE—called ActiveX and Component Object Model (COM)—aren't supported by Publisher. Windows recognizes ActiveX and COM objects as OLE objects, but they can't be inserted into a Publisher document.

Are linked pictures really OLE links? No. Linked pictures aren't true OLE links; they are merely pointers to an external file. There are superficial similarities to OLE links. For example, if you change the external picture file, the image in your Publisher document is updated when you print the document. However, you can't edit a linked picture by double-clicking the picture. Furthermore, you must manage linked pictures using the Graphics Manager, accessed through the Commercial Printing Tools command on the Tools menu.

For more information on linked pictures, see Chapter 10.

Create a New OLE Object While Working in Publisher *(continued)*

5 In the source application, create the object you want to embed.

6 Do one of the following:

- If you are working within Publisher's window, click anywhere outside the OLE object to accept your changes and return to the Publisher document.

- If you are working in a separate window, open the source application's File menu and select Exit And Return. A dialog box appears that asks whether you want to update your publication. Click Yes to embed the object.

Link or Embed an Externally Stored File as an OLE Object

1 Open the Insert menu and choose Object. The Insert Object dialog box appears. Publisher scans your system and lists all the applications that support OLE as source programs.

Display information as an icon. The Display As Icon check box appears in both the Insert Object and Paste Special dialog boxes. This option is useful when you want easy access to information from another file but don't want the information to appear in your publication. Instead of viewing the contents of a file, you can use this option to insert an icon into your document. Double-clicking the icon activates the source program and displays the file.

For more information about the Windows Clipboard, see Chapter 3.

Why can't I access the Paste Link option in the Paste Special dialog box? Not all applications support OLE in the same way. If the Paste Link option is grayed out, you can't create a link between Publisher and the source application.

Link or Embed an Externally Stored File as an OLE Object *(continued)*

2 To use a file that exists on disk, select Create From File.

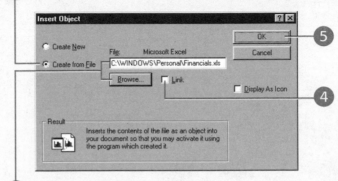

5 Click OK. The object is inserted into your document.

4 Activate the Link check box to create a link, or clear it if you want to embed the object.

3 Specify the location and name of the file, or click Browse to search through the drives and folders on your system and then click Insert to return to the Insert Object dialog box.

Link or Embed a Portion of a File as an OLE Object

1 Open a source program that supports OLE, such as Microsoft Word or Microsoft Excel.

2 In the source application, create or open the file you want to link. If you create a file, be sure to save it as a file on disk before you continue.

3 In the source application, select the portion of the file you want.

4 Open the Edit menu and select Copy to place the selection on the Windows Clipboard.

5 Switch to Publisher.

6 Open Publisher's Edit menu and choose Paste Special. The Paste Special dialog box appears.

Publisher treats OLE objects like pictures.
You can alter the appearance of OLE objects by using Publisher's picture-editing tools.

@ You can increase or decrease the size of OLE objects by dragging a selection handle or by entering sizing percentages into the Scale Object dialog box (accessed from the Format menu).

@ The Recolor Object command (found on the Format menu) applies varying tints of a chosen color to an OLE object.

@ The Crop Picture tool on the Formatting toolbar lets you hide or reveal portions of an OLE object by resizing the frame without resizing the information it contains.

For more information on Publisher's picture editing tools, see Chapter 10.

Link or Embed a Portion of a File as an OLE Object *(continued).*

7 To embed the object, choose Paste. To link the object, choose Paste Link.

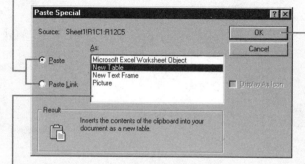

9 Click OK to return to your Publisher document.

8 In the As list box, choose the appropriate format for the object. The choices in the As list box vary depending on the type of data stored on the Clipboard. For example, if you have placed an Excel worksheet on the Clipboard, you can choose among Microsoft Excel Worksheet Object, New Table (which creates a Publisher table), New Text Frame, or Picture.

Determining How OLE Links Behave

After you create an OLE link, you can choose whether the correspondence between the OLE object in your publication and the external file with which it is associated is updated automatically or manually.

Select Link Options for a Particular File

1 Open the Edit menu and select Links. The Links dialog box appears.

2 Select the linked object you want to update from the file list.

Clicking versus double-clicking. A single click selects an OLE object, which allows you to either move it or edit it with Publisher's picture editing tools. A double-click starts the source program, which allows you to change the content and internal formatting of the object.

 Does clicking the Close button in the Links dialog box cancel the changes I've made? No. The Close command returns you to your document. The functions of the Links dialog box take effect immediately when you click an option or a button. If you want to cancel the modifications you've made, you must change the options back to the previous settings.

Select Link Options for a Particular File *(continued)*

3 Tell Publisher how often to update the link from the external file.

- Click Automatic if you want Publisher to check the status of the external file each time you open your document. If the external file has been changed, Publisher updates the contents of the OLE frame with the latest version of the source file.

- Click Manual if you want to control the frequency of the updates. Manual updates occur whenever you click the Update Now button, activate the source application by double-clicking the OLE object, or print the publication containing the OLE object.

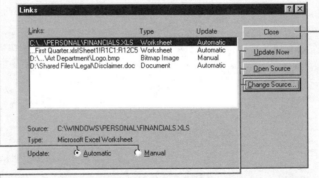

5 When you have finished modifying links and updating files, click the Close button.

4 Optionally, take one or more of the following actions:

- Click Update Now to import the latest version of the file.

- Click Open Source to activate the source application and display the contents of the OLE object.

- Click Change Source to choose a different source file or to reestablish a link with a source file that is in a different location. In the Change Source dialog box that appears, locate and select the new file, and then click OK.

Creating Web Pages

Microsoft Publisher 2000 can generate Web pages. In contrast to regular desktop publishing documents, which are typically printed on paper, the following is true of Web pages:

@ Web pages are intended to be read directly from the computer screen.

@ Web pages can include multimedia objects, so you can listen to sound files and view animations or digital videos.

@ Hyperlinks, in the form of hypertext or picture hot spots, allow you to move (or "surf") to other pages in a Web site, to other Web sites, or to other externally stored files regardless of their physical location.

@ Web pages can contain electronic forms that allow the reader to enter text, make selections from drop-down lists, click check boxes, and submit the completed electronic form.

@ Web pages allow readers to respond to authors by sending an e-mail message.

@ Web pages in the Hypertext Markup Language (HTML) format are easy to distribute by way of disk, network, or the Internet.

How do I find an Internet Service Provider? You'll find that most well-known online services, including the Microsoft Network (MSN), America Online (AOL), and CompuServe, offer Internet access. Major phone companies are providing national service. Look into AT&T WorldNet, Sprint, or MCI WorldCom. Another option is to look up a local Internet Service Provider in your hometown yellow pages.

Procuring a Web browser. In most cases, your Internet Service Provider (ISP) will supply you with a suite of Internet applications, including a browser program. Once you have access to the Internet, you can download a browser directly from a vendor's Web site. This guarantees that you'll have the most current version of a browser program, which is essential if you want to access the hottest features of the Web, such as online animation or video, frame-based Web designs, and animated interface elements produced with JavaScript or Dynamic HTML code.

What is an intranet? An intranet is simply an internal network that looks and behaves like the Internet but provides access to a limited number of users. For example, a corporation might use an intranet to disseminate information privately to company employees.

Gaining Access to the Web

In order to take full advantage of Publisher's Web tools, you should have access to the Internet (or an intranet). You can think of the Internet as a collection of public and private networks that enables computers of all sorts—PCs, Macintoshes, and Unix boxes—to communicate and exchange data around the world. The Internet provides easy access to the World Wide Web (also referred to as WWW, or simply the Web). Use the following checklist to be sure that your computer is properly configured to access the Internet.

@ You must have a modem to physically connect your computer to a phone line. If you are using regular analog telephone lines, your modem speed should be at least 28.8 Kilobits per second (Kbps) or, better yet, 56 Kbps.

@ You must have an account with an Internet Service Provider (ISP). An ISP supplies communication software that connects you via the phone line to the Internet.

@ In order to perform tasks on the Internet, you must have appropriate applications installed on your computer. For example, a Web browser application, such as Microsoft Internet Explorer, allows you to read documents online.

Publisher's HTML Tools

When you generate a Web page, it must be converted from Publisher's native file format (.pub) to HTML, which is the standard document format used on the Web. The HTML specification doesn't support many of the design capabilities normally found in a desktop publishing program. Therefore, whenever you create a Web page, Publisher limits your layout options. In some cases, new commands and buttons appear on the toolbars or menus. In other cases, dialog boxes present you with only those choices that are appropriate for Web publishing. The following discussion is not meant to replace the detailed explanations of Publisher's design and layout tools covered in Chapters 2 through 10. Instead, it highlights the modified functions and new tools that are specific to Web design.

What do those abbreviations and acronyms for communications hardware and software mean? Computer lingo can be confusing. Here are definitions of a few key terms that you'll encounter when you hook up your computer to the Internet.

- The device that sends and receives data over the phone lines does so by MOdulating and DEModulating a signal—hence the name "modem."

- Modem speed is always measured in bits per second (bps). The speeds are typically noted in units of thousands (indicated by the letter *K*), so a 28.8K modem operates at 28,800 bits per second.

Why does the HTML specification limit the design options for Web pages? HTML was developed as a file format for online viewing. HTML's developers limited its layout and formatting options in order to facilitate the speedy transmission of documents over standard phone lines.

Beginning Work on a Web Publication

You should always begin work on a Web publication by choosing the Web Page layout. Doing so signals Publisher to make its special Web publishing tools available to you. You should also take a few moments to define global properties for your Web site and the pages it contains.

In many other ways, however, creating a Web publication is identical to creating a print publication. You should set up the page size, background, scheme colors, and layout guides.

Begin a New Web Publication

1. Access the Catalog dialog box, either by opening Publisher or by choosing New on the File menu.

2. Select the Blank Publications tab.

3. Select the Web Page layout.

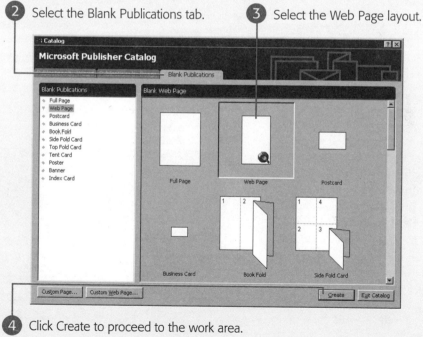

4. Click Create to proceed to the work area.

Use Publisher's automated design tools to create a Web page. If you click the Publications By Wizard tab in the Catalog dialog box, you can choose from 45 different Web site designs that are appropriate for a business, a community group, or home use. The wizard generates a multiple page document complete with hyperlinks. You can also insert individual Web elements, such as a masthead or navigation bar, from Publisher's Design Gallery.

For more information about Publisher's wizards and the Design Gallery, see Chapter 14.

Choose a page size that matches the screen resolution used by your readers. VGA resolution refers to a screen display that is 640 pixels wide by 480 pixels high. SVGA resolution refers to a screen display that is 800 pixels wide by 600 pixels high. When choosing the page width of your Web publication, remember that your readers may not have the same high-resolution monitor that you do. For example, if you choose the Wide (or SVGA) option, readers with a VGA monitor will be forced to scroll horizontally as well as vertically to read the entire page.

Setting Up a Web Page

Although HTML documents are referred to as having pages, they are meant to be read on-screen. So when you access the Page Setup dialog box (available from the File menu), Publisher gives you width options that correspond to standard VGA and SVGA screen resolutions.

Set Up a Web Page

1 Choose Page Setup on the File menu or click the Custom Web Page button on the Blank Publications tab in the Catalog dialog box. The Web Page Setup dialog box appears.

2 Choose one of these three options.

- Select Standard for a screen width that corresponds to the VGA resolution of 640 pixels wide.

- Select Wide for a screen width that corresponds to the SVGA resolution of 800 pixels wide.

- Select Custom to set the specific width and height of your Web page.

When you choose the Standard or Wide page formats, the width is predetermined and cannot be changed. If you want to specify a different width, choose the Custom option.

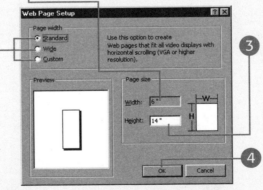

3 Enter a value from 0.25 through 240 inches in the Height text box. The page you create can be longer than a typical screen because Web browsers allow users to scroll down to view more information.

4 Click OK.

How will the keywords and description I enter in the Web Properties dialog box be used? Search engines—Web utilities that help people to find Web sites—use this information to catalog and describe your Web site. An Internet user looks for sites of interest by typing search criteria into a search engine, such as Yahoo!, LYCOS, or InfoSeek. If one of your keywords matches the search, your Web site is listed as a good source of information. The search engine may display the text in the Description box to further identify your Web site.

Special considerations for multilingual documents. Only newer browsers that support the HTML 4.0 (or later) specification can display multilingual documents properly. If you are creating a multilingual document, select the Microsoft Internet Explorer Or Netscape Navigator 4.0 Or Later (High Fidelity) option in the Web Properties dialog box. You must also identify the language for each paragraph in a multilingual document by highlighting the text and choosing a language in the Set Language dialog box (found on the Language submenu on the Tools menu).

Choosing Web Properties

Publisher allows you to choose properties for your entire Web site and for the individual pages it contains. Publisher's global Web site properties allow you to use file naming conventions required by your ISP, provide information about your site to Web-based search engines, and choose compatibility levels for different versions of the HTML specification. You can also can publish your Web page(s) in a language other than your system's default language by choosing a specific character set (or a multilingual character set) in the Web Properties dialog box.

You can configure individual pages in a Web site to play a background sound or automatically update navigation bars generated with a Publication wizard or the Design Gallery.

Change Properties for the Entire Web Site

1 On the File menu, choose Web Properties. The Web Properties dialog box appears.

2 Click the Site tab.

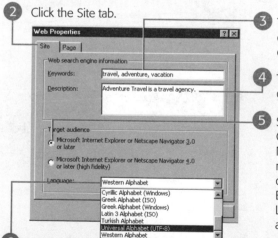

3 Type short phrases to identify the content of your Web site. Separate each phrase with a comma.

4 Type a general description of your Web site.

5 Select an HTML compatibility option. Choose Microsoft Internet Explorer Or Netscape Navigator 3.0 Or Later if you need compatibility with a broad range of programs. Choose Microsoft Internet Explorer Or Netscape Navigator 4.0 Or Later (High Fidelity) if you want to take advantage of the latest HTML functions.

6 Open the Language drop-down list and choose a character set to use when displaying the text in your Web site. Choose Universal Alphabet (UTF-8) if your Web pages contain text in several different languages.

7 Click OK.

Add hyperlinks automatically when you add pages. If you click the Add Hyperlink To Web Navigation Bar option in the Page tab of the Web Properties dialog box, Publisher will automatically insert a hyperlink to that page in any navigation bar that you create using a wizard or the Design Gallery. When you are working in a Web document, the same option is available in the Insert Page dialog box (accessed from the Insert menu).

How do background sounds differ from sound files I insert using the Clip Gallery? When you insert a sound file using the Clip Gallery, it appears as an object in the layout. Although background sounds are associated with a specific page, they never appear on-screen. In addition, your reader can't control the playback of a background sound. It plays as soon as the page is opened according to the parameters you have chosen in the Web Properties dialog box.

Change Properties for an Individual Page in a Web Site

1 Move to the page in your publication whose properties you want to change.

2 On the File menu, choose Web Properties. The Web Properties dialog box appears.

3 Click the Page tab.

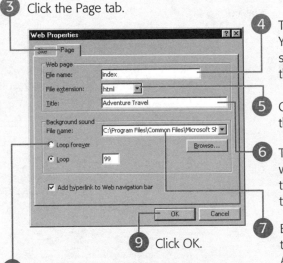

4 Type the file name for this page. Your ISP may require you to use a specific name, such as "index" for the first (or home) page.

5 Choose the file extension for the pages in your document.

6 Type a title for this page. The title will appear in the Web browser's title bar when a reader accesses the page.

7 Enter the file name and location of the sound file you want to play. Alternatively, you can open the drop-down list to access recently used sound files, or click the Browse button to find the file using the Background Sound list box.

8 Click Loop Forever to play the sound continuously, or click Loop and then enter a value between 1 and 99 in the text box to play the sound a specified number of times.

9 Click OK.

Choosing a Web Page Background and Color Scheme

You can choose to add a color, a texture, or both to the background of a Web Page layout. You can choose from 225 background patterns supplied with Publisher, or you can create your own background pattern.

Which file extension should I choose for my Web site? You should conform to the file naming convention used by your ISP. For example, DOS-based servers require file names to have a three-letter (.htm) file extension; they don't support four-letter (.html) file extensions.

Do I have to change the file extension for each page in my Web site? No. Whenever you choose a file name extension for one page in your publication, the change is automatically copied to all of the pages.

Create a custom color scheme for the Web. Macs and PCs use different color palettes to display Web pages. To be sure that the colors in your Web page display properly on a wide variety of computers, create a Web-specific color scheme. It's easy. Just be sure that when you specify an RGB color, you use one of the following values for each of the primary colors: 255, 204, 153, 102, 51, or 0.

Web pages also use a color scheme that contains a main color and five accent colors. In addition, a Web color scheme contains two special colors to identify hyperlinked text (text that triggers an event when clicked) and followed hyperlinked text (text referring to a link that has already been explored).

Choose a Color or Texture for a Web Page Background

1 On the Format menu, select Color And Background Scheme. The Color And Background Scheme dialog box appears.

2 Select either the Standard or Custom tab. The options for background color and texture are identical on both tabs.

3 In the Background area, open the Solid Color drop-down list and choose one of the available colors, tints, or shades.

Use the Preview area to see how Publisher will repeat the texture on the page. Some textures, such as the one shown here, fill only a portion of the page. Other textures fill the entire page.

4 Select this check box to add a texture to the background.

5 Click the Browse button to locate a picture file to be used as a background texture.

6 Click OK.

Create an efficient custom background texture. Don't use a large bitmapped graphic as the background texture for your Web page. A picture with large dimensions, high resolution, and many colors takes a long time to download—and will keep your readers waiting for your Web page to appear. Instead, use a small picture with a file size of 20 KB or less. For example, the picture of leaves below measures only 2 by 2 inches and occupies only 22 KB of disk space. Make sure the picture is "in repeat," which means that the top, bottom, left, and right edges form a seamless match when multiple copies of the image are tiled to fill the screen. When a reader accesses your Web page, only the small original picture is transmitted. The Web browser repeats the image to form a continuous pattern.

 For more information about creating a custom color scheme, see Chapter 15.

Choose Standard or Custom Colors for a Web Page

1 On the Format menu, click Color And Background Scheme. The Color And Background Scheme dialog box appears.

2 Click the Standard tab and select one of the predefined color schemes. Publisher automatically chooses the best colors for the Main Text, Hyperlink Text, and Followed Hyperlink Text elements. Alternatively, click the Custom tab to choose your own colors.

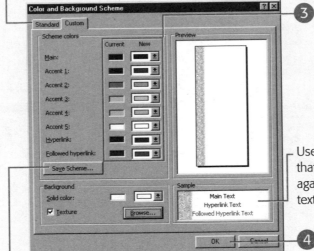

3 If you clicked the Custom tab, open each color drop-down list to choose an available color, tint, or shade.

Use the Sample area to be sure that the text colors are legible against the background color or texture you've chosen.

4 Click OK.

Click the Save Scheme button to store and reuse the custom colors under a new scheme name. Publisher lists this name along with the predefined color schemes on the Standard tab.

For more information about layout and ruler guides, see Chapter 3. For more information about graphic regions and how they are created, see "Managing Art in a Web Page" later in this chapter.

Why shouldn't I overlap objects in a Web publication? Older Web browsers, such as Internet Explorer or Netscape Navigator 3.0, can't display overlapping objects. If you overlap objects in a publication targeted for these browsers, Publisher automatically converts the objects (even text objects) into a graphic region. Graphic regions can increase file size and download times for your Web publications.

Setting Up Layout Guides

Publisher's layout and ruler guides function normally within a Web publication. You should use column, row, and ruler guides to be sure that text and picture frames don't overlap, as shown in the following illustration.

Divide the page with rows if you need to create a Web page design that is compatible with very old browsers that can't display tables or frames. All of the text and pictures will be aligned along the left margin.

You can also use column and row guides to create a multiple column layout. A viewer's browser application must be able to display tables or frames in order to view this page properly.

Managing Art in a Web Page

In order to create efficient Web pages, you must understand how both HTML and Publisher handle pictures, sounds, and motion clips.

Inline Graphics: GIF and JPEG Images

Inline graphics are an integral part of a Web page. They appear within the browser window and are embedded in the text flow. Currently, only the GIF (CompuServe Graphics Interchange Format) and JPEG (Joint Photographic Experts Group) bitmapped file formats are widely supported by graphical Web browsers. Both the GIF and JPEG formats offer cross-platform compatibility (meaning that they

Which graphics formats does Publisher convert to the JPEG format? Publisher maintains imported JPEG images in the JPEG format. It also converts TIFF images to JPEG. It converts all other graphics formats, as well as any shapes that you create with Publisher's drawing tools, to the GIF format.

For more information about picture file formats, see Chapter 10.

Why don't certain features of my GIF file, like transparency and animation, work in my Web page? Check your layout. If you overlap an animated GIF file with other objects or rotate it, Publisher doesn't preserve the animation sequence. Alternatively, you may have pasted the GIF file into your document from an application that doesn't support GIF transparency or animation. Delete the problematic GIF file from the Publisher document. Insert a new copy of the file using the Insert Picture command or by dragging the file from Windows Explorer into Publisher. When you preview or save the Web page again, these features should work.

can be viewed on PCs, Macintoshes, and Unix machines) and sophisticated compression schemes. This last point is very important because bitmapped pictures can grow quite large. Your goal is to produce the smallest, most efficient graphics files without sacrificing image quality.

Publisher converts all imported graphics to either the GIF or the JPEG format. Publisher decides whether the GIF or JPEG format is appropriate based on the following factors:

⊚ The original file format of a picture. For example, TIFF images are usually converted to the JPEG format, and WMF images are converted to the GIF format.

⊚ The target browser you have chosen in the Web Properties dialog box. If you have chosen Microsoft Internet Explorer or Netscape Navigator 3.0 or later browsers, Publisher converts overlapping objects (including imported pictures) to a graphic region, which is saved as a GIF file.

When Publisher converts an imported picture to the GIF or JPEG format, it doesn't take the content of the picture into consideration. In addition, Publisher always uses standard settings to optimize the file. You can often achieve better-looking graphics if you convert pictures to the GIF or JPEG format prior to importing them into a Web page. In general, the JPEG format is preferable for a photographic image containing lots of colors and smooth tonal variation. The GIF format is the best choice for a drawn image (and the occasional photograph) that contains text, hard edges, and flat areas of color. In order to produce the best-looking pictures with the smallest possible file size, you should use the optimization techniques summarized in the following table.

Optimize GIF and JPEG Images for Web Publications

Feature	Description	Optimization Technique
Dimensions	The size of a picture in a Web page should be measured in pixels because monitors are measured in pixels. For example, a picture measuring 200 by 200 pixels fills nearly one-seventh of a 640 by 480 monitor.	Create pictures that measure between 80 and 150 pixels (vertically and horizontally). Images that will be used as button icons should be even smaller—as small as 30 by 30 pixels.
Resolution	Resolution is defined as the number of dots (or pixels) that occur in a particular unit of measurement. Most scanning utilities measure the number of dots per inch (dpi).	It is preferable to size a picture using the actual dimensions measured in pixels (see "Dimensions" above). If your scanning utility requires you to enter a resolution, scan at 72 dpi—the resolution of most monitors. If you scan at a higher resolution, Publisher reduces the resolution of the picture when generating the HTML document.
Colors	A bitmapped graphic contains a specific number of colors. The color capability of a bitmapped file is measured by bit depth. A 4-bit file contains 16 colors, an 8-bit file contains 256 colors, and a 24-bit file contains potentially 16.7 million colors.	Use a graphics program to reduce the number of colors in a GIF picture to 256 colors or less, as the GIF format supports a maximum of 256 colors. JPEG pictures are always saved as full-color, 24-bit files, which makes them more suitable for photographic images.
Compression	The GIF format uses the Lempel-Zir and Welch (LZW) compression routine. LZW compression doesn't discard any picture data and typically squeezes a file down to half of its original size. The JPEG format offers multiple levels of compression, but discards data (and potentially degrades the quality of the image) in order to achieve small file sizes.	In your graphics utility or image editing program, save the image using the GIF format. The LZW compression scheme is automatically applied. When saving a JPEG image, use a utility that allows you to judge the tradeoff between compression level and quality. Choose the highest compression level that still delivers a good-looking picture.
Incremental downloads	Interlaced GIF files and progressive JPEG files use an encoding method that appears to download an image more quickly. From the user's point of view, the full image, though blurry, appears on-screen in less time than it would take the full image to appear. The image comes into focus as the remaining image data is downloaded to complete the picture. Note that interlacing and progressive encoding increase the *apparent* transmission speed of the image, not the actual speed.	To take advantage of this feature, your graphics utility or image editing program must be able to export interlaced GIF files or progressive JPEG files.

Feature	Description	Optimization Technique
Transparency	When a picture is displayed, one or more colors within it appear to be transparent. This technique is especially useful if you want to create silhouettes, an effect where the irregular outline of a picture appears against the background of an HTML page. Instead of filling the picture with the same color or pattern as the background page, you designate the fill color as transparent. Publisher allows you to use transparent GIFs as background textures. The solid background color you've chosen shows through the transparent areas of the background GIF file.	To take advantage of transparency, your graphics utility or image editing program must be able to export version 89a of the GIF format. The JPEG format doesn't support transparency.
Animation	A single GIF file can contain a series of images. When viewed sequentially, these images flow together to create the illusion of movement.	When viewed in a Web browser, a GIF file plays continuously. You should create an animation loop where the movement or gesture in the last image flows seamlessly into the movement or gesture in the first image. The JPEG format doesn't support sequential images.

Turn off the display of graphic regions. If you don't want Publisher to alert you to the creation of graphic regions as you work, you can turn off the display of the special red boundary rectangle. On the Tools menu, select Options. On the General tab, clear the Show Rectangle For Text In Web Graphic Region check box.

Graphic Regions

If you targeted your Web publication for Microsoft Internet Explorer or Netscape Navigator 3.0 browsers, Publisher converts any objects that aren't compatible with these older applications into a graphic region. Graphic regions preserve your layout. Older browsers don't support overlapping objects, for example. But when converted to a graphic region, they appear on the reader's screen exactly as you intended.

When Publisher generates the HTML document, graphic regions are converted to GIF images and behave just like any other bitmapped picture. This means that the download time for such images increases substantially.

Why do overlapping objects appear in a linear layout when I view my Web page in my browser?
You have targeted the Web page for high-fidelity browsers, such as Microsoft Internet Explorer or Netscape Navigator 4.0, that are capable of displaying Cascading Style Sheets. However, you are viewing the Web page using an older browser (such as Microsoft Internet Explorer or Netscape Navigator 3.0) that isn't capable of displaying Cascading Style Sheets. Either retarget the document for an older browser, or upgrade to a newer version of Internet Explorer or Netscape Navigator.

Use graphic regions to incorporate unusual fonts in your Web pages. You can use an unusual font in your Web page for special text elements, such as headlines. You must convert the font into a picture—or graphic region—to be sure that the typeface will be displayed properly by your reader's browser application. The easiest way to convert text to a picture is to create it using WordArt. WordArt is always converted to a graphic region.

If you overlap frames, Publisher alerts you that it will create a graphic region by outlining the objects with a red boundary rectangle. It does this only once—at the moment when the two objects overlap. The flashing red box delineates the size of the graphic region, which is equal in size to a rectangle large enough to encompass all of the objects.

Any objects that fall within the red boundary box are included in the graphic region and will also be converted to a picture, even if they don't overlap any other objects.

Within a Web page, Publisher creates a graphic region whenever one of the following conditions occurs:

- You overlap frames. This applies if you position a picture frame over a text frame in order to create a text wrap or if you overlap two text frames.

- You create a WordArt object.

- You rotate a text frame.

- You add BorderArt to a text frame.

- You fill a text frame with a pattern or gradient.

Displaying a Text Description of a Picture

There are several instances in which the pictures (and graphic regions) in your Web page won't appear on your reader's screen. Your reader may be using a text-only browser. Many browser applications allow users to turn off the display of graphics in order to speed up performance. Even if the reader chooses to display graphics, a slow Internet connection or an overloaded server (either yours or theirs) may prevent pictures from appearing. In anticipation of these common problems, you should associate a label with each picture in a Web page. This description, known as alternate text (or ALT text), downloads quickly and is compatible with even the oldest browser that a reader may use.

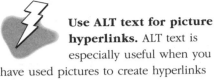 **Use ALT text for picture hyperlinks.** ALT text is especially useful when you have used pictures to create hyperlinks in your Web site, because it allows the reader to navigate the site without viewing the images.

Associate ALT Text with a Picture or Object

① Select a picture, OLE object, or WordArt object.

② Select Picture Frame Properties or Object Frame Properties on the Format menu. The modified Picture Frame Properties (or Object Frame Properties) dialog box appears.

③ In the Alternate Text Representation area, enter a descriptive phrase in the Text To Display text box.

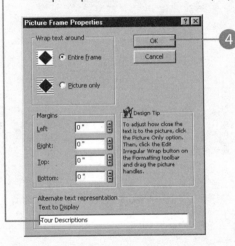

④ Click OK.

When viewed in a Web browser, the ALT text appears in place of a missing picture or whenever you place your cursor over the picture.

Managing Multimedia Objects in a Web Page

Using Publisher's Clip Gallery, you can easily insert multimedia objects, such as sounds, digital videos, and GIF animations, into a Web page. Publisher allows you to import any multimedia format supported by the Windows Media Player. For example, you can import sound files in the WAV format and videos in the AVI format because the drivers for these standard formats were loaded when you installed the Media Player as part of Windows.

Can I play a sound file or view a motion clip from within Publisher?
Yes, simply double-click a multimedia file. The sound or movie plays, provided that the format is supported by the Windows Media Player. Alternatively, you can preview sounds and motion clips using the Play button in the Clip Gallery. This latter method also works for the animated GIF format, which isn't supported by the Windows Media Player.

For more information about the Clip Gallery, see Chapter 10.

What are the differences between the Component Object Model, a plug-in, and MIME? These three specifications allow Web browsers to display file formats not directly supported by HTML and to play multimedia files. The MIME specification, which is older, allows the browser to open a window and run a separate helper application in order to play the multimedia file. Browsers that support Microsoft's Component Object Model (also known as ActiveX controls) and Netscape's plug-in specification can display files and access multimedia objects within the main browser window.

When imported into a document, multimedia files appear to be static images. Sound files are represented by an icon. Clicking the icon while running a Web browser plays the recording. Motion clips are represented by the first frame of the movie or animation.

A WAV file is identified by a picture of a speaker.

GIF animations play continuously when viewed in a Web browser.

The icon for a MIDI file always includes the file name.

Digital video files are always identified with a file name. Clicking the image while running a Web browser plays the movie.

Users who wish to play the multimedia files in your Web page must have the proper hardware and software on *their* systems, including:

- A sound card to play sound files and the soundtracks associated with video files.
- A color monitor to display videos.
- The Windows Media Player and appropriate sound and video drivers.
- A browser that can display animated GIF files.
- A browser that supports Microsoft Component Object Model or ActiveX controls, the Netscape Plug-in specification, or MIME (Multipurpose Internet Mail Extension) helper applications.

Why does the text in my HTML document take a long time to download? You may simply be experiencing the transmission delays that normally occur when there is a lot of traffic on the World Wide Web. However, your document may contain graphic regions rather than true text. Open the original .pub file and check for any conditions that may have forced Publisher to convert true text into a graphic region.

Managing Text Elements in a Web Publication

Text is the most important element in a Web page. It conveys most, if not all, of the information in your publication. Equally significant is that text downloads much more quickly than a picture. Your goal as a Web publisher is twofold:

@ To produce a text design that fits within the limitations of the HTML specification.

@ To avoid converting true text objects into graphic regions, which, as pictures, download much more slowly.

The HTML specification doesn't offer absolute control over the appearance of text. It primarily defines the relationship between text elements. Think of this structure as a big outline where you define the relative importance of text—for example, headings versus body copy. You can request specific text formatting attributes, such as font and point size, but the reader's browser program might not be able to fulfill those requests and might make undesirable substitutions.

In addition, many standard text formatting attributes, such as line spacing and tabs, are simply not supported by HTML. When Publisher converts the .pub document to an HTML document, much of this formatting is lost. The following comparison illustrates this process.

Unusual font choices, such as Eras Bold ITC, might look correct in your Publisher document, but they will be replaced with a standard font, such as Times New Roman, if your readers don't have the same fonts installed on their computer systems.

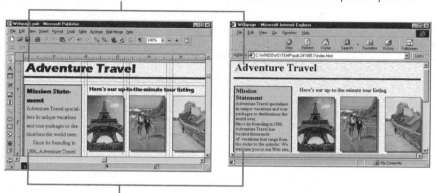

Because HTML supports only plain text, many formatting attributes, such as the additional line spacing, hyphenation, or indented paragraphs shown in this Publisher document, won't appear in the final Web page.

The table below summarizes formatting attributes that may prove to be troublesome when a .pub document is converted to HTML, or when a reader accesses the document using a Web browser (especially if the reader is using an older browser).

Text and Text Frame Formatting Guidelines for Web Publications			
Text Attribute	**In a Publisher Document**	**In an HTML Document**	**Recommended Text Formats**
Font	You can format text with any font installed on your system.	Publisher inserts a request for the font into the HTML document. If your reader doesn't have the same font installed, a standard font will be substituted.	Format text in a Web page with the following standard fonts: Arial, Arial Black, Comic Sans MS, Courier New, Georgia, Impact, Symbol, Times New Roman, Trebuchet MS, Verdana, and Wingdings. You can enhance these typefaces with font styles, such as regular, italic, bold, and bold italic.

Text and Text Frame Formatting Guidelines for Web Publications *(continued)*			
Text Attribute	**In a Publisher Document**	**In an HTML Document**	**Recommended Text Formats**
Point size	Publisher can format text from 0.5 through 999.5 points in 0.5-point increments.	HTML supports only seven font size designations. The reader's browser application determines the actual point size at which type appears on screen.	Format text ranging from 8 through 30 points.
Font effects	Publisher lets you format text with eight different effects.	HTML doesn't support shadowed, small capital, outlined, embossed, or engraved text effects.	Use only Subscript, Superscript, and All Caps effects in your Web pages.
Line spacing	Publisher allows you to set line spacing from 0.25 through 124 spaces in quarter-space increments (or from 3 through 1488 points in 0.5-point increments).	HTML documents are displayed with single line spacing. All line-spacing attributes within the Publisher document are ignored.	Set all copy using single line spacing.
Indents	Publisher allows you to create indents for the left side, right side and first line of a paragraph.	HTML doesn't allow indents. Any indents within the Publisher document are ignored.	Distinguish the beginning of a paragraph with an extra line space. As an alternative to indents, increase the text frame margins.
Bulleted and numbered lists	Publisher can automatically create bulleted and numbered lists.	HTML supports both bulleted and numbered lists. Many of the advanced formatting options within Publisher (such as the ability to specify the style of bullet or change the indent) are ignored when the publication is converted to HTML.	Create simple bulleted and numbered lists.
Alignment	Publisher gives you four alignment options: left, right, center, and justified.	HTML supports left, right, and center alignment only.	For maximum legibility, keep most of your text left aligned. Reserve the center alignment option for headlines and short lists.
Tabs	Publisher allows you to set four kinds of tab stops: left, right, center, and decimal.	HTML doesn't recognize tabs of any kind. When you insert a tab, Publisher converts it to a space.	Avoid tabs.

Text and Text Frame Formatting Guidelines for Web Publications *(continued)*

Text Attribute	In a Publisher Document	In an HTML Document	Recommended Text Formats
Hyphenation	Publisher offers both automatic and optional hyphenation.	HTML doesn't support automatic or optional hyphenation.	Turn off automatic hyphenation and refrain from using optional hyphens. However, you can manually insert the hyphen character or a nonbreaking hyphen.
Spacing between characters	Publisher allows you to modify the spacing for an entire paragraph (called tracking) or for selected characters (called kerning).	HTML doesn't support tracking or kerning. All adjustments that you make in the Publisher document are ignored.	Don't apply tracking or kerning to text in a Web page.
Underlining	Publisher allows you to choose among 17 underlining effects.	HTML displays only a single solid underline. Publisher's other underlining styles are converted to a single solid underline.	In Web pages, underlining often signals hypertext links. You should therefore avoid underlining other types of text elements because it can confuse your readers.
Text color	You can choose colors to identify normal text, hyperlinked text, and followed hyperlinked text. Publisher also lets you assign any color, tint, or shade to selected text.	The color you assign to text is maintained in the HTML document.	Because readers may view your Web page on a 16- or 256-color monitor, you should choose solid text colors that contrast with the background color. Don't confuse readers by choosing the same or similar colors for normal text and hyperlink text.
Table text	Publisher can produce true tables that are arranged like a spreadsheet, in rows and columns.	The current version of HTML does accept tables. However, some older browsers don't display tables properly.	Include tables in your Web publications if you are certain that your readers will be using full-featured browsers that can display tables.
Multiple columns	In a standard publication, you can create up to 63 columns in a text frame. In a Web publication, however, this option is unavailable.	HTML doesn't support multiple columns.	If you want to create multiple text columns, draw individual text frames and link them to accommodate text flow.

Text Attribute	In a Publisher Document	In an HTML Document	Recommended Text Formats
Object fill	Publisher lets you fill a text frame with any color, tint, shade, pattern, or gradient.	If you have targeted the document for older browsers, text frames containing a fill are converted to a graphic region. If you have targeted the document for high-fidelity browsers, the text frame is preserved with a Cascading Style Sheet.	Use transparent text frames.
Borders and BorderArt	Publisher allows you to assign either a line border or BorderArt to a text frame.	If you have targeted the document for older browsers, text frames formatted with BorderArt are converted to a graphic region. If you have targeted the document for high-fidelity browsers, the text frame is preserved with a Cascading Style Sheet.	Avoid using BorderArt on text frames. Use line borders with discretion. If a reader views your Web site with an older browser, the line border might not be displayed. The text itself, however, displays normally.
Shadow	Publisher can create a drop shadow for a text frame.	Older browsers may not be able to display shadows on text frames.	Use shadows on text frames with discretion. If a reader views your Web site with an older browser, the shadow might not be displayed. The text itself, however, displays normally.
Rotation	Publisher can rotate a text frame in 1-degree increments.	The rotated text frame is converted to a graphic region.	Avoid rotated text.

Converting a Print Publication to a Web Publication

Publisher can create a Web page from a standard publication that has been designed for printed output. Although this function is convenient, it should be used with caution. Many design elements commonly used in print publications (such as overlapping objects, WordArt elements, and rotated text) aren't supported by

For more information about the Design Checker, see Chapter 3.

Wizards easily convert documents between print and screen versions. If you use a wizard to create a print document, such as a newsletter or a brochure, you can also use the wizard to convert the document to a Web publication. The command appears in the wizard window. Because wizards keep track of the objects in a publication, the conversion is more intelligent and less likely to generate an inefficient Web publication. For example, the wizard can automatically generate hyperlinks, and it doesn't allow objects to overlap. But be warned—the wizard doesn't include any objects, text frames, or pictures you may have added to the document when it converts the print publication to a Web publication.

To learn more about wizards, see Chapter 14.

HTML. If you convert a print publication to a Web page without a careful examination of the layout and an intelligent redesign, you will produce an inefficient Web page. Luckily, Publisher's Design Checker can alert you to potential problems.

Create a Web Page from an Existing Publisher Document

1 Open the publication file you wish to convert to a Web page.

2 Choose Create Web Site From Current Publication from the File menu. Publisher displays an alert box prompting you to save the file. Click Yes.

3 Publisher then displays an alert box asking if you want to run the Design Checker.

4 Click Yes to activate the Design Checker in order to discover problems specific to Web pages.

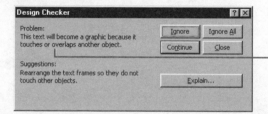

The Design Checker looks for Web-specific layout problems, such as objects that will be converted to graphic regions or large graphics that will slow down performance (not shown).

5 When you have finished running the Design Checker and making any necessary changes, save the publication file with a new name.

6 When you are ready to create an HTML document, use the Save As Web Page command found on the File menu.

Creating and Managing Hyperlinks in a Web Page

You've probably heard the Internet described as the information highway. In keeping with the road map metaphor, hyperlinks are the signs that point to specific addresses on the World Wide Web. A Web address is called a URL, or Uniform Resource Locator.

Hyperlinks can be associated with text, in which case they are called hyperlink text. Hyperlinks associated with graphic objects, such as imported pictures and drawn shapes, are called hot spots. The following diagram illustrates how hyperlinks work.

Hyperlinks can be associated with text or a picture. When you move your cursor over a hyperlink, the hand pointer appears.

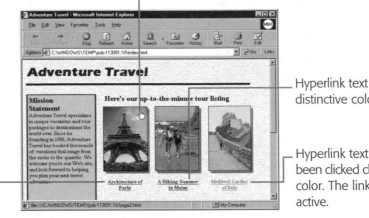

Hyperlink text is identified by a distinctive color and underlining.

Hyperlink text that has already been clicked changes to a different color. The link, however, is still active.

Clicking a hyperlink moves you to the address (or URL) assigned to that link. Hyperlinks are not linear; they can move you forward or backward in a document. Or they can move you to a completely different location on the Web.

Creating Hyperlinks

A hyperlink can be assigned to a text phrase, a picture, a shape, or a hot spot. The Hot Spot tool is especially useful when you want to add more than one hyperlink to an object. For example, you could assign different URLs to various parts of a picture.

Whenever you create a hyperlink, you must choose one of four hyperlink types, as explained in the following table.

Types of Hyperlinks

Create this hyperlink...	To perform this action...	Based on this information...
To another page in your Web site.	This is an exploring hyperlink. It moves the reader to another page in the current Web publication.	You must specify a relative or absolute page number. Relative pages (first page, previous page, and next page) are useful for generic controls, such as page turn icons that appear on every page of a document. Absolute page numbers are useful when you are cross-referencing specific information or creating a navigation bar.
To another document already on the Web.	This is an exploring hyperlink. It moves the reader to another address anywhere on the Web.	You must specify a Web address (or URL).
To an Internet e-mail address.	This is a response hyperlink. When clicked, it allows the reader to send a message to the specified address.	You must enter a valid Internet e-mail address. If you enter your own e-mail address, your readers can contact you or your company easily.
To a file on a Web server.	This hyperlink downloads a file from your Web server (which can be your local hard disk) to the reader's hard disk.	Type the full path, including the drive designation, the folders, and the file name with its extension. If you don't know the full path, click the Browse button (in the Hyperlink dialog box) to search for the file. When you select the file and click Open, Publisher enters the correct path information in the text box.

Create a Hyperlink

1 Highlight text, or select a picture or a drawn shape.

2 On the Insert menu, choose Hyperlink, or right-click the object and choose Hyperlink from the shortcut menu. The Hyperlink dialog box appears.

You can activate the Hyperlink dialog box by clicking the Insert Hyperlink icon on the Standard toolbar.

Entering Internet addresses correctly. If you want the hyperlinks in your Web pages to function properly, you must enter the URL correctly. Look closely at the following sample URL, and note what each part of the address signifies.

Identifies the Hypertext Transfer Protocol, the method used on the Web to locate files.

Identifies the World Wide Web.

`http://www.microsoft.com`

Identifies the domain or host name.

Identifies the organization type. Abbreviations include .com (commercial), .edu (education), .gov (government), .mil (military), and .org (organization).

Create a Hyperlink *(continued)*

3 Choose the type of hyperlink you want to associate with the selected object.

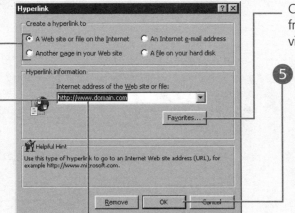

Click here to select an address from a list of the Web sites you visited most recently.

5 Click OK. If your selected object is a text phrase, Publisher changes its color and underlines it. If your selected object is a picture or a shape, Publisher creates the hyperlink but doesn't change the appearance of the selected object.

The type of hyperlink you create determines what kind of information you must enter in the Hyperlink Information area. For example, if you create a hyperlink to a document on the Web, you must enter an Internet address. If you create a hyperlink to a file on your hard disk, you must enter the path to locate that file.

4 Enter the appropriate information in the Hyperlink Information area. In this case, you must enter an Internet address.

Create a Hot Spot

1 Select the Picture Hot Spot tool (shown below) from the toolbar. The pointer changes to the crossbar pointer.

2 Position the crossbar over the area where you want to add a hot spot.

Why is the Hot Spot Tool grayed out? Publisher makes the Hot Spot Tool available when you are working on a Web publication—and only then. If the Hot Spot Tool appears grayed out, you are probably designing a standard print publication. You need to open an existing Web publication, start a new Web publication, or convert the current publication to a Web publication.

Why do I have trouble selecting hot spot objects? By default, the Hot Spot Tool creates transparent, borderless rectangles. Like all other objects in a Publisher document, hot spots have object boundaries (which disappear when you generate an HTML document). Object boundaries are light gray dotted lines, which can be difficult to see on-screen, especially when the hot spot is stacked on top of a picture. You can, however, temporarily format a hot spot object with attributes such as a line border or a fill color to make it easy to see and select.

You can also group a hot spot with a picture. When you select, move, or resize the picture, the hot spot will also be selected, moved, or resized.

Create a Hot Spot *(continued)*

③ While pressing and holding the mouse button, drag the mouse diagonally to create a transparent rectangle. You may create a rectangle that completely surrounds an object (such as a picture), or you may create a rectangle that surrounds only a portion of the underlying object.

④ When the shape and size of the hot spot are to your liking, release the mouse button. The Hyperlink dialog box appears.

⑤ Choose the type of hyperlink you want to assign to the hot spot.

⑥ Enter the appropriate information in the Hyperlink Information area.

⑦ Click OK to create the hyperlink.

Editing Hyperlinks

You can change the characteristics of a hyperlink, including its type, file path, and color. You can also delete a hyperlink from your document. The ability to edit the URL associated with a hyperlink is especially important because the Web is constantly in flux. New Web sites are created, existing Web sites are altered or abandoned, and files are moved. As a Web publisher, you have an obligation to your readers to keep the URLs up-to-date.

Change the Type or Destination of a Hyperlink

① Select a hyperlinked text, picture, picture hot spot, or drawn shape object.

② Select Hyperlink on the Insert menu, or right-click the object and choose Hyperlink from the shortcut menu. The Hyperlink dialog box appears.

③ Make the appropriate changes by choosing a new hyperlink type or by entering new information in the Hyperlink Information area.

④ Click OK.

ScreenTips identify hyperlinks. When you position the pointer over a hyperlink, a ScreenTip appears. The tip identifies the type of hyperlink by displaying the associated page reference, URL, e-mail address, or file name, as shown below.

A Biking Summer
in Maine Hyperlink to Next Page

Remove a Hyperlink

1 Select a hyperlinked text, picture, picture hot spot, or drawn shape object.

2 Choose Hyperlink on the Insert menu, or right-click the object and choose Hyperlink from the shortcut menu. The Hyperlink dialog box appears.

3 Click the Remove button to delete the hyperlink associated with the currently selected object. The appearance of a picture, drawn shape, or hot spot remains unchanged when the hyperlink is removed. Text color reverts to the Main Text color, and the underline disappears when the hyperlink is removed.

4 If necessary, use Publisher's standard tools to delete the text, picture, drawn shape, or hot spot.

Creating and Formatting Forms in a Web Page

Web pages can contain electronic forms. Electronic forms appear in Publisher as static objects, but when viewed in a Web browser they are interactive and can be filled out by the reader. You compose an electronic form by creating and combining six different Form Control objects that in turn determine the type of information a reader can enter. When you design a form, you must choose the appropriate form control object for the type of information you want to gather, as described in the table below.

Types and Uses of Form Control Objects		
Use this form control...	**To have the reader...**	**Enter this kind information...**
Single-line text box	Type a short text phrase.	A name or address.
Multiline text box	Type longer text blocks.	A product evaluation or customer comment.
Check box	Turn a single item on or off or select multiple items from a list where more than one choice might apply.	The answer to a Yes-or-No question. A list of products a customer may want to purchase.

Types and Uses of Form Control Objects *(continued)*

Use this form control...	To have the reader...	Enter this kind information...
Option button	Select a single item from a group of related, but mutually exclusive, items.	An answer to a multiple-choice question or a choice on a rating scale.
List box	Make a single selection or multiple selections from a scrollable list box or drop-down list box.	A listing of state names in an address form, or a listing of colors in a catalog.
Command button	Click a button to execute a command.	Submit the information or reset the form.

 Why can't I resize a form control? Certain form controls, such as option buttons or check boxes, are created at a standard size. Although you can resize the label associated with these objects, you can't resize the actual button or box.

 For more information about resizing objects, see Chapter 3.

Create a Form Control

① Select the Form Control tool on the Objects toolbar (shown below).

② From the menu, select the type of form control you would like to insert. The pointer changes to the crossbar pointer.

③ Place the crossbar pointer where you want the center of the form control object to appear, and then click.

④ If necessary, drag a selection handle to resize the form control object or its label.

⑤ Repeat steps 1 through 4 for each control you want to add to the form.

Why don't the form controls work when I view them in my Web browser? You have overlapped one or more form controls with other objects in your document. Publisher doesn't prevent you from overlapping a form control with another object, but it does display a warning. When you view the Web page in a browser, however, the form control will be inactive.

Can I apply effects to a form control object? No, you can't apply rotation, fill color, fill effects, shadows, borders, or BorderArt to a form control. However, you can apply some of these attributes, such as fill color or a border, to a form control label.

Entering Form Control Item Labels

Item labels are the text phrases that appear next to each object in the electronic form. Keep these labels clear and concise. Remember that self-explanatory labels help your readers to complete the form quickly and correctly.

Check boxes and option buttons (not shown) contain item label text frames. Highlight the default text and type new text. You can change the appearance of the item label using Publisher's standard text formatting tools.

You can choose or type an item label for a command button in the Command Button Properties dialog box. You can't change the font, point size, or alignment of this label.

You can enter item labels in list boxes and type default text for text boxes (not shown) using the associated properties dialog box. You can't change the font, point size, or alignment of this text.

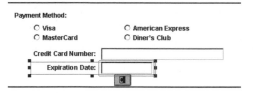

You can draw standard text frames to create labels for form control objects. Group a text frame with the form control object it describes to move them together easily.

Setting Form Control Properties

In order to have your electronic form function properly and return information to you in a usable format, you must set properties for each form control object in your document. With the exception of the object's appearance, these properties remain hidden from your reader. They work behind the scenes to help you process and evaluate the reader's responses. The properties you can set vary from object to object but fall into four main categories, as detailed in the following table.

Form Control Properties

Property Type	Available for...	Description
Default appearance	All form control objects	Can include the default state (selected or unselected) of an item, an item label, or sample text that can be replaced by the reader.
Function	Command button, list box, single-line, or multiline text box	Can associate a specific action with a button, allow or disallow multiple list box selections, or make a text box mandatory.
Data processing label	Single-line and multi-line text box, check box, option button, list box	An internal label (hidden from the reader) that identifies the data when it is returned to you. For example, "Payment Method" could be used to identify a reader's credit card choice.
Data processing value	Single-line and multi-line text box, check box, option button, list box	The actual data returned to you. In most cases, the value should match the item label. For example, if a reader chooses "Visa" as the payment method, the value for the option button should be "Visa."
Data retrieval method and information	Command button	The manner and file format in which the completed form is delivered to you.

 Fast access to form control properties dialog boxes. You can right-click any form control object to open a shortcut menu. On the shortcut menu, select the Properties command to open the associated form control properties dialog box. Alternatively, you can double-click a form control object (not its label) to immediately open the associated properties dialog box.

Set Properties of a Single-Line or Multiline Text Box

1 Select the single-line text box or the multiline text box you want to modify.

2 Choose the Single-Line Text Box Properties or Multiline Text Box Properties command on the Format menu.

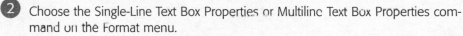

Why can't I enter a value for a Single-Line or Multiline Text Box?

Publisher assumes that the value of a Single-Line or Multiline Text Box is the text typed in by the reader. For example, the value of a First Name text field is the reader's given name.

Set Properties of a Single-Line or Multiline Text Box *(continued)*

③ Type default text, such as "Enter Your Text Here." The text you type will appear in the form but will be replaced when the reader enters new information.

④ Enter a value from 0 to 255 to limit the number of characters that can be typed into a Single-Line Text Box. This option isn't available for a Multiline Text Box.

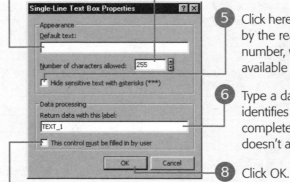

⑤ Click here to hide the information typed by the reader, such as a credit card number, with asterisks. This option isn't available for a Multiline Text Box.

⑥ Type a data processing label. This label identifies the reader's response when the completed form is returned to you; it doesn't appear in the form.

⑧ Click OK.

⑦ Check this box to make a response to this form control mandatory. The reader won't be allowed to submit the form unless this item is completed.

Set Properties of a Check Box

① Select the check box you want to modify and choose the Check Box Properties command on the Format menu.

Set Properties of a Check Box *(continued)*

2 Choose the default appearance of the check box—Selected or Not Selected.

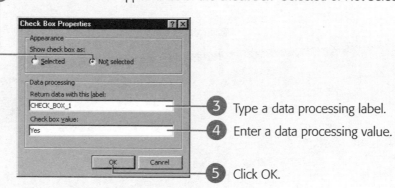

3 Type a data processing label.

4 Enter a data processing value.

5 Click OK.

Why can I select more than one option button in a list when I view the form in my Web browser? You haven't assigned all of the option buttons in the list to the same group (designated by the data processing label). Return to your Publisher document, select each option button in the list, and choose the same data processing label in the Option Button Properties dialog box (accessed from the Format menu). When you next view the form in your Web browser, the option button choices will be mutually exclusive.

Set Properties of an Option Button

1 Select the option button you want to modify and then choose the Option Button Properties command on the Format menu.

2 Choose the default appearance of the option button—Selected or Not Selected.

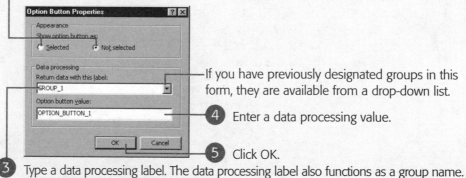

If you have previously designated groups in this form, they are available from a drop-down list.

4 Enter a data processing value.

5 Click OK.

3 Type a data processing label. The data processing label also functions as a group name. The reader can select only one option from among all the items belonging to this group.

Are there cases where the data processing value should not match the item label? There are valid reasons to have the data processing value differ from the item label. Here are two possible scenarios:

@ In your form, you ask a Yes-or-No question. For example, if the item label reads, "Click Here to Receive Our Catalog," the data processing *value* should be "Yes" (and the data processing *label* should be "Send Catalog").

@ In your form, you present a list of English-language choices to the reader, but you want to associate those items with internal code numbers. For example, your reader chooses five music CDs based on an album or artist name from a list. In the Properties dialog box for each item, you enter the recording company's catalog number to facilitate your purchase order process.

Set Properties of a List Box

① Select the list box you want to modify and then choose the List Box Properties command on the Format menu.

② Type a data processing label to identify the list box.

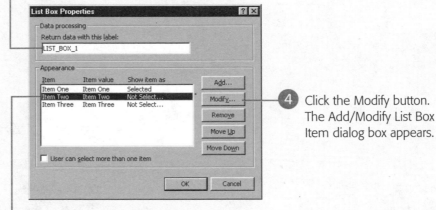

④ Click the Modify button. The Add/Modify List Box Item dialog box appears.

③ Select one of the default items.

⑤ Type a new label for the item. This label will appear in the form.

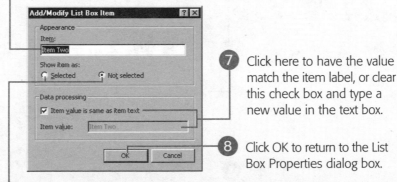

⑦ Click here to have the value match the item label, or clear this check box and type a new value in the text box.

⑧ Click OK to return to the List Box Properties dialog box.

⑥ Choose the default appearance of the list box item button—Selected or Not Selected.

Create a scrollable list box or a drop-down list box. To create a scrollable list box, draw the frame large enough to display two or more item labels. Publisher automatically adds a vertical scroll bar. To create a drop-down list box, draw a small frame that displays only one item label. Publisher automatically adds a drop-down arrow button. These controls won't be functional within your Publisher document but will operate when viewed in a Web browser.

| Alpiine White ▾ |

Drop-down list

| Alpiine White ▲ |
| Burgundy |
| Cranberry ▼ |

Scrollable list box

Set Properties of a List Box *(continued)*

Click to add a new item to the list. The Add/Modify List Box Item dialog box appears.

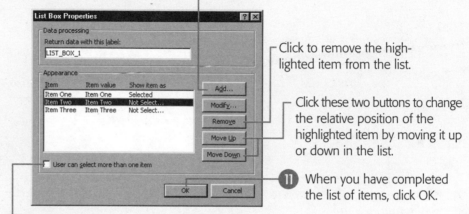

Click to remove the highlighted item from the list.

Click these two buttons to change the relative position of the highlighted item by moving it up or down in the list.

11 When you have completed the list of items, click OK.

9 Click here if you want to enable multiple selections in the list. Leave the item unchecked if you want the reader to select only one item from the list.

10 If necessary, modify, add, or remove other items in the list box.

Set Properties of a Command Button

1 Select the command button you want to modify and then choose the Command Button Properties command on the Format menu.

Why can't I resize a command button? The size of a command button is determined by the length of its label. When you create a command button, the frame is just large enough to contain the default label (either Reset or Submit). You can't change the size of a command button by dragging a resize handle, but you can change the size by typing a new, longer label in the Command Button Properties box.

If I opt to save form data on my Web server, which file format should I choose? Choose a file format based on the method and program you will use to evaluate the reader's responses. For example, if you intend to read the completed form, choose HTML to view the file in your Web browser or Formatted Text to view the file in your word processing program. If you plan to import the completed form into a database, spreadsheet, or forms processing program, choose the Comma-Delimited Text or Tab-Delimited Text format. Delimited text uses a designated character (in this case, either a comma or a tab) to separate the data from each form control object. When you import delimited text into the appropriate program, the data from each form control object is treated as a separate field.

Set Properties of a Command Button (continued)

2 Choose the actual command that will be executed when the reader clicks this button. The Submit button returns the completed form to you. The Reset button clears all of the reader's data and redisplays the default values.

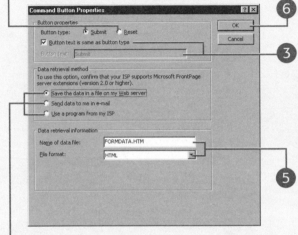

6 Click OK.

3 Check this box to have the button label read either "Submit" or "Reset." To rename the button, clear this check box and type a new label in the text box. The label you type will appear in the form.

5 If this is a Submit button, enter the information needed to complete the data retrieval method you've chosen. This option isn't available for a Reset button.

4 If this is a Submit button, choose a data retrieval method. This option isn't available for a Reset button.

Retrieving the Completed Form

To retrieve a completed form, you must match Publisher's capabilities with the services offered by your ISP (or supported by your Web server software). The information you'll need and the decisions you should make are summarized in the following table.

Retrieval Options for Electronic Forms		
If your Web server or ISP...	**Choose this method...**	**In the Command Button Properties dialog box, enter...**
Supports Microsoft FrontPage Server Extensions 2.0 or later.	Save The Data In A File On My Web Server.	A file name. You must also specify the file format. Publisher can save the data as HTML, Formatted Text, Comma-Delimited Text, or Tab-Delimited Text.
Supports Microsoft FrontPage 98 Server Extensions 3.0 or later.	Send Data To Me In E-Mail.	Your e-mail address. You can also specify the subject of the message.
Doesn't support Microsoft FrontPage Server Extensions.	Use A Program From My ISP.	The URL of the ISP's transfer program. You must also contact your ISP to determine whether you should use the Get or Post transfer method, and if you must insert identifying or handling information (in hidden fields) into the file.

What is JavaScript?

JavaScript is a scripting technology that allows you to add interactive elements to your Web site. JavaScript is commonly used to generate rollover effects, which are images that change appearance in a Web browser when you move the mouse over them or click them. Many Web graphics programs can create JavaScript code for you, which you can then cut and paste into Publisher's HTML Code Fragment dialog box.

JavaScript is only one of several different scripting languages. You can also use Dynamic HTML or Visual Basic scripting to generate special effects, such as pop-up boxes, scrolling text and graphics, or animated objects that appear, disappear, or move around the screen.

Inserting an HTML Code Fragment

When you save or publish a Web page, Publisher automatically generates HTML code. There are certain HTML functions, however, that Publisher can't generate. For example, Publisher can't generate rollover buttons with JavaScript. Nor can Publisher create a hyperlink that jumps to a particular anchor point on a page (Publisher's hyperlinks always jump to the top of a page).

The HTML Code Fragment tool gives you the power to circumvent Publisher's limitations by typing or pasting HTML code into a special dialog box. The following illustration shows you how an HTML code fragment appears in the Publisher document.

```
<script language="JavaScript">
<!-- hide this script from
non-javascript-enabled browsers
// pre-cache 'filename' button
state images
```
— In a Publisher document, the HTML code fragment appears as simple text in a frame. You can't format the text in an HTML Code Fragment object. In this example, JavaScript code creates a rollover button.

— When viewed in a Web browser, a rollover button appears at the location of the HTML Code Fragment frame. This button changes its appearance when a mouse pointer is positioned over it or in response to a mouse click.

Why do I get an error message when I view a Web site containing an HTML code fragment in my browser? Many HTML commands include a URL that refers to an externally stored file. You must include both the correct name of the file *and* its location (or URL) in the HTML Code Fragment Properties dialog box.

HTML supports two kinds of URLs. Absolute URLs show the entire address on the Web, such as *www.domain.com/publish/images/button.gif.* Relative URLs show only a portion of the address, where the location of the file is dependent on the folder of the current Web page. For example, if you have created a folder to hold your images within the folder that holds your Web site, you would type */images/button.gif.* Relative URLs use standard DOS commands: a slash (/) moves you to the next lower folder; two periods (..) move you to the next higher folder. Ask your ISP if you should use absolute or relative URLs when publishing your Web site.

Insert an HTML Code Fragment

1 Click the HTML Code Fragment tool on the Objects toolbar (shown below), and draw a frame where you would like the HTML object to appear. The HTML Code Fragment Properties dialog box appears.

2 Type or paste the HTML code. Publisher doesn't check the code for accuracy, so be sure the spelling and syntax are correct.

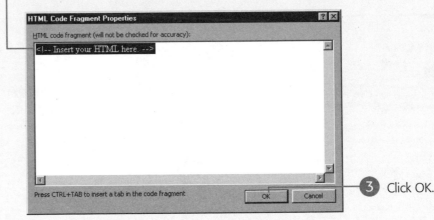

3 Click OK.

To create a preview of your Web site, click the Web Page Preview button on the Standard toolbar.

Press Ctrl-Shift-B to preview a Web site.

Turn On the Preview Troubleshooter. By default, the Preview Troubleshooter doesn't appear on-screen when you preview a Web site. You can, however, instruct Publisher to show the Preview Troubleshooter whenever you preview a Web site. Choose Options on the Tools menu. Click the User Assistance tab, and select the Preview Web Site With Preview Troubleshooter check box.

Previewing a Web Publication

Before you actually publish your Web site on the Internet, you should preview the document on your own system. A preview will reveal any formatting changes Publisher makes to accommodate the limitations of the HTML specification. A preview allows you to test all of the functions you've built into your Web page. For example, you can play sound and video files. You can also follow the hyperlinks to their destinations. Ideally, you should preview the document on a variety of computers to determine if the document looks the same when it is viewed:

- On different platforms, such as a PC and a Mac.

- Using different browsers, such as Microsoft Internet Explorer and Netscape Communicator, or different versions of the same browser, such as Microsoft Internet Explorer 3.0 versus later versions.

- At different resolutions, such as a standard VGA screen and a high-resolution SVGA screen.

- With different numbers of screen colors, such as a 16-color display versus a 256-color or full-color display.

Preview a Web Site

1 Open the Web page you want to preview.

2 On the File menu, select Web Page Preview. If your publication contains more than one page, Publisher displays the Web Page Preview dialog box.

3 Click Web Site to preview all the pages in the publication, or click Current Page to preview only one page of the document.

4 Click OK.

Test your Web site. When you preview your Web site, take the time to carefully explore the document. Use this checklist to be sure that you've examined the document thoroughly.

- Has any of the text changed in appearance?

- Do GIF animations play continuously?

- When clicked, does each multimedia object play properly?

- When clicked, does each hyperlink to another page in your Web site move you to the proper page?

- When clicked, does each hyperlink that contains a URL move you to the appropriate Web site?

- When clicked, do e-mail hyperlinks activate an e-mail application and insert your Internet address?

- When clicked, does each hyperlink that allows readers to download a file find the correct file on your hard disk?

- Can you select check boxes, option buttons, and list items in a form?

- Can you enter text in a single-line or multiline text box in a form?

- When clicked, do the Reset and Submit command buttons perform the correct action?

Preview a Web Site *(continued)*

5 Publisher displays a progress indicator while it converts the .pub file to HTML. Publisher then activates your browser application.

6 Using the functions of your Web browser, explore the HTML document. If you are previewing the entire Web site, you can move from page to page. If you have chosen to preview a single page, hyperlinks to other pages within the site won't work.

7 If you have chosen to use the Preview Troubleshooter, it appears on-screen in a separate window.

Click hyperlinks to move through the various Preview Troubleshooter screens.

Use the scroll bar to review a list of possible problems.

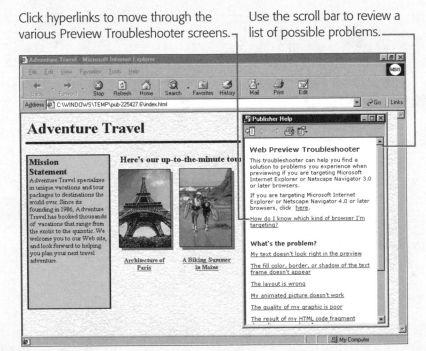

8 Close the browser and Preview Troubleshooter windows to return to Publisher.

What is the difference between previewing a Web site and publishing a Web site? When you preview your Web site, you are viewing the document using a Web browser, but all of the files reside on your local hard disk. When you publish your Web site, you transfer the document and all related files to a Web server that resides on the Internet or an intranet. Anyone with access to the server can access and read your publication.

Use separate folders for each Web site. Publisher alerts you if you attempt to save a Web site to a folder that already contains a Web site. If you proceed, Publisher overwrites existing files and erases the Web site that already resides there. You can, however, use this system to update an existing Web site with new information.

Generating a Web Page

To produce the finished version of a Web publication, Publisher performs the following operations:

- Converts your document to HTML. The first page of the document, or the home page, is normally saved as "Index.html." Subsequent pages are normally saved as "Page2.html," "Page3.html," and so on.

- Exports all imported pictures as either JPEG or GIF files, and all drawn objects and graphic regions as GIF files. Each image is stored in a separate file identified by a number. As an example, a Web site containing two GIF files and one JPEG file would contain Img0.gif, Img1.jpg, and Img2.gif.

- Copies any hyperlinked or externally stored files to the local folder or to the World Wide Web. Files that fall into this category include sound and video files and any files that the reader can download using a hyperlink.

The simplest way to generate a Web page is to save a file in the HTML format to a local folder on your hard disk (or network). However, you must subsequently use Microsoft's Web Publishing Wizard or transfer software provided by your ISP to publish the Web site on the Internet.

Save a Web Page to a Local Folder

1. On the File menu, choose Save As Web Page.
2. In the Save As Web Page dialog box, select a folder where you want to generate the Web site.
3. Click OK.

For more information on the Web Properties dialog box, see "Choosing Web Properties" earlier in this chapter.

Once I have published my Web site, can I update it with new information? You must return to the original .pub file in order to update your Web page. The .pub file contains standard desktop publishing objects, which can be edited. Make your changes using Publisher's standard tools, and then generate a new HTML file using the Publish To Web or Save As Web Page command.

Publishing to an Intranet or to the Web

Before you attempt to publish your Web site, contact your ISP (or your intranet network administrator) to be sure that the following conditions are true:

- You have chosen the correct global parameters for your Web site in the Web Properties dialog box, such as the file naming convention, language character set, and the compatibility level for different browsers.

- Your ISP or the network administrator supplies space on a server where you can store your Web site. ISPs usually make several megabytes available to customers for this purpose.

- You have direct access to an Internet or intranet server and are not accessing it through a proxy server or network gateway.

- You have the appropriate write privileges to be able to save your Web publication on the server.

- You know the correct URL and the name of the folder where you will publish your Web site on the server.

- You know the file transfer protocol required by your ISP or network administrator.

Publisher provides three different ways for you to publish your Web site, as explained in the following table.

Web Publishing Methods		
If...	Use the...	To...
You have saved your Web site to a local folder.	Web Publishing Wizard	Provide requested information, connect to the server, and copy the entire Web site to the designated folder.
Your ISP supports Microsoft FrontPage 97 (or later) server extensions.	Save As Web Page command on the File menu	Convert your document to HTML, and copy all necessary files to a remote Web folder that you have created on your ISP's server.
Your ISP requires you to upload files via FTP (File Transfer Protocol).	Save As Web Page command on the File menu	Convert your document to HTML, and copy all necessary files to a remote FTP location on your ISP's server.

Which file transfer protocols does the Web Publishing Wizard support? The Web Publishing Wizard can transfer files using the FTP, HTTP Post, Microsoft Content Replication System (CRS), or FrontPage Extended Web format. Contact your ISP to learn its preferred protocol.

 How can I access the Web Publishing Wizard? You can access the Web Publishing Wizard in one of two ways:

⊚ On the Windows Start menu, choose either Microsoft Web Publishing or Internet Explorer, then choose Web Publishing Wizard.

⊚ In Windows Explorer, right-click a single file name, a group of files, or an entire folder to display the shortcut menu. Select the Send To command and choose the Web Publishing Wizard from the submenu.

Transfer a Web Site Using the Web Publishing Wizard

1 Begin an online Internet (or intranet) session.

2 On the Windows Start menu, choose either Microsoft Web Publishing or Internet Explorer, then choose Web Publishing Wizard.

3 In the Web Publishing Wizard dialog box, click Next to start the Wizard.

4 Proceed through the dialog boxes, and when prompted, enter information about your Web site, including the location, a descriptive name, and a URL.

5 After the wizard has uploaded the files, end your online session.

What is a Web folder? A Web folder is a shortcut to a location on a Web server.

Why can't I create a Web folder? In order to create a Web folder, your ISP must support Microsoft FrontPage 97 (or later) server extensions. If your ISP does not offer this support, you can publish your Web site using an FTP Location or the Microsoft Web Publishing Wizard.

Publish a Web Site to a Web Folder

① Begin an online Internet or intranet session. If you have already created a Web folder, proceed to step 5.

② To create a Web folder, double-click the My Computer icon on the Windows desktop.

③ Double-click the Web Folders icon, and then double-click the Add Web Folder icon. The Add Web Folder Wizard appears.

④ Proceed through the dialog boxes by entering information when requested, such as the URL of your Web folder. After you have provided the necessary information, your Web folder will appear in the Web Folders list.

⑤ Open your Web publication in Publisher.

⑥ On the File menu, choose Save As Web Page.

⑦ In the Save As Web Page dialog box, click the Web Folders shortcut. In the list box, select the Web folder you created in step 4.

⑧ Click OK.

⑨ After Publisher has saved the Web site to the designated folder, end your online session.

Do I have to be connected to the Internet or an intranet to create an FTP Location? No, you can create an FTP location when you are not connected to the Internet or an intranet. However, if you are offline when you attempt to save a file to an FTP location, Publisher will prompt you to begin an online session.

Alternate access to the Add/Modify FTP Location dialog box. You can also access the Add/Modify FTP Location dialog box from the Open Publication dialog box or the Save As dialog box.

Publish a Web Site to an FTP Location

(1) Begin an online Internet or intranet session.

(2) Open Publisher. Then open your Web publication.

(3) On the File menu, choose Save As Web Page.

(4) If you have already created an FTP location, proceed to step 8. If you want to create an FTP Location, on the File menu, open the Look In drop-down list, and select Add/Modify FTP Location. The Add/Modify FTP Locations dialog box appears.

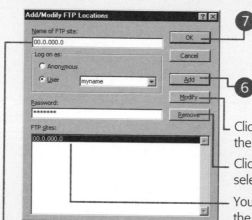

(7) Click OK to return to the Save As Web Page dialog box. The FTP Location will now appear in the Look In drop-down list.

(6) Click Add to enter the location in the FTP Sites list.

Click Modify to update the information for the currently selected FTP location.

Click Remove to delete the currently selected FTP location.

You can select an existing FTP location in the FTP Sites list box.

(5) Enter the information, such as the FTP address, and (optionally) the user name and password that you received from your ISP.

(8) Select the FTP Location you created in step 5 from the Look In drop-down list box.

(9) Click OK.

(10) After Publisher has saved your Web site to the FTP location, end your online session.

Working with Mailing Lists

Direct mail remains a cost-effective way to get your message out to your customers. Microsoft Publisher 2000 provides special tools, known collectively as mail merge, that help you to manage the standard tasks associated with direct, high-volume mailings, such as automatically addressing envelopes or inserting a subscriber's address into a newsletter.

Publisher's mail merge functions require you to create an address list and to insert field codes into your publication. The following illustration diagrams the relationship between these two key components and provides an overview of the mail merge process.

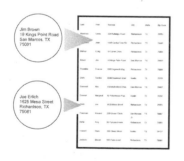

You must connect the Publisher document to the address list.

Jim Brown
19 Kings Point Road
San Marcos, TX 75081

Joe Erlich
1625 Mesa Street
Richardson, TX 75081

The address list contains information that you want to insert in your document. You can create an address list in Publisher or an external application.

A field code inserted into the document points to a category heading (or field) within the address list, such as a first name or a zip code. A field code is always surrounded by double angle brackets (<< >>).

When you merge a document, Publisher replaces the field code with specific information, such as a name or an address.

Can I use Publisher's mail merge feature with electronic Web documents? No. Publisher's mail merge feature works with printed publications only.

 Organize data into discrete fields. When designing your address list, break the information down into small categories, so that each category is a separate field. For example, split city and state information into different fields. You can then search, sort, and filter the information in the address list with greater precision.

 Use the same address list for multiple publications. When you create an address list using Publisher's mail merge functions, you are prompted to save the file to disk. Doing so allows you to create one central address list and then use it over and over for a wide range of projects.

Creating and Modifying an Address List in Publisher

An address list is simply a database of information. Typically, the data will be contact information, such as a name, an address, a telephone number, and perhaps an e-mail address. You can create and modify an address list using database functions built into Publisher.

Create an Address List in Publisher

1 On the Mail Merge menu, choose Create Publisher Address List. The New Address List dialog box appears.

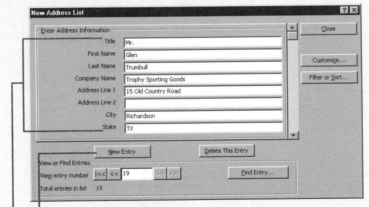

3 Click the New Entry button to have Publisher save the current fields as an entry. Empty field boxes appear for the next entry.

2 Enter the appropriate information in each field, using the scroll bar to move through the fields. You may leave fields blank.

4 Repeat steps 2 and 3 until you have finished adding entries to the address list.

5 Click the Close button to close the address list. The Save As dialog box appears.

Can I work simultaneously on an address list and the Publisher document to which it is attached? If you have created your address list within Publisher, you can modify the list at any time. There is no need to close the current publication in order to access the address list connected to the publication. If, however, you are using an address list created with another program, you must close the publication file before you attempt to edit the address list connected to it.

Why can't Publisher find an entry in the address list? You have misspelled the text phrase in the Find Entry dialog box. Correct the spelling and try again.

Create an Address List in Publisher (continued)

⑥ In the Save As dialog box, choose a location for the address list.

⑦ Enter a filename for the address list.

⑧ Click Save to create the address list. Publisher stores address lists in the Microsoft Access database format with the .mdb extension.

Edit Entries in a Publisher Address List

① On the Mail Merge menu, choose Edit Publisher Address List.

② In the Open Address List dialog box, locate and select the address list you want to modify. Click Open to display the address list dialog box.

③ Locate the entry you want to change.

④ Edit or insert information.

⑤ Click here to save your changes and close the address list.

Click here to delete all of the fields in the current entry.

Click here to search for an entry. In the Find Entry dialog box that appears, type a text phrase. You can search all fields or specify a particular field.

Click the left or right double angle brackets to move to the adjacent entry, or type an entry number in the text box and press Enter. The double angle bracket and bar icon moves you to the first or last entry in the address list.

Trophy dialog box:

Enter Address Information
- First Name: Glen
- Last Name: Trumbull
- Company Name: Trophy Sporting Goods
- Address Line 1: 15 Old Country Road
- Address Line 2:
- City: Richardson
- State: TX
- ZIP Code: 75081

Close | Customize... | Filter or Sort...

New Entry | Delete This Entry

View or Find Entries
View entry number |<< << 19 >> >>|
Total entries in list 20

Find Entry...

Manage existing fields in an address list. You can easily reorganize the fields in an address list, or remove fields you no longer use. By clicking the clearly labeled buttons in the Customize Address List dialog box, you can:

- ⊘ Delete unwanted fields.
- ⊘ Rename a field.
- ⊘ Move a selected field up one position in the list box.
- ⊘ Move a selected field down one position in the list box.

Use Publisher's address list for nonaddress information. Publisher's address list functions just like a traditional database. By adding and modifying fields, you can customize the address list for any kind of information. You could, for example, add a field to identify large corporate customers in order to offer them special volume prices. You might want to keep a list of your customers' birthdays, to offer them a personal discount one day a year.

Add a New Field to a Publisher Address List

① On the Mail Merge menu, choose Create Publisher Address List or Edit Publisher Address List to customize an existing address list.

② If you are customizing an existing address list, the Open Address List dialog box appears. Select the file containing the address list you want to customize, and then click Open.

③ In the address list dialog box, click the Customize button. The Customize Address List dialog box appears.

④ Click a field to select it.

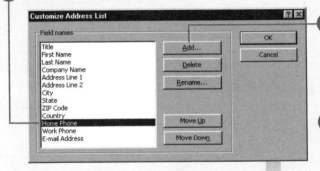

⑤ Click here to add a new field to the address list. The Add Field dialog box appears.

⑧ Click OK to add the field and return to the Customize Address List dialog box.

⑥ Type a name for the new field.

⑦ Specify whether the new field should be before or after the currently selected field.

⑨ Repeat steps 4 through 8 to add more fields to the address list.

⑩ Click OK to save your changes.

Can I use my program to generate an address list even if Publisher doesn't list my database or spreadsheet program in the Open Data Source dialog box? Yes. Publisher accepts external data sources if they are in a standard file format. Generate your address list in a standard file format, such as .xls or .dbf.

 Can I use a text file as an external data source? Yes, you can use a text file as an external data source if the information is organized properly. You must be sure to separate each field from the next with a special character (known as a delimiter), such as a comma or tab.

Connecting a Publication to an Address List or Other Data Source

Before you can use an address list with a Publisher document, you must associate the document with the data source that contains the list. Only one data source can be associated with a publication at any given time. However, you can replace a data source with a new data source at any time. Publisher can access address list data stored in many different formats, as the following table summarizes.

Address List File Formats	
File Extension	**Program**
.dbf	Borland dBASE III, dBASE IV, dBASE 5, Microsoft FoxPro
.mdb	Microsoft Access, Microsoft Publisher address list
.xls	Microsoft Excel
.pab	Microsoft Outlook
.doc	Microsoft Word address list or table
.wdb	Microsoft Works Database
.db	Borland Paradox
.txt, .csv, .tab, .asc	Text files

Connect a Publication to a Data Source

1. On the Mail Merge menu, choose Open Data Source. The Open Data Source dialog box appears.

2. Take one of the following actions:

Create and connect to an address list in one operation. If you choose Create An Address List In Publisher in the first Open Data Source dialog box, Publisher presents you with the New Address List dialog box. When you've finished entering your information, Publisher will ask if you want to merge the information from this address list into the current publication. Click Yes to connect the current publication to the address list.

Why does another dialog box appear when I attempt to connect to an external data source? You are attempting to connect to a database file that contains multiple tables, or a spreadsheet file that contains multiple worksheets. Publisher requires you to choose the specific table or worksheet containing the information you want to merge with your publication. The dialog box that appears may display a list of the various tables contained in a database file. Alternatively, the dialog box may require you to type in the exact name of the worksheet or table.

Connect a Publication to a Data Source *(continued)*

Click here to connect the publication to an address book you've created with Microsoft Outlook.

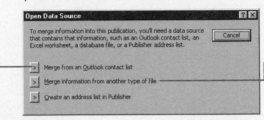

Click here to connect the publication to a compatible database, spreadsheet, or text file.

③ In the second Open Data Source dialog box that appears, use the Look In drop-down list box and the Files list box to locate and select the data source.

④ Click Open to create a connection between the data source and the current publication. The Insert Fields dialog box appears.

⑤ You can insert a field code or you can click Close to return to your document. Even if you click Close without inserting any field codes, the connection between the current publication and the data source remains active, allowing you to insert field codes later in the work session.

Choose a New Data Source

① On the Mail Merge menu, choose Open Data Source. Publisher asks you if you want to replace the currently selected data source with a new data source.

② Click Yes to access the Open Data Source dialog box and choose a new data source. If you have not inserted any field codes in the publication, you can proceed with the mail merge normally. However, if you have inserted field codes that refer to fields that don't exist in the new data source, Publisher won't be able to retrieve information for those field codes. Publisher identifies these field codes by changing the text to read <<Missing mail merge field>>.

Inserting Field Codes into a Publication

A field code is a generic placeholder in your publication. It tells Publisher where to insert information from the address list. In the working view of your publication, field codes are identified by double angle brackets, and they display the name of the field to which they refer, such as <<First Name>>.

Why can't I connect my publication to an external data source? In all likelihood the data source is open. Return to the application in which you created the data source and close the file.

Why is the Insert Field command dimmed? You can't insert a field code until you connect your publication to a data source. After you have used the Open Data Source command to associate the current publication with a data source, the Insert Field command becomes available.

Why does the Insert Fields dialog box remain on-screen after I click the Insert button? Instead of closing, the Insert Fields dialog box simply becomes inactive. It remains on-screen so that you can easily click elsewhere in the document and continue adding additional field codes in new locations. While the Insert Fields dialog box is inactive, you can add text or punctuation to your publication without affecting the field code. Click the Insert Fields dialog box to make it active again.

Insert Field Codes in a Publication

1 Select a text frame in the publication and move the text insertion point where you want the first field code to appear.

2 Choose Insert Field on the Mail Merge menu. The Insert Fields dialog box appears.

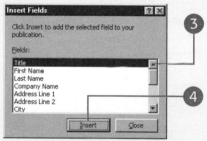

3 Scroll through the list box and select the field code you want to insert.

4 Click Insert to place a field code in your publication.

5 To insert additional field codes, repeat steps 3 and 4.

6 Click Close to exit the Insert Fields dialog box and return to your publication.

7 In your publication, click the field code to select it. Publisher highlights the entire field code.

8 Use Publisher's normal text formatting tools to change the appearance of the field code. You can also Cut, Copy, or Paste the field code.

Why can't I change the text in the field code? It doesn't matter if you are viewing a field code or previewing an entry in a merged publication, you can't change the text using Publisher's standard text editing tools. To edit the field names or the content of a field, you must return to the Publisher address list, or to the external application where you originally created the data source.

Why is Show Merge Results dimmed on the Mail Merge menu? The Show Merge Results command is available only after you have connected your publication to a data source, inserted at least one field code, and issued the Merge command.

Cancel a mail merge operation. If you select Cancel Merge on the Mail Merge menu, Publisher displays an alert box. Click Yes to disconnect the publication from the data source and to convert any field codes in the publication to normal text.

Merging and Previewing a Publication with an Address List or Data Source

Before you can print a mail merge document, you must substitute the address list entries for the field code placeholders. The Merge command accomplishes this task and shows you an on-screen preview of the results. Once you've merged an address list with a publication, you can choose to view the merge results (or the field codes) at any time.

Merge and Preview a Publication with an Address List

1 Choose Merge on the Mail Merge menu. Publisher replaces the field codes with the first entry from your address list and displays the results in the document window. The Preview Data dialog box appears.

2 Use the left and right double angle brackets to move through the entries, or type an entry number in the text box and then press Enter.

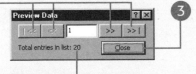

3 When you have finished previewing the merged document, click Close to return to your publication. Publisher replaces the displayed entry with the field code designations.

Publisher displays the total number of entries in the address list.

Toggle the Display of Merge Results and Field Codes

1 Open the Mail Merge menu.

Choose Show Merge Results to open the Preview Data dialog box. The first entry will appear in place of the field codes.

Choose Show Field Codes to close the Preview Data dialog box and once again display generic field codes in the document.

Does sorting or filtering change the contents of the address list? No. Sorting doesn't actually change any of the entries in the address list; it merely changes the order in which entries appear on-screen and print. Likewise, when you apply a filter to an address list, entries aren't deleted. Entries that don't meet the selection criteria are skipped when Publisher merges the address list with the publication.

Why can't I view or print all of the entries in my data source? In all likelihood, you have applied a filter to the data source. You must remove the filter before Publisher can display, preview, or print all the entries in the address list.

Sorting and Filtering Information in an Address List

Publisher provides two powerful capabilities to help you manage address lists: sorting and filtering. Sorting allows you to change the order of entries in the address list, which typically appear in the order in which you type them. For example, you might sort entries alphabetically by last name to locate an item more easily. And you can comply with bulk mailing regulations more easily by sorting and then printing all zip codes sequentially.

Filters allow you to use only a portion of a larger address list. Think of filters as selection criteria. Only the entries that meet the selection criteria will be displayed or printed. One common filtering technique targets specific geographic areas by using entries from a particular city, state, or zip code. You can also create specialized filters. For example, you can filter a mailing by the age or income of the recipient, provided that you created the appropriate fields in the address list.

You can apply up to three different sorting and filtering criteria to an address list. Furthermore, you can apply sorting rules and filters in two different locations—with two different results.

- The address list dialog box lets you sort and filter entries. The results are visible only within the dialog box and don't affect the merge operation.

- The Mail Merge menu lets you sort and filter an address list. The results are visible in your document when you preview the merge on-screen or print the merged publication.

Change the Order of Entries

1 To change the order in which entries are previewed and printed, choose Filter Or Sort on the Mail Merge menu. To change the order in which entries appear within the address list dialog box, click the Filter Or Sort button in the dialog box itself. The Filtering And Sorting dialog box appears.

Mailing Lists

What is the difference between the And and Or choices in the Filtering And Sorting dialog box? If you choose the And operator, entries must meet both criteria to be merged with the document or displayed in the address list dialog box. If you choose the Or operator, entries must meet only one criteria to be merged with the document or displayed in the address list dialog box. For example, if you create a filter in which the City field is equal to Paris *and* the State field is equal to TX, Publisher will find entries for Paris, Texas. But, if you create a filter in which the City field is equal to Paris *or* the State field is equal to TX, Publisher will find entries for Paris, Texas; for all other cities in Texas; for Paris, France; and for all other cities named Paris.

Change the Order of Entries *(continued)*

② Select the Sort tab.

③ Open the drop-down list box and choose a field to sort by.

④ Select Ascending to sort entries from A to Z or from 0 to 9. Select Descending to sort entries from Z to A or from 9 to 0.

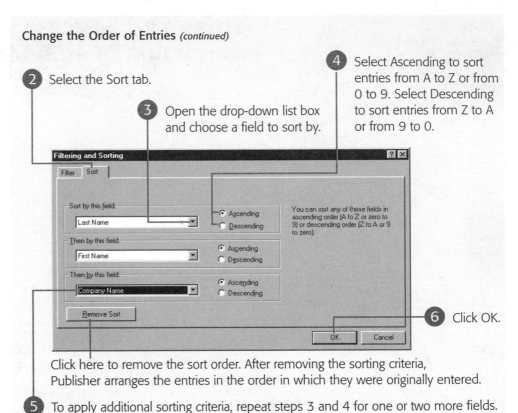

⑥ Click OK.

Click here to remove the sort order. After removing the sorting criteria, Publisher arranges the entries in the order in which they were originally entered.

⑤ To apply additional sorting criteria, repeat steps 3 and 4 for one or two more fields.

Apply a Filter to an Address List

① To merge only selected entries from an address list with a publication, choose Filter Or Sort on the Mail Merge menu. To locate and display specific entries within the address list dialog box, click the Filter Or Sort button in the dialog box itself. The Filtering And Sorting dialog box appears.

Why does Publisher tell me that no entries match my filter criteria when I know there are matching entries? You have probably misspelled the phrase in the Compare To text box. Publisher ignores capitalization but requires you to spell the phrase in the text box exactly as you have spelled it in your data source. For example, a filter won't work if you search for entries in the city of "Ausin" and your data source contains entries for the city of Austin.

 Use filters to proofread entries in an address list. You can check the accuracy of the information in an address list by creating filters that search for potential problems. For example, if you want to find incomplete mailing addresses, create a filter where the zip code field is equal to an empty Compare To field.

Apply a Filter to an Address List *(continued)*

2 Select the Filter tab.

3 Open the drop-down list box and choose a field that will be part of the filter criteria.

4 Choose one of the four comparison phrases: Is Equal To, Is Not Equal To, Is Less Than, or Is Greater Than.

5 Type a text phrase or a number to be compared to the contents of the Field box.

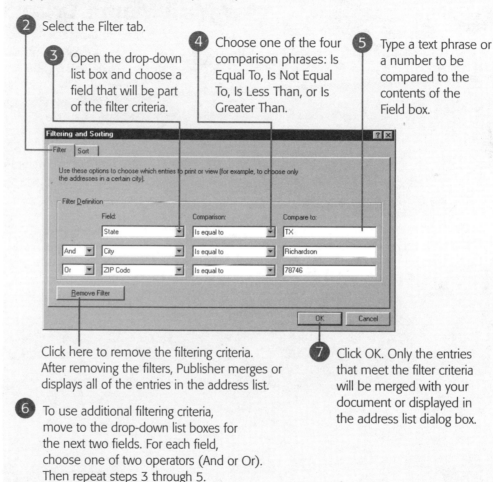

Click here to remove the filtering criteria. After removing the filters, Publisher merges or displays all of the entries in the address list.

6 To use additional filtering criteria, move to the drop-down list boxes for the next two fields. For each field, choose one of two operators (And or Or). Then repeat steps 3 through 5.

7 Click OK. Only the entries that meet the filter criteria will be merged with your document or displayed in the address list dialog box.

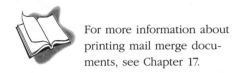

For more information about printing mail merge documents, see Chapter 17.

Printing Considerations for Mail Merge Documents

When you output a mail merge document, Publisher replaces the Print command with the Print Merge command. Publisher's Print Merge command helps you generate mail merge documents more efficiently by offering specialized functions that allow you to do the following:

ⓠ   Print a test to be sure that the mail merge is working properly.

ⓠ   Specify a range of entries (rather than a page range) for printing.

ⓠ   Specify where on a sheet of labels Publisher should begin printing. For example, if you've already used two rows of labels, you can begin printing at the third row.

14

Wizards, Design Gallery, and Templates

Microsoft Publisher 2000 offers powerful tools, in the form of wizards and the Design Gallery, that quite literally automate the design process. Wizards are interactive programs that allow you to choose the layout options that Publisher uses to assemble documents. The Design Gallery contains a wide variety of fully formatted objects that can add a professional touch to your documents at the click of a button.

Two technologies, Smart Objects and synchronization, make it equally easy to change a publication. Smart Objects are design elements that you create with a wizard or the Design Gallery. Unlike standard text and picture frames, Smart Objects remain linked to a wizard. Modifying a Smart Object is as simple as asking the wizard for help. Synchronization links similar objects within the current publication to each other. Making a change to one synchronized object automatically updates the other synchronized elements.

Once you've created a document, either with a wizard or from scratch, you can reuse it easily by saving it as a template. Templates allow you to build new publications on the solid foundation of an existing design.

What kinds of publications can I create with a wizard?

The Publications By Wizard tab in the Catalog dialog box contains the following publication types:

- 6 advertisements
- 4 airplanes
- 14 award certificates
- 40 banners
- 71 brochures
- 29 business cards
- 200 business forms
- 27 calendars
- 20 catalogs
- 29 envelopes
- 81 flyers
- 20 gift certificates
- 91 greeting cards
- 64 invitation cards
- 52 labels
- 29 letterheads
- 12 menus
- 34 newsletters
- 4 origami designs
- 105 postcards
- 3 programs
- 51 quick publications
- 28 signs
- 45 Web sites
- 20 "With compliments" cards

Creating a Publication with a Wizard

You first encounter Publisher's wizards when you begin a new document, where options in the Catalog dialog box allow you to start a wizard in order to create an entire document. You can access the same wizard you used to create the publication in order to modify its layout at any time.

Publisher comes with wizards to create hundreds of different documents. To help you locate a specific wizard more quickly, Publisher organizes the wizards in two different ways.

- Publications By Wizard groups the same type of publication together. As an example, Newsletters constitute one group.

- Publications By Design groups the same design styles together. As an example, the Arcs group (under the Master Sets heading) includes a newsletter, a flyer, a brochure, and a Web site that all share a look.

The publications created with wizards vary dramatically in both content and complexity. This variety is reflected in the questions that the wizard poses as you move through the creation process. For example, the Newsletter Wizard asks you how many columns of text you want on each page. This question would be inappropriate for a calendar. Instead, the Calendar Wizard asks whether you want to create a monthly or yearly calendar.

Publisher lets you control how the wizards work. You can choose to have the wizards ask you specific questions or present you with a checklist of options. You can even opt to have a wizard available when you start a blank publication.

Why would I want to create a blank document with the Quick Publication Wizard? The Quick Publication Wizard automates basic tasks associated with setting up a publication, such as choosing a color scheme or changing the page orientation. It also can create decorative backgrounds and simple layouts.

Choose Wizard Functions

1 On the Tools menu, select Options.

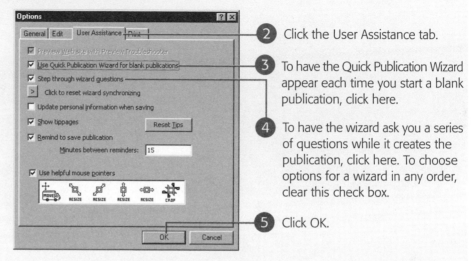

2 Click the User Assistance tab.

3 To have the Quick Publication Wizard appear each time you start a blank publication, click here.

4 To have the wizard ask you a series of questions while it creates the publication, click here. To choose options for a wizard in any order, clear this check box.

5 Click OK.

Create a New Publication with a Wizard

1 Access the Catalog dialog box by starting Publisher or by choosing New on the File menu.

2 Select either the Publications By Wizard tab or the Publications By Design tab.

A circle indicates that there are no subcategories in a group.

A triangle indicates that there are subcategories in a group. Click the triangle to show or hide the subcategories.

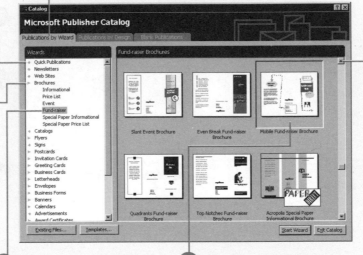

4 Scroll through the publication types (represented by detailed thumbnail sketches), and decide which one you want to use.

3 Select a category from the list of available wizards.

5 Double-click the thumbnail, or single-click the thumbnail and then click Start Wizard. If you have chosen to answer a series of questions, Publisher displays the document in the workspace and simultaneously displays the step-by-step wizard in a special window along the left side of the screen.

Choose the printer before you start the wizard. Wizards assume that you will use the default printer already designated in the Windows Control Panel. If you create a publication using a wizard and then change printers in the Print Setup dialog box (accessed from the File menu), your publication might not print correctly. If you want to change to a different printer, be sure to do so before you start the wizard.

For more information about how to change the default printer, see Chapter 17.

Create a New Publication with a Wizard *(continued)*

6 Make a choice (or enter text) in response to the wizard's question.

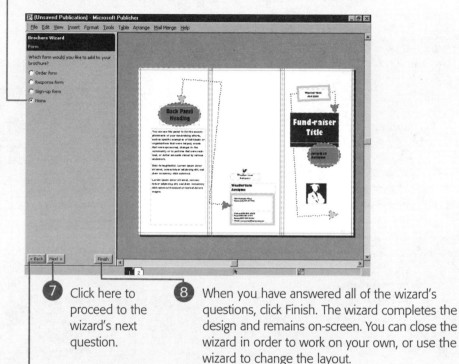

7 Click here to proceed to the wizard's next question.

8 When you have answered all of the wizard's questions, click Finish. The wizard completes the design and remains on-screen. You can close the wizard in order to work on your own, or use the wizard to change the layout.

Click here to return to the previous question in order to review or change your answer.

Why doesn't the wizard ask me step-by-step questions as it creates the publication? You have turned off the Step Through Wizard Questions option on the User Assistance tab in the Options dialog box. When this check box is cleared, Publisher creates the document using default settings. However, you can still use the wizard to modify the layout.

 When should I choose the Publications By Design tab in the Catalog dialog box? You should choose the Publications By Design option when you want to create multiple documents with a single design theme. For example, you can create a consistent company identity by using the same design motif for your printed correspondence (letterhead, business card, and envelope), your company newsletter, and your promotional publications (such as a flyer or brochure).

Modify a Publication Created with a Wizard

1 If the wizard isn't displayed, open the View menu and select Show Wizard. Alternatively, click the Show Wizard button, located at the lower left corner of the work area. The wizard appears in a separate window at the left side of the screen.

2 Select the aspect of the layout that you would like to change.

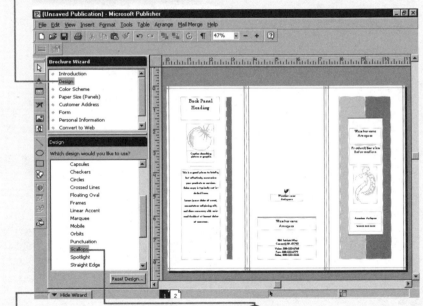

5 When you are satisfied with your modifications, click the Hide Wizard button (or select Hide Wizard on the View menu).

3 Answer the wizard's question by choosing a new option, typing new information, or executing a command.

4 If you would like to change other aspects of the layout, repeat steps 2 and 3.

Why isn't the Show Wizard command available? You are working in a publication that you created from scratch using the Blank Page option on the User Assistance tab in the Catalog dialog box and you have turned off the Use Quick Publication Wizard For Blank Publications option on the User Assistance tab in the Options dialog box. To activate this feature, follow the instructions in the procedure "Choose Wizard Functions" earlier in this chapter.

Can I modify individual elements within a publication? Yes. You must first determine whether the element you want to modify is a standard text or picture frame or a Smart Object. You can use Publisher's standard formatting tools to modify text and picture frames and to insert text and pictures into a Smart Object. You must, however, use a wizard to modify the appearance of a Smart Object.

Why isn't the Reset Design button available? The Reset Design button is available only when you have selected the Design item in the wizard window.

Remove Modifications You've Made to a Publication Created with a Wizard

① If the wizard isn't displayed, select Show Wizard from the View menu. Alternatively, click the Show Wizard button, located at the lower left corner of the work area. The wizard appears in a separate window at the left side of the screen.

② In the wizard window, select the Design option.

③ Click the Reset Design button, shown below. The Reset Design dialog box appears.

④ Choose some or all of the options in the dialog box.

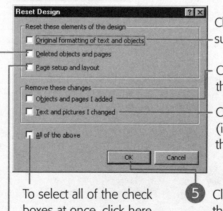

Click here to restore formatting attributes, such as font choice and color scheme.

Click here to remove pages or objects that you added to the original layout.

Click here to remove all of the content (including text, pictures, and hyperlinks) that you added to the publication.

To select all of the check boxes at once, click here.

⑤ Click OK to reset the selected items.

Click here to return pages and objects to their original sizes, orientation, and positions.

Click here to restore objects or pages that you deleted from the original layout. The default text, pictures, and hyperlinks are restored. This command also reestablishes the text frame links, text wrap options, and picture cropping in the original layout.

What kinds of elements can I insert from the Design Gallery? Your choices in the Design Gallery, which are listed below, change depending upon whether you are working with a print publication or a Web site.

- 11 accents for barbells, boxes, checkerboards, and dots
- 33 accent styles for accent boxes, accessory bars, borders, linear accents, marquees, and punctuation
- 6 advertisements
- 36 attention getters
- 23 calendars
- 3 coupons
- 10 logos
- 1 phone tear-off
- 8 picture captions
- 34 print or 45 Web mastheads
- 34 print or 15 Web pull quotes
- 9 print or 3 Web reply forms
- 34 print or 15 Web sidebars
- 34 tables of contents or 45 Web navigation bars
- 30 Web buttons

Using the Design Gallery

You can think of the elements in Publisher's Design Gallery as the building blocks of a publication. You can create an entire layout by selecting and combining elements from the Design Gallery, or you can use one or two elements to enhance a publication that you design from scratch. Publisher's Design Gallery contains hundreds of fully formatted elements, and most of them are composed of Smart Objects. To help you locate a specific element more quickly, Publisher organizes the Design Gallery in two different ways.

- Objects By Category groups the same type of publication together. As an example, Calendars constitute one group.

- Objects By Design groups the same design styles together. As an example, the Capsules group includes a masthead, a calendar, a pull quote, and a sidebar that all share a look.

You can customize the Design Gallery by adding your own creations to it. Elements that you add to the Design Gallery are composed of standard objects, including drawn shapes, text, pictures, and table frames. Unlike Smart Objects, custom Design Gallery elements don't have special functions attached to them, nor can you modify them with a wizard.

Insert a Design Gallery Object in a Publication

 Click the Design Gallery Object tool or choose Design Gallery Object on the Insert menu. The Design Gallery dialog box appears.

Use design motifs consistently throughout a publication. The name of each element in the Design Gallery refers to a design motif, such as Arcs or Marble. Using elements with the same design motif guarantees that objects "match," or complement, one another throughout your publication.

Insert a Design Gallery Object in a Publication *(continued)*

2 Click either the Objects By Category tab or the Objects By Design tab. If you added custom objects to the Design Gallery, you can access them by clicking the Your Objects tab.

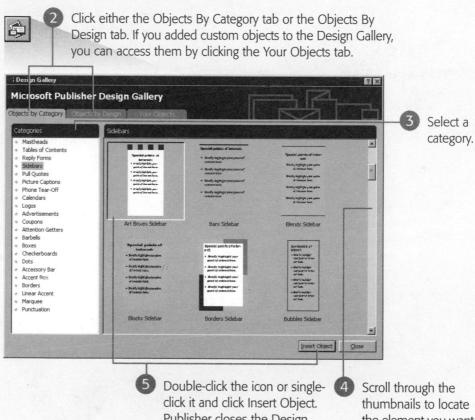

3 Select a category.

5 Double-click the icon or single-click it and click Insert Object. Publisher closes the Design Gallery window and inserts the object in the center of the screen.

4 Scroll through the thumbnails to locate the element you want to use.

Can I add more than one object at a time to the Design Gallery? Yes, you can perform a multiple selection and add several objects to the Design Gallery simultaneously. However, Publisher adds the multiple selection to the Design Gallery as a single grouped object, not as a series of individual objects.

Customizing the Design Gallery

You can customize the Design Gallery by adding to it elements that you have created. When you add an object or a group to the Design Gallery, Publisher saves it with the current publication only. You can use it over and over again in the current publication. But if you want access to the same custom object in more than one publication, you must either copy the object from document to document using the Clipboard or import the object from the publication in which you originally saved it.

You can identify the objects you add to the Design Gallery with names, organize them into categories, and delete them when they are no longer needed.

Add a Custom Object to the Design Gallery

① Select the object you want to add to the Design Gallery.

② Choose Add Selection To Design Gallery on the Insert menu. Alternatively, click the Design Gallery Object tool, select the Your Objects tab, click the Options button, and then select Add Selection To Design Gallery. The Add Object dialog box appears.

③ Type an object name.

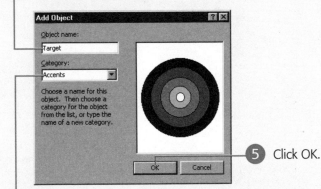

⑤ Click OK.

④ Type a category name. If you have previously added objects to the Design Gallery, open the drop-down list and choose a category.

Why can't I see the custom Design Gallery objects for the current publication in the Design Gallery dialog box? You have used the Browse button to view custom Design Gallery objects saved with other publications. If you want to see the custom Design Gallery objects saved with the current publication, click the Options button and then choose View Gallery For Current Publication from the submenu.

Import Design Gallery Objects from Other Publications

1. Open the publication to which you want to add custom Design Gallery objects.

2. Click the Design Gallery Object tool on the Objects toolbar, or choose Design Gallery Object on the Insert menu. The Design Gallery dialog box appears.

3. In the Design Gallery dialog box, click the Your Objects tab.

4. Click the Options button that appears at the tab's lower left corner. Then choose Browse on the menu. The Other Designs dialog box appears.

5. Locate the file containing the custom objects you want to copy.

6. Highlight the file name.

7. Click OK. All the custom objects, along with their names and category designations, are copied to the Design Gallery associated with the current publication.

8. Save the current publication to make the changes permanent.

Rename, Delete, or Create a Category in the Design Gallery

1. Open the publication that contains the category you want to modify.

2. Click the Design Gallery Object tool on the Objects toolbar, or choose Design Gallery Object on the Insert menu. The Design Gallery dialog box appears.

3. Click the Your Objects tab.

4. Click the Options button and then choose Edit Categories from the submenu.

Use the shortcut menu to modify the Design Gallery. You can delete, rename, and create categories directly from the Design Gallery dialog box. In the Categories list box, right-click the category you want to modify. On the shortcut menu, choose the appropriate command.

Rename, Delete, or Create a Category in the Design Gallery *(continued)*

5 If you want to delete or rename a category, select it.

6 Do one of the following:

Click here to create a new category. In the Create New Category dialog box, type a name and then click OK.

Click here to rename the selected category. In the Rename Category dialog box, type a new name and then click OK.

Click here to delete the selected category. In the confirmation dialog box that appears, click Yes.

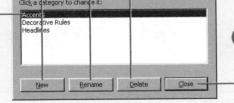

7 Click Close in the Edit Categories dialog box, and then click Close in the Design Gallery dialog box to return to your publication.

8 Save the publication to make the changes permanent.

Delete or Rename Objects in the Design Gallery

1 Open the publication that contains the Design Gallery object you want to delete or rename.

2 Click the Design Gallery Object tool on the Objects toolbar or choose Design Gallery Object on the Insert menu. The Design Gallery dialog box appears.

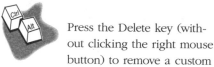 Press the Delete key (without clicking the right mouse button) to remove a custom object from the Design Gallery. In the confirmation dialog box, click Yes.

Delete or Rename Objects in the Design Gallery *(continued)*

3 Click the Your Objects tab.

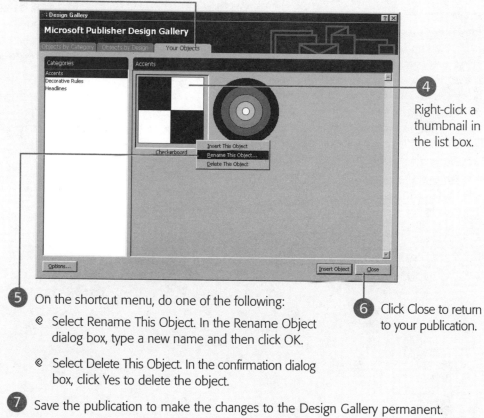

4 Right-click a thumbnail in the list box.

5 On the shortcut menu, do one of the following:

❧ Select Rename This Object. In the Rename Object dialog box, type a new name and then click OK.

❧ Select Delete This Object. In the confirmation dialog box, click Yes to delete the object.

6 Click Close to return to your publication.

7 Save the publication to make the changes to the Design Gallery permanent.

Convert a Smart Object to standard text and picture frames. If you want to alter the relative size, position, rotation, layering, or alignment of the objects within a Smart Object, you can convert the Smart Object to standard text and picture frames. Select the Smart Object and choose Ungroup Objects from the Arrange menu. Publisher displays an alert box warning that you will no longer be able to change the design of the Smart Object with the wizard. Click Yes to proceed with the conversion.

Using Smart Object Wizards

Many of the publications that you create using a wizard contain Smart Objects. In addition, most of the elements in Publisher's Design Gallery are Smart Objects. On the simplest level, a Smart Object is a group of text, table, and picture frames. In order to add your own content, you select an individual frame within the Smart Object and type text or insert a picture. You can also select individual elements and change the object's formatting attributes using Publisher's standard tools. For example, you can change the font used in a text frame or recolor a picture.

Smart Objects, however, are not ordinary groups. As shown in the following illustration, Smart Objects don't display a group button. Instead they display a Wizard button, which you can click to open the associated wizard and change the design of the Smart Object.

You can select individual objects within a group, such as the picture shown here.

You can select individual objects within a Smart Object.

Standard groups are identified by a Group button.

Smart Objects are identified by the Wizard button. Click the button to open the associated wizard.

Use the Format Painter to copy attributes from Smart Objects to standard text and picture frames. If you've already inserted a Smart Object into your document, you can use the Format Painter to copy its attributes to other objects in the document. Using the Format Painter allows you to choose which formats you copy. For example, you can select a drawn object in order to copy its fill color and border width to another object. Here's how—select the individual element within the Smart Object whose formats you want to copy. Click the Format Painter tool on the Standard toolbar. Then using the Paintbrush pointer click the object you want to reformat.

 Can I resize, move, rotate, or change the layering and alignment of individual elements within a Smart Object? No. You can use Publisher's standard tools to change the size, position, rotation, layering, or alignment of a Smart Object, but Publisher applies the changes to the entire Smart Object. For example, if you use the Send To Back command, Publisher sends the entire Smart Object to the bottom of the stack. Within the Smart Object itself, the layering of the individual elements remains unchanged.

Use a Wizard to Modify a Smart Object

1 Select the Smart Object you want to change.

2 Click the Wizard button, found along the lower right edge of the Smart Object. The Wizard dialog box appears.

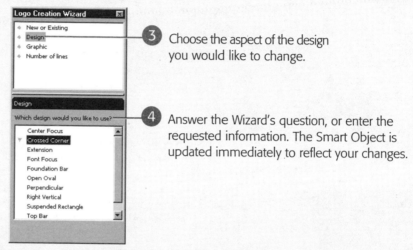

3 Choose the aspect of the design you would like to change.

4 Answer the Wizard's question, or enter the requested information. The Smart Object is updated immediately to reflect your changes.

5 When you are satisfied with your changes, click the Close button on the wizard's title bar.

Understanding Synchronization

Certain elements should be consistent throughout a document. For example, your logo, which may appear several times within a promotional brochure or company newsletter, should be identical each time it occurs. Publisher makes it easier to maintain consistency by synchronizing certain kinds of objects. Synchronized objects are linked to one another within the current publication. If you change one instance of a synchronized object, the change ripples through to all the other linked instances. To use the previous example, if you change the font of a logo,

**Synchronize colors
using a color scheme.**
Publisher 2000 lets you
manage the colors in your document
using a color scheme (a defined set of
colors). Any object in a document (not
just a synchronized object) that has
been formatted with a color from a color
scheme is updated automatically whenever you change the scheme.

For more information on
Publisher's color schemes,
see Chapter 15.

Publisher automatically changes all the copies of the logo to match your font choice
(provided you created the logo with a wizard).

Synchronization is always under your control. You can turn synchronization
on or off for a group of synchronized objects within the current publication. You
can't synchronize objects across different publications. Nor can you update only
a single object within a group of synchronized objects.

In some cases, Publisher updates the content of an object but not the formatting, or the formatting but not the content. Though it may seem confusing at first,
there is an inherent logic to this approach. For example, Publisher always updates
the content of a Personal Information component, because your name, address,
and phone number shouldn't vary from page to page. But because Publisher
doesn't update the formatting of a Personal Information component, you can
change the font on an individual basis to match the surrounding text. The table
below summarizes the types of objects Publisher can synchronize and the ways
in which Publisher implements synchronization.

A Summary of Synchronized Elements			
If you created...	**Using...**	**Publisher synchronizes...**	**In these locations...**
A logo	The Personal Information command on the Insert menu.	The content of text and picture frames and all formatting attributes.	All copies of the logo on all the pages in the current publication.
A Personal Information component	A wizard or the Personal Information command on the Insert Menu.	The content of the text frame but not the formatting attributes of the text.	On all the pages in the current document where the Personal Information component appears.
A multi-page, yearly calendar	A wizard	The formatting attributes of the names of the months, days of the week, and dates.	On all the pages in the current publication.

A Summary of Synchronized Elements *(continued)*

If you created...	Using...	Publisher synchronizes...	In these locations...
Phone tear-offs	A wizard or the Design Gallery	The content of the text frames, as well as formatting attributes applied to the entire text object.	Subsequent instances of the phone tear-off within the Smart Object. Publisher won't update other copies of the Smart Object within the publication.
A running header and footer in a newsletter	A wizard	The content of the text frames but not the formatting attributes.	All copies of the header and footer on all pages within the current document.
Web navigation bars	A wizard or the Design Gallery	The content of the text and picture frames but not the formatting attributes.	All copies of the navigation bar on all pages in the current Web site.
Graphic accents (such as barbells, boxes, checkerboards, and dots)	A wizard or the Design Gallery	The formatting attributes.	Subsequent instances of the drawn shape within the Smart Object only. For example, if you change the color of one dot, all other dots in the selected object will change. However, Publisher doesn't update other copies of the graphic accent within the publication.
Accent Styles (including accent boxes, accessory bars, borders, linear accents, marquees, and punctuation)	A wizard or the Design Gallery	The formatting attributes.	All instances of the drawn shape throughout the document and all object types that share a style, such as a masthead or a pull quote.

Edit a Synchronized Element

1. Select the synchronized element you want to change.

2. Edit the synchronized object, either by entering new text, inserting a new picture, or changing the formatting attributes.

3. Click away from the object. Publisher applies the changes you've made to all instances of the synchronized object.

Automatically update hyperlinks in a Web site navigation bar. The navigation bar in a Web site is an electronic table of contents; it contains hyperlinks that move a reader from page to page.

You can have Publisher track the pages in your Web site and automatically add (or remove) entries in the navigation bar when you add or remove pages. Move to the page to which you want to add the navigation bar. Choose Web Properties on the File menu. In the Web Properties dialog box, click the Page tab. Click Add Hyperlink To Web Navigation Bar and then click OK.

 Why haven't my changes been synchronized with other similar elements in my publication? There are several reasons why Publisher may not be synchronizing your changes.

- You may not have clicked away from the object you edited.

- You are working with an object that can't be synchronized, such as a standard text, picture, or table frame.

- You have turned off synchronization.

Turn Off Synchronization

① Select a synchronized object.

② Change the object's text content, picture content, or formatting attributes. Then click away from the object. Publisher updates all synchronized objects.

③ Choose Undo Synchronize on the Edit menu. Publisher changes all of the synchronized objects back to their previous state. These elements remain unsynchronized until you once again activate synchronization.

Note that other object types that remain synchronized continue to be updated automatically whenever you make a change. For example, when you turn off synchronization for a Web navigation bar, it doesn't affect synchronization for any Personal Information components that may be in your document.

Turn On Synchronization

① Choose Options on the Tools menu.

② Click the User Assistance Tab.

③ Click the button labeled Click To Reset Wizard Synchronizing.

④ Click OK. The next time you modify a synchronized object, Publisher applies the change to all other instances of that element.

Why can't I find the Undo Synchronize command on the Edit menu? You are attempting to turn off synchronization for a Personal Information component. The command reads, "Undo Propagate Personal Information." Though the language is different, the effect is identical to the Undo Synchronize command.

Learn by example. Taking apart a group of objects created with a wizard or the Design Gallery can teach you quite a lot about design, such as how to combine text, table, and picture elements. After you've dismantled the design, you can simply discard it because it can be recreated easily.

For information about page setup and layout guides, see Chapters 2 and 3.

Align guides to objects. You'll find it easier to align guides with existing frames if you turn off Snap To Ruler Marks and Snap To Guides, but turn *on* Snap To Objects.

Modifying Wizard Publications and Smart Objects

Using a wizard to create a publication or inserting an object from the Design Gallery can jump-start your design process. However, you will probably need to modify your document's layout using Publisher's standard text, table, picture, and WordArt tools. Before you start importing text and pictures, take a few moments to analyze—and optimize—the publication.

Layout Issues

Publisher's wizards don't generate an underlying structure for a document. They don't set up layout guides and they don't place repeating elements on the background. You can make the publications easier to modify if you:

- Confirm which Publication Layout, Paper Size, and Orientation options have been selected in the Page Setup dialog box. For example, if the Normal layout option has been selected, the actual page size of the publication will vary depending on the size of the paper set for your printer.

- Create layout guides or ruler guides based on the wizard's design. If you subsequently decide to rearrange the elements in the layout, you'll be able to move and align them with precision.

- Select objects such as page numbers or headers and footers, and select the Send To Background command on the Arrange menu.

Object Attributes

Identifying an element properly can help you edit it more efficiently. Click each object in the layout and note the following:

- Determine whether it is a Smart Object or a standard text, table, picture, WordArt, or drawn object. For example, if you identify a logo design as a Smart Object, you know you can change the design using a wizard.

@ Determine whether a particular design element is composed of one object with complex formatting or of multiple objects. It's much easier to edit a single text frame with attributes for borders, object color, and shadow than it is to edit a group consisting of a text frame, a tinted rectangle, and several lines.

Type Styles

Wizards and Design Gallery objects don't contain defined type styles; instead, they contain preformatted text frames. If you type your copy, Publisher preserves the formatting attributes of the wizard or Design Gallery object. However, if you import copy and your word processing file contains type styles, Publisher attempts to replace the formatting attributes of the wizard or Design Gallery object with the imported type formatting attributes.

In order to preserve the text formatting in wizard publications or Design Gallery objects, take the following actions before you type or import copy:

@ Analyze the design to identify potential text styles, such as body copy, headlines, subheads, table of contents entries, or captions.

@ Select the preformatted text and use the Create Style By Example dialog box to save (and reuse) the text formatting attributes.

Fonts

For more information on creating a text style by example, see Chapter 6. For more information about text frames, see Chapter 4.

Publisher's wizards and the Design Gallery use standard TrueType fonts that ship with Windows or Publisher. You should change the selected font if any of these statements are true:

@ The font doesn't complement other text objects in your document.

@ The font doesn't appeal to you aesthetically.

@ You've deleted fonts from your system, and the wizard or Design Gallery object uses a font that is no longer installed on your computer.

@ You are creating a Web site, which shouldn't contain unusual fonts.

Text Flow

When you import text into a preformatted document, it flows through all the connected text frames. To control the text flow process, you should:

- Locate all of the connected text frames in the publication by clicking the Frame Jump buttons that appear at the upper left or lower right corner of a selected text frame.

- Disconnect the text frames before you import the text. Then reconnect the frames as needed to handle text overflow.

Object Organization

Elements inserted from the Design Gallery are often Smart Objects. Publications created with wizards can contain Smart Objects or groups.

- You can resize and reposition all of the elements in a group or a Smart Object simultaneously without ungrouping them.

- If you want to change the size, position, rotation, or stacking order of an individual element within a group or Smart Object, you must first ungroup the objects or the Smart Object.

- You can change the content and formatting of an individual element within a group or Smart Object without ungrouping or converting it. Simply click the individual object to select it.

Templates

A template is like a standard Publisher document, with one important difference—when you open a template file, Publisher opens a copy of the template for your use and leaves the original template file undisturbed.

Publisher's template feature is a powerful tool that allows you to save your own custom designs for reuse. For example, you can save a customized letterhead as a template. Then, whenever you write a letter, you can start with a clean document

Why can't I find a Templates tab in the Catalog dialog box or a Template folder on my hard disk? Publisher doesn't list templates on a separate tab in the Catalog. Instead, you access templates by clicking the Templates button on either the Publications By Wizard tab or the Publications By Design tab in the Catalog. If you are installing Publisher for the first time, no templates exist. Publisher automatically creates a Templates folder the first time you save a publication as a template.

Where should I store my template? Don't worry about the Save In drop-down list box or the Files list box. When Publisher saves a document as a template, it always stores the file in a specially designated Templates folder.

(equivalent to a fresh piece of stationery) with your logo, your company address, and predefined type styles for the body of the letter.

You can also use Publisher's template feature to modify the working environment. Before you save a template, change the settings (called the defaults) for many of Publisher's tools, including the layout guides, default unit of measure, and frame attributes for text, picture, table, and drawn objects. For example, you could create a flowchart template where lines are automatically created with arrowheads and the layout guides have been set up as a .25-inch drawing grid.

Save a Publication as a Template

1. Choose Save As on the File menu. The Save As dialog box appears.

2. Type a meaningful name for the document that does not duplicate the name of an existing template. For example, "Letterhead" could identify your company stationery. (Don't type a file extension; the extension ".pub" is added automatically.)

3. Open the Save As Type drop-down list and select Publisher Template (*.pub).

4. Click Save. Now when you look through the list of available templates, your template appears in the list in alphabetical order.

Create a Document Based on a Template

1. Click New on the File menu.

2. In the Catalog, click the Publications By Wizard or Publications By Design tab and then click the Templates button.

3. Use the Open Template dialog box to locate the template you want to use as a basis for the current publication.

4. Click Open. Publisher opens a copy of the template as an Unsaved Publication.

Can I modify Publisher's working environment without saving a template? Yes, you can change the defaults for many of Publisher's tools in a standard document. However, the changes you make remain in effect only for the current work session or for the current document. The next time you open Publisher or start a new publication, the application reverts to the original "factory settings."

Change Publisher's Default Settings

1 Open a new blank publication.

2 Change any of the following settings:

    Page setup, including paper size and orientation, and the publication layout

    Layout guides for page margins and column/row division

    Ruler guides

    The default unit of measurement

    Text frame properties, including fill color, line and border style, shadow, frame margins, and text columns

    Picture frame properties, including fill color, line and border style, shadow, and picture frame margins

    Table frame properties, including fill color, line and border style, shadow, and table cell margins

    Drawn shape properties, including fill color, line and border style, shadow, and (in the case of lines) dashes and arrowheads

3 Save the document as a template.

4 Close the publication. Publisher uses the new settings for all of the future publications you create based on the template.

Color and Fill Effects

Microsoft Publisher 2000's color functions, including a full range of color models, Color Schemes, and the Microsoft Image Color Matching (ICM) system, can help you to choose colors that are aesthetically pleasing and that look good on-screen or in print. In addition, fill effects—such as tints, shades, patterns, or gradients—can help you to add variety to a design without adding more colors.

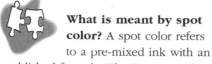

What is meant by spot color? A spot color refers to a pre-mixed ink with an established formula. The Pantone color matching system, for example, contains standardized colors that are referred to by number, such as 320 CVC. Traditionally, spot colors are applied only to small areas—spots—to accent a basically black-and-white design. A spot color document is often referred to as a two-color (or less frequently a three-color) document. It contains only black and one or two accent colors.

Color Models

Publisher supports four different color models: RGB, CMYK, HSL, and the Pantone color matching system. Each color model is uniquely suited to a particular type of output.

@ The RGB and HSL color models are best used for Web documents. They can be used for locally printed paper-based documents, especially if color matching isn't crucial.

@ The CMYK color model is ideal for full-color documents printed on paper, especially when color matching is important. It's suitable for both desktop printers and for projects that are ultimately sent to commercial printing services.

@ The Pantone Solid color matching system is used for spot color documents that are sent to commercial printing services. The Pantone Process color matching system is used for CMYK documents that are sent to commercial printing services.

Each color model also has it own unique way of describing color, as explained in the following table:

Comparison of Color Models			
Color Model	**Associated Hardware**	**Primary Colors**	**Number of Available Colors**
RGB	Color monitors and scanners.	Red, green, and blue pixels in values ranging from 0 (for pure black) through 255 (for full color intensity).	Up to 16.7 million colors. The RGB color system can simulate CMYK colors when images are displayed on-screen.
CMYK	Desktop printers and four-color process commercial printing presses.	Cyan, magenta, yellow, and black in values ranging from 0 through 100 percent.	Color printers vary widely in resolution and consequently in the number of colors they can produce. Color printers can reproduce only a small subset of the RGB spectrum.
HSL	None. HSL mimics the way in which artists mix paints.	Hue in values from 0 through 359. Saturation in values from 0 (for pure gray) through 100 (for full saturation). Luminescence in values from 0 (black) through 100 (white).	Up to 16.7 million colors, because Publisher automatically translates HSL values to RGB equivalents.
Pantone Solid	Spot color commercial printing presses.	None. Pantone Solid colors consist of pre-mixed inks. You specify a color with an identifying code number, such as 1265 CVU.	The Pantone color library contains thousands of colors. For practical purposes, spot color documents are limited to 1 or 2 spot colors, plus black.
Pantone Process	Desktop printers or four-color process commercial printing presses.	Pantone Process colors refer to CMYK colors, but the percentage of each color is determined by a formula. You specify a color with an identifying code number, such as S316-7 CVP.	Color printers vary widely in resolution and consequently in the number of colors they can produce. Low-resolution printers may not be able to accurately reproduce a specific Pantone Process color.

Do older Publisher files contain a color scheme?
A publication file created with a version earlier than Publisher 98 doesn't contain a color scheme. When you open this type of document, Publisher 2000 analyzes the colors used in the design and automatically creates a custom color scheme.

To access the Color Scheme dialog box from the Format toolbar, select a frame or a drawn object, click the Fill Color button (shown below) and select More Color Schemes from the drop-down menu.

Color Schemes

Publisher helps you to choose colors that work well together by providing sets of compatible colors—called Color Schemes. When you start a new publication, Publisher uses a default color scheme (named Bluebird). However, you can choose a different color scheme from the list of 62 predefined color schemes that ship with Publisher or you can create a custom color scheme. At any time, you can associate only one color scheme with a publication.

A color scheme contains five slots. When you format an object with a color scheme, Publisher keeps track of the color slot number and the name of the scheme. As shown in the following illustration, when you change color schemes, Publisher automatically changes the colors of all the objects in your publication that use color schemes.

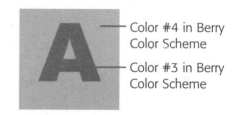

Color #4 in Fjord Color Scheme

Color #3 in Fjord Color Scheme

Color #4 in Berry Color Scheme

Color #3 in Berry Color Scheme

Choose a Standard Color Scheme

1 Start a new publication or open an existing publication.

2 If you are working with a Web document, choose Color And Background Scheme on the Format menu. If you are working with a print document, choose Color Scheme on the Format menu. The Color And Background Scheme dialog box (not shown) or the Color Scheme dialog box appears.

Color and Fill Effects

Why can't I find the Color Scheme command on the Format menu?

The Color Scheme (or the Background And Color Scheme) command is available only when you are working on a full-color RGB or CMYK document. If you have created a spot color document for a commercial printing service, the Color Scheme command is replaced by the Change Spot Color command.

For more information on preparing spot color documents for a printing service, see Chapter 16. For more information on the Color and Background Scheme dialog box, see Chapter 12.

Choose a Standard Color Scheme *(continued)*

3 Click the Standard tab.

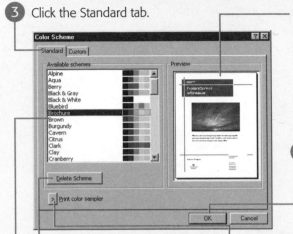

The Preview area displays the actual objects on the current page of your document as they appear with the selected color scheme.

5 Click OK. Publisher recolors all of the objects in your publication that use color schemes.

Click the Delete Scheme button to remove a Custom color scheme from the list of available schemes.

4 Scroll through the list of color schemes and select one. The list includes Publisher's predefined color schemes and any Custom schemes you have saved.

Click Print Color Sampler to print a document that contains all of Publisher's standard color schemes and the colors in the basic palette. This printout helps you to determine which colors print well on your printer.

Create a custom color scheme for the Web.

Computer systems—notably Macs and PCs—use different color palettes to display Web pages. To be sure that the colors in your Web page display properly on a wide variety of computers, create a Web-specific color scheme. It's easy. Just be sure that when you specify an RGB color for the Web, you use one of the following values for each of the primary colors: 255, 204, 153, 102, 51, or 0.

Create a Custom Color Scheme

1 Start a new publication or open an existing publication.

2 If you are working with a Web document, choose Color And Background Scheme on the Format menu. If you are working with a print document, choose Color Scheme on the Format menu. The Color And Background Scheme dialog box (not shown) or the Color Scheme dialog box appears.

The Preview area displays the actual objects on the current page of your document as they appear with the custom color scheme.

3 Click the Custom tab.

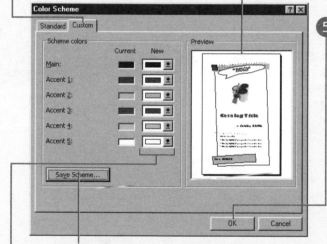

5 Click OK. Publisher lists the color scheme you've created—with the name "Custom"—in the Standard tab of the Color Scheme dialog box under Available Schemes. Publisher recolors all of the objects in your document that use color schemes.

Click the Save Scheme button to store and reuse the custom colors. Publisher lists this name along with the predefined color schemes on the Standard tab.

4 In the New area, open the drop-down list for the color you want to define. Choose one of the available colors, tints, or shades.

How do color schemes work with wizards and Design Gallery objects?

When you use a wizard to create a publication, the wizard asks you to choose a color scheme. When you insert an object from the Design Gallery, it uses the colors in the current scheme.

You can change the color scheme any time, either by using the Color Scheme command on the Format menu or by opening the Quick Publication Wizard (click the Show Wizard button at the lower left of the work area). In the Quick Publication Wizard panel, choose the Color Scheme category in the top panel and then select a color scheme from the list.

 For more information on wizards and Design Gallery objects, see Chapter 14.

Associate a Color Scheme with a Personal Information Set

① Choose Personal Information from the Edit menu. The Personal Information dialog box appears.

② Choose one of the four personal information sets.

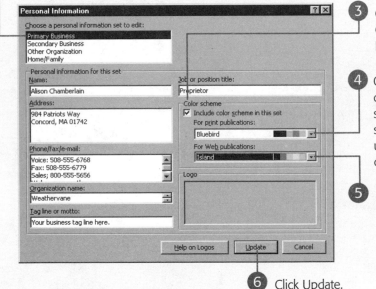

③ Click Include Color Scheme In This Set.

④ Open the drop-down list and select a color scheme to be used for print documents.

⑤ Open the drop-down list and select a color scheme to be used for Web documents.

⑥ Click Update.

Publisher uses this color scheme whenever you associate a publication with the personal information set you chose in step 2.

Choosing Colors for Fills, Lines, Borders, and Text

To a large extent, the color choices available to you and the colors that Publisher uses to display imported pictures are dependent upon the printing process you choose when you set up your document, as explained in the following table.

Color Availability in a Publisher Document		
If you set up...	Available colors include...	Publisher displays imported pictures using...
A black-and-white document for a commercial printing service.	Black, white, and shades of gray.	Black, white, and shades of gray.
A spot-color document for a commercial printing service.	Black, white, and the spot color (or colors) you have chosen. Each Publisher document can contain a maximum of two spot colors. The Pantone color library is still available, so you can change the designated spot color.	Black, white, and shades of gray. However, you can recolor imported artwork using the spot colors in the document.
A full-color RGB document.	The full range of computer-generated colors. You can create colors using any color model—RGB, HSL, CMYK, or Pantone.	The colors contained in the original picture.
A full-color CMYK document.	CMYK and Pantone colors only.	The colors contained in the original picture.

What is a non-scheme color? A non-scheme color is any color that is not contained in the current color scheme. When you choose a new color scheme, objects with non-scheme colors aren't automatically updated with the new colors.

You can assign colors, especially scheme colors, to a selected object quickly by using the buttons on the Formatting toolbar. The buttons available to you differ depending upon the type of object you have selected, but they include:

The Fill Color button —
The Font Color button
The Line Color button

You can fill the interior of a frame or drawn object with color, apply color to the border of a frame or drawn object, change the color of a line, change the color of text, and even recolor imported pictures.

In a full-color document, Publisher provides a multi-tiered palette system that includes Color Scheme colors, the most recently used non-scheme colors, a basic palette of standard computer colors, and a custom palette where you can mix your own colors using the RGB, HSL, CMYK, or Pantone color models. You can access Publisher's color palettes from several different locations within the program, as explained in the following table.

How to Access Publisher's Color Palette	
To change the color of...	**Access the Color menu by...**
The interior, or fill, of a selected object.	Selecting the Fill Color command on the Format menu.
A selected line or the border of a selected object.	Selecting Line/Border Style on the Format menu. Click the More Styles command on the submenu. Click the Color drop-down list in the Line/Border Style dialog box.
Highlighted text.	Selecting the Font command from the Format menu. Click the Color drop-down list in the Font dialog box.
A selected picture, Word Art object, or OLE object.	Selecting Recolor Picture or Recolor Object from the Format menu. Click the Color drop-down list in the dialog box.
A drop cap in a selected paragraph.	Selecting Drop Cap or Change Drop Cap from the Format menu. Click the Custom Drop Cap tab and click the Color drop-down list.

For more information on tints, shades, patterns, and gradients, see "Fill Effects" later in this chapter.

Why don't objects in my publication change color when I choose a new color scheme? If objects in your publication don't change color when you choose a new color scheme, they aren't formatted with a scheme color. You can choose the Color Scheme command on the Format menu. When Publisher displays an alert box asking if you want to change non-color schemes to the closest matching color in the new color scheme, click Yes. Though Publisher does its best to choose appropriate colors, the results may not be what you expect.

If you want more control, you must select each object that uses a non-scheme color and choose a color from the current color scheme.

Choose a Color from the Current Color Scheme

1 Select the object to which you want to apply a color and then access the color palette.

The No Fill option makes an object transparent.

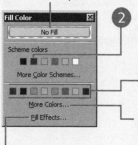

2 Select a color by clicking a swatch. As soon as you select a color, Publisher applies it to the object and you automatically return to the document or dialog box.

Publisher also displays swatches for up to eight of the most recently used non-scheme colors, tints, or shades.

Click More Colors to access the Basic Colors and All Colors palettes.

Click Fill Effects to access tints, shades, patterns, and gradients.

Choose a Non-Scheme Color from the Basic Palette

1 Select the object to which you want to apply a color and then access the color palette.

2 In the color palette, click the More Colors button. The Colors dialog box appears.

Access the basic colors from the drop-down color dialog box. If you routinely use colors from the basic palette, click Show Basic Colors In Color Palette (found in the Colors dialog box). This displays all of the basic colors on the Fill Color, Line Color, and Font Color drop-down menus, making it unnecessary to subsequently open the Colors dialog box.

Why can't I activate the option to mark colors that will not print well on my printer? This option is offered only for color printers and even then it is available only if the printer supports the Image Color Matching (ICM) system. In order to have this option fully functional, you must also click the Improve Screen And Printer Color Matching check box on the General tab in the Options dialog box (available from the Tools menu) and choose the appropriate Image Color Matching options in your printer's Properties dialog box.

For more information about the Windows Image Color Matching system, see "Screen Color and Printer Color Compatibility" later in this chapter.

Choose a Non-Scheme Color from the Basic Palette *(continued)*

3 Select the Basic Colors option.

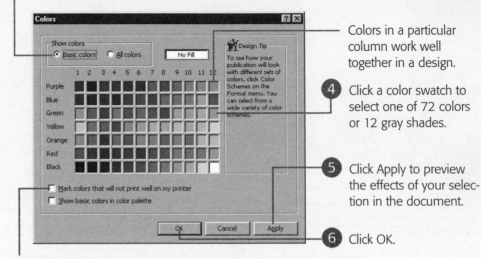

Colors in a particular column work well together in a design.

4 Click a color swatch to select one of 72 colors or 12 gray shades.

5 Click Apply to preview the effects of your selection in the document.

6 Click OK.

Click this check box to use the Image Color Matching (ICM) system.

Specify a CMYK, RGB, or HSL Color

1 Select the object to which you want to apply a color and then access the color drop-down menu.

2 Click the More Colors button. The Colors dialog box appears.

What do the numerical values for RGB, HSL, and CMYK colors mean?

The RGB, HSL, and CMYK color models specify color differently.

- RGB colors are based on 256 intensity levels where 0 produces no color (or black) and 255 produces maximum color (solid red, green, or blue). A value of 255 for all three primary colors produces white.

- The HSL color model is based on a color wheel in which each degree represents a different hue. The spectrum starts at 0 (or red) and cycles through all hues back to an almost-red color at 359. You specify saturation values in percentages from 0 (for pure gray) through 100 (for full saturation). Luminescence values are also specified in percentages, where 0 represents black and 100 represents white.

- The CMYK color model combines tints of the primary colors. A low percentage number represents a light tint. For example, 0 is white. A high percentage represents a more intense tint, and 100 percent produces a solid color of cyan, magenta, yellow, or black.

Specify a CMYK, RGB, or HSL Color *(continued)*

Instead of typing numerical values, you can move this crossbar to choose a hue and saturation interactively. Move the crossbar left and right to pick a hue. Move the crossbar up and down to pick a saturation. Colors are at full saturation at the top of the box and are grayer toward the bottom of the box.

3 Select the All Colors option to display the color picker.

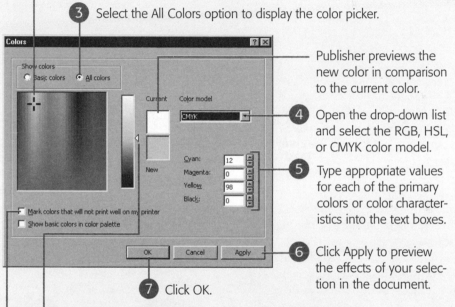

Publisher previews the new color in comparison to the current color.

4 Open the drop-down list and select the RGB, HSL, or CMYK color model.

5 Type appropriate values for each of the primary colors or color characteristics into the text boxes.

6 Click Apply to preview the effects of your selection in the document.

7 Click OK.

Instead of typing numerical values, you can move this arrow up or down to adjust the luminescence, or lightness, of a color.

Click this check box to use the Image Color Matching system.

How can I see an accurate representation of a Pantone Solid color ink? In order to see an accurate representation of a Pantone Solid color ink, you must purchase a printed Pantone swatch book, available at any art supply store.

Why might the Colors dialog box contain a button called Change Color, instead of the numerical input boxes to mix primary colors? You selected an object formatted with a Pantone color before you opened the Colors dialog box. You can't mix Pantone colors; you can only choose a swatch from the library of predefined colors. To access the Pantone dialog box, click the Change Color button. To view numerical input boxes where you can mix primary colors, open the Color Model drop-down list and select the RGB, CMYK, or HSL color model.

Specify a Pantone Solid Color

① Select the object to which you want to apply a Pantone color and then access the color drop-down menu.

② Click the More Colors option. The Colors dialog box appears.

③ Select the All Colors option to display the color picker.

④ Open the Color Model drop-down list and select Pantone. The Pantone dialog box appears. If this is the first time you have accessed Pantone colors, an alert box appears, explaining that screen representations don't necessarily provide accurate previews of Pantone Solid colors. Click OK to proceed to the Pantone dialog box.

⑤ If it is not already selected, click the Pantone Solid tab.

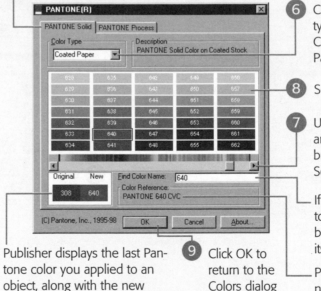

⑥ Choose one of three color types from the drop-down list: Coated Paper, Uncoated Paper, or Convert To Process.

⑧ Select a color swatch.

⑦ Use the scroll bars or click an area in the color spectrum to browse the library of Pantone Solid colors.

If you know the identifying Pantone number, type it in this text box and press Enter to jump to its location in the swatch library.

Publisher lists the reference number identifying the currently selected Pantone color.

Publisher displays the last Pantone color you applied to an object, along with the new color that is currently selected.

⑨ Click OK to return to the Colors dialog box. Click OK.

Convert Pantone solid colors to CMYK equivalents. If your document will ultimately be printed using CMYK inks, it is best to specify colors using the Pantone Process color library. However, Publisher can convert Pantone Solid colors to CMYK equivalents. You can see the transformation on-screen in one of two ways.

First, select the object containing the Pantone Solid color you want to convert to CMYK. In the Pantone dialog box, open the Color Type drop-down list and choose Convert to Process. The preview area, in the lower-left corner of the dialog box, clearly displays the difference between a true Pantone Solid color and the closest possible match using CMYK inks.

Alternatively, select the object containing the Pantone Solid color you want to convert to CMYK. In the Pantone dialog box, click the Pantone Process tab. Publisher automatically chooses the Pantone Process color that most closely matches the current Pantone Solid color.

Specify a Pantone Process Color

1. Select the object to which you want to apply a Pantone color and then access the color drop-down menu.

2. Click the More Colors option. The Colors dialog box appears.

3. Select the All Colors option to display the color picker.

4. Open the Color Model drop-down list and select Pantone. The Pantone dialog box appears. If this is the first time you have accessed Pantone colors, an alert box appears, explaining that screen representations don't necessarily provide an accurate preview of Pantone Solid colors. Click OK to proceed to the Pantone dialog box.

5. If it isn't already selected, click the Pantone Process tab.

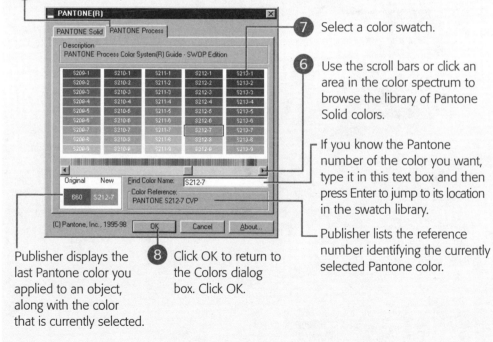

7. Select a color swatch.

6. Use the scroll bars or click an area in the color spectrum to browse the library of Pantone Solid colors.

If you know the Pantone number of the color you want, type it in this text box and then press Enter to jump to its location in the swatch library.

Publisher lists the reference number identifying the currently selected Pantone color.

Publisher displays the last Pantone color you applied to an object, along with the color that is currently selected.

8. Click OK to return to the Colors dialog box. Click OK.

Why can't I choose a color from the basic palette or create a custom color? You aren't working in a full-color document. If you are working in a black-and-white document, Publisher limits your choices to black, white, and 14 shades of gray. If you are working in a spot color document, Publisher limits your choices to 16 percentages of black, Spot Color 1, and Spot Color 2, as shown in the following illustration.

Fill Effects

In addition to filling an object with a solid color, Publisher lets you create special effects, including tints, shades, patterns, and gradients.

Publisher can mix a selected color with white to create tints or with black to create shades.

Publisher provides 18 fill patterns. You can also make an object transparent so that filled objects placed further back in the stacking order show through.

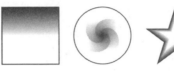

A gradient fill creates a transition from one color to another. Publisher provides 44 styles of gradient fills.

Choose a Tint or a Shade

1 Select the frame or drawn shape you want to fill.

2 Choose Fill Color on the Format menu or click the Fill Color button on the Formatting toolbar.

3 Select Fill Effects on the cascading menu. The Fill Effects dialog box appears.

Why aren't darker shades of my chosen color available? If you've set up a black-and-white or spot-color document, Publisher restricts your choices to tints only. In order to access tints *and* shades, you must change your print options using the Commercial Printing Tools command (found on the Tools menu).

For more information about preparing a file for a commercial printing service, see Chapter 16.

Add a tint or a shade to a custom Color Scheme. When you create a custom color scheme, you can fill a color slot with a tint or a shade. In the Color Scheme dialog box, click the Custom tab. Open the color palette by clicking the New drop-down arrow. Select Fill Effects. The tint or shade you specify appears as part of the custom color scheme.

Choose a Tint or a Shade *(continued)*

④ Select the Tints/Shades option.

⑤ Open the Base Color drop-down list box and select one of the available colors.

⑥ Scroll through the tint and shade options. Either click one of the 11 predefined tints to create a lighter version of the current color or click one of the 10 predefined shades to create a darker version of the current color.

Fill Effects dialog box:

Style
- ○ Tints/Shades ○ Patterns ○ Gradients

Color
- Base color:
- ☐ Mark colors that will not print well on my printer

Sample

Design Tip
Use tints and shades of a color to create a sophisticated color scheme.

Color: 20% tint

OK   Cancel   Apply

⑦ Preview the effect in the Sample area or click Apply to see the tint or shade in your publication.

⑧ Click OK.

Choose a Pattern

① Select the frame or drawn shape that you want to fill with a pattern.

② Choose Fill Color on the Format menu or click the Fill Color button on the Formatting toolbar.

③ Select Fill Effects on the cascading menu. The Fill Effects dialog box appears.

To make an opaque object transparent or to make a transparent object opaque, select it and press Ctrl-T.

Why doesn't the fill pattern get bigger when I increase the size of an object? Publisher's patterns are a type of formatting attribute—like a color or a tint. You wouldn't expect an object to change its color if you enlarged it. In the same way, no matter how large or small an object may become, the pattern that fills it remains the same size.

Choose a Pattern *(continued)*

The very first box contains a circle with a vertical line through it to indicate that it is the transparent, or clear, option. Objects or frames formatted with the Clear pattern allow objects further back in the stacking order to show through.

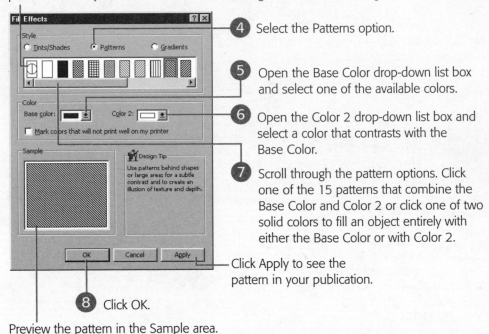

④ Select the Patterns option.

⑤ Open the Base Color drop-down list box and select one of the available colors.

⑥ Open the Color 2 drop-down list box and select a color that contrasts with the Base Color.

⑦ Scroll through the pattern options. Click one of the 15 patterns that combine the Base Color and Color 2 or click one of two solid colors to fill an object entirely with either the Base Color or with Color 2.

Click Apply to see the pattern in your publication.

⑧ Click OK.

Preview the pattern in the Sample area.

Remove tints, shades, patterns, and gradients.
If you want to remove a special fill from an object, select the object and then select either a new color or the No Fill option from the color palette.

If you want to change the color of an object *without* removing the special fill, pick a new color from within the Fill Effects dialog box.

Choose a Gradient

1. Select the object you want to fill.

2. Choose Fill Color on the Format menu or click the Fill Color button on the Formatting toolbar.

3. Select Fill Effects from the cascading menu. The Fill Effects dialog box appears.

5. Open the Base Color drop-down list box and select one of the available colors.

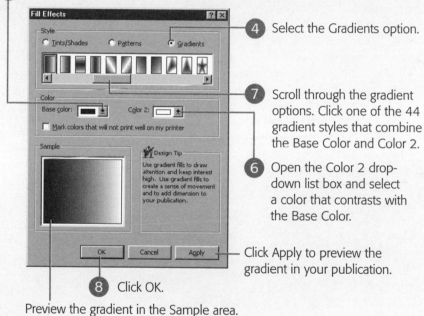

4. Select the Gradients option.

7. Scroll through the gradient options. Click one of the 44 gradient styles that combine the Base Color and Color 2.

6. Open the Color 2 drop-down list box and select a color that contrasts with the Base Color.

Click Apply to preview the gradient in your publication.

8. Click OK.

Preview the gradient in the Sample area.

For a more detailed comparison of RGB and CMYK colors, see "Color Models" earlier in this chapter.

See accurate colors on-screen. The number of colors that you see on your computer monitor varies depending on the video mode you are using. The standard VGA resolution, for example, can reproduce only 16 colors. Any other colors are simulated with a process known as dithering. Dithered colors aren't accurate. If your document contains only flat color (meaning solid colors, tints, and shades), a 256-color video mode should be sufficient. But for the most accurate view of the colors in your document (and especially in imported pictures), your monitor and video card should be capable of displaying the full 16.7 million colors. This video mode is often referred to as True Color, or 24-bit color.

For more information on the Commercial Printing Tools, see Chapter 16.

On-Screen Color and Printer Color Compatibility

Computer monitors and color printers use different—and not entirely compatible—color systems. As a result, the bright, saturated RGB colors you see on-screen may appear dark and dull when printed with CMYK inks on paper.

Windows provides a color matching mechanism called Image Color Matching (ICM). You don't need to understand exactly how ICM works in order to use it, but an overview of its functionality is useful here. The ICM engine reads special files called ICC (International Color Consortium) device profiles. These profiles contain information about how a particular device, such as a monitor or printer, defines colors. The ICM engine then translates from one device profile to another.

Publisher takes advantage of ICM in two different ways. In CMYK mode, Publisher provides an accurate preview of the final printed color. For example, if you set up a Process Color document for a commercial printing service, Publisher limits your color choices to mixtures of cyan, magenta, yellow, and black. You can also select an object filled with an RGB color, open the Colors dialog box, and then switch to the CMYK color model. Publisher immediately translates the current color to the nearest CMYK match.

In addition, Publisher can alert you to colors that won't print well on your chosen output device. But Publisher can display this alert only if all of the following are true:

@   You have properly identified your monitor in the Display Properties dialog box. (Double-click the Display icon in the Control Panel folder.)

@   Your printer supports ICM and you have turned on the feature in the printer Properties dialog box.

@   You have activated ICM in Publisher.

Why don't I have the same Image Color Matching options available for my printer? The exact structure of the printer Properties dialog box changes depending on your particular printer. For example, some color printers can't perform color matching calculations and offer only an option to perform image color matching on the host computer. Use the instructions given here as a guideline.

 Have the printer perform color matching calculations. You can increase your system's speed by using the printer's processor, rather than your computer's processor, to perform the calculations for color matching. This technique works only if you have a PostScript Level 2 or Level 3 color printer, which uses a color dictionary to map screen colors to printer colors. To take advantage of this feature, choose Perform Image Color Matching On The Printer to download a color dictionary to the printer with each job or choose Print Using Printer Calibration to use a color dictionary that has already been downloaded to the printer. Though this method of color matching frees up your system resources, it may result in less accurate color matching.

Turn On the ICM Feature in the Printer Properties Dialog Box

1 On the Windows Start menu, choose Settings. On the submenu, choose the Printers folder.

2 In the Printers folder, right-click the icon for your color printer and then choose Properties on the shortcut menu.

3 In the printer Properties dialog box, click the Graphics tab if it is available. If your printer does not have a Graphics tab, proceed to step 4.

4 Click the Color button. The Graphics-Color dialog box appears.

5 Select this option to turn on ICM.

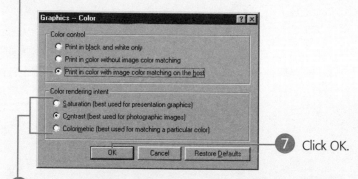

7 Click OK.

6 Choose a rendering model.

- Saturation is best for solid-colored pictures (such as charts and diagrams).
- Contrast works best for photographic images.
- Colorimetric requires the printer to have the exact color of ink you specify in your documents.

Why has Publisher marked every color in the color palette as a potential printing problem? You are working in RGB mode. Publisher alerts you to the fact that RGB colors don't print well on CMYK printers. To circumvent this situation, work in Process Color (CMYK) mode by choosing that option in the Color Printing dialog box (found on the Commercial Printing Tools submenu).

For more information on Publisher's Commercial Printing Tools, see Chapter 16.

Activate ICM in Publisher

1 Open the Tools menu and choose Options. The Options dialog box appears.

2 Select the General tab.

3 Click the Improve Screen And Printer Color Matching check box.

4 Click OK. If the current printer doesn't have an ICC profile or if the printer hasn't been configured to use ICM, an alert box appears. If this happens, return to the "Turn On the ICM Feature in the Printer Properties Dialog Box" section of this chapter and configure ICM in the printer Properties dialog box. Then return to step 1.

5 Select an object.

6 On the Format menu, choose Fill Color and then More Colors from the submenu. The Colors dialog box appears.

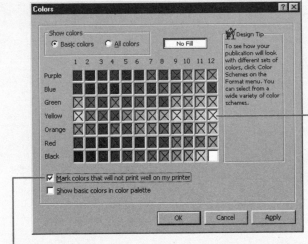

Publisher puts an X through the color swatches that won't reproduce well on your printer.

7 Click the Mark Colors That Will Not Print Well On My Printer check box.

Why don't the special paper designs print along with the rest of my publication? The Special Paper designs are screen previews only; Publisher doesn't print them. If you want these designs to appear in your publications, you need to buy the papers from Paper Direct at 1-800-272-7377.

Why is the Special Paper command on the View menu grayed out? Your publication is set up for a commercial printing service. The Special Paper command is available only if you are printing to a local or network printer. Open the Color Printing dialog box and select Composite RGB.

Use a wizard to create designs for special papers. You can use a wizard to create a design that works perfectly with a preprinted specialty paper. When you begin a new publication, click the Publications By Design tab in the Catalog and choose the category called Special Papers.

Printing on Colored Paper

Even if you own a black-and-white printer, you can easily add color to your publications by printing on colored paper. Papers compatible with laser and ink jet printers come in a wide variety of colors. Many specialty papers are available in multicolor designs. If you design your document to be printed on one of these papers, you might find it helpful to see a screen preview of it. Publisher provides screen previews of over 40 popular papers for letterheads, brochures, postcards, and business cards. The papers are all available from Paper Direct, a paper manufacturer.

Turn the Display of Special Papers On and Off

1. On the View menu, choose Special Paper. The Special Paper dialog box appears.

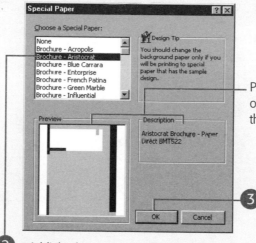

Publisher always displays a preview of the selected design along with the Paper Direct product ID.

3. Click OK to add a screen preview of the paper to the current document.

2. Highlight the paper you want to use or select None to deactivate the display of special paper.

Working With a Commercial Printing Service

I f you plan to reproduce a publication in large quantities, you should consider using a commercial printing service. You should also consider a commercial printing service if your design calls for output that you cannot generate with a desktop printer. Commercial printing services typically offer the following benefits:

@ Professional quality output from high resolution or continuous tone printers.

@ Oversized paper stock for banners or posters.

@ Heavy or unusual papers, such as textured paper, colored paper, and cover or card stock.

@ Double-sided printing (provided that your desktop printer doesn't support duplex printing).

@ Finishing operations such as trimming, folding, binding, or laminating the printed piece.

Commercial printing services are incredibly varied, both in terms of the kinds of documents they can produce and the prices they charge. You should procure quotes from several different services in order to find the best combination of quality and cost. In general, commercial printing services fall into three categories, as summarized in the following table.

A Comparison of Commercial Printing Services				
This type of service...	Supports these color models...	At these resolutions...	For this number of copies...	Generates this kind of output...
A traditional offset printer.	Black and white, spot color, and process CMYK color.	1270 dpi through 2540 dpi (or higher).	More than 500 copies. As the number of copies increases, the price per copy is reduced.	Either film or press plates from your electronic file. The printer subsequently uses press plates on an offset printing press to mass-produce your publication.
Copy shop.	Black and white and process CMYK color. Spot colors must be simulated with process CMYK colors.	300 dpi through 600 dpi.	Fewer than 500 copies.	Photocopies. A copy shop requires you to create a production-quality printout of the publication.
Digital graphics service bureau (or a high end copy shop).	Black and white and process color. Spot colors must be simulated with process CMYK colors.	300 dpi through 720 dpi (or higher).	Fewer than 500 copies. The price per copy may not decrease as the quantity of copies increases.	Multiple copies of your publication directly from an electronic file.

 How can I find a digital graphics bureau that offers full color output?

You may be able to find a local graphics service bureau that offers digital printing by looking up "Desktop Publishing Services" in the yellow pages. You can also take advantage of an online printing service, called Printovation, that allows you to place an order and transfer your output file by modem. You can contact Printovation at 1-800-386-7127 or download software from their Web site at http://www.printovation.com.

Choosing a Color Printing Mode

Depending upon your design *and* your budget, Publisher can generate process color, spot color, and black-and-white files for a commercial printing service. Obviously, full color output is the most expensive option. Spot color is a good alternative, because it allows you to add one (or two) accent colors to a design at a relatively low cost. And the black-and-white option almost guarantees that your publication will be inexpensive to produce, because it restricts your color choices to black, white, and shades of gray.

You should choose a color printing mode *before* you design your publication in order to guarantee that what you see on your screen will match what appears in the final printout.

For more information on the various color models Publisher supports, see Chapter 15.

Why would I want to limit my design to black and white only? When you choose the Black And White Only option in the Choose Spot Color dialog box, Publisher limits your color choices to black, white, and shades of gray. In addition, all imported pictures are displayed and printed in black and white. This limitation prevents you from including color objects in your publication, which can cause time-consuming and costly printing problems at a commercial printing service.

Choose a Color Printing Mode

1 On the Tools menu, choose Commercial Printing Tools.

2 On the submenu, select Color Printing. The Color Printing dialog box appears.

3 Choose one of the three color options.

Choose Spot Color(s) if you plan to print your document with a maximum of black plus two accent colors.

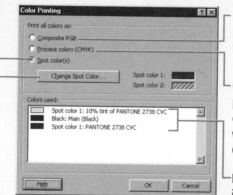

Choose Composite RGB if you are using a desktop printer and want access to all the color models that Publisher supports.

Choose Process Colors (CMYK) if you plan to print a full color document at a commercial printing service, or if you would like Publisher to accurately preview CMYK colors you specify.

Publisher lists the colors currently in use within the publication.

4 If you choose the Spot Color(s) option, click the Change Spot Color button. The Choose Spot Color dialog box appears.

5 Select Black And White Only to create a monochrome document, or select Black Plus to activate the Spot Color 1 option.

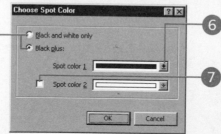

6 Open the drop-down list box for Spot Color 1 and choose an available color.

7 If you want to add another spot color to your publication, click the check box to activate Spot Color 2. Then open the drop-down list box and choose an available color.

Convert composite RGB colors to process or spot color. Even if you design an entire publication in Publisher's default color mode—composite RGB—you can still generate process (CMYK) or spot color separations. Simply follow the instructions in the procedure, "Choose A Color Printing Mode."

If you are converting to process colors, Publisher converts the colors of text, drawn shapes, OLE objects, and most graphics to the closest matching CMYK color. Publisher does not convert bitmapped graphics embedded in a vector EPS file or textures and gradients created with Microsoft Draw 2000. Instead, Publisher prints those objects on the black plate.

If you are converting to spot colors, Publisher converts colored text and the colors of drawn objects and OLE objects to tints of Spot Color 1. If you are using a second spot color, only those objects that match exactly will be printed on the plate for Spot Color 2. All imported color graphics will be converted to black and white.

Sending a Publisher File to a Commercial Printing Service

In most cases you'll want to send a native Publisher file (in the .pub format) to the commercial printing service. Doing so allows the commercial printer to run a preflight check—a process in which the printer examines the document for potential printing problems. If necessary, the commercial printing service can change internal settings that influence printing, modify a design to eliminate a printing problem, or correct a last-minute error in the document.

There is one caveat: the printing service must use the current version of Publisher. Confirm that the printing service has a copy of Microsoft Publisher 2000. Older versions of Publisher cannot open or print Publisher 2000 files.

Publisher takes most of the guesswork out of sending a publication file to a commercial printing service. The new Pack And Go command gathers all of the necessary files and compresses them for easy transport. Specifically, it:

- Embeds TrueType fonts into the publication.
- Creates links for embedded graphics.
- Collects linked graphics.
- Packs and compresses all of the files into a single archive file.
- Copies the packed file to a drive or folder of your choice. If you are saving the packed file to a floppy disk and the file is too large to fit on a single disk, Publisher spans the file across several disks.
- Copies a decompression utility called Unpack.exe to the same drive or folder containing the packed file.
- Prints both composite and separation proofs of the document on your desktop printer.

For more information about OLE objects, see Chapter 11.

Use the Design Checker to create efficient files.
Before you send your publication to a commercial printing service, run the Design Checker to find and eliminate potential problems—such as empty frames and hidden objects. The result will be a smaller, cleaner publication file that is less prone to printing errors.

OLE Object Issues

OLE objects in your Publisher document point to other applications installed on your computer system. The printing service must have the same source programs installed on its computer system in order to make any last-minute content changes to the OLE objects before printing. If the source program is not available, the printing service will be able to display the OLE object on-screen and print it, but it won't be able to alter the OLE object.

Be aware that the Pack And Go command doesn't automatically update OLE objects that are linked to (rather than embedded in) your document. To be sure that any linked OLE objects in your publication contain the latest information, use the Links command (found on the Edit menu) to update the file before you pack the publication.

Transfer a Publication to a Commercial Printing Service

1 On the File menu, select Pack And Go. On the submenu, choose Take To A Commercial Printing Service.

2 The first screen of the Pack And Go Wizard appears. It describes the operations it can perform. Click Next.

3 Choose a location for the packed files. You can select the A:\ drive option, enter a path and folder name into the text box, or click the Browse button to search for a drive or folder. Then click Next.

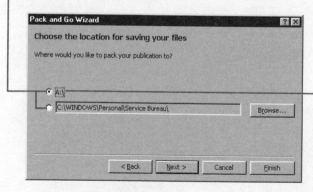

If you choose the A:\ drive and the packed file is too large to fit on a single floppy disk, Publisher automatically spans the file across multiple disks.

For more information about embedded TrueType fonts, see "Embedding Fonts" later in this chapter. For more information about linked graphics, see "Managing Linked Graphics" later in this chapter.

 What happens if the Pack And Go Wizard cannot locate a linked graphic file? The Pack And Go Wizard displays an alert box listing the file name of the missing linked graphic. The alert box allows you to skip the file or to browse for the file. If you click the Browse button, Publisher displays the standard Link To Graphic dialog box.

 What is Unpack.exe and why do I need this file when I transfer my publication to a commercial printing service? When Publisher packs a publication for transport to a commercial printing service, it compresses the files to make them as small as possible. While compressed, the files are not usable—or printable. Unpack.exe is a utility program that uncompresses the files, allowing them to be opened in Publisher and printed.

Transfer a Publication to a Commercial Printing Service *(continued)*

4 Select the appropriate options.

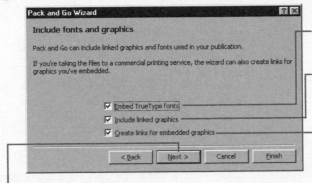

Select this option to embed TrueType fonts used in this publication.

Select this option to copy linked graphics to the destination folder or drive.

Select this option to export any embedded graphics as linked graphics.

5 Click Next.

6 The wizard presents a dialog box, listing the operations it will perform and the destination folder or drive. Click the Finish button. Publisher saves your publication and linked graphics to a file called Packed01.puz, along with a copy of Unpack.exe and a Readme.txt file.

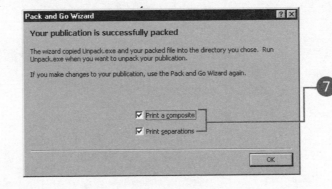

7 In the final dialog box, click the appropriate options to print a composite and/or a separated proof. Then click OK.

Take your publication to another computer. The Pack And Go Wizard can help you to transport your publication to another computer. The process is nearly identical to packing a publication to take to a service bureau. On the File menu, select Pack And Go. On the submenu, select Take To Another Computer. Follow the on-screen instructions, with these possible changes:

◎ If you know that the computer to which you are transporting the document contains the fonts you have used, clear the check box that tells Publisher to embed fonts.

◎ If you plan to print the document to a desktop printer, clear the check box that tells Publisher to export embedded graphics as linked graphics.

Finally, if you use the Pack And Go Wizard to take your publication to another computer, the wizard doesn't print proofs of the publication. You can use the Print dialog box to generate composite or separated proofs of the publication if necessary.

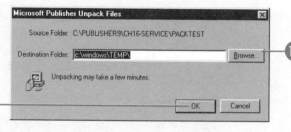

Transfer a Publication to a Commercial Printing Service *(continued)*

⑧ Transfer the files to your commercial printing service.

⑨ At the commercial printing service, run Unpack.exe. The Microsoft Publisher Unpack Files dialog box appears.

⑩ Specify a location for the unpacked files or click the Browse button and choose a location for the unpacked files.

⑪ Click OK. Publisher unpacks the publication file and appends the letters "png" to the file name. For example, if your original publication name was News01.pub, look for a file called News01PNG.pub. Publisher also unpacks any linked graphics stored in the .puz file. A dialog box then reports that the files have been unpacked successfully. Click OK.

⑫ Locate the publication file you unpacked in step 11. Open it in Publisher.

Publisher's Commercial Printing Tools

The printing process is a complex procedure that can involve a combination of digital, photochemical, and mechanical operations. Publisher provides a number of specialized functions to address the needs of a commercial printing service. Publisher can:

◎ Convert all of the colors in a publication file to percentages of CMYK inks or to a spot color ink.

◎ Generate traps on both a global and per-object basis.

◎ Embed TrueType fonts.

◎ Create and manage links to externally stored graphics.

What is the difference between digital, photochemical, and mechanical processes? There really are no absolute divisions between these processes, but at the risk of over-simplification:

- ◎ A digital process produces output directly from an electronic file, as when you print a Publisher or PostScript file directly to paper.

- ◎ A photochemical process uses light-sensitive materials to form an image, as when you expose printing plates to light filtered through film separations of your publication.

- ◎ A mechanical process physically transfers an image to paper, as when an offset printing press transfers ink from a plate to paper.

If the printing service you have chosen accepts Publisher 2000's native file format, you can safely ignore many of these advanced tools. The printing service can choose the proper settings prior to generating output from the Publisher file.

However, if the printing service you have chosen does not accept Publisher 2000's native file format, you must properly configure the commercial printing options prior to generating PostScript separations. Be warned—choosing the wrong options or entering the wrong values can cause serious press problems and degrade the quality of your publication. Before attempting to generate PostScript separations, speak with your commercial printing service and determine the best settings for their equipment. Then follow their instructions exactly.

Trapping

When printing plates (for either CMYK or spot color documents) don't align—or register—perfectly on press, gaps can appear between adjacent, differently colored objects. For example, an unsightly white space can appear between red text and a blue background. A trap is a high-end printing technique that overlaps adjacent objects in order to avoid gaps created by misregistration on press.

Publisher traps objects (ever so slightly) by extending the lighter colors of one object into the darker colors of an overlapping or adjacent object. Trapping amounts are typically very small. For example, the standard trapping amount is only 0.25 point—or 0.0035 inch. Publisher supports the full range of industry-standard traps, including spread, choke, and centerline traps (as shown in the following schematic drawing). In addition, Publisher can produce knockouts or overprint objects.

What is the difference between a knockout and overprinting? A knockout occurs when a color object prints against a white background, even if "holes" must be cut into (or knocked out of) the background color. Overprinting does not create a knockout, but instead prints a color object over a color background.

A knockout

Overprinting

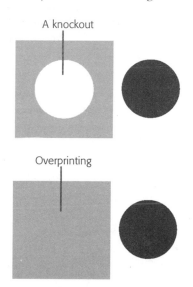

In this diagram, the black line clearly shows the position of the trap. The actual color of a trap will be much more similar to the colors of the foreground object and background.

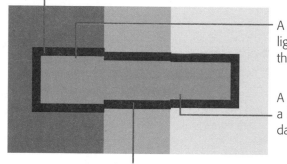

A spread extends the colors of a lighter foreground object into the background.

A choke extends the colors of a lighter background into the darker foreground object.

A centerline trap is used when the foreground object and the background have similar color values. It extends from the boundary between two objects equally into the foreground object and the background.

Publisher uses a complex set of rules and a host of default settings to create automatic traps. You can override automatic trapping in two different ways:

@ You can modify the settings in the Trapping Preferences dialog box.

@ You can select individual objects and create custom trap values.

Before you can change any of these settings with confidence, you must understand three key concepts: luminance, thresholds, and indeterminate objects.

Are there cases where Publisher does not create a trap for overlapping objects? Yes. If Publisher determines that trapping is unnecessary, no trap is created. Based on the default threshold settings for automatic trapping, Publisher won't trap overlapping or adjacent objects when:

- The objects are the same color or use different percentages of the same color.

- The objects have 50 percent (or more) of one CMYK ink color in common or 30 percent (or more) of two CMYK ink colors in common.

- One object's color consists of CMYK values that are all greater than the other object's CMYK values.

- One object is white, unless you have specified white as a color in a spot color document or unless you have created a keepaway trap in a CMYK document.

 For more information about keepaway traps, see "How Publisher Traps Objects" later in this chapter.

Luminance

As the first step in the trapping process, Publisher must determine the lightness (or luminance) value of any objects that overlap or share a border. For process colors, Publisher determines the luminance value automatically, because it knows the industry standard luminance for CMYK inks. For spot colors, Publisher allows you to modify the luminance value, based on the actual ink color that the commercial printing service will use.

Thresholds

In general, Publisher extends the colors of the lighter object into the colors of the darker object. However, in some cases, two objects have colors in common. In those cases, Publisher either creates a centerline trap or no trap. It makes this decision based on percentage values in the Trapping Thresholds dialog box. For example, Publisher creates a centerline trap when the ratio of luminance between two objects reaches or surpasses a threshold of 70 percent. You can override Publisher's default threshold settings, but you should do so only on the advice of your commercial printing service.

Indeterminate Objects

An indeterminate object is any object that contains multiple colors. The presence of multiple colors makes it difficult for Publisher to assign a luminance value to the object. Indeterminate objects include any object filled with a gradient or pattern, imported images, WordArt, BorderArt, and Microsoft Draw objects. Publisher allows you to specify a width for traps that are applied to indeterminate objects.

Turn off automatic trapping. To deactivate automatic trapping, open the Trapping Preferences dialog box (by opening the Tools menu and selecting the Commercial Printing Tools, Trapping, and Preferences commands). Clear the check box for Automatic Trapping.

How can I restore Publisher's default values in the Trapping Preferences dialog box? In the Trapping Preferences dialog box, click the Reset All button. This action returns all values for all of the objects in the publication, including objects with individual trapping values, to the default automatic trapping values.

Set Up a Document for Automatic Trapping

1 On the Tools menu, select Commercial Printing Tools. On the submenus, select Trapping and Preferences.

2 Click Automatic Trapping.

3 Enter values in the Width and Indeterminate text boxes.

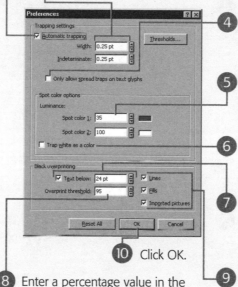

4 Click Only Allow Spread Traps On Text Glyphs if your document contains script fonts that you want to trap.

5 If you are working in a spot color document, enter a Luminance value for Spot Color 1 and, if necessary, for Spot Color 2.

6 If you are working in a spot color document and you want to trap white objects, click Trap White As A Color.

7 In the Black Overprinting area, make sure that a check mark appears beside the Text Below option. Enter a point size in the text box.

8 Enter a percentage value in the Overprint Threshold text box.

9 Select any combination of check boxes to overprint lines, fills, or imported pictures when they contain a percentage of black higher than or equal to the value in the Overprint Threshold text box.

10 Click OK.

What is a rich black object? The black ink in a CMYK document, even when printed at 100%, can sometimes appear washed out. To compensate, rich black mixes black ink with one or more tints of another process color (typically cyan). The most common use for a rich black is as a black background for white text.

Publisher defines rich black as any object, drawn shape, border, or line in a CMYK document that is formatted with 100% black plus any percentage of another CMYK ink that overlaps a white object. However, you can change the definition of rich black by specifying a lower ink percentage of black in the Trapping Preferences dialog box.

 How does the one-color or two-color threshold affect trapping? When you increase the one-color or two-color threshold setting, you also increase the likelihood that Publisher will create a trap for two overlapping or adjacent objects. When you decrease the one-color or two-color threshold setting, you decrease the number of traps in a document.

Change Trapping Thresholds

1 On the Tools menu, select Commercial Printing Tools. On the submenus, select Trapping and Preferences.

2 Click Automatic Trapping.

3 Click the Thresholds button. The Trapping Thresholds dialog box appears.

4 Enter a new one-color threshold value. Objects that have this percentage (or more) of one color in common are not trapped.

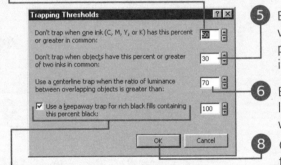

5 Enter a new two-color threshold value. Objects that have this percentage (or more) of two colors in common are not trapped.

6 Enter a new threshold value for the luminance ratio at which Publisher will create a centerline trap.

8 Click OK twice to return to your document.

7 Select this check box to create keepaway traps for rich black objects. Then enter a percentage of black that Publisher will use to identify rich black objects.

Set Up Per-Object Trapping

1 Select an object or highlight the text for which you want to set custom trapping values.

2 On the Tools menu, select Commercial Printing Tools. On the submenu, select Trapping. On the next submenu, select Per Object Trapping. The Per Object Trapping dialog box appears.

View the current trapping settings for a selected object or highlighted text. If you create custom trapping settings, you can view them at any time. First select an object or highlight text. On the Tools menu, select Commercial Printing Tools, Trapping, and Per Object Trapping. In the Per Object Trapping dialog box, click the Details button for the type of trap you want to review. Publisher displays the Trapping Details dialog box, as shown below. The top portion of the dialog box describes the foreground object (in this case the border of a text frame). The list box describes the background object and the custom trap.

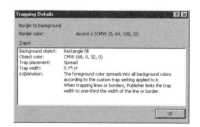

Set Up Per-Object Trapping *(continued)*

3 If you want to change the trapping of the object's border to the background, open the Border To Background Setting drop-down list box and then choose Default, Overprint, Knockout, or Custom.

4 If you choose the custom setting, open the Placement drop-down list and then select Centerline, Spread, or Choke.

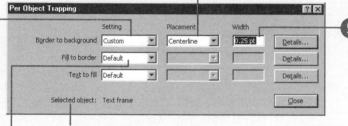

5 If you choose the custom setting, enter a value in the Width text box.

Publisher always tells you which object is currently selected.

The Default option applies the threshold and trapping values specified in the Trapping Preferences dialog box. Select the Default option whenever you want to remove custom trap settings from a selected object or text.

6 If necessary, repeat steps 3 through 5 for the Fill To Border and Text To Fill items.

7 Click Close.

How Publisher Traps Objects

If you plan to use trapping when you print your publication, you should be aware that Publisher (like most desktop publishing programs) cannot trap all objects in exactly the same way. The following table explains how Publisher traps different types of objects.

Automatic Trapping in Publisher		
Object type	**Publisher traps...**	**Publisher doesn't trap...**
Text.	TrueType fonts. PostScript Type 1 fonts, provided that you are using Windows NT as your operating system and have Adobe Type Manager installed. Process and spot color, and all text (including black text) larger than the point size threshold specified in the Trapping Preferences dialog box. Text formatted as regular, bold, italic, bold italic, superscript or subscript, or as a drop cap.	PostScript Type 1 fonts if you are using Windows 95 or Windows 98 as your operating system. Black text at small point sizes, as defined by the point size threshold in the Trapping Preferences dialog box. Instead, this text is overprinted. Text printed over other text or an imported picture, text in WordArt objects, or text in linked or embedded OLE objects. Text formatted with the outline, underline, shadow, engrave, or emboss effects. Any objects overlying text.
Drawn shapes, lines.	Process and spot color drawn shapes and lines.	Black lines and black fills whenever these objects have a black percentage greater than the overprint threshold value specified in the Trapping Preferences dialog box.
Borders.	Any process or spot color border.	BorderArt. Borders that have a black percentage greater than the overprint threshold value specified in the Trapping Preferences dialog box.

Add a black hairline border to imported pictures. Publisher does not trap imported pictures, which are considered indeterminate objects. You can, however, create a trap by formatting the picture with a thin hairline border. Publisher can then trap or overprint the border against a colored background.

What is a keepaway trap? Normally, Publisher does not trap white objects. A keepaway trap forces Publisher to trap white objects when they are positioned next to or on top of rich black objects. Specifically, Publisher chokes the tinted color in the rich black in order to keep it away from the edge of the white object. In traditional print production, keepaway traps are used to ensure that white text placed against a rich black background remains clean and legible.

For more information about how Publisher identifies rich black fills, see the procedure, "Change Trapping Thresholds" earlier in this chapter.

Automatic Trapping in Publisher *(continued)*		
Object type	**Publisher traps...**	**Publisher doesn't trap...**
Indeterminate Objects (imported pictures, WordArt, OLE objects, gradients, and patterns).	The borders applied to the frame (if any). Gradients and patterns that overlap with or are adjacent to a solidly colored object. Publisher uses the Indeterminate trap value specified in the Trapping Preferences dialog box.	Overlapping or adjacent indeterminate objects. The contents of imported pictures. However, if these objects contain trapping information, Publisher retains it. An imported picture recolored to black within Publisher, when the black percentage is greater than the overprint threshold value specified in the Trapping Preferences dialog box.
Tables.	The table frame border, interior cell borders, fill colors for cells, and text.	Diagonally split cells. Any objects overlapping the table.
White objects.	White objects in a spot color document, but only when you have specified white as a spot color and have activated Trap White As A Color in the Trapping Preferences dialog box. White objects in a CMYK document that are adjacent to a rich black object, but only when you have turned on Keepaway Traps in the Thresholds dialog box.	Objects filled with white in a spot color document if white has not been defined as a spot color.

For more information about Publisher's Pack And Go command, see "Sending a Publisher File to a Commercial Printing Service" earlier in this chapter.

Should I use TrueType fonts or PostScript fonts? Many printing services have a collection of PostScript Type 1 fonts. If you plan to produce a lengthy document or a significant number of publications, you should consider purchasing PostScript fonts that duplicate at least a portion of the printing service's font library. However, there are two drawbacks concerning PostScript fonts. Publisher cannot embed PostScript Type 1 fonts in a publication file. If you are using Windows 95 or 98, Publisher cannot trap PostScript Type 1 fonts.

Publisher's fonts can be embedded into a document. All of the fonts that ship with Publisher 2000 are fully licensed for embedding. You can therefore use these fonts with confidence, knowing that you can legally embed them and send them to a commercial printing service.

Embedding Fonts

Normally a Publisher document doesn't actually contain fonts; it contains instructions that refer to fonts installed on your system. If the printing service doesn't have the fonts you are using in your design, different fonts will be substituted at print time. With a standard Windows font such as Arial or Times New Roman, the substitution might be nearly impossible to detect. When you use a decorative or unusual font, the substituted font probably won't be acceptable.

Publisher addresses this problem by allowing you to embed TrueType fonts into a publication file. When you use the Pack And Go command before transporting a publication file to a commercial printing service, Publisher automatically embeds fonts in the file. In addition, you can use Publisher's commercial printing tools to embed fonts into a publication file. There are, however, several restrictions that you must keep in mind.

- Publisher embeds only TrueType fonts. It cannot embed PostScript Type 1 fonts or printer resident fonts.

- Publisher can embed only TrueType fonts that are properly licensed for this type of distribution.

When a file that contains embedded fonts is opened, Publisher presents a special dialog box that allows you to temporarily install the embedded fonts. The fonts can be used in the current publication only. When the publication is closed, the fonts are removed from the computer system.

What are the advantages and disadvantages of embedding a subset of a font? When you embed a subset of a font, Publisher embeds only those characters that are actually used in the publication. As a result, the file size is smaller and easier to transport to a commercial printing service. However, if you ask the commercial printing service to make text changes to your publication (to correct a spelling or price error, for example) they may be unable to do so, because the necessary characters were not included in the font subset.

Embed Fonts

① On the Tools menu, select Commercial Printing Tools. On the submenu, select Fonts. The Fonts dialog box appears.

② Click this check box to embed TrueType fonts in the publication.

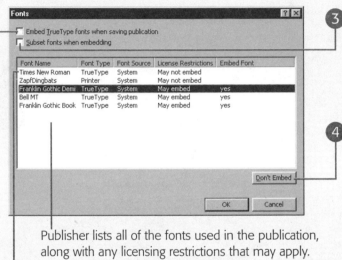

③ Click this check box to embed only the characters you have used in the document and not the entire font.

④ If you don't want to embed a font, select it in the list box and then click the Don't Embed button.

Publisher lists all of the fonts used in the publication, along with any licensing restrictions that may apply.

Publisher doesn't embed system-level TrueType fonts, because these fonts are typically available at a commercial printer.

⑤ Click OK.

What kinds of licensing restrictions might apply to an embedded font? Some fonts can be embedded but are licensed for previews only. If you open a publication that contains preview-only fonts, you can make changes to the publication and print the publication, but you cannot save the publication with the changes.

What is meant by "Duplicate" in the Load Fonts dialog box? If you are about to install a font that has the same name as a font already installed on your system and if you are positive that the fonts are identical, you can choose not to install the duplicate font. If, however, you suspect that two different fonts have the same name, install the embedded font. Publisher uses the embedded font to display and print the publication and removes the duplicate font name from your system when you close the publication.

Open a Publication Containing Embedded Fonts

1. On the File menu, select Open. In the Open dialog box, locate the publication (containing embedded fonts) that you want to open and then click Open. The Load Fonts dialog box appears.

2. Select options to load or not load embedded fonts.

Publisher indicates fonts that will be loaded with the word "Yes," and those that won't be loaded with the word "No."

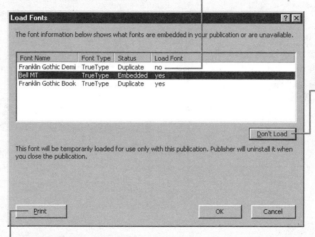

To not load a font, click the font name and then click the Don't Load button. To load a font, click the font name and then click the Load button (which replaces the Don't Load button).

Click Print to print out a report of all fonts used in the publication, including embedded fonts with licensing restrictions and fonts that will be substituted at print time.

3. Click OK. Publisher temporarily installs the fonts and opens the publication.

Managing Linked Graphics

In many cases, a commercial printing service will want direct access to the graphics in your publication. They may want to adjust colors, change the resolution, or save the picture in a different format. Publisher accommodates this requirement by creating links to externally stored pictures.

For more information about inserting pictures, see Chapter 10.

Preserve process color separations. Certain file formats, notably TIFF and EPS files, can contain CMYK information—which is, in effect, a preseparated image. You can preserve the CMYK data by linking these file formats to your publication. This guarantees the best color fidelity when you send your publication to a commercial printing service.

However, if you embed these file formats into a publication, the picture is converted to composite RGB color. Even if you subsequently export the embedded picture, the image file that Publisher saves will contain only composite RGB colors. As a result, you may see dramatic color shifts when you subsequently send your publication to a commercial printing service.

Publication files that contain linked graphics are typically smaller than publications that contain embedded graphics. The reason is obvious. When you embed a graphic in a publication, all of the high resolution data must be stored in the publication—bloating file size. When you import a picture as a linked graphic, Publisher stores only a low resolution screen preview in the publication along with a pointer to the location of the high resolution file.

Whenever you insert a picture into a publication, you have the option of embedding the picture or linking to it. At any time, however, you can use the Graphics Manager dialog box to check or change the status of a graphic. You can update links, embed linked pictures, or create links for embedded pictures.

Embed a Linked Graphic

1 On the Tools menu, select Commercial Printing Tools. On the submenu, select Graphics Manager. The Graphics Manager dialog box appears.

2 In the list box, select the linked file you want to embed.

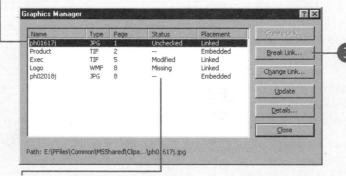

3 Click Break Link. The Break Link dialog box appears.

Publisher always reports the status of a linked graphic as OK, Unchecked, Missing, or Modified.

Why would I want to embed a linked file in my publication? Because embedded graphics are stored as part of the publication file, they are automatically transported along with the publication if you move it or send it to a commercial printing service.

 Check the status of a linked file. You can easily check all of the important statistics of a linked graphic by clicking the Details button in the Graphics Manager dialog box. Publisher displays the Details dialog box, which displays a preview and reports the location, size, color model, and the date the linked file was last modified, as shown below. If you decide to replace the picture with a different one, click the Change Link button and then use the Link To Graphic dialog box to insert a new file.

Embed a Linked Graphic *(continued)*

④ Choose to embed the full resolution image or the low resolution preview that you see on-screen. If you embed the full resolution image, Publisher searches for the file at the link location. If it cannot find the file, Publisher displays the Break Link To Graphic dialog box.

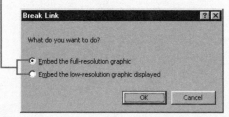

⑤ In the Break Link To Graphic dialog box, browse to locate the file. Then click Break Link.

⑥ Click Close. Publisher embeds the graphic in the publication file.

Update or Change a Graphic Link

① On the Tools menu, select Commercial Printing Tools. On the submenu, select Graphics Manager. The Graphics Manager dialog box appears.

② Select the linked graphic you want to update or modify.

③ Choose one of the following options:

      ❂ Click the Update button. Publisher updates the link based on the previous known location of the file. If the file is missing, Publisher displays the Link To Graphic dialog box.

      ❂ Click the Change Link button. Publisher displays the Link To Graphic dialog box.

④ In the Link To Graphic dialog box, locate the new file you want to insert into the publication as a linked graphic. The new file will replace the existing image.

⑤ Click Link To File to return to the Graphics Manager dialog box.

⑥ Click Close.

Link to Publisher's clip art. When you insert a picture from Publisher's Clip Gallery Tool, the picture is always embedded into the publication. You can use the Graphics Manager dialog box to create links to Clip Gallery images.

Export embedded graphics. If you no longer have the original picture file, you can export an embedded graphic to an external file and create a link to it. In the Create Link dialog box, select the second option: Create A Link From The Full Resolution Graphic Stored In The Publication And Link To That. In the Save As dialog box that appears, choose a location, type a file name, and then click Save.

Be warned, however, that Publisher can save only a handful of graphics file formats, as noted below:

- Bitmapped graphics, including .bmp, .gif, and .jpg, are converted to .tif.

- Transparent .gif files are exported as .gif.

- Vector graphics and .eps files are exported as .wmf.

- The first frame of motion graphics, including .avi video and animated .gif, is exported as .tif.

Create a Link for an Embedded Graphic

① On the Tools menu, select Commercial Printing Tools. On the submenu, select Graphics Manager. The Graphics Manager dialog box appears.

② In the list box, select the embedded graphic you would like to link.

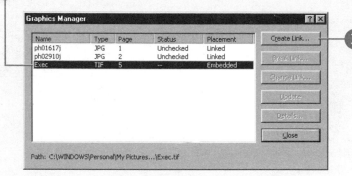

③ Click the Create Link button. The Create Link dialog box appears.

④ Select this option to browse for the original file and link to it.

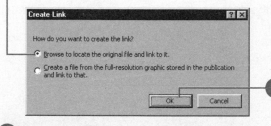

⑤ Click OK. Publisher displays the Link To Graphic dialog box.

⑥ In the Link To Graphic dialog box, locate the file you want to insert into the publication as a linked graphic.

⑦ Click Link To File to return to the Graphics Manager dialog box.

⑧ Click Close.

Publisher's outside printer drivers. When you install Publisher, two generic printers are added to your system: MS Publisher Color Printer and MS Publisher Imagesetter. These are generic PostScript drivers that prepare a document properly for medium resolution full color output or high resolution output, respectively.

Choose the correct PostScript format. When you generate a PostScript file, specify the most reliable format to reduce printing errors. In the printer Properties dialog box, click the PostScript tab and choose the PostScript (Optimize For Portability—ADSC) option to create a file that conforms to the Adobe Document Structuring Conventions.

For more information on changing settings in the printer Properties dialog box, see Chapter 17. For more information about printer device options, see "Device Output Options" later in this chapter.

Sending a PostScript File to a Printing Service

When you create a PostScript print file, you are translating Publisher's native file format into a format that contains all the information needed to print the file, including all of the font information and all of the commands necessary to operate the printer.

Publisher supplies a generic PostScript printer driver that is compatible with the high resolution, professional-quality output devices found at copy shops, service bureaus, and commercial printing services. Because PostScript output is not device-specific, the same PostScript file can print on any PostScript printer.

Save a PostScript File

1. On the Tools menu, choose Commercial Printing Tools. On the submenu, select Color Printing.

2. In the Color Printing dialog box, confirm that the publication is set up for either process color (CMYK) or spot color printing.

3. On the File menu, choose Save As.

4. In the Save As dialog box, open the Save As Type drop-down list and then select PostScript (*.ps).

5. Use the Files and Folders list box to choose a location for the PostScript file.

6. Enter a name into the File Name text box.

7. Click Save. The Save As PostScript File dialog box appears.

Transporting large files to a printing service. A 3.5-inch floppy disk can hold 1.44 megabytes of information. If the PostScript file is too large to fit on a floppy disk, you can transport the file using one of the following methods:

- Use a third party compression utility, such as PKZIP or WinZip, which reduces the size of the file. The printing service must have the same version of the utility to decompress the file.

- Use high-capacity removable media, provided that both you and your printing service have access to the same type of Syquest, Bernoulli, Zip, or Jaz drive.

- If your computer is equipped with a modem and Internet access, ask if the printing service accepts files by way of standard telecommunications software or their Web site.

- Use a backup utility (such as the Norton Utilities or Windows Backup) to copy the file to several disks. The printing service must have the same utility in order to restore the file.

Save a PostScript File *(continued)*

8 Open the drop-down list box and select a PostScript printer driver.

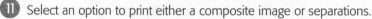

9 Click the Properties button to change hardware printer settings.

12 If you are printing separations, open the drop-down list box and select a color plate, or select All to print all color plates.

10 Click the Advanced Print Settings button to access device options.

13 Click Save.

11 Select an option to print either a composite image or separations.

14 When the PostScript file has been saved, transfer it to the commercial printing service on floppy disk (or other removable media).

Create an Encapsulated PostScript File

Some printing services, especially Mac-based printing services, prefer to receive files in the Encapsulated PostScript (EPS) format. Unfortunately, you cannot use the Save As command to generate an EPS file. However, you can produce EPS files using Publisher's standard Print command. To do so, you'll have to change a configuration option in the PostScript printer driver.

Change your view of the document. If you are working in a multiple-page document and you are viewing spreads, open the View menu and clear Two-Page Spread. You must be viewing a single page in order to print a single page as the current page of the document.

Can I generate an EPS file if I am using Windows NT? No. The Windows NT PostScript printer driver doesn't support EPS output.

Import EPS files into a publication. You can import an EPS file that you created from Publisher (as described in the procedure titled, "Create An Encapsulated PostScript File") into a publication. Publisher doesn't save EPS files with a screen preview. Instead, you will see only a bounding box that contains the name of the file, the date on which it was created, and the PostScript driver version number. The EPS file will print properly when sent to a PostScript printer. It cannot, however, be printed on a non-PostScript device.

Create an Encapsulated PostScript File

1. On the Tools menu, choose Commercial Printing Tools. On the submenu, select Color Printing.

2. In the Color Printing dialog box, confirm that the publication is set up for either process color (CMYK) or spot color printing.

3. If you are printing a multiple-page document, move to the page you want to generate as an EPS file. Encapsulated PostScript files cannot contain multiple pages.

4. On the File menu, choose Print.

5. In the Print dialog box, open the drop-down list and select a PostScript printer.

6. Click the Properties button.

7. In the Properties dialog box, click the PostScript tab.

8. Open the PostScript Output Format drop-down list and then select Encapsulated PostScript (EPS).

9. Click OK to return to the Print dialog box.

10. Click the Print To File check box.

11. If you are printing a multiple-page document, select Current Page in the Create PostScript File dialog box.

12. Select the Composite option.

13. Click OK. The Printing and Print To File dialog boxes appear.

14. In the Print To File dialog box, specify a location and a file name for the EPS file. The file name extension must be .eps.

15. Click OK in the Print To File dialog box. The Printing dialog box reports on Publisher's status as it converts the current page to an EPS file and saves it to disk.

Use a printer that isn't connected to your computer. You can print a publication on a printer that isn't physically connected to your computer. For example, you might create a publication at home but print it at the office where you have a high resolution or color printer.

In Publisher's Print dialog box, select the offsite printer as the output device and click the Print To File check box. After you've saved the output file to your hard disk, transfer it to the hard disk of the computer that is attached to the printer you want to use.

On the Windows Start menu, select Programs and then select MS-DOS Prompt. At the MS-DOS prompt, type the following command to send the file to the printer:

copy *filename*.prn lpt1: /b

Replace "filename.prn" with the full path and name of your output file. Type the correct parallel port information for the printer you are using. For example, the printer might be attached to LPT2. The "/b" ensures that the entire file will be printed, even if it contains more than one page.

For more information about printer ports and the MS-DOS prompt, see the Windows online help system.

Device Output Options

Publisher's Device Options dialog box lets you choose the output options required by your commercial printing service. Depending upon the particular process used to generate film or printing plates, you can print your publication upside down, flipped right to left, or as a negative. In addition, the Device Options dialog box gives you the power to control the resolution at which the document is printed.

Choose Device Options

1 On the Tools menu, select Commercial Printing Tools. On the submenu, select Color Printing.

2 In the Color Printing dialog box, confirm that you are printing either a process color (CMYK) or spot color document. Then click OK.

3 Open the File menu and select Print. In the Print dialog box, open the Name drop-down list and choose a high resolution PostScript output device.

4 Click the Advanced Print Settings button. The Print Settings dialog box appears.

How is printer resolution measured?
Printer resolution is measured in dots per inch (dpi). However, in order to print photographic images or tints of a color, printers employ halftone screens. Halftone resolution is measured in lines per inch (lpi), also known as screen frequency.

Choose publication options before you create a PostScript file.
Before you generate a PostScript file, you should also determine how you want to handle font substitution, image quality for linked graphics, printer marks, bleeds, and color plates that don't contain any image data. The controls for these functions are found on the Publication Options tab of the Print Settings dialog box.

For more information about publication options, see Chapter 17.

How do I determine the correct screen frequency and screen angle values? Consult with your commercial printing service. Only the printer can tell you the optimal screen values required by his equipment.

Choose Device Options *(continued)*

5 Click the Device Options tab.

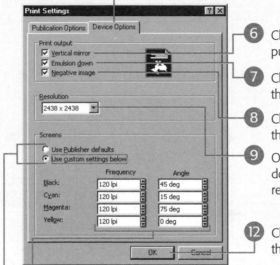

6 Click Vertical Mirror to print the publication upside down.

7 Click Emulsion Down to flip the printout left-to-right.

8 Click Negative Image to reverse the tonal values in the printout.

9 Open the Resolution drop-down list and select a printer resolution, measured in dpi.

12 Click OK to return to the Print dialog box.

11 If you choose to use custom settings, enter screen frequency and screen angle values into the text boxes for each of the color plates.

10 Click Use Publisher Defaults for the screen settings, or click Use Custom Settings Below.

Desktop Printing

For a complete description of the Printers folder, refer to the Windows online help system.

Microsoft Publisher 2000 lets you print a wide range of projects right from your desktop—including folded cards, multiple-page books, oversized banners and posters, undersized business cards and labels, and mail-merge documents. Even if you intend to send your publication to a commercial printing service, you can still print proofs using your desktop printer. You can improve overall printing speeds, enhance the final appearance of your publication, and even save paper by taking control of the printing process.

Publisher's Print dialog box offers both basic and advanced options that let you specify how a document will be printed. In addition, you can configure the actual printer hardware, using either Publisher's Print Setup dialog box or your printer's Properties dialog box (which can be accessed from within Publisher or from the Printers folder in Windows).

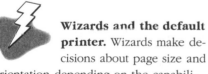

Wizards and the default printer. Wizards make decisions about page size and orientation depending on the capabilities of the default printer. Make sure you choose the correct printer as the default printer *before* you create a publication using a wizard.

Changing Printer Properties

The Printers folder in Windows and Publisher's Print Setup command offer options for changing printer characteristics.

Choosing a Default Printer

When you begin a new publication, Publisher assumes that you want to use the printer designated as the default printer in Windows. If you have more than one printer installed on your computer, you can select the printer you would like to use as the default.

Is the Set As Default command found only on the shortcut menu?
No. In the Printers folder, you can select the icon that represents the printer you want to use as the default. Then choose Set As Default on the File menu.

Is there any difference between accessing the printer Properties dialog box from the Windows Printers folder and accessing the printer Properties dialog box from within Publisher? Yes, there is an important difference. If you use the Properties button in Publisher's Print or Print Setup dialog box to access the printer Properties dialog box, the changes you make apply to the current document only. If you use the Printers folder in the Windows Control Panel to access the printer Properties dialog box, the changes you make apply to all print jobs sent from any application to that printer.

Select the Default Printer

1 On the Windows Start menu, choose Settings. On the Settings submenu, choose Printers.

2 In the Printers folder, right-click the icon that represents the printer you want as your default. The shortcut menu appears.

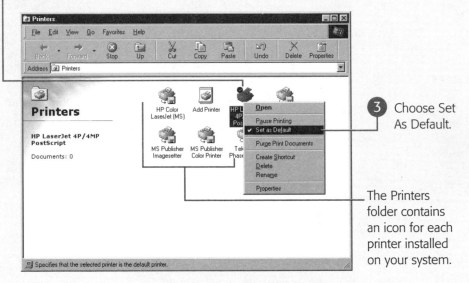

3 Choose Set As Default.

The Printers folder contains an icon for each printer installed on your system.

Choosing Printer and Paper Options

By using Publisher's Print Setup dialog box, you can choose a new printer and specify unique paper options for each document you create.

Select Printer and Paper Options Within Publisher

1 Choose Print Setup on Publisher's File menu. The Print Setup dialog box appears.

2 Select the options you want.

When to use the Manual Feed paper option.
Specify Manual Feed if you want to feed envelopes, small cards, or heavier stocks through your printer. Feeding small or thick paper by hand can help you avoid paper jams.

Where can I change the paper orientation? You can change the orientation of the printer paper in three places:

⊚ The printer Properties dialog box, accessed from the Printers folder, sets the default orientation for the printer.

⊚ The Print Setup dialog box, accessed from Publisher's File menu, sets the orientation for the current document.

⊚ The Page Setup dialog box, accessed from Publisher's File menu, sets the orientation for the current document.

Select Printer and Paper Options Within Publisher *(continued)*

Open the Size drop-down list box to choose one of the standard paper sizes.

Open the Name drop-down list box to choose a printer.

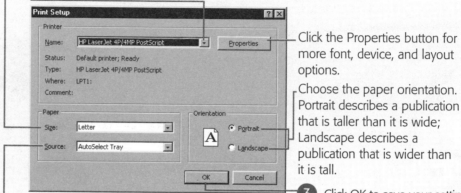

Click the Properties button for more font, device, and layout options.

Choose the paper orientation. Portrait describes a publication that is taller than it is wide; Landscape describes a publication that is wider than it is tall.

3 Click OK to save your settings.

Open the Source drop-down list box to choose paper tray options or Manual Feed.

Customizing the Paper Size

You can give your designs an aesthetic boost by using special paper stocks, such as note paper, folded cards, and postcards. Many stationery stores, office supply stores, and mail order companies carry specialty papers that work with a desktop laser or inkjet printer. To print on these nonstandard papers, you must define a custom paper size in the printer Properties dialog box.

Select an Atypical Paper Size for Your Document

1 Choose Print or Print Setup on the File menu.

2 In the Print or Print Setup dialog box, click the Properties button. The printer Properties dialog box appears. The actual options you see will depend upon the capabilities of your printer. The following dialog box displays options for a PostScript laser printer.

Why isn't the Custom button available in the Properties dialog box for my printer? The Custom button is available only for printers that accommodate custom paper sizes. In all likelihood, your printer doesn't support custom paper sizes. To produce unusually sized publications, you must print your document to a full-size sheet of paper and then trim the excess paper.

Why can't I select a custom paper size from the Size drop-down list in Publisher's Print Setup dialog box? If you attempt to select a custom-sized paper directly from the drop-down list of paper sizes available in the Print Setup dialog box, Publisher doesn't recognize the paper size and defaults your selection to a different size. Therefore, you should always choose a custom paper size in the Properties dialog box, as described in the procedure "Select an Atypical Paper Size for Your Document."

Select an Atypical Paper Size for Your Document *(continued)*

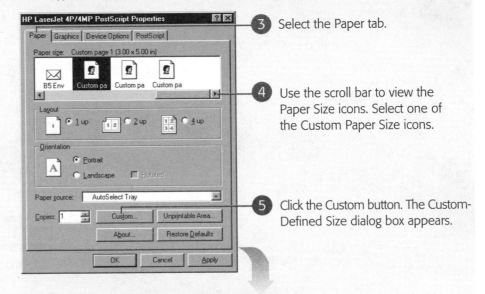

3. Select the Paper tab.

4. Use the scroll bar to view the Paper Size icons. Select one of the Custom Paper Size icons.

5. Click the Custom button. The Custom-Defined Size dialog box appears.

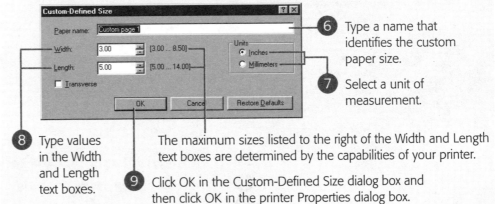

6. Type a name that identifies the custom paper size.

7. Select a unit of measurement.

8. Type values in the Width and Length text boxes.

The maximum sizes listed to the right of the Width and Length text boxes are determined by the capabilities of your printer.

9. Click OK in the Custom-Defined Size dialog box and then click OK in the printer Properties dialog box.

How can I determine nonprinting margins on an older printer?

Older printers typically do not supply Windows with information about nonprinting margins. You can still determine the size of the nonprinting margins empirically. Create a new publication. In the Print Setup dialog box, select the largest paper size your printer can accomodate. In the Page Setup dialog box, choose the Normal option. Using the Rectangle tool, draw a rectangle that covers the entire page. With the rectangle selected, choose Fill Color on the Formatting toolbar and then choose a color or gray tint in the drop-down list that appears. Don't choose the Clear or White options. Print the page. The unshaded areas around the edge constitute the nonprinting margins.

To bypass the Print dialog box and output a publication with the current printer settings, click the Print button on the Standard toolbar.

Accommodating Nonprinting Margins

Most printers are alike in one important way: they reserve a portion of the page to grip the paper and feed it through the printing mechanism. This portion of the page can't contain any images or text. Whenever you plan a full-page publication, be sure you set page margins that are at least as wide as your printer's nonprinting margins.

Determine the Standard Nonprinting Margins for Your Printer

1. Choose Print or Print Setup on the File menu.

2. In the Print or Print Setup dialog box, click the Properties button. The printer Properties dialog box appears. The options you see will depend upon the capabilities of your printer.

3. Select the Paper tab.

4. Click the Unprintable Area button. The Unprintable Area dialog box appears.

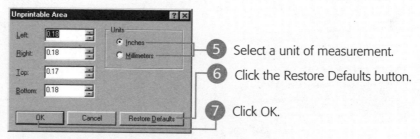

5. Select a unit of measurement.

6. Click the Restore Defaults button.

7. Click OK.

Choosing Printing Options

Publisher streamlines the printing process by placing only the most frequently used options in the first level of the Print dialog box. However, the Advanced Print Settings dialog box provides control over many details of the printing process, such as font usage, image quality, and printer marks.

You can access the Print dialog box by pressing Ctrl-P.

 Drag-and-drop printing. You can print a document by dragging a Publisher file and dropping it on top of the icon for your printer. Windows then opens Publisher in order to print the file.

 For more information about book printing options, tile printing options, and page options, see "Printing Atypically Sized Publications" and "Printing Folded Publications" later in this chapter.

 Interrupt printing. When you issue the Print command, Publisher displays the Printing dialog box, which tells you how much of the file has been processed. You can interrupt printing by clicking the Cancel button. Publisher immediately stops sending information to either your printer or the Windows print queue. However, any pages that have already been sent to the printer and stored in its memory will print.

Choose Printer Options

1 On the File menu, select Print. The Print dialog box appears.

2 Change the settings as appropriate.

Open the drop-down list box to select a different printer installed on your system.

Click here to access the printer Properties dialog box.

Select this check box to save the print version of your document to disk, instead of sending it directly to a printer.

Enter the number of copies you want to print.

Click this check box to collate copies. Publisher prints each copy of your publication in the correct page order. You can speed up printing by turning collation off. When this check box is cleared, Publisher prints every page 1, then every page 2, and so on.

Click here to access the Advanced Print Settings dialog box.

3 Click OK.

Choose the range of pages to print. If you decide to print a section of a larger publication, enter the starting and ending page numbers in the From and To text boxes, respectively.

The Book Printing Options button, Page Options button, or the Tile Printing Options button appears here and allows you to determine the arrangement of publication pages on the sheet of paper.

Choose Advanced Print Settings

1 On the File menu, select Print. In the Print dialog box, click the Advanced Print Settings button. The Print Settings dialog box appears.

Why should I add printer's marks to my document? Printer's marks provide identifying information and quality control marks. Specifically:

- Registration marks are used to align printing plates for color separated documents.

- Job information includes the publication name, a date and time stamp, the page number, and the color of ink.

- Density bars and color bars provide a 10-step scale that allows commercial printers to evaluate and control the ink density.

Choose device options for color separations. The Device Options tab in the Advanced Print Settings dialog box lets you change printer settings for resolution, halftone screens, and image orientation. Alter these settings only if you are generating color separations and you have received specific instructions from your commercial printing service.

For more information about Publisher's color separation functions and the Device Options tab, see Chapter 16. For more information about ICM, see Chapter 15.

Choose Advanced Print Settings *(continued)*

2 Click the Publication Options tab.

3 Select the appropriate options for the current print job.

Choose one of three resolution options for linked graphics. Full resolution graphics provide the best quality but take longest to print. For quick proofs, you can choose to print low resolution graphics or no graphics (which print as X-filled rectangles).

Choose a font handling option. Font substitution allows Publisher to use printer resident fonts that are a close (but not necessarily exact) match to the specified font. If you want the printout to match the screen image exactly, select Use Only Publication Fonts.

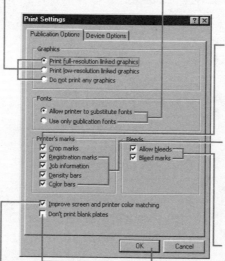

Select the Crop Marks check box to print guides that help you trim a publication to the final size.

If you have set up your publication for a commercial printing service, you can add information to the margins of the printout. Publisher requires at least 1 inch of free space on the paper to add printer's marks to the output.

Select Allow Bleeds if you want to print images and text off the edge of your page. If you select Bleed Marks, Publisher prints a second set of trim marks 0.25 inch beyond the crop marks.

Select this option to activate the Image Color Matching (ICM) system.

4 Click OK to return to the Print dialog box. Click OK in the Print dialog box to begin printing.

If you are printing a process color or spot color document, select this option to print only those color plates that contain text or images.

Why aren't the tiling options available in the Print dialog box? Tiling is available only when you use the Special Size option in the Page Setup dialog box *and* the printer's paper size is smaller than the document's page size.

Print a single tile of your poster or banner. You don't have to reprint an entire banner or poster to check a section of your design—to correct a spelling mistake, for example. Instead, select Print One Tile From Ruler Origin in the Poster And Banner Printing Options dialog box. Before you use this option, however, you must change the zero points of both the horizontal and the vertical rulers in your publication so that they align with the upper left corner of the tile you want to print.

For more information about the Page Setup command, see Chapter 2. For more information about changing the position of a ruler's zero point, see Chapter 3.

Printing Atypically Sized Publications

It doesn't matter to Publisher how big or small your publication might be. An oversized banner or a poster is still considered to be a single page. If the paper size happens to be smaller than the document page size, Publisher prints the publication page across several sheets of paper in a process known as tiling. If the paper size happens to be larger than the document page size, Publisher lets you print either a single copy or multiple copies on a single sheet of paper.

Print a Poster or a Banner

1. On the File menu, select the Page Setup command and confirm that the Special Size layout option for a poster or banner is selected. Click OK to close the Page Setup dialog box.

2. On the File menu, select the Print command. The Print dialog box appears.

3. Click the Tile Printing Options button. The Poster And Banner Printing Options dialog box appears.

4. Select Print Entire Page

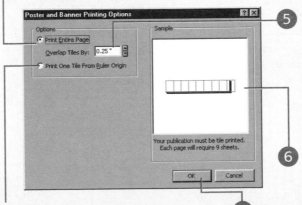

5. Enter a value from 0 through 6.25 inches in the Overlap Tiles By text box. By default, Publisher overlaps the image by 0.25 inch to avoid any white gaps between sections of the poster or banner.

6. Preview the layout of the poster or banner in the Sample area.

Select this option to print a single section, or tile, of the poster or banner.

7. Click OK to return to the Print dialog box.

Why isn't the Page Options button available in the Print dialog box? Page options that allow you to print more than one copy of a publication on a single sheet of paper are available only when you use the Special Size or Labels option in the Page Setup dialog box *and* the printer's paper size is large enough to accommodate more than one copy of the document's page size.

The trouble with 0-value margins. Although Publisher allows you to enter a value of 0 in the Side Margin and Top Margin text boxes, you would rarely want to do so. Setting these margins at 0 places a portion of the page into the printer's nonprinting margin. When you print the publication, part of your design might be cut off.

For more information about nonprinting margins, see "Accommodating Nonprinting Margins" earlier in this chapter.

Print a Small Publication

1 On the File menu, choose the Page Setup command and confirm that the Special Size layout option for a small publication, such as a business card, is selected. Click OK to close the Page Setup dialog box.

2 On the File menu, select the Print command. The Print dialog box appears.

3 Click the Page Options button. The Page Options dialog box appears.

4 Choose an option to either print one copy of the publication centered on the page, or to print multiple copies of the publication on a single sheet of paper.

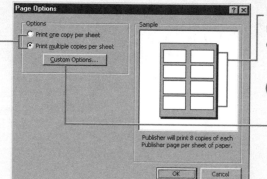

Publisher always shows the number of copies that will fit on a single sheet of paper.

5 Click the Custom Options button to display the Custom Options–Small Publications dialog box, where you can modify the arrangement of copies on the paper.

6 Enter new values in the margin and gap text boxes. The minimum value you can enter is 0. The maximum value is determined by the paper size and the page size.

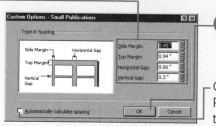

7 Click OK in the Custom Options–Small Publications dialog box. Then click OK in the Page Options dialog box.

Click this check box to have Publisher automatically calculate the spacing between copies.

Why are the pages for my folded document printed upside-down or out of order? When Publisher prints the pages for a folded publication, they may appear to be upside-down or out of order. Don't be concerned. This odd-looking arrangement, called the imposition, ensures that the pages will appear in the correct order when you fold the paper to create the final document.

Printing Folded Publications

Publisher can print documents that are ready to be folded into a card or book. If you are printing a card, Publisher prints all of the pages on one sheet of paper. A multiple-page book, however, requires you to bind the pages together.

Print a Card

1. On the File menu, choose the Page Setup command, and confirm that the Special Fold layout for a tent card, a side-fold card, or a top-fold card is selected. Click OK to close the Page Setup dialog box.

2. On the File menu, select the Print command. The Print dialog box appears.

3. In the Print Range area, click All Pages to have Publisher print two pages on each sheet of paper (for a tent card) or four pages on each sheet of paper (for a side- or top-fold card).

4. Click OK.

5. To complete the card, fold it in half (for a tent card) or in quarters (for a top- or side-fold card).

Print a Book

1. On the File menu, choose the Page Setup command, and confirm that the Special Fold layout for the book fold is selected. Click OK to close the Page Setup dialog box.

2. On the File menu, select the Print command. The Print dialog box appears.

Print a normal publication as a book. If you print a normal 8.5 x 11-inch publication to a printer that can accommodate tabloid size paper, Publisher allows you to print it as a book. Simply click the Book Printing Options button in the Print dialog box (accessed from the File menu) and select the Print As Book option, as shown below.

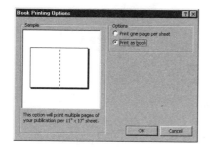

Why does Publisher insert blank pages when I print my book?
The book layout works only if the number of pages in your document is a multiple of 4 (4, 8, 12, and so on). If the number of pages isn't a multiple of 4, you will have "blanks" at the end. If you want to insert blank pages in specific locations, use the Page command on the Insert menu.

Print a Book *(continued)*

③ In the Print Range area, select an appropriate option:

 ◉ Click All Pages to have Publisher create an imposition for the entire document.

 ◉ Click Pages and enter page numbers in the From and To text boxes to print a section of the book.

 ◉ Click Current Page to print a single selected page of the document.

④ Click OK.

⑤ If you are printing only a portion of a book, a confirmation dialog box appears. Click Yes to print the selected pages as a separate booklet. Publisher recalculates the imposition for the selected pages so that the first page in the range becomes a right-hand page. Click No to print the selected pages as part of the entire book. Publisher preserves the imposition for the entire book by printing the selected pages along with the appropriate facing page in each spread.

Arranging the Pages of a Book by Hand

Most laser printers print on only one side of the paper, but you can still create a book using Publisher, your laser printer, and a copy machine. Look at the following illustration of an eight-page book, which will help you understand how a book, newsletter, or magazine is constructed. You perform two basic operations when assembling a book:

 ◉ Use a copy machine to make double-sided pages.

 ◉ Bind the book by folding, assembling, and stapling the pages.

Duplex printing. If your laser printer supports duplex printing, Publisher can print on both sides of the paper simultaneously.

 For more information on customizing page options, see "Print A Small Publication" earlier in this chapter.

 Why can't I find the Print Merge command on the File menu? If the Print Merge command is not available, it means that you have not properly set up the publication for mail merge. Connect the publication to a data source and insert at least one field code in the publication. The Print Merge command should now be available.

 For detailed instructions on mail-merge operations, see Chapter 13.

When Publisher prints the pages in a book, it starts from the outside and works toward the center two facing pages, also called the center spread. When you assemble your book, you must also work your way toward the center.

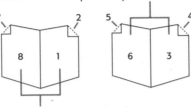

The first page of your book must be a right-hand page, and the last must be a left-hand page.

For an eight-page publication, copy the sheet containing pages 8 and 1 onto the back of the sheet containing pages 2 and 7.

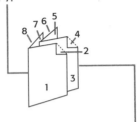

Then copy the sheet containing pages 6 and 3 onto the back of the sheet containing pages 4 and 5.

Printing Mail Merge Documents

When you print a mail merge document, Publisher prints the results of the merge operation, meaning that each copy of the publication contains a different entry from the address list. The Print Merge command offers specialized options that can help you test whether the mail merge is working properly. In addition, several of Publisher's standard print options have new significance when you are printing a mail merge publication.

Print a Merged Document

 On the File menu, choose Print Merge. The Print Merge dialog box appears.

Page layout options for mail merge labels. In the Page Setup dialog box (available from the File menu), Publisher offers 80 page layouts for Avery labels—the standard brand for sheets of multiple labels. An Avery product number identifies each layout choice.

Even if you are working with labels from another manufacturer, you still can print labels efficiently. Create a special size publication, where the page size equals the size of one label. In the Print dialog box, click the Page Options button to open the Page Options dialog box, where you can adjust the placement of labels on the page.

 Are there special options to print envelopes in the Print dialog box? No, the Print dialog box does not contain any special commands to print envelopes. Instead, you must coordinate the settings you have chosen in the Options dialog box (opened from the Tools menu), the Page Setup dialog box (opened from the File menu), and the Print Setup dialog box (opened from the File menu).

Print a Merged Document *(continued)*

 Select All Entries to print all of the entries in your data source, or enter a range of entries to be printed. These print options reflect any filter or sort criteria you applied to the data source.

Open this drop-down list box to specify where on a sheet of labels Publisher should begin printing. For example, if you've already used two rows of labels from a sheet of labels, you can begin printing at row 3. If you are not printing labels, this option is unavailable.

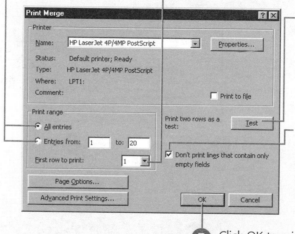

Click the Test button to print only one publication (or two rows of labels) as a test. This functions as a quick preview and can help you discover printing problems at the outset.

Click this check box to remove blank lines from the printed publication. Blank lines are caused by empty fields in the data source.

Click OK to print the merged document.

Printing Envelopes

Printers differ in their ability to print envelopes. Some printers support envelopes as a standard paper size; others require custom settings. Publisher offers special configuration options that can help you output envelopes correctly on your particular printer.

Why don't envelopes print correctly? The answer depends upon the settings you chose on the Print tab in the Options dialog box.

@ If you chose Automatically Use Envelope Paper Sizes, you must select one of the envelope publication layouts in the Page Setup dialog box.

@ If you chose Print Envelopes To This Printer Using These Settings, you must be sure that the orientation and placement options you've selected on the Print tab in the Options dialog box match those required by your printer. You must also be sure to specify a paper size that is equal to the size of your envelope in the Print Setup dialog box.

Print on colored paper. Even if you own a black-and-white printer, you can easily add color to your publications by printing on colored paper. Laser-compatible and inkjet-compatible papers come in a wide variety of colors and designs.

For more information about specialty papers, see Chapter 15.

Choose Envelope Printing Options

1 Choose the Options command on the Tools menu.

2 Click the Print tab.

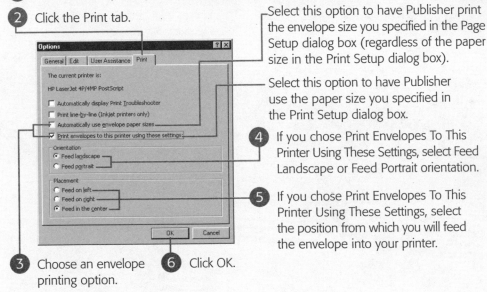

Select this option to have Publisher print the envelope size you specified in the Page Setup dialog box (regardless of the paper size in the Print Setup dialog box).

Select this option to have Publisher use the paper size you specified in the Print Setup dialog box.

4 If you chose Print Envelopes To This Printer Using These Settings, select Feed Landscape or Feed Portrait orientation.

5 If you chose Print Envelopes To This Printer Using These Settings, select the position from which you will feed the envelope into your printer.

3 Choose an envelope printing option.

6 Click OK.

Printing Color Documents

Publisher can print black-and-white, full color, and spot color documents to any Windows–compatible printer. If you print a color document to a black-and-white printer, Publisher converts all of the colors in the publication to black, white, and shades of gray.

Whenever you print a process color (CMYK) or spot color document, the Print dialog box contains special commands that allow you to print proofs on a desktop printer.

Why don't the spot colors I specified look the same on screen as in the printed proof? When you set up a spot color document, Publisher lets you choose a color from either a pre-defined palette of 35 standard hues or from the Pantone color library. Publisher must represent the spot color on the screen using RGB values and must print the color to a color desktop printer using CMYK values. Both the screen color and the proof are merely simulations. The spot color, especially if you have chosen a Pantone color, refers to a pre-mixed ink. To accurately judge the spot color you have chosen, you must refer to a swatch book, such as the Pantone Color Imaging Guide. Industry standard swatch booklets are available at graphic art supply stores.

Printing Color Proofs

Publisher allows you to print two kinds of proofs: composite proofs and color separations. A composite proof prints all colors on a single sheet of paper. As shown in the following illustration, this proof allows you to check how different color elements on the page register with one another.

A spot color composite proof  A process color composite proof

When printed to a black-and-white printer, Publisher converts colors in a composite proof to shades of gray.

Publisher also allows you to print spot color or process color separations for a document. A separated proof prints each color on a different sheet of paper (or film). As shown in the following illustration, this proof shows the structure of the separation—including overprinting and knockouts.

Spot color separations  Process color separations

Notice that Publisher prints the true tint percentage of each color. A 100 percent tint of a light yellow, for example, prints as solid black.

Print a Proof of Your Process Color or Spot Color Document

1 On the Tools menu, choose Commercial Printing Tools. On the submenu, select Color Printing to confirm that you are printing either a process color or spot color document. Click OK to close the Color Printing dialog box.

2 On the File menu, select the Print command. The Print dialog box appears.

3 In the Print Range area, select one of the following options: All Pages, From (specifying page numbers), or Current Page.

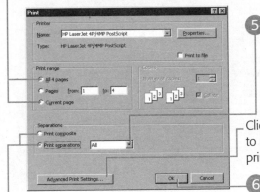

5 If you have chosen to print separations, open the drop-down list and choose a specific color plate from the list of available colors. To print all color plates, choose All.

Click the Advanced Print Settings button to control font usage, image quality, and printer marks.

6 Click OK.

4 Select the kind of proof you want to print—either a composite or separations.

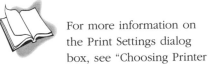

For more information on the Print Settings dialog box, see "Choosing Printer Options" earlier in this chapter.

Common Printing Problems and Solutions

Publisher is a *WYSIWYG* (What You See Is What You Get) desktop publishing program, which means that the screen preview attempts to show you how the final printed page will appear. There are situations in which the printed output will not match the screen preview. The following table summarizes some of the most common problems you might encounter and offers possible solutions.

Printing Problems and Solutions

If you're having this problem...	Because of these circumstances...	Try this solution...
Rotated or white text isn't printing.	You are printing special text, such as text that has been rotated for a card layout, to an inkjet printer (or to an older dot matrix printer).	Optimize printing for an inkjet printer by selecting Print Line-By-Line (Inkjet Printers Only) on the Print tab in the Options dialog box (opened from the Tools menu). Alternatively, you can convert all of the problematic text to WordArt. WordArt is sent to the printer as a picture—not as text.
The printed font looks different from the font on screen.	You are using a printer-based font that Publisher cannot accurately preview on screen.	Use TrueType fonts, which Publisher can preview on screen. Or, if you are using PostScript fonts, install a type manager utility such as Adobe Type Manager, which generates accurate screen previews.
The printer generates a memory error message or prints only half of the page.	You are printing a document that contains many pages, large or numerous pictures, or a wide variety of fonts.	Reduce the memory required for the current document by printing only one page (or a small range of pages) in a multiple-page document, reducing the resolution of imported pictures, or reducing the number of fonts used in the publication. Alternatively, you can install more memory in your printer.
The printed colors do not match the colors as they appear on screen.	You are printing colors specified with RGB values or a Pantone Solid color to a CMYK printer.	Click Image Color Matching (ICM) in the printer Properties dialog box and within Publisher to mark those colors that will not reproduce well on your printer. Alternatively, convert all of the colors in your document to Process CMYK values.

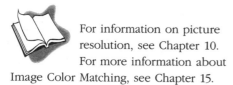

For information on picture resolution, see Chapter 10. For more information about Image Color Matching, see Chapter 15.

To learn about non-printing margins, see "Accommodating Nonprinting Margins" earlier in this chapter.

 Use printer-resident fonts to reduce printer memory requirements for long, text-intensive publications. A printer typically has a small selection of scalable fonts built into its ROM (Read Only Memory). Unlike software-based fonts (which must be downloaded to the printer's memory), hardware-based fonts don't use up any additional printer memory. If you are receiving memory error messages when you attempt to print a lengthy, text-based document, try substituting printer-resident fonts for fonts (such as TrueType fonts) that must be downloaded to the printer. An icon of a printer precedes a printer-resident font in the Font drop-down list.

Printing Problems and Solutions *(continued)*

If you're having this problem...	Because of these circumstances...	Try this solution...
Text and pictures aren't properly positioned on the page, or they are cut off at the edge of the paper.	You have ignored the non-printing margins required by your printer, or you are printing on a paper size that differs from the paper size you specified in the printer Properties dialog box.	Create page margins (using the Layout Guides dialog box opened from the Arrange menu) that are larger than the non-printing margins of your printer. Confirm that the paper size you have specified in the Print Setup or printer Properties dialog box matches the size of the paper you have actually inserted into your printer.
Images and text that should extend past the trimmed edges of the paper have been cropped.	You have not instructed Publisher to bleed the image off the page.	In the Print dialog box (opened from the File menu), click the Advanced Print Settings button. In the Bleed area, select Allow Bleeds.
Gradient fills print as a series of stripes or bands.	You are printing on a low-resolution printer that cannot produce a sufficient number of shades to create a gradual tonal transition.	Minimize banding by turning on error diffusion or dithering, using settings found on the Graphics tab in the printer Properties dialog box. Not all printers support this feature.

Special effects influence printer performance. Certain types of objects or formatting attributes can increase the size of the file sent to the printer, require more printer memory, and increase printing times. If you are having problems printing your document, search the publication for OLE objects, such as Microsoft Draw pictures or WordArt effects. Printing pages that contain these objects separately, can, in many cases, solve the output problems. You should also look for large drawn shapes or frames that are formatted with pattern fills. Simply changing a pattern fill to a solid color, tint, or shade can improve the printer's performance dramatically.

For more information about Publisher's Help system, see Chapter 1.

The Print Troubleshooter

The Print Troubleshooter is part of Publisher's online Help system. It pinpoints the cause of many common printing problems and suggests solutions to them. You can access the Print Troubleshooter in one of two ways:

@ Click Automatically Display Print Troubleshooter on the Print tab in the Options dialog box (opened from the Tools menu).

@ Choose Print Troubleshooter from the Help menu.

The Print Troubleshooter appears in Publisher's standard Help window.

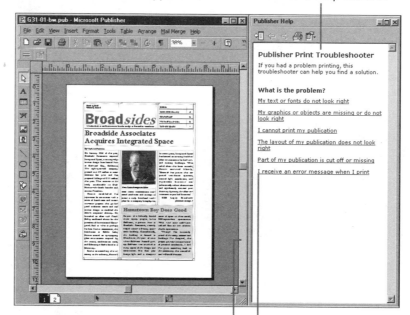

Use the scroll bar to review a list of possible problems.

Click hyperlinks to move through the various Print Troubleshooter screens.

PART 2

Design Projects

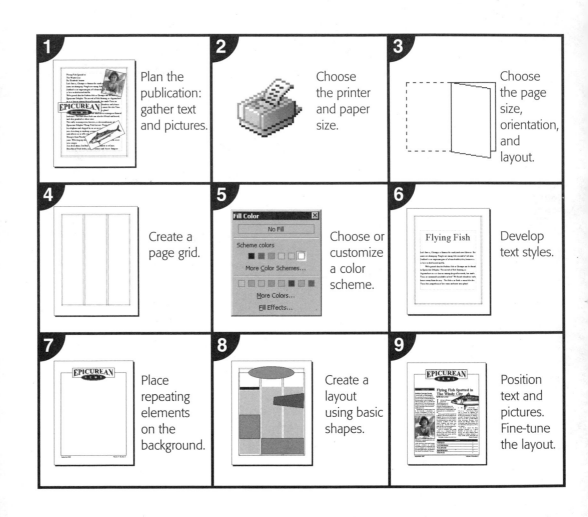

1. Plan the publication: gather text and pictures.

2. Choose the printer and paper size.

3. Choose the page size, orientation, and layout.

4. Create a page grid.

5. Choose or customize a color scheme.

6. Develop text styles.

7. Place repeating elements on the background.

8. Create a layout using basic shapes.

9. Position text and pictures. Fine-tune the layout.

An Overview
of the Design Process

There is no denying that the design process begins with inspiration. But there are certain concrete tasks—shown in the diagram on the facing page—that are common to all design projects. This chapter provides essential background information to help you tackle each of these tasks.

As you develop your own layouts, you'll discover that the design process is iterative. The only way to achieve the right combination of words, pictures, and graphic elements is to experiment with variations of a layout.

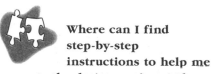

Where can I find step-by-step instructions to help me recreate the design projects? If you want step-by-step instructions to help you use Publisher's tools and dialog boxes, you must refer to the appropriate chapters in Part 1, "Publisher 2000 Fundamentals." The chapters in Part 2, "Design Projects," focus on design theory and practice and contain only general instructions concerning Publisher's tools.

Planning a Publication

Every publication should have a specific purpose. The purpose can be modest or ambitious. You may merely want to print a throwaway banner to welcome your son home from college. Or you may need to produce a full-color brochure that explains your company's products to potential customers. Once you've defined the goal of your publication, you'll be able to gather appropriate pictures and write meaningful text. You'll also be able to answer other questions about your project regarding the design strategy and production budget. For example, you won't want to spend a lot of money on a banner that will be displayed for only a few hours.

The following table lists the essential questions you must consider and also provides the answers for three (very different) sample projects. As you examine them, try to see the relationship between the purpose of the project and the production or design decisions.

Sample Projects			
Question	**Sale Flyer**	**Company Brochure**	**Web Site**
What is the purpose of this publication?	To alert customers about an upcoming sale and encourage them to visit the store.	To provide information about company products and services.	To deliver up-to-the-minute product information and elicit customer feedback.
Who is the intended audience?	Local customers.	Potential corporate clients.	Existing and potential customers.
What is the life span of this publication?	2 weeks.	1 year.	3 months.
How will you deliver the publication?	Store handout, direct mail.	Personal sales calls, mail.	On the World Wide Web.
How will you print the publication?	Desktop laser printer.	Commercial printing service.	Not applicable.
What is an appropriate document size?	1 standard letter-sized page.	8-page booklet measuring 7-by-10 inches.	Standard VGA screen.
What type of paper will you use?	Laser-compatible paper.	High-quality paper.	Not applicable.
What type of artwork will you include?	Black-and-white clip art.	Spot-color artwork.	Full-color bitmapped images.
What is the budget?	Inexpensive.	Expensive.	Moderate.

For more information about selecting a printer and choosing printer options, see Chapter 17. For more information about preparing a document for a commercial printing service, see Chapter 16.

Choosing a Printer

The printer you choose sets limits on many of the design choices you can make. Your choice of printer determines:

@ Available paper sizes. Publisher uses the current paper size when determining the imposition of pages for specially sized and folded publications. For example, if you intend to print an 8.5-by-11-inch booklet, you must be sure that the printer can handle paper that measures at least 11-by-17 inches.

@ Resident fonts. Printers have a collection of fonts built into read-only (ROM) memory, but the fonts vary from model to model. If you use printer resident fonts in a design and then switch to a different printer, the fonts you have chosen may not be available on the new printer.

Standardize your project to save time and money. The more you standardize your publication, the cheaper it is to produce. Begin by trying to design your publication to fit on standard size paper and—if necessary—in a standard size envelope.

Even if you do vary the size of the publication, make sure that you are adhering to the requirements of printing and mailing equipment. Consult your printer to find a document size that avoids paper waste, unnecessary handling, and extra trimming (all of which increase the cost of the job). Confirm that your publication size (meaning the envelope size, not just the page size) meets postal requirements for automated, or machinable, handling. Finally, if you are mailing your publication, be aware that oversized pages and heavy paper can dramatically increase the cost of postage.

For more information about setting up pages, see Chapter 2. For more information about Web documents, see Chapter 12.

◎ Document color. If you are printing to a local printer, Publisher gives you access to the full spectrum of computer-generated colors. Preparing your document for a commercial printing service, however, restricts the number of colors to match the capabilities of your chosen output device. As an example, setting up a document for a high-resolution black-and-white printer limits your color choices to black, white, and shades of gray.

Choosing Page Size and Orientation

The page layout you choose will, to a large extent, determine the number of pages in the document, the amount of paper needed to print it, and the amount of time spent trimming and folding it. The following illustration compares three different page layouts.

The Book Fold layout requires that the total number of pages in a publication be a multiple of 4. A printing service may require multiples of 8 or 16 pages.

Small publications require extra production time (or money) to trim excess paper. This is especially time consuming if you are trimming paper manually.

The Web page layout can extend past the bottom of the reader's screen, but it then requires the reader to scroll through the page vertically.

Create combination grids. You can easily develop a flexible grid to accommodate pictures and text frames of various sizes. In general, the grid or guides should be based on the smallest common denominator of the various elements in your layout. For example, if your publication contains pictures measuring 1/3 or 1/2 of a page wide, use a six-column grid. One-sixth (1/6) is the smallest common denominator of 1/2 and 1/3. A six-column grid lets you size elements at a number of different column measures: 1/6, 1/3, 1/2, or 2/3 of the page width.

Setting Up a Grid

The key to a well-designed publication is an underlying structure, called a grid, that helps you size, position, and align elements consistently. Before you set up the grid, think about the number and the type of elements you will add to your document.

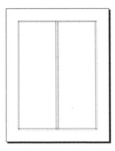

A one-column, wide-column, or two-column format accommodates long text lines and is suitable for books and technical reports.

Custom column widths accommodate differently sized elements, such as ID numbers, photographs, and product descriptions in a catalog. Consistent row height allows readers to find information quickly.

Newsletters that contain pictures of varying sizes require a flexible grid composed of several columns.

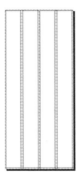

In a Web publication, grids can prevent you from overlapping objects—a condition that causes Publisher to create graphic regions.

Add visual interest to monochromatic documents. Even if you don't own a color printer, you can add visual interest to your designs by using black, white, and shades of gray in combination. For example, you can place white text against a black background or fill a text frame with a gray tint.

What is a dithered color? Dithering is a process in which small printer dots or individual screen pixels of two or more colors are juxtaposed to create the optical illusion of a new color. For example, blue and yellow dots close to one another produce the illusion of green. Excessive dithering can make images look grainy and degrade the appearance of thin lines and text.

For more information on Publisher's color functions, see Chapter 15.

Choosing or Customizing a Color Scheme

You can add visual interest to a page and draw the reader's attention to important information by adding color to your publications. Publisher's predefined color schemes can help you to choose colors that work well together. However, you can develop your own custom color schemes. If you do, you should choose colors carefully, making sure that the color combinations meet the following standards:

@ They are pleasing to the eye and don't produce jarring juxtapositions. Bright red type against a bright green background, for example, appears to vibrate.

@ They provide sufficient contrast between the text and the background color. For example, black text against a dark blue background is unreadable.

@ They are used consistently throughout a document to structure and enhance your message. For example, you could print all of the subheads in a long article in a contrasting color to signal the beginning of each section and to help your reader skim the story.

@ They look good when printed. Colors that appear on your screen as bright, pure hues may look washed out, dark, or muddy when printed on paper.

@ They look good when viewed on the World Wide Web. Colors that appear on your PC's full-color screen as bright, pure hues may look totally different or exhibit dithering when viewed by your reader on a computer that displays fewer colors.

Use TrueType or PostScript software fonts. TrueType fonts stored on your computer system are available regardless of the printer you select when you set up your publication. If your printer doesn't directly support TrueType, the Windows printer driver can send the fonts as vector outlines.

PostScript fonts can also be stored on your computer system and downloaded to any PostScript printer at output time. You can print PostScript fonts to a non-PostScript printer only if you have installed a font utility, such as Adobe Type Manager. Such utilities convert the PostScript information into a format your printer can understand.

A font's x-height influences the legibility and length of a story. When you need type that's highly legible at small point sizes, select a typeface with a larger x-height. When you need to fit a large amount of text into a few pages, select a typeface with a shorter x-height.

Choosing Type

The power of your message depends in large part on the fonts you choose. Once you understand the basic characteristics and categories of type, you can choose fonts with confidence and combine fonts to add visual interest to your documents.

Font Categories

Fonts are divided into three categories, as explained in the following illustration:

Goudy Old Style

Serif fonts employ small lines or curves (called serifs) at the ends of each stroke of a character.

Century Gothic

Sans-serif fonts are fonts without serifs. Note the straighter lines.

Lucida Handwriting

Script fonts resemble cursive handwriting.

Font Structure

Serif, sans-serif, and script fonts all share a similar structure. The following illustrations help you to identify the various parts of a letter and to select an appropriate font for your designs.

Book Antiqua — Ascenders and descenders are the portions of a lowercase letter that rise above or drop below the main body (x-height) of the letter.

 A font's x-height refers to the height of the lowercase letter x in relation to the capital letters of that font. The letter x is the standard because it has no ascenders or descenders. A font with a large x-height has lowercase letters almost as tall as the capital letters (as shown here). A font with a small x-height has lowercase letters that are much shorter in relation to the capital letters.

Weight refers to the thickness of the strokes that form the characters themselves. A font's weight is often designated by words such as light, heavy, bold, and ultra bold.

Gill Sans Ultra Bold Condensed

The width of a font is referred to as either condensed or expanded. The letters in a condensed font are narrower, so you can fit more text on a line. The letters in an expanded font are wide and widely spaced. You can usually tell whether a font is condensed or expanded by its name.

Lucida
Sans
Typewriter

Leading (pronounced "ledding") is the distance from the bottom (or baseline) of one line of text to the baseline of the next line of text. Leading is typically measured in points.

Letterspace refers to the white space between letters.

The Difference Between Display Type and Body Copy

When you create your text designs, separate text elements into categories according to their purposes, as either display type or body copy.

Display type refers to text that organizes or decorates a publication. Headlines, subheads, drop caps, jump heads, pull quotes, and logos are all examples of display type.

Body copy or body text refers to the running text of a story. Body copy is most often organized into sequential paragraphs; it can flow from column to column and from page to page.

What is a pull quote? A pull quote is a quotation from the main text, often set in a larger point size or otherwise emphasized.

Display type suffers most from font substitution. There are several circumstances in which a font that you specify might be replaced with a different font. This unintentional substitution can happen when you send a .pub file to a service bureau for output or when a reader opens a Web document. In either case, if the requested font isn't installed on the other computer system or embedded into the document, a standard font will be used instead. Although such a substitution might not be detectable for standard body copy fonts, it is quite noticeable for display typefaces. Use one of these techniques to avoid font substitution:

- Use only standard fonts, such as Times New Roman or Arial, in your designs.

- Contact your service bureau to be sure they have the fonts you need installed.

- Use WordArt (which is generated as a graphic region) to employ unusual display fonts in a Web publication.

Sans-serif fonts are widely used for display type because their simple outlines are suited to bold messages. However, at large point sizes (30 points or more), serif fonts work equally well in headlines. When you choose a font for display type, think about the personality it projects. The following illustration demonstrates that fonts can be formal or casual; they can project an aggressive corporate image or an avant-garde attitude.

Cooper Black

Cooper Black adds weight to your words—quite literally—with very heavy strokes.

Eras Medium ITC

Eras Medium ITC gives your text an ultramodern look.

COPPERPLATE GOTHIC LIGHT

Copperplate Gothic Light looks like a traditional engraver's typeface and adds a formal note to a design.

Snap ITC

Snap ITC exaggerates and distorts letterforms for a playful effect.

When you choose a font for body copy, consider legibility first. Documents with hard-to-read type can lower comprehension. Because readers score higher on comprehension tests in which the text is set in serif fonts, designers frequently use serif fonts for body copy. You don't need to completely avoid sans-serif fonts for body copy, but you should use them with discretion. Restrict your use of sans-serif type to short or moderately short text blocks, such as captions or catalog entries.

Publisher offers a wide variety of body copy fonts. Publisher ships with a number of fonts that are particularly well-suited for use as body copy, such as Baskerville Old Face, Garamond, Lucida Sans, and Perpetua. As you look at the following samples, take note of the variations among these fonts. It is especially dramatic when you consider that all the fonts are technically the same size—11 points.

Baskerville Old Face

Garamond

Lucida Sans

Perpetua

Can I combine two serif fonts or two sans-serif fonts in a type design? In general, unless you have a lot of typography experience, you should never combine different serif fonts or different sans-serif fonts in a single publication. Your goal when combining different fonts is to create contrast and variety. Two serif fonts (or two sans-serif fonts) don't provide enough contrast. Instead, they are just different enough to distract the reader.

Let's face it. Chicago is famous for stockyards not fisheries. But times are changing. People are eating fish instead of red meat. Seafood is an important part of a heart-healthy diet, because it is low in cholesterol and fat.

The decorative flourishes, or serifs, at the ends of a font's vertical and horizontal lines help readers group words together. The thin and thick strokes vary more than the strokes of sans-serif fonts. This visual variety among letters can prevent fatigue when someone is reading a long text passage.

Let's face it. Chicago is famous for stockyards not fisheries. But times are changing. People are eating fish instead of red meat. Seafood is an important part of a heart-healthy diet, because it is low in cholesterol and fat.

Modern sans-serif fonts vary the letter thickness to make the text more legible.

Font Combinations

Most designers create visual interest in a publication by choosing fonts that have contrasting yet complementary letterforms. There are no hard and fast rules where type design is concerned, but here are a few basic guidelines:

- Use no more than two font families in a document. (A font family is the set of fonts depicting different styles of a single typeface. For example, Arial, Arial Black, and Arial Narrow are all contained within the same font family.)

- Use different styles within a font family—regular, bold, italic, and bold italic—for variety and emphasis.

- Combine a serif and a sans-serif typeface for contrast.

- Look for variations on the font you're using. For example, some fonts are available in condensed or expanded widths or in heavier or lighter weights.

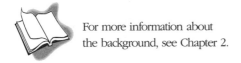

For more information about the background, see Chapter 2.

Creating Background Elements

Consistency is an important part of any design. You can create visual consistency by including (on your background page design) many of the following organizational elements, which repeat on every page in your publication.

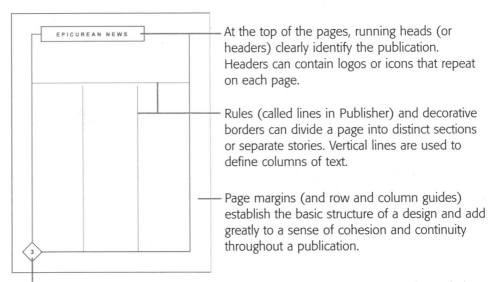

At the top of the pages, running heads (or headers) clearly identify the publication. Headers can contain logos or icons that repeat on each page.

Rules (called lines in Publisher) and decorative borders can divide a page into distinct sections or separate stories. Vertical lines are used to define columns of text.

Page margins (and row and column guides) establish the basic structure of a design and add greatly to a sense of cohesion and continuity throughout a publication.

At the bottom of pages, running feet (or footers) usually contain a page number to help readers locate information easily. Footers can provide volume, chapter, or date information.

Positioning Text and Pictures

You can move, resize, and—most important—edit text and pictures to create an integrated layout. When arranging a layout, forget that text frames are full of words and that picture frames contain images. You'll find it easier to begin your design using colored and shaded drawn objects and frames before you import actual text and pictures. This preliminary design helps you determine approximately how much text you'll need, as well as the size, shape, and position of artwork.

Identify visual problems with text.

Editors and designers use the following terms to identify situations that disrupt the appearance and flow of text.

@ Widows consist of a single word, a portion of a word, or a few short words left on a line by themselves at the end of a paragraph.

@ Orphans are created when the last line of a paragraph prints alone at the top of a page or column of text.

@ Rivers refer to the excessive space between words in a justified paragraph, creating a distracting pattern of white space.

@ Ladders are formed when there are too many consecutive hyphens (3 or more) in a block of hyphenated text.

Normally, these problems are corrected by changing the text or the text formatting so that lines rebreak to fill out lines or lose lines.

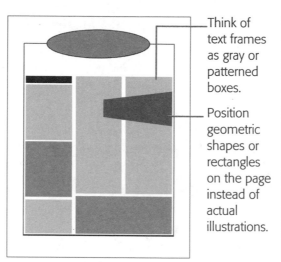

Think of text frames as gray or patterned boxes.

Position geometric shapes or rectangles on the page instead of actual illustrations.

The shapes and differing gray densities create a pattern for your eyes to follow.

Notice how the text and pictures follow the same overall pattern as the mockup.

Fine-Tuning the Layout

Even when a layout is "mostly right," text and pictures often need minor adjustments. The following checklist can help you to fine-tune your documents.

Edit the Text

In most cases, you'll edit the text in your publications for sense—meaning that you'll change the copy to make sentences more understandable and to correct grammar and spelling errors. However, you should also edit text to improve the appearance of the publication. Be prepared to add, delete, or modify words in order to:

@ Change the length of a story to fit the layout. This process, known as copyfitting, shouldn't require you to substantially rewrite the story. But you may have to cut or add several lines of text.

For more information about Publisher's text editing tools, see Chapter 5. For information about Publisher's text formatting functions, see Chapter 6.

Avoid narrow columns. As you can see in the following illustration, narrow text columns cause all sorts of typesetting problems. Narrow columns contain only a few words on each line. This forces Publisher to make much larger spacing adjustments to each word. In contrast, wider text columns contain more words on each line. This gives Publisher the opportunity to make smaller—and less noticeable—adjustments to each word.

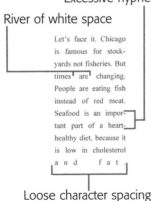

Excessive hyphenation

River of white space

Let's face it. Chicago is famous for stock-yards not fisheries. But times are changing. People are eating fish instead of red meat. Seafood is an important part of a heart-healthy diet, because it is low in cholesterol and fat.

Loose character spacing

- Eliminate widows and orphans by cutting text to lose lines or by adding text to lengthen sentences.

- Search for typewriter-style characters and replace them with typographic characters for a professional appearance.

- Add texture and visual contrast with display type such as captions, subheads, pull quotes, or drop caps. Many display text blocks, such as pull quotes and "Continued" notices, should be added only after a layout has been roughed out.

Modify Text Formatting

On a practical level, you can expand a story to fill a layout or fit a long story into a tight layout by tweaking text formats. On an aesthetic level, you can use these same techniques to increase the legibility of the text, improve line breaks, and change the density of text on the page.

- Alter the point size and line spacing of body copy by a fractional value. A decrease or increase of a tenth of a point won't be noticeable to your reader, but it can significantly contract or expand a story.

- Change the hyphenation zone. Increasing this value eliminates consecutive hyphens (or ladders) but can lengthen a story. Decreasing the value eliminates rivers by tightening up loose lines, creates more hyphens, and shortens a story.

- Adjust the tracking values. Tighter tracking fits more words on each line. Looser tracking can help to fill out a story that is short by a few lines. Looser tracking can also increase the legibility of sans-serif fonts, highly condensed fonts, or small point sizes.

- Avoid awkward white spaces that can occur at large point sizes by decreasing line spacing and by kerning the letters in a headline.

Think metaphorically (and creatively) when choosing clip art. Try not to be too literal when you search for the "perfect" clip art image. Clip art pictures can be used as illustrations, but they can also evoke a mood or convey a concept. A picture of a handshake, for example, communicates the idea of cooperation more clearly than a literal image of two people working together at a desk.

A literal image of cooperation.

A symbolic image of cooperation.

For more information on Publisher's picture tools and Clip Gallery, see Chapter 10. For more information on Microsoft Draw, see Appendix A.

Highlight Important Information

As a designer, you want to direct the reader's attention to the important information in your publication. You can use any of the following techniques:

@ Use a design device, such as a drop cap or a rule, to signal the beginning of an article or a section of a long story.

@ Place a separate but related story into a text box, called a sidebar. Fill the text box with a color or a gray tint.

@ Assign color to text elements based upon their function. Functional color choices are especially important in a Web publication, where colors are used to flag hyperlinks.

Edit Imported Artwork

Whether you use one of the many images supplied with Publisher or artwork from another source, you often have to adjust it in order to make it work with your layout. Here are a few suggestions:

@ Crop pictures instead of resizing them. Cropping a picture can save space, hide part of an unnecessary background, or create drama by showing only the essential part of an image.

@ Recolor images to create artistic effects. For example, you can colorize a black-and-white image with a spot color, or you can create an interesting background (called a watermark) by tinting artwork with a very light color that is similar to the paper color.

@ Combine pictures to create your own more complex illustrations. This technique works well when you can find pictures executed in the same style. In addition, the individual pictures should have transparent backgrounds so they can be overlapped to create what looks like a single illustration.

@ Use Microsoft Draw to change the content of a clip art image. Draw allows you to change the shape or color of a vector drawing or change the brightness and contrast of a bitmapped image.

The
Martin Krump
Trio

Friday, July 24ᵗʰ and
Saturday, July 25ᵗʰ
At 10 P.M.

City Lights Café
449 Harrison Street
Cincinnati, Ohio

Call for Reservations
513-555-2222

The clip art has been recolored to match the gray palette of the other elements in this design.

JAZZ

The Martin Krump Trio
At City Lights Café
Saturday and Sunday
July 24ᵗʰ and 25ᵗʰ

A decorative font works especially well for an invitation containing short text blocks.

Rules can organize and emphasize text.

Postcard Announcement

A postcard announcement contains only a few essential pieces of text, such as the name (or purpose) of the event, the location, and the date and time. It provides an opportunity to build a design around a strong central image, such as the picture of the jazz band used in this project.

Preparing the Publication

Microsoft Publisher 2000's unique page layout options make it easy to create small documents such as this postcard.

Set Up the Page

Postal regulations influence design decisions. In order to mail your postcard announcements without incurring postal surcharges, you must meet the U.S. Postal Service requirements for automated handling. These regulations determine the size of the postcard (which must be between 3.5-by-5 inches and 4.25-by-6 inches) and the type of paper used for printing (a heavy card stock with a thickness, or caliper, between .007 and .0095 inch). For more information and a template to check the size of your postcards, contact your local post office.

1 Create a new document, with a special page size measuring 4.25-by-5.5 inches.

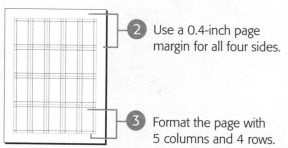

2 Use a 0.4-inch page margin for all four sides.

3 Format the page with 5 columns and 4 rows.

4 Select the printer you will use and confirm that the current paper size is 8.5-by-11-inch letter size, in Portrait orientation.

Because the project will be printed in black and white, select the Black & Gray color scheme to limit your color choices.

Creating the First Page

This small postcard has a big design impact, thanks to bold shapes and a few well-chosen words.

Create a Background for Text

 Using the pink guidelines on the underlying grid, create 2 rectangles.

     @ The first rectangle spans columns 1, 2, 3, 4, and 5 and rows 3 and 4.

     @ The second rectangle overlaps the first. It spans columns 1 and 2 and row 4.

2 Format the rectangles as indicated.

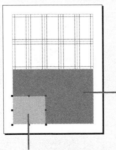

Format the first rectangle with a border of None and a 40 percent black tint.

Format the second rectangle with a border of None and a 20 percent black tint.

Why should I use the pink guides instead of the blue guides? The blue guides include a safety margin (or gutter allowance) of 0.10 inch. While this is essential for separating text columns, it isn't appropriate when you are using the guides as a drawing grid, as you are in this exercise. The pink guides provide precise page divisions and allow you to create objects that abut one another.

Preserve the aspect ratio of an imported image. Even when you are trying to fit a picture into a layout, you shouldn't distort a picture's aspect ratio. In this exercise you use two different techniques to preserve the aspect ratio of the musicians' image.

- Use the Scale Picture command on the Format menu to resize the width and height of the picture equally.

- Use the Crop Picture tool to enlarge the frame without enlarging the picture.

Create groups to organize elements in a design. Grouping can help you manage and manipulate your designs more efficiently. Once grouped, the rectangles, picture, and rules that form the backdrop function as a single object—making the text frames you're about to add easier to select. Even if you accidentally select and move a grouped object, the elements in the group remain properly aligned with one another.

Import and Recolor the Picture

1 Without drawing a picture frame, insert the picture file PE00737.wmf (found on the Publisher CD-ROM). You can find the image easily by searching for the word *musicians* using the Clip Gallery.

2 Scale the picture to 117 percent of its original size.

3 Recolor the picture with a 40 percent tint of black.

4 Fill the picture frame with a 10 percent tint of black.

5 Position the picture along the top blue row guide. It should span the width of the page.

6 Using the Crop Picture tool, extend the top of the picture frame to the pink margin guide. This provides some breathing room for the sax player's head.

Add Rules

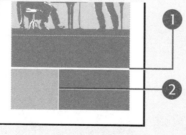

1 Draw a 4-point white line along the pink guide that separates rows 3 and 4. The line should span all 5 columns.

2 Draw a 2-point white line along the pink guide that separates columns 2 and 3. The line should match the height of row 4.

3 Select all the objects on the page and group them together.

For the text of the announcement, see Appendix B.

Experiment with informal fonts. This announcement is a perfect opportunity to use an informal font. The Britannic Bold font exhibits rhythmic variation in the stroke that's reminiscent of the syncopation in jazz music, but there are other decorative alternatives that would work just as well. Look at the single word *Jazz* formatted with Bauhaus 93 (top), Colonna MT (center), and Forte (bottom). Ask yourself what different flavors of jazz (bebop, big band, fusion) would correspond to each font.

JAZZ

JAZZ

JAZZ

Add Display Type

1 Using the pink guides, draw a text frame that spans columns 1, 2, 3, 4, and 5 and row 3.

2 Change the left, right, top, and bottom text frame margins to 0.10 inch. Format the text frame with a transparent fill, and align text vertically at the bottom of the frame.

3 Using the pink guides, draw a second text frame that spans columns 3, 4, and 5 and row 4.

4 Change the left, right, top, and bottom text frame margins to 0.10 inch. Format the text frame with a transparent fill, and align text vertically at the top of the frame.

5 Enter the text and format it as indicated.

Britannic Bold font, 70 points, white characters, left alignment, with 1 space of line spacing.

Britannic Bold font, 12 points, white characters, left alignment, with 1 space of line spacing.

Use typographic characters. When you enter the text for this project you should insert an accented *é* (from the Symbol dialog box) in the word *Café*. You should also apply the small caps attribute to the time designation *P.M.* and the superscript attribute to the letters *th* following each date.

How can I draw the objects in this project accurately? In this project (and in others), you are asked to draw objects of unusual sizes, such as a height of 2.35 inches. By far the easiest way to create these objects is to draw a frame at an arbitrary size. With the frame selected, open the Size And Position dialog box (found on the Format menu) and enter the exact dimensions in the Height and Width text boxes.

Creating the Message for Page Two

Brevity is the watchword when writing the message for a postcard, because you must be sure to leave an appropriate amount of space for the address information.

Enter and Format Text

1 Insert a new page. Create a text frame measuring 2.35 inches wide by 3.45 inches high.

2 Enter the text and format it as Britannic Bold, 12 points, black characters, left alignment, with 1 space of line spacing.

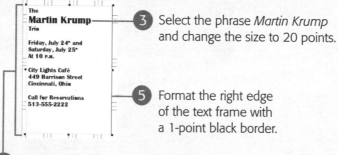

3 Select the phrase *Martin Krump* and change the size to 20 points.

5 Format the right edge of the text frame with a 1-point black border.

4 Center the text in the frame.

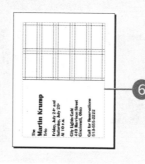

6 Rotate the entire text frame to the left 90 degrees and position it at the bottom of the page.

Why do I have to feed the card stock through the printer twice? If you have a standard laser printer, you must feed the card stock through your printer twice in order to print on both sides of the same piece of paper. Notice that you have been instructed to print page 2 of the postcard first. This page contains only text, requires the least amount of toner, and should not cause any problems when feeding the card through the printer for a second pass. If you own a duplex printer, have installed the correct Windows driver, and have enabled duplex printing, Publisher can print both sides of the postcard simultaneously.

Use specialty paper stocks. You can improve the quality of your publications by purchasing specialty papers. For this project, you can buy card stock measuring 8.5-by-11 inches that has already been divided into 4 postcards. These cards are produced from heavy stock that is appropriate for mailing. They're perforated to make the job of trimming them down to size a matter of tearing the paper along a dotted line. You can find laser printer-compatible postcards in stationery stores or through mail order sources, such as Paper Direct.

Completing the Announcement

Print the Document

1. In the Print dialog box, click the Page Options button and select the Print Multiple Copies Per Sheet option. The Sample area shows that 4 copies of the document fit on a single sheet of paper.

2. Insert a piece of perforated 8.5-by-11-inch card stock into the printer's manual feed.

3. Under the Advanced Print Settings button, clear the Crop Marks option and print only page 2 of the document. Publisher prints 4 instances of page 2.

4. Feed the same piece of card stock through the printer, but invert it in order to print on the opposite side.

5. Print only page 1 of the document. Publisher prints 4 instances of page 1.

6. Separate the cards along the perforations to produce the final mailing piece.

Emphasize text by printing white letters against a black background.

Position artwork to lead the reader's eye toward your message.

Tournament Bikes
Sales ◆ Custom Orders ◆ Expert Repairs

Visit Our
Web Site
www.domain.com

◆ Racing Bikes
◆ Touring Bikes
◆ Mountain Bikes
◆ Children's Bikes
◆ Jogging Strollers

215-555-8989
1653 Newfield Ave.
Norristown, PA 19401

A bulleted list can summarize important information about your business.

Phonebook Advertisement

By designing ad copy in Microsoft Publisher 2000, you can avoid both the cost of an outside designer and the typesetting fee charged by the publication in which your ad appears.

Preparing the Publication

This advertisement will ultimately be printed on a page in a phonebook, alongside other display ads and company listings. Phonebooks, magazines, and newspapers typically print partial-page display ads at standard sizes. The size may be a fraction of the overall page size (such as one-half page or one-third page) or may be measured by the column-inch (with a standard column determining the width of the ad). Ultimately, these sizes are relative. The exact dimensions will vary depending on the trim size and column layout of the publication. Before you begin your design, ask the publication in which you intend to advertise for exact dimensions.

Why set the page margins to zero? This design will be printed on a sheet of paper that is larger than the dimensions of the ad. You can therefore make the page margins as small as you want, and not be in danger of placing objects in the nonprinting margin. Setting a margin of 0 inches for this project creates a 0.1-inch safety area between the pink margin guides and the blue column guides. Normally, when the page size and the paper size are identical, the page margins must be large enough to prevent you from placing text and pictures in the nonprinting area of the paper.

Crop and bleed artwork to create a bolder design. You can increase the impact of a picture by cropping it. In this project, cropping the image and placing it at the edge of the advertisement creates the illusion that the biker is riding into the reader's field of view. It adds a sense of movement to the design. Notice how the position of the artwork, which points toward the text, helps to direct the reader's attention to the message.

Set Up the Page

① Create a new special-size publication measuring 5.5 inches wide by 2.5 inches high.

② Set page margins to 0 for all four sides.

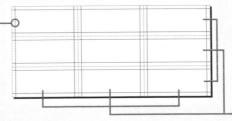

③ Create 3 columns and 3 rows.

④ Select the printer you will use and confirm that the current paper size is 8.5-by-11 inches in Landscape orientation.

Importing and Editing the Clip Art

A well-chosen clip art image provides instant identification of a business. Look for a picture that has both the right content *and* the right mood. For example, the picture used in this project conveys the idea of racing, not just biking.

Import and Crop Clip Art

① Without drawing a picture frame, insert the clip art image SL00286_.wmf found on the Publisher CD. You can easily find the image by searching for the word "biker" in the Clip Gallery.

② Scale the picture to 225 percent of its original size.

Import and Crop Clip Art *(continued)*

3 Using the bottom-right handle, crop the image to measure 2.43 inches wide by 2.41 inches deep.

4 Move the picture until it aligns with the bottom-right edge of the page.

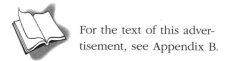

For the text of this advertisement, see Appendix B.

Creating the Ad Copy

Most people don't read the phonebook; they skim it. Make sure that your message is clear and concise. Your company's name and phone number are the most important pieces of information in a phonebook ad. They should virtually jump out at the reader.

Type and Format the Company Name and Contact Information

1 Using the blue column guides, create a text frame that fills columns 1 and 2 and row 1.

2 Draw a second text frame that fills columns 1 and 2 and row 3.

3 Draw a third text frame that fills the intersection of column 1 and row 2.

4 Make all three frames transparent.

Choose an appropriate font. A bold, modern typeface—like Eras ITC—has a sporty look that is appropriate for a bike shop.

Make use of font variants to rank the information from most to least important. In a small design like this advertisement, you should use only one typeface, but you should choose a typeface with variants. This design employs two different weights of the same font family: Eras Bold ITC and Eras Medium ITC. Notice how the most important information, such as the company name and the phone number, has been set in the bold face. The different weights also add visual interest to the type treatment.

Type and Format the Company Name and Contact Information *(continued)*

5 Type the contact information and format the text as indicated below:

Eras Bold ITC, 22 points, center alignment

Eras Bold ITC, 11 points, center alignment

Eras Bold ITC, 12 points, center alignment

Eras Medium ITC, 9 points, center alignment

Tournament Bikes
Sales, Custom Orders, Expert Repairs

Visit Our Web Site
www.domain.com

215-555-8989
1653 Newfield Ave.
Norristown, PA 19401

Eras Bold ITC, 9 points, center alignment

Create the Body Copy

1 Draw a text frame that measures 1.63 inches wide by 1.03 inches high. It should fill column 2 and fit snugly against the top and bottom of the existing text frames.

2 Enter the copy, which is a simple list of the kinds of bicycles Tournament Bikes carries. Format the bulleted list as indicated.

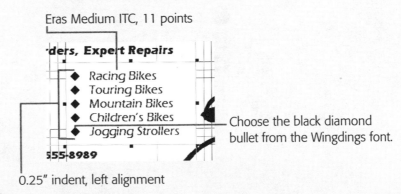

Eras Medium ITC, 11 points

·ders, Expert Repairs

◆ Racing Bikes
◆ Touring Bikes
◆ Mountain Bikes
◆ Children's Bikes
◆ Jogging Strollers

Choose the black diamond bullet from the Wingdings font.

55-8989

0.25" indent, left alignment

3 Center the text vertically in the text frame.

Fine-Tuning the Design

You can add geometric shapes and symbols to a design to emphasize and organize text. In this project, you'll correct three noticeable shortcomings:

- The subhead identifying the company contains too many commas to be effective as display copy.

- The text inviting readers to visit the company Web site is floating in an awkward white space.

- The ad has no boundary to separate it from the other partial-page ads that will appear on the same page in the phonebook.

Edit the text for a quick read. Short, immediately understood messages are what advertising is all about. If you take the time to edit your text, you'll find that you can communicate your message with just a few words. In this design, three words underneath the store name sum up the entire scope of the business, and the bulleted list succinctly details the wide range of products available

Add Bullets to the Display Copy

1. Highlight the comma and the space after the word *Sales.*

2. Using the Symbol dialog box, replace the highlighted characters with a black diamond-shaped bullet from the Wingdings font.

3. Highlight the last letter in the word *Sales,* the bullet, and the first letter in the word *Custom.* Expand the kerning by 1.75 points.

Tournament Bikes
Sales ◆ Custom Orders, Expert Repairs

Visit Our Web Site
www.t_bikes.com

- ◆ Racing Bikes
- ◆ Touring Bikes
- ◆ Mountain Bikes
- ◆ Children's Bikes

4. Repeat steps 2 and 3 to replace the comma and space after the word *Orders* with a bullet.

White text pops. You can give a simple text element the impact of a picture by reversing the color from black to white. You must be sure to keep the text legible by contrasting it with the background color. In this project, the white text against the black starburst highlights important information and balances the layout.

Why does the display type for the phone number move to the right when I nudge the starburst? The starburst shape is forcing the display type to wrap around its boundary. You can solve the problem and return the display type to the correct position by selecting the starburst and text frame group and sending it to the bottom of the stack.

Add a Starburst Background to the Web Address

1 Using the pink guides, draw a starburst shape that spans column 1 and row 2.

2 Fill the starburst with 100 percent black.

3 Send the starburst behind the text frame containing the Web address.

4 Change the color of the text to white and (using Shift+Enter) break the text into three lines.

5 Center the text over the starburst and group the two objects.

6 Rotate the group counterclockwise by 20 degrees.

7 Nudge the group down and to the right by 0.06 inch.

8 Send the group to the bottom of the stack.

Create the Ad Border

1 Draw a box measuring 5.5 inches wide by 2.5 inches high. Position the box directly over the page edges.

2 Format the box with a 3-point black border.

Use reproduction-quality paper to generate camera-ready art. In order to generate printouts that are suitable for reproduction, you must print on special paper (called Repro paper) that provides a high-contrast white background for black text and black-and-white illustrations. This paper is available from stationery stores and mail order companies.

Completing the Advertisement

If you have a printer that prints 600 or more dots per inch, you can produce either proofs or camera-ready printouts on your laser printer.

Print the Document

1. In the Print dialog box, click the Page Options button and select the Print One Copy Per Sheet option. The Sample area shows that one copy of the document is centered on the paper.

2. In the Advanced Print Settings dialog box, turn on Crop Marks.

3. Insert a sheet of reproduction-quality paper into your printer.

4. Print the document normally.

The crop marks align with the black border that surrounds your advertisement. These crop marks help the phonebook publisher trim and position the ad on the final publication page.

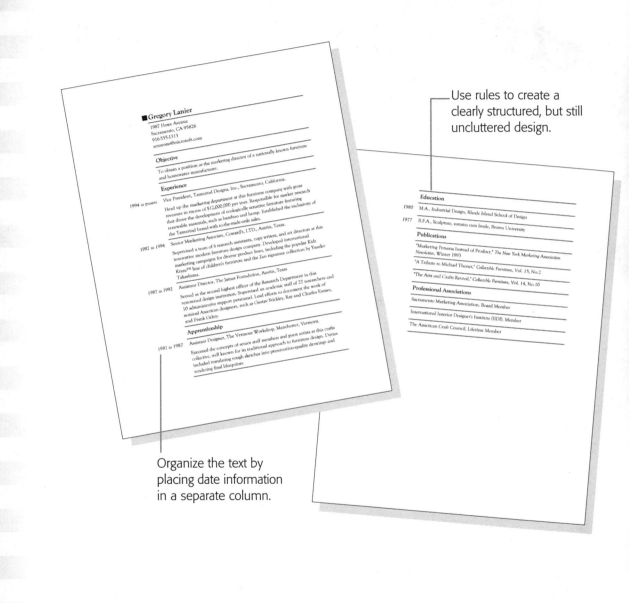

Use rules to create a clearly structured, but still uncluttered design.

Organize the text by placing date information in a separate column.

■ Gregory Lanier
1987 Howe Avenue
Sacramento, CA 95826
916-555-1313
someone@microsoft.com

Objective

To obtain a position as the marketing director of a nationally known furniture and housewares manufacturer.

Experience

1994 to present — Vice President, Tamarind Designs, Inc., Sacramento, California.
Head up the marketing department at this furniture company with gross revenues in excess of $12,000,000 per year. Responsible for market research that drove the development of ecologically sensitive furniture featuring renewable materials, such as bamboo and hemp. Established the exclusivity of the Tamarind brand with to-the-trade-only sales.

1992 to 1994 — Senior Marketing Associate, Coward's, LTD., Austin, Texas.
Supervised a team of 6 research assistants, copy writers, and art directors at this innovative modern furniture design company. Developed international marketing campaigns for diverse product lines, including the popular Kidz Kraze™ line of children's furniture and the Zen signature collection by Yasuko Takashima.

1987 to 1992 — Assistant Director, The James Foundation, Austin, Texas
Served as the second highest officer of the Research Department in this renowned design institution. Supervised an academic staff of 27 researchers and 10 administrative support personnel. Lead efforts to document the work of seminal American designers, such as Gustav Stickley, Ray and Charles Eames, and Frank Gehry.

Apprenticeship

1981 to 1987 — Assistant Designer, The Vermont Workshop, Manchester, Vermont.
Executed the concepts of senior staff members and guest artists at this crafts collective, well known for its traditional approach to furniture design. Duties included translating rough sketches into presentation-quality drawings and rendering final blueprints.

Education

1980 — M.A., Industrial Design, Rhode Island School of Design

1977 — B.F.A., Sculpture, summa cum laude, Brown University

Publications

"Marketing Persona Instead of Product," *The New York Marketing Association Newsletter*, Winter 1993

"A Tribute to Michael Thonet," *Collectible Furniture*, Vol. 15, No.2

"The Arts and Crafts Revival," *Collectible Furniture*, Vol. 14, No.10

Professional Associations

Sacramento Marketing Association, Board Member

International Interior Designer's Institute (IIDI), Member

The American Craft Council, Lifetime Member

Résumé

A well-designed résumé is so distinctive that it stands out from the résumés of other job applicants. However, there should be a clear hierarchy of information. In this project, note the use of white space, rules, and headings to organize the elements of the résumé.

Preparing the Publication

Business documents, such as this résumé, use standard paper size and margin settings.

Set Up the Page

1 Create a new full-page document measuring 8.5-by-11 inches.

2 Select the printer you will use and confirm that the current paper size is 8.5-by-11-inch letter size in the Portrait orientation.

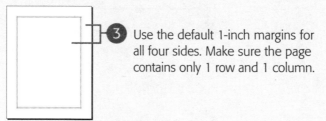

3 Use the default 1-inch margins for all four sides. Make sure the page contains only 1 row and 1 column.

The power of custom cell borders. Custom borders are responsible for the airy, elegant design of this résumé. By applying borders to only the top and bottom margins of a selected range of cells, this design avoids a cramped, boxy look.

Creating a Layout with the Table Frame Tool

You'll create a more flexible layout if you use Publisher 2000's Table Frame Tool rather than layout guides, to create rows and columns. The structure of a résumé, with dates in one column and descriptions in another, makes it ideally suited to a table format.

Set Up the Table Structure

1 Draw a table frame that begins at the 2.5-inch mark on the vertical ruler and that aligns with the left, right, and bottom row and column guides.

2 Set up the table with 19 rows, 2 columns, and the None table format.

3 Press and hold the Shift key while dragging the division between the two columns to 2.5 inches on the horizontal ruler.

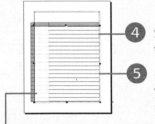

4 Select the right column. Assign a 1-point border to the top, middle, and bottom sides of the column.

5 Format the right column with cell margins of 0.04 inch for the top, right, and left sides. Change the bottom cell margin to 0.06 inch.

6 Select the left column. The top, left, and bottom cell margins can remain at 0.04 inch. Change the right cell margin to 0.15 inch. Increasing this margin provides an appropriate amount of room between the date information and the text information.

Inserting and Formatting Text

Publisher's powerful tools, such as drag-and-drop text editing and the capability to format all the text in a column at one time, allow you to create a table quickly and easily. Begin by creating text styles for the Description, Date, and Category items.

The résumé text was created in a word processing program and formatted as standard paragraphs. If you insert the text directly into the table, Publisher places all the copy in the first cell. For more flexibility, place the text into a temporary text frame on Publisher's scratch area.

Build related styles easily. You can base a new text style on an existing text style. Simply highlight the style name you want to use as the starting point. Publisher picks up all the formatting attributes when you click the Create A New Style button. You can then make a few changes to create a new style.

Create Text Styles

1 Using the Text Style dialog box, create a style named *Description*, and specify the following attributes:

    @ Goudy Old Style font

    @ 11-point font size

    @ 14 points of line spacing

    @ 7 points after paragraphs

    @ Left alignment

2 Create a new text style named *Date*. Base this style on the *Description* style, but make the following changes:

    @ Italic

    @ 0 points after paragraphs

    @ Right alignment

3 Create a new text style named *Category*. Base this style on the *Description* style, but make the following changes:

    @ Bold

    @ 13-point font size

    @ 0 points after paragraphs

For the text of this résumé, see Appendix B.

Removing predefined formats. When you insert a text file into a document, Publisher attempts to retain any formatting attributes—such as font, point size, and alignment—that were assigned within the word processing program. Assigning the Normal text style to the imported text deletes any associated style names and makes it easier to apply new text styles.

Note that Publisher always retains local attributes of imported text, such as boldface or italic styling. In this example, the titles of publications remain in italics even after you apply the Description text style to the copy.

Insert Text on the Scratch Area

1. Using your favorite word processing program, create and save a file called *Resume*.
2. Draw a text frame on the scratch area that is approximately the same size as the page.

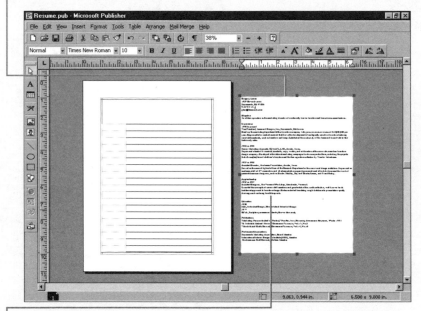

3. Insert the *Résumé* text file.
4. Highlight the entire text file and format it with Publisher's default Normal text style.

Import a table from an-other application. You can bypass many of the procedures in this project—including the creation of the table itself—by importing a table from another Microsoft Office application. For example, if you copy or insert a table from Microsoft Excel or Microsoft Word, Publisher automatically creates a new table object.

Drag the Text to the Résumé

1 Before you move the text into the table, confirm that the Grow To Fit Text command on the Table menu is active.

2 Select and then drag each item to an appropriate position in the table. Date items are positioned in the left column. Category and Description items are positioned in the right column. After you enter all the text, the table extends past the bottom of the page margin.

3 Select the entire left column and format it with the Date text style.

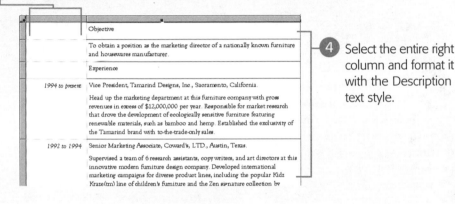

4 Select the entire right column and format it with the Description text style.

Fine-Tuning the Table

You must now address several minor flaws in the table:

- Assign the correct text style to category headings.
- Center category headings vertically in each cell.
- Eliminate bad line breaks by turning off hyphenation.
- Insert a true trademark symbol to replace typewriter-style characters.
- Move the portion of the table that extends past the page margins onto a second page.

Format Category Headings

1 Scroll through the text, and assign the Category text style to categories.

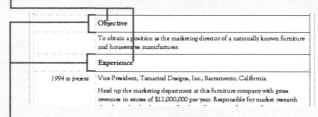

Objective	
	To obtain a position as the marketing director of a nationally known furniture and housewares manufacturer.
Experience	
1994 to present	Vice President, Tamarind Designs, Inc., Sacramento, California.
	Head up the marketing department at this furniture company with gross revenues in excess of $12,000,000 per year. Responsible for market research

2 With each category item still selected, align the text vertically in the cell.

Why can't Publisher's AutoCorrect function automatically insert the trademark symbol? Publisher's AutoCorrect function substitutes a true trademark symbol (™) for the typewriter-style characters (tm) only when you type or paste those characters directly into a Publisher document. If you import those characters as part of a word processing file, one of two things will happen:

- ℮ If the word processing file contains a true trademark symbol, Publisher will preserve it.

- ℮ If the word processing file contains only typewriter-style characters, you must make the change using Publisher's text editing tools.

Adjust Text

1 Select the entire column containing category and description items, and turn off hyphenation.

2 Locate the typewriter-style trademark character within parentheses—*(tm)*—and replace it with the trademark symbol ™.

Continue the Table on a Second Page

1 Select all the rows beginning with the category *Education*. Cut these rows to the Clipboard.

2 Delete the empty rows from the table.

3 Insert a second page.

4 From the Edit menu, choose Paste Special and then choose Paste New Table. Publisher retains the format of the table, including borders and text styles.

5 Align the new table with the top, left, and right column guides.

Choose a font that fits your personality and the message. A typeface evokes a particular feeling in a reader. When you choose a font for your résumé, think about the characteristics of the type. Does a particular font match your personality? Is the position you are applying for serious or more relaxed? Goudy Old Style, used in this project, is formal and restrained but has a light touch. Experiment with possible typefaces. Remember that the most important quality of the typeface you choose is its readability.

Adding Name and Address Information

Adding a second table is the easiest way to add the name and address information to this résumé. Duplicating key attributes such as the alignment and the one-point rule integrates the second table into the design.

Insert and Format the Name

1 Starting at the 2.5-inch mark on the horizontal ruler, draw a table frame to the right column margin. It should measure 1.25 inches deep.

2 Set up the table with 2 rows, 1 column, and the None table format.

3 Use the Adjust pointer while you press and hold the Shift key to move the row division to the 1.5-inch mark on the vertical ruler.

4 Drag the name and address from the text frame on the scratch area and format it as shown below.

Goudy Old Style font, 16-point font size, bold, left alignment, aligned at the bottom of the cell

Goudy Old Style font, 11-point font size, left alignment, 14 points of line spacing

Emphasize important information. The most important piece of information in a résumé is the subject's name. In this design you draw attention to the name with a graphic accent—the black rectangle.

Clean up the .pub file. At the beginning of this project you created a text frame on the scratch area in order to temporarily store text. Take a moment to delete the now-empty text frame. Objects left on the scratch area won't print; however, they do increase the file size.

Collate as you copy. If you are mailing your résumé to a long list of recipients, consider duplicating it at a service bureau. Service bureaus often offer high-quality stationery, and today's high-speed copiers can collate and even staple publications faster than you could ever do it by hand.

Add Decorative Elements

1 Pull down two horizontal ruler guides to align with the baseline and ascenders of the name. Make the text frame transparent in order to view the ruler guides.

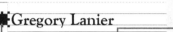

1987 Howe Avenue
Sacramento, CA 95826
916-555-1313

2 Assign a 1-point border to the bottom of the top cell.

3 Use the Rectangle tool to draw a square bullet that is exactly as high as the letter G. It should align with the two horizontal ruler guides and abut the left edge of the table frame. Format the box with a border of None and a black fill color.

Printing the Publication

Select Print Options

1 Choose the appropriate options in the Print dialog box to print both pages of the document.

2 If you are printing more than one copy, consider turning off collation. Doing so dramatically speeds up the print time, although it requires you to collate by hand.

3 Click Advanced Print Settings. In the Print Settings dialog box, activate the Use Only Publication Fonts option and turn off Crop Marks. Click OK to accept these settings.

4 Click OK to print the document.

Set the tone with a friendly and informal typeface.

Combine and overlap drawn shapes to mimic the artistic style of imported pictures.

Use a WordArt effect to add visual interest to a simple list.

Flyer

A successful flyer grabs a reader's attention with a strong image and bold headlines. As you work on this project promoting a winter sports festival at the local high school, notice how the various elements—including the clip art, the font choice, and graphic accents—work together to create a unified design.

Preparing the Publication

Flyers are typically printed on one side of standard letter-sized paper. Use column and ruler guides to align objects in the layout, and choose a color scheme that complements the design.

Set Up the Page

1. Start a new full-page document.

2. Select the printer you will use and confirm that the current paper size is 8.5-by-11-inch letter size in Portrait orientation.

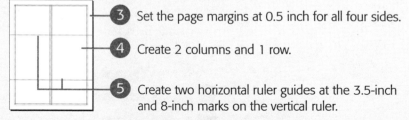

3. Set the page margins at 0.5 inch for all four sides.

4. Create 2 columns and 1 row.

5. Create two horizontal ruler guides at the 3.5-inch and 8-inch marks on the vertical ruler.

6. In the Color Scheme dialog box, select the Floral scheme.

Resizing vector artwork. If you were to look in the Scale Picture dialog box you would see that you have just enlarged this picture by more than 120 percent. However, because this is a vector drawing, you can enlarge it and print it without degrading the quality of the image. This artwork will print at the highest quality of which your printer is capable.

For more information about vector art, see Chapter 10.

Inserting Artwork

The image of a snowman illustrates one of the events at the festival—a competition to see who can build the best snowman. But the style of the image is as important as its content. The bright colors and flowing lines create a festive mood.

Insert the Picture

① With the Picture Frame Tool, draw a picture frame that aligns with the two horizontal ruler guides. The frame should span the entire width of the page from the left margin to the right margin.

② Insert the picture So00333_.WMF from Publisher 2000's CD clip art library. You can find the picture by searching for the keyword "snowman" in the Clip Gallery.

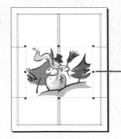

Publisher resizes the picture frame to maintain the aspect ratio of the image and centers the picture on the page.

Creating a Background

The picture of the snowman seems to float in space. You can ground him by drawing a background.

Draw and Format a Rectangle

① Draw a rectangle that aligns with the top, bottom, left, and right pink margin guides.

② Send the rectangle behind the picture.

Use the background to hide objects temporarily. When it is visible, the rectangle in this design obscures the layout and ruler guides. In order to see the guides, send the rectangle to the background page and turn off the display of the background. When you are ready to print the document, simply turn the display of the background on again.

For more information about Publisher's background page, see Chapter 2.

Draw and Format a Rectangle *(continued)*

③ Format the rectangle with a 4-point black rule.

The transparent background of the vector clip art image lets you see the fill color of the rectangle lower in the stack.

④ Fill the rectangle with a 40 percent tint of the color Accent 3 (turquoise).

⑤ Select the rectangle and send it to the background.

⑥ On the View menu, select Ignore Background to hide the rectangle temporarily.

Creating the Headline

The text treatment for the headline should complement the image you've chosen. The Forte font contains script letters that echo the bold and casual lines in the drawing. Notice how the free-flowing lines in the drawing don't adhere strictly to the outlines of the shapes. In the same way, the letters in the Forte font don't adhere strictly to the baseline of the text block.

Create the Headline

① Starting at the top blue row guide, draw a text frame that spans both columns. The text frame should measure 2.9 inches deep. The bottom of the text frame should align with the horizontal ruler guide at the 3.5-inch mark on the vertical ruler.

② Change the text frame margins to 0 inches for all four sides.

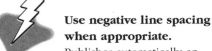

Use negative line spacing when appropriate.

Publisher automatically applies one line space to text you type or import. Publisher defines one line space as 120 percent of the type's point size, which is too much spacing for text set at large point sizes. The amount of space between the lines of text in this headline is even more noticeable because the words contain no descenders (the parts of letters that fall below the baseline). To make the text look correct, you should use a negative value of 0.65 space to delete the extra leading between the lines.

Repeat design motifs to create a cohesive design.

You can create a visual pattern to hold a layout together by repeating design motifs. In this project, the second snowball creates a sense of perspective. It appears to be in the background, while the larger snowball appears to be in the foreground of the picture.

Create the Headline *(continued)*

3 Make the text frame transparent.

4 Enter the following text on 3 lines:
The 5ᵗʰ Annual
Winter
Festival

5 Highlight the text and assign the following formats:

- 0.65 line spacing
- Center alignment
- Align text vertically at the bottom of the frame

Adding Drawn Objects and a List

The list of events at the festival uses a playful type treatment, where curved text is placed against a snowball. When you add graphic accents to a design, take the time to visually incorporate the drawn elements with the imported artwork. Here, for example, an off-center, partial black outline mimics the line style in the drawing.

Create complex drawings by overlapping geometric shapes. The second, smaller snowball is composed of four overlapping shapes that create the illusion of two freely drawn black lines on top of a white circle. The individual objects (shown below with size and formatting information) consist of three circles and one oval, none of which have borders. Begin by placing the large white circle on top of the large black circle, offset slightly up and to the right. Add the smaller black circle, making sure to leave a rim of white on the right edge of the composition. Top it all off with the small oval, leaving an interior crescent of black.

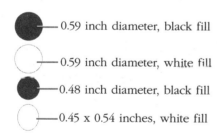

— 0.59 inch diameter, black fill

— 0.59 inch diameter, white fill

—0.48 inch diameter, black fill

—0.45 x 0.54 inches, white fill

Create the Snowball Drawings

① Starting at the blue guide for column 2 and the 7-inch mark on the vertical ruler, draw a true circle (shown below) 3.25 inches in diameter.

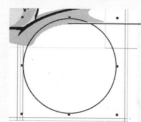 The circle should slightly overlap the clip art image.

② Format the circle with a white fill and a border of None.

③ Duplicate the circle, and fill the duplicate with black.

④ Position the black circle 0.1 inch to the left of the white circle.

⑤ Using the Send Backward command, send the black circle behind the white circle.

⑥ Group the two objects.

⑦ Create another smaller snowball by overlapping four oval shapes. The group of objects should measure approximately 0.65 inches in width.

⑧ Move the smaller snowball to the left of the snowman's scarf at the 1-inch mark on the horizontal ruler and the 3.75-inch mark on the vertical ruler.

Create the WordArt Elements

① Draw a WordArt frame measuring 3.5 inches wide by 1.25 inches deep.

② Type or paste the text "Snowman Competition" in the WordArt text box.

③ Format the text with the Forte font at 28 points.

For the text for this flyer, see Appendix B.

Use the Size And Position dialog box to increase precision. Instead of moving the grouped WordArt elements with the mouse, take advantage of the Size And Position dialog box. You can't resize a grouped object using this dialog box, but you can enter exact coordinates (as shown below) to place the object anywhere on the page.

Create the WordArt Elements *(continued)*

④ Choose the Arch Up (Curve) text shape and an Arc Angle of 110 degrees.

⑤ Duplicate the WordArt frame three times and replace the text.

⑥ Overlap the WordArt frames by a 0.5-inch vertical offset.

⑦ Group the WordArt frames and rotate the entire group to the left by 20 degrees.

⑧ Position the grouped object at the 4.15-inch mark on the horizontal ruler and the 6.6-inch mark on the vertical ruler.

Entering and Formatting Text

The remaining text in this flyer informs the reader of the festival's location, date and time, and admission price.

Type and Format Body Copy

① Draw a text frame measuring 3.55 by 2.5 inches in the left column. Align the top of the frame with the ruler guide at the 8-inch mark on the vertical ruler.

② Make the text frame transparent and change all four text frame margins to 0 inches.

③ Insert or type the location, admission, and date and time information.

Format display type at relatively large point sizes. The Forte font is a display typeface. It should always be formatted at a fairly large size, such as 14 points or larger. At smaller point sizes, decorative display fonts simply aren't legible. In addition, at the larger point sizes (normally 14 points or above) Publisher automatically kerns letters to improve character spacing.

For more information on character spacing, see Chapter 6.

Type and Format Body Copy *(continued)*

4 Highlight the text and format it with the Forte font at 14 points.

5 Center the text in the text frame.

6 Fine-tune the text by adjusting the line breaks and inserting symbols as shown below.

Create a blank line between each paragraph, and insert the round bullet character from the Wingdings font.

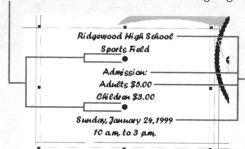

Use the Shift-Enter shortcut keys to insert line breaks after the words School, Admission, $5.00, and 1999.

Completing the Publication

Before you can print the publication, you must make the background page—and the rectangle it contains—visible.

Print the Flyer

1 Clear the Ignore Background option on the View menu. The light blue rectangle becomes visible.

2 Open the Print dialog box, click the Advanced Print Settings button, and turn off Crop Marks and Bleeds. Click OK to return to the Print dialog box.

3 Specify the number of copies you want to print.

4 Print the document.

Use WordArt to produce a splashy text banner.

THE **CLARK**

FAMILY BULLETIN

Standard-sized frames are easy to update with new photos and captions.

Becky Nunnelley (though she prefers Becca these days) is entering her junior year in high school. Like her Dad, she's a talented athlete. In fact, she's the youngest member of the varsity softball team.

Grandma Sylvia just got back from a visit with Lori and Mike's family in Minneapolis. Here's her summary of the trip, "The weather was simply spectacular. And all of my grandkids were a blast!"

Patrick Sean Clark II is about to turn 4. He's fascinated with computers, as you can see in this totally adorable picture taken by his Mom. If you're pondering a birthday present for Patrick, think computer games.

As we all know from the last family reunion, Diane is unusually camera shy. But her Dad captured this rare smile for the camera during a Sunday game of touch football. In case you're wondering, her team won.

REUNION TIME

It's time to finalize the plans for our 4th biennial family reunion. Helen and George are lobbying for San Francisco in October. By October the fog has departed, leaving clear skies and warm temperatures. And there are lots of other things to do in San Francisco, like visit museums or take quick trips to the wine country.

Add a repeating background texture to your Web pages.

WEBMASTER

Click here to contact Margaret Clark Russell.

Dave wants to go on a cruise. He has found a reasonably priced cruise that sails from Puerto Rico to Aruba. We'd have to change the date, because October is the rainy season in the Caribbean. But in Dave's words, "A cruise is perfect. You can sun or swim, go dancing after dinner, or indulge at the all-you-can-eat buffet!" Dave has agreed to keep track of everyone's vote. So please call him (not me!) with your opinions.

Family Web Page

This personal Web page contains lots of fun elements, like a speckled background, colorful accents, and a banner created with WordArt. However, the design respects the limitations of the World Wide Web by keeping the pictures small and the text formatting simple.

Preparing the Web Publication

Microsoft Publisher 2000's Web authoring tools appear when you choose the Web Page option on the Blank Publications tab of the Catalog dialog box.

Create layouts with no overlapping objects to avoid graphic regions.

When Publisher generates an HTML document, it converts all overlapping objects into graphic regions, which are pictures that take longer to download. As you complete each procedure in this sample project, notice the precise placement of design elements and the use of column guides and ruler guides to prevent objects—especially text frames—from overlapping other objects.

Set Up the Web Page

1 Create a new Web publication.

2 In the Page Setup dialog box, choose the Standard page layout option. Change the page height to 9 inches.

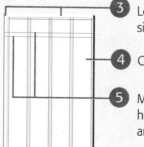

3 Leave the page margins at 0 for the bottom and right sides. Change the top and left page margin to 0.25 inch.

4 Create a grid consisting of 4 columns and 1 row.

5 Move to the background page and create two horizontal ruler guides at the 1.25-inch mark and the 1.5-inch mark on the vertical ruler.

Set Up the Web Page *(continued)*

6 Return to the foreground.

7 In the Web Properties dialog box, click the Site tab. Then type an appropriate keyword (such as "Clark") and a description (such as "The Clark family Web site"). Specify that the target audience will be using HTML 3.0 (or later) browsers and the Western Alphabet.

8 In the Web Properties dialog box, click the Page tab. Then type an appropriate title for the page, such as "The Clark Family Bulletin."

 Choose Web-safe colors. Computer systems—notably Macs and PCs—use different color palettes to display Web pages. To be sure that the colors in your Web page display properly on a wide variety of computer systems, you should choose colors from a Web-safe palette. You can find a Web-safe palette by searching graphics sites on the Web, or you can create your own Web-specific color scheme. It's easy. Just be sure that when you specify an RGB color, you use one of the following values for each of the primary colors: 255, 204, 153, 102, 51, or 0.

Create a Custom Background and Color Scheme

1 In the Color And Background Scheme dialog box, select the Custom tab.

2 Click the Texture check box (or the Browse button) and select the file J0143748.GIF for the background.

3 Create a custom color scheme using the following RGB values, which are listed in order as red, green, blue:

- Main: 0, 0, 0
- Accent 1: 0, 102, 102
- Accent 2: 51, 102, 153
- Accent 3: 204, 102, 0
- Accent 4: 204, 51, 51
- Accent 5: 255, 255, 255
- Hyperlink: 0, 51, 153
- Followed Hyperlink: 102, 0, 102

Choose text colors based on function.
When choosing colors for text elements in your Web page, keep the following functional considerations in mind:

- The text must be legible on a wide variety of monitors, including 16- and 256-color monitors. Choose text colors that contrast with the background in both hue (color) and value (lightness or darkness).

- Readers must be able to distinguish normal text from hyperlinks and unfollowed hyperlinks from followed ones. Choose noticeably different colors for the Main, Hyperlink, and Followed Hyperlink items in the Custom Color Scheme dialog box.

Overriding the default body text color. Using Publisher's normal text styles function, you can change the color of text on a case-by-case basis. In the current project, for example, the Web Head text style is formatted as white, not black. Employ this feature sparingly; too many text colors in a Web document can make it difficult to distinguish normal text from hyperlink text.

Creating Text Styles

You should limit your text styles to standard fonts and simple text styles. This will enable Publisher to convert your document to HTML without any loss of formatting.

HTML Text Styles			
Text Style	**Character Type and Size**	**Indents and Lists**	**Line Spacing**
Web Body	Arial, 10 points	Left alignment	1 sp (space)
Web Head	Arial, bold, white, 11 points	Center alignment	1 sp

Creating the Banner

Though this Web page is intended to disseminate family information, anyone with access to the World Wide Web can read it. Therefore, you should clearly identify the purpose of the Web site with a banner.

Create the First WordArt Element

1. Go to the Background.

2. Draw a WordArt frame that measures 3.95 inches wide by 0.8 inch deep. The frame should align with the top pink row guide and the blue guide for column 2.

3. Type the word "CLARK." Choose the following WordArt formats.

Why must I use two separate WordArt elements to create the shadow effect? In order to have the first word in the banner appear in a Web-safe color (Accent 1), you must recolor the WordArt element using Publisher's Recolor Object command. Unfortunately, this would also recolor the shadow to a pale shade of green. By creating a second WordArt element, you can preserve the more appropriate gray color for the shadow. When you publish this document to the Web, Publisher combines the two overlapping objects into a single picture.

Create the First WordArt Element *(continued)*

- @ Plain text shape
- @ Arial Black font
- @ Best Fit size
- @ Black characters

4 Assign a margin of 0.02 inch to all four sides of the WordArt frame.

5 Using Publisher's Recolor Object command, change the color of the text to Accent 1 (green).

6 Duplicate the WordArt object.

7 Recolor the duplicate with a light gray color (use an RGB value of 204, 204, 204).

8 Move the duplicate down 0.1 inch, to the left 0.1 inch, and to the bottom of the stack.

Create the Second and Third WordArt Elements

1 Draw a second WordArt frame that measures 1.44 inches wide and 0.25 inch deep. The frame should align with the two horizontal ruler guides and the left guide for column 2.

2 Type "FAMILY." Apply the following WordArt formats:

Create the Second and Third WordArt Elements *(continued)*

- ⟲ Plain Text shape
- ⟲ Arial Black font
- ⟲ Best Fit size
- ⟲ White fill for the letters
- ⟲ Letter Justify alignment

3 Fill the frame with the Accent 2 (blue) color.

4 Assign a margin of 0.05 inch to all four sides of the WordArt frame. Duplicate the WordArt frame.

5 Increase the width of the duplicate to 2.88 inches. It should abut the right edge of the "FAMILY" object and span columns 4, 5, and 6.

6 Change the text to read "BULLETIN."

7 Change the fill color of the frame to Accent 4 (red).

Use the background as a safety zone. This Web project contains only one page. However, you should still place the banner on the background for safety's sake. While you are working on the foreground, you can't select—and inadvertently change or delete—objects placed on the background.

Add the Final WordArt Element

1 Duplicate the "FAMILY" WordArt object again.

2 Change the text to read "THE."

3 Decrease the width of the frame to 0.7 inch.

4 Fill the WordArt frame with the Accent 3 color (orange).

5 Rotate the frame 90 degrees to the left.

6 Position the frame at the 1.44-inch mark on the horizontal ruler and the 0.35-inch mark on the vertical ruler. It should align with the top and left side of the "CLARK" WordArt frame.

7 Return to the foreground.

Adding Pictures to the Web Page

A Web site is a great way to show off the latest crop of family photos. The formatting applied to the picture frames mimics the colors and outline treatment of the WordArt banner.

What will happen if I resize bitmapped pictures in Publisher?

Resizing a bitmapped picture in Publisher isn't normally recommended because it can degrade image quality. In this case, however, you are decreasing the size of the picture, which results in less image degradation than if you were to increase the size of a bitmapped picture. In addition, when Publisher generates the final HTML file, it takes a snapshot of the screen, automatically changing the resolution of these images to a resolution appropriate for monitor output.

Import and Format the First Picture

1. Insert the Clip Gallery picture J0101857.BMP. You can find the picture easily by searching for the keywords, "baseball players, photos."

2. Position the picture at the 2.0-inch mark on the vertical ruler, aligned with the first column guide.

3. Using the lower-right selection handle, resize the picture until it spans column 1.

4. Using the Crop Picture tool, hide the bottom of the picture. The cropped picture should measure 1.5 inches tall.

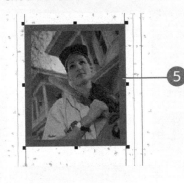

5. Format the picture frame with a 6-point border, using Accent 4 (red).

Insert and Edit the Second Picture

1. Insert the Clip Gallery picture J0101864.BMP. You can find the picture easily by searching for the keywords, "golf, photos."

2. Position the picture at the 2.0-inch mark on the vertical ruler, aligned with the second column guide.

Change the shape of pictures. This Web page design features a row of nearly square pictures. When inserted into the document, the photographs are actually horizontal or vertical rectangles. Changing the shape of the pictures is the only way to make the images work with the layout. Notice that the Crop Picture tool is used extensively, because it allows you to change the shape of a picture without distorting the aspect ratio.

Insert and Edit the Second Picture *(continued)*

3 Using the middle-right selection handle, crop the picture to span only column 2.

4 Format the picture with a 6-point border, using Accent 1 (green).

5 If necessary, resize the height of the picture to 1.5 inches, to match the height of the picture in column 1.

Insert and Edit the Third Picture

1 Insert the Clip Gallery picture J0101860.BMP. You can find the picture easily by searching for the keywords, "science, photos."

2 Position the picture at the 2.0-inch mark on the vertical ruler, aligned with the third column guide.

3 Using the lower-right selection handle, resize the picture until it spans column 3.

4 Using the Crop Picture tool, hide the bottom of the picture. The cropped picture should measure 1.5 inches tall.

5 Format the picture frame with a 6-point border, using Accent 3 (orange).

Trim opposite sides of a picture simultaneously and equally. Here's a technique that can help you to keep a picture centered in its frame when you crop it. Simply press and hold the Ctrl key when you use the Crop Picture tool. If you use the middle-right selection handle, for example, Publisher trims the left side of the picture by the same amount. If you press and hold the Ctrl key and crop a picture from one of the corner selection handles, Publisher trims all four sides of the picture by an equal amount.

Insert and Edit the Fourth Picture

1. Insert the Clip Gallery picture, PH01728J.JPG. You can find the picture easily by searching for the keywords, "football, photos."

2. Scale the picture's width and height to 44 percent of its original size.

3. Using the Crop Picture tool, hide portions of the left, right, and bottom of the picture. The cropped picture should span column 4 and should measure 1.5 inches tall.

4. Position the picture at the 2.0-inch mark on the vertical ruler, aligned in column 4.

5. Format the picture with a 6-point border, using the Accent 2 color (blue).

Creating Display Type

Simple text frames filled with accent colors continue the design motif of this Web page. They also add much needed structure to the page.

Create and Format Display Type

1. At the 6.0-inch mark on the vertical ruler, draw a text frame that spans columns 2, 3, and 4 and measures 0.25-inch tall.

2. Type the text "REUNION TIME" and format it as follows.

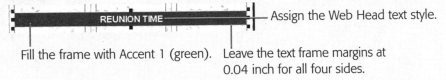

Assign the Web Head text style.

Fill the frame with Accent 1 (green).   Leave the text frame margins at 0.04 inch for all four sides.

Design efficiently by reformatting duplicate objects. You can create a layout much more quickly if you duplicate an object, reposition it on the page, and then change one or two of its attributes. In this procedure, for example, duplicating the display type text frame and then editing the text is more efficient than creating a new text frame.

For the text of this Web site, see Appendix B.

Turn off automatic hyphenation. HTML doesn't support automatic hyphenation of any kind. You should therefore select each text frame in your Web publication and disable automatic hyphenation. This guarantees that the line breaks you see in your working version of the document will match the line breaks your readers see when they view the document using a Web browser.

Copy and Modify the Display Copy

1 Place a duplicate of the text frame containing the display copy in column 1 at the 7.75-inch mark on the vertical ruler. Reduce the width of the text frame to span only column 1.

2 Change the text to read "WEBMASTER."

3 Change the fill color to Accent 2 (blue).

Inserting Body Copy

This Web page uses the Arial font for body copy. It's acceptable to use a sans-serif font, because the text blocks are relatively short and therefore easier to read. In fact, the text that appears below each photograph functions as an extended caption.

Insert Extended Photo Captions

1 Place a horizontal ruler guide at the 3.625-inch (3-5/8") mark on the vertical ruler.

2 Draw four separate text frames, as shown below, with one frame in each of the four columns. Each frame should span one column and measure 2.25 inches tall.

3 Type the extended captions or insert the copy from a text file.

4 Format the text as follows:

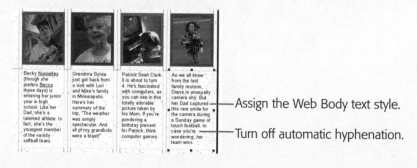

Assign the Web Body text style.

Turn off automatic hyphenation.

Isn't it improper to separate paragraphs with a blank line? When you design a print publication, it's considered bad form to separate paragraphs with a blank line. However, older Web browsers don't support sophisticated text formats, such as indented paragraphs, tabs, or custom line spacing. Inserting a blank line is the only way to separate paragraphs.

For more information about creating hyperlinks, see Chapter 12.

Shouldn't the e-mail address appear in the Web page? No, it isn't necessary for the actual e-mail address to appear in the text of a document. You can attach an e-mail address to any object or text phrase in your document.

Insert Body Copy

1 Starting at the 6.375-inch (6-3/8″) mark on the vertical ruler, draw a text frame that spans columns 2, 3, and 4. The bottom of the text frame should align with the bottom row guide.

2 Type or insert the text about the family reunion. Remember to separate the paragraphs with a blank line.

3 Assign the Web Body text style and turn off automatic hyphenation.

4 Starting at the 8.125-inch (8-1/8″) mark on the vertical ruler, draw a second text frame that spans column 1. The bottom of the text frame should align with the bottom row guide.

5 Type or insert Margaret Clark Russell's contact information.

6 Assign the Web Body text style and turn off automatic hyphenation.

Creating a Hyperlink

A Web document isn't truly complete until you add interactivity in the form of hyperlinks. Even though this publication contains only one Web page, you can still add a link to the Webmaster's e-mail address.

Create an E-mail Hyperlink

1 Highlight the contact information for Margaret Clark Russell.

2 In the Hyperlink dialog box, click the An Internet E-mail Address option and type the e-mail address "someone@microsoft.com" in the text box.

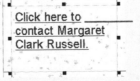

Publisher flags the text with the hyperlink color and underlining.

Check the conversion to HTML. Whenever you proofread a Web document, you should do more than just read the text. You should double-check the HTML formatting and the functionality of hyperlinks. Specifically:

- Confirm that the title you typed in the Web Properties dialog box appears in the browser's title bar.

- Confirm that the text formatting in the Web browser matches the text formatting you created in Publisher.

- Position the pointer over a hyperlink. The hand pointer should appear. Click the hyperlink to activate it.

Use the Web Publishing Wizard. The Microsoft Web Publishing Wizard is a separate utility that ships with Publisher. After you have saved a document as a Web page, you can use the Web Publishing Wizard to post your documents to the World Wide Web.

For more information about the Web Publishing Wizard, see Chapter 12.

Previewing and Producing the Web Site

Before you publish your document to the Web, you should use Publisher's special preview feature to see what the document will look like when it's viewed using a Web browser. Using a Web browser also allows you to check the hyperlink in the document.

Preview the Web Site and Test Hyperlinks

1. On the File menu, choose the Web Page Preview command. Publisher opens your browser and loads the Web page.

2. Proofread and explore the Web page.

3. When you are satisfied that the document appears as it should and that the hyperlink works as it should, close your Web browser.

Generate an HTML File

1. In the Web Properties dialog box, click the Page tab and confirm that you are using the filename and the extension required by your Internet Service Provider (ISP).

2. On the File menu, choose Save as Web Page. Select or create a folder, and then click OK. Publisher creates an HTML document and converts all pictures and graphic regions to the .gif format at a resolution that is appropriate for on-screen viewing.

3. Contact your ISP for more information about posting your HTML document to its server.

Use a silhouette or a symbol as part of a logo design. The simple shape is easy to identify and can help readers recognize your company.

Juxtapose both thick and thin line weights in a design to increase visual interest.

Integrate the company name with background shapes. Here, WordArt elements conform to the circular shapes in the logo.

Company Logo

A sophisticated logo can help a small business make a big impression. This logo embellishes the company name with WordArt effects and drawn shapes. The result is a recognizable symbol that can be used for standard business documents, such as stationery or a business form, and for promotional items, such as a shopping bag or baseball cap.

Preparing the Publication

This project focuses on the logo design and therefore doesn't require you to set up page guides. However, you should use ruler guides to help you properly align and position elements.

Set Up the Page

1. Start a new full-page document.

2. Select the printer you will use and confirm that the current paper size is 8.5-by-11-inch letter size in Portrait orientation.

3. Leave the page margins at 1 inch for all four sides. The number of rows and columns should remain at one.

Set Up the Page *(continued)*

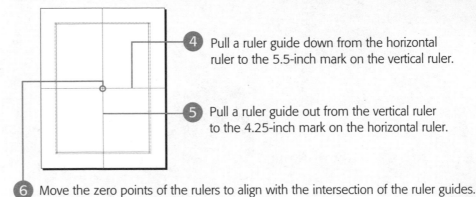

4 Pull a ruler guide down from the horizontal ruler to the 5.5-inch mark on the vertical ruler.

5 Pull a ruler guide out from the vertical ruler to the 4.25-inch mark on the horizontal ruler.

6 Move the zero points of the rulers to align with the intersection of the ruler guides.

 Why should I draw an element from the center outward? Drawing an element from the center outward ensures that it is centered. For each object, start from the intersection of the ruler guides and press and hold the Ctrl and Shift keys as you draw.

 Format lines before you draw them. Before you draw the nine parallel lines in this design, select the Line tool and open the Line/Border Style dialog box. Choose the 2-point line thickness and click OK. All the subsequent lines you draw in this publication will be formatted correctly.

Creating the Background Shapes

Draw the Background Shapes

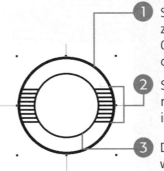

1 Starting from the intersection of the ruler guides (the new zero point), draw (from the center outward) a circle with a 0.75-inch radius. The diameter is 1.5 inches. Format the circle with a solid white fill color and a 3-point black border.

2 Starting in the center of the circle, draw nine parallel rules that intersect the circle. Space the rules 0.063 (1/16) inch apart, and format them with a 2-point line thickness.

3 Draw a second circle—once again, from the center outward—with a 0.5-inch radius (the diameter is 1 inch). Format the circle with a solid white fill color and a 2-point black border.

4 Group these elements.

Create logos quickly with clip art. You can often create a logo quite easily by combining an appropriate piece of clip art with the name of your company. Even when you are simply placing clip art next to text, look for a special visual relationship between the two. In the following logo design, the banner is positioned very close to (and flies high above) the most important word in the company name, "Trophy."

Combine multiple WordArt elements. Publisher offers several WordArt shapes that can wrap text around a circle or curve. You could create a version of this logo using the Circle or Button shapes. But you have much more control over how the words in this logo wrap around a circle if you create two separate WordArt elements by using the Arch Up and Arch Down shapes.

Creating WordArt Elements

You can make text conform to the outline of a drawn shape by creating the text object in Publisher's WordArt module.

Create the Main WordArt Element

1 Draw a WordArt frame that is 1.25 inches wide by 1.25 inches high.

2 Type TROPHY in uppercase letters in the text box.

3 Assign the following attributes to the text:

- Arch Up (Pour) shape
- Arial font
- 12-point font size
- Bold
- Center alignment

4 In the Spacing Between Characters dialog box, choose the Very Loose (150 percent) option.

5 In the Special Effects dialog box, change the Arc Angle value to 105 degrees, which will flatten the curve to match the circular background shapes.

6 In the Shadow dialog box, choose the three-dimensional shadow (third option from the right). Assign a shadow color of silver.

7 Click outside the WordArt frame to return to the document.

8 If necessary, reposition the WordArt frame to center it on the upper band of the circular background.

Create the Second WordArt Element

1 Copy the TROPHY WordArt element and paste a duplicate in the publication.

2 Double-click the duplicate to activate WordArt.

Why does Publisher keep asking me if I want to resize the WordArt frame? You have typed a longer text phrase but haven't yet changed the point size. As a result, the WordArt object is—at least temporarily—too large for the frame. In the alert box, click No to maintain the current size of the WordArt frame, and then reduce the size to 8 points.

3 Change the text to read SPORTING GOODS (in uppercase letters).

4 Change the formatting to Arch Down (Pour) and 8-point font size. Leave the following options unchanged: Arial font, bold, center alignment, and three-dimensional shadow.

5 In the Spacing Between Characters dialog box, choose the Loose (120 percent) option.

6 In the Special Effects dialog box, change the Arc Angle to 120 degrees.

7 Click outside the WordArt frame to return to your document.

8 If necessary, reposition the WordArt frame to center it on the lower band of the circular background.

**Crop WordArt to avoid
text wrapping problems.**
When you finish assembling the WordArt elements, notice that the WordArt frames extend past the circle. If you place the logo on top of a text frame, you'll create an undesirable text wrap. You can avoid this problem by using the Crop Picture tool to hide some of the white space in the WordArt frames. Using the Crop Picture tool allows you to resize the frame without changing the size or aspect ratio of the WordArt effect. Don't resize the frames or you will distort the effect.

Crop the WordArt Frames

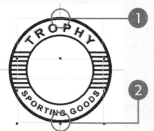

1 Using the Crop Picture tool, move the top selection handle of the Trophy object down. Reduce the size of the WordArt frame to 0.85 inch.

2 Using the Crop Picture tool, move the bottom selection handle of the Sporting Goods object up. Reduce the size of the WordArt frame to 0.90 inch.

3 Group the WordArt elements with the background shapes.

Drawing a Picture

Simple images, like the silhouette of a trophy used here, are often the best choices for a logo design. Instead of using clip art, you can create this picture using Publisher's drawing tools.

Draw Geometric Shapes

 Draw, position, and format a series of geometric shapes as listed in the following table.

Drawing Tool and Shape	Width x Height	Horizontal Position	Vertical Position	Fill Color
Custom Shapes, Pie Segment, adjusted to 1/2 circle	0.70 x 0.52 inch	-0.35 inch	-0.42 inch	Black
Custom Shapes, Pie Segment, adjusted to 1/2 circle	0.56 x 0.36 inch	-0.28 inch	-0.30 inch	White

Use the Size And Position toolbar. You can use the Size And Position dialog box to quickly assemble the individual geometric shapes in this drawing. For even easier access, click the Show Toolbar button in the Size And Position dialog box. Publisher creates a floating toolbar that remains open even when you draw or select a new object.

Draw Geometric Shapes *(continued)*

Drawing Tool and Shape	Width x Height	Horizontal Position	Vertical Position	Fill Color
Custom Shapes, Pie Segment, adjusted to 1/2 circle	0.46 x 0.80 inch	-0.23 inch	-0.60 inch	Black
Rectangle	0.10 x 0.23 inch	-0.05 inch	0.13 inch	Black
Custom Shapes, Octagon	0.20 x 0.08 inch	-0.01 inch	0.32 inch	Black
Rectangle	0.34 x 0.08 inch	-0.17 inch	0.36 inch	Black
Custom Shapes, Octagon	0.43 x 0.11 inch	-0.21 inch	-0.28 inch	Black
Custom Shapes, Hexagon	0.16 x 0.12 inch	-0.08 inch	-0.35 inch	Black
Custom Shapes, Octagon	0.06 x 0.12 inch	-0.03 inch	-0.44 inch	Black

(2) Select all of the drawn objects and group them, as shown in the following illustration.

(3) Group the drawing of the trophy with the WordArt objects.

Create a logo library. As you develop publications for your business, you'll discover that you need variations of the logo. You might require a smaller size for your business card or, as shown below, a tinted logo for use as a watermark (a light image that prints behind text). As you create different versions of the logo, save them as custom Design Gallery objects. Soon you'll have a library of logo-related design effects that you can reuse in all of your publications.

Completing the Logo

You should always print your designs in order to proofread the text and to check the design. Once you've developed a strong logo, you should use it in all of your publications. Storing the logo in the Design Gallery makes it easy to access. Whenever you need the logo, you can simply import it from this publication.

Print a Proof of the Design

1. Open the File menu and choose Print.
2. Clear Crop Marks in the Advanced Print Settings dialog box.
3. Click OK.

Add the Logo to the Design Gallery

1. Select the logo.
2. On the Insert menu, choose Add Selection To Design Gallery. In the Add Object dialog box, type an Object Name (such as *Trophy*) and a Category designation (such as *Logo*).
3. Save the file to finalize the addition of the logo to the Design Gallery.

Purchase Order

Trophy Sporting Goods
15 Old Country Road
Richardson, TX 75081
Voice: 214-555-1313
Fax: 214-555-1414

Vendor:	Date:
Address:	Resale Number:
	Terms:
	Ship Via:
Phone:	Ordered By:
Fax:	Authorized By:

Qty.	Description	Unit Price	Discount	Total
			Subtotal	
			Freight	
			Total	

Use the company logo on all correspondence to establish a corporate identity.

Design an order form with sufficient room for the requested information to be entered.

Apply tints to alternating rows of a table—checkbook style—to make it easy to track information across the page.

Business Form

A well-designed business form is easy to understand and easy to use. The person who fills out the form should be able to figure out exactly what information is needed and should have enough room to enter text legibly. The person who receives the form should be able to read and process the information without errors.

Determine the number of columns or rows that you need. You should always base the number of column and row guides on the width and height of the smallest element in your layout. In this business form project, for example, the narrowest text block is 1/8 page wide. Therefore, you should divide the page into 8 vertical sections or columns.

Preparing the Publication

Creating an underlying grid for this business form allows you to position and size a wide range of elements—including the internal column divisions of a table—with precision.

Set Up the Page

1 Start a new blank, full-page document.

2 Select the printer you will use and confirm that the current paper size is 8.5-by-11-inch letter size in Portrait orientation.

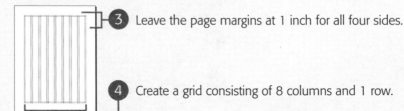

3 Leave the page margins at 1 inch for all four sides.

4 Create a grid consisting of 8 columns and 1 row.

What should I do if I haven't completed the project in Chapter 24?
The following procedures assume that you have already designed the logo in Chapter 24. You can still complete this project by making one simple adjustment. When asked to import the Trophy Sporting Goods logo, substitute a piece of clip art.

Creating the Header

Typically, the top portion of a business form contains the company logo, the title of the form, and contact information, such as an address and telephone number. Inserting the logo gives you an opportunity to take advantage of the Design Gallery.

Insert the Company Logo

1. Open the Design Gallery and click the Your Objects tab.

2. Use the Browse command (accessed through the Options button) to locate the .pub file containing the logo you created in Chapter 24, and insert the logo into the current publication.

3. Align the exterior circle of the logo with the leftmost column guide and the top row guide.

Publisher always shows you a gray outline of the elements in a group to help you position objects precisely.

Draw the Page Division

1. Starting at the 2.75-inch mark on the vertical ruler, draw a horizontal line that spans all 8 columns.

2. Change the line width to 2 points.

Draw the Page Division *(continued)*

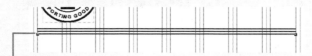

3 Create two duplicates of the line. Position each duplicate 0.063 inch (1/16") below the preceding line.

4 Group the three lines.

When to use relative line spacing. Publisher computes line spacing relative to the point size of the font. In this project, for example, the line spacing for all text lines is set at the default of 1 space. Publisher computes the line spacing for the 24-point text as 28.8 points, for the 12-point text as 14.4 points, and for the 9.5-point text as 11.4 points. Use relative line spacing so that you can mix font sizes in a single text frame without worrying about the descenders on one line of text crashing into the ascenders on the next line.

Alternatively, you can use absolute line spacing, which uses points (rather than spaces) as the unit of measure. But you'll have to compute the appropriate amount of line spacing for each point size.

Insert the Address and Phone Information

1 Draw a text frame that spans columns 3, 4, 5, and 6 and measures 1.5 inches high. Align the top of the text frame with the top row guide.

2 Enter the text in the illustration and format it as indicated.

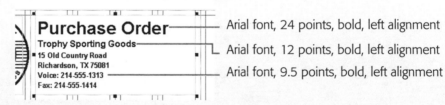

3 Draw a second text frame that spans columns 7 and 8 and measures 0.5 inches high. Align the top of the text frame with the top row guide.

4 Enter the order number, *#90065-30-421*. Format it as Arial, 12 points, bold, right alignment.

Use tools in combination to create accurate layouts. You can create and align duplicate text frames easily using Publisher's layout tools. First, turn on Snap To Objects. This command enables you to quickly snap each frame into the proper alignment. Then press and hold the Ctrl and Shift keys to drag a duplicate of the text frame straight up. Repeat this process, remembering to press and hold the constraint keys, for the remaining four text frames.

Creating the Vendor and General Information Items

When you create an order form, think about who will be relying on it for information. For example, if you don't want a vendor to charge you sales tax, you must leave room to enter your resale number. If all orders require approval, you need to include a place for a supervisor's signature.

You can expedite your work in this section of the form by duplicating individual frames and groups of frames and then moving them to the proper positions.

Create the Vendor Information Area

1 Pull down a horizontal ruler guide. Position it at the 4.5-inch mark on the vertical ruler.

2 Draw a text frame that spans columns 1, 2, 3, and 4 and measures 0.25 inch high. The bottom of the text frame should align with the horizontal ruler guide.

3 Type *Fax:* in the text box.

4 Format the text with the following attributes:

- Arial font

- 8 points

- Bold

- Left alignment

5 Format the text frame with a clear fill color and a 1-point border at the bottom of the frame.

6 Duplicate this text frame. Move the duplicate up so that the bottom of the copied frame aligns with the top of the previous frame.

Consider design alternatives. In this purchase order project, you create the vendor and general information items using standard text frames. However, you could create these elements using a table instead. Using Publisher's ability to apply custom borders to table cells, you could create a single table that looks exactly like the group of six text frames in the adjacent procedure.

How to edit text within groups. You don't have to ungroup objects in order to edit text. Simply select the text frame. Publisher indicates the selected frame with a red outline. Then highlight the existing text, and type the new text.

Create the Vendor Information Area *(continued)*

7 Repeat step 6 four more times. You should create a total of six text frames.

8 Enter labels for address and phone information as shown.

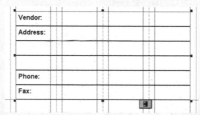

9 Select these six text frames and group them.

Create the Order Information Area

1 Create a duplicate of the text frame group, and position it so that it spans columns 5, 6, 7, and 8. The bottom of the group should align with the horizontal ruler guide at the 4.5-inch mark on the vertical ruler.

2 Enter the labels shown here.

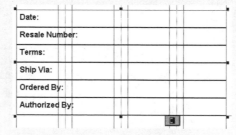

Creating the Order Form

Use a table to ensure consistent alignment of rules and text.

Draw and Format the Table

1 Starting at the 4.75-inch mark on the vertical ruler, draw a table frame that spans all 8 columns and aligns with the bottom row guide.

2 In the Create Table dialog box, specify 16 rows, 5 columns, and the Checkbook Register table format.

3 Select the entire table. In the Border Style dialog box, select the Line Border tab and assign a 1-point rule to the grid.

4 Select the top row and format it with the following attributes:

- Arial font
- 10-point font size
- Bold
- Center alignment

5 Select a range of cells comprising all the rows in columns 1 and 2 except the first row. Format them with the following attributes:

- Arial font
- 10-point font size
- Left alignment

Column guides versus page guides. Publisher distinguishes between column guides (shown in blue) and page guides (shown in pink). Whenever you use the layout guides as a grid, align objects to the pink guidelines instead of the blue guidelines.

Align numbers at the decimal point. When you enter numbers—especially prices—in a form, you should align the information at the decimal point. This sample form uses simple right alignment for all columns containing numbers. However, it requires you to enter each number with a decimal point and two trailing zeros, as in "$00.00." Alternatively, you can create a true decimal tab stop. When you subsequently enter the numbers, you must be sure to use the special key-combination (Ctrl-Tab) to insert the tab characters and align the numbers at a decimal point.

For more information on decimal aligned tabs, see Chapter 6.

Draw and Format the Table *(continued)*

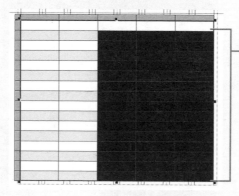

6 Select a range of cells comprising all the rows in columns 3, 4, and 5 except the first row. Format them with the following attributes:

- ℮ Arial font
- ℮ 10-point font size
- ℮ Right alignment

7 Pressing and holding the Shift key, use the Adjust pointer to resize the columns of the table in relation to the underlying pink grid, as indicated below.

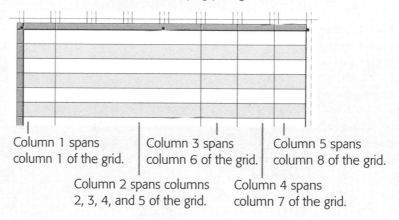

Column 1 spans column 1 of the grid.

Column 2 spans columns 2, 3, 4, and 5 of the grid.

Column 3 spans column 6 of the grid.

Column 4 spans column 7 of the grid.

Column 5 spans column 8 of the grid.

Enter the Table Labels

① Type the labels into each cell of the first row of the table, as shown below.

② Create summary labels in the bottom 3 cells of table column 4.

③ As you type, Publisher formats the text with the 10-point Arial font. Select each label and boldface the text.

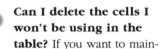

Can I delete the cells I won't be using in the table? If you want to maintain the alignment of text in the table, don't delete the cells at the bottom of columns 1, 2, and 3. Instead, make this section of the table invisible by changing the formatting attributes. Doing so doesn't change the structure of the table, but it does produce the illusion that the cells have been deleted from the table.

Hide Unneeded Cells and Customize the Table Border

① Select the bottom three rows in columns 1, 2, and 3 of the table.

② Fill the selected cells with a solid white color.

③ In the Border Style dialog box, select the Line Border tab. Select the left edge, the bottom edge, and the interior vertical and horizontal dividers (but not the top or right edges), and format them with no rule. The selected section looks like the following illustration.

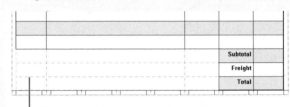

Though dotted cell boundaries appear on screen, they don't print.

Forms built from tables are easy to fill out electronically. When you design a form with Publisher, you can print it out and enter the information by hand. Alternatively, you can fill out the form electronically, using Publisher as a forms processor. Using the Table tool to build a form makes the form easier to fill out electronically because the Tab key moves you from cell to cell in the table. If you create a table using text frames, you must lift your hands from the keyboard and use the mouse to select the next text frame.

Completing the Purchase Order

Save this file as a template so that you can use the form over and over again.

Save the File as a Template

1 In the Save As dialog box, open the Save As Type drop-down list and choose Publisher Template (*.pub).

2 Type an appropriate filename, such as Purchase Order, in the text box.

3 Click OK.

Print the Document

1 Open the File menu and choose Print.

2 Click the Advanced Print Settings button, and clear the check mark from the Crop Marks and Allow Bleeds options.

3 In the Print dialog box, enter the number of copies you want to print.

4 Click OK.

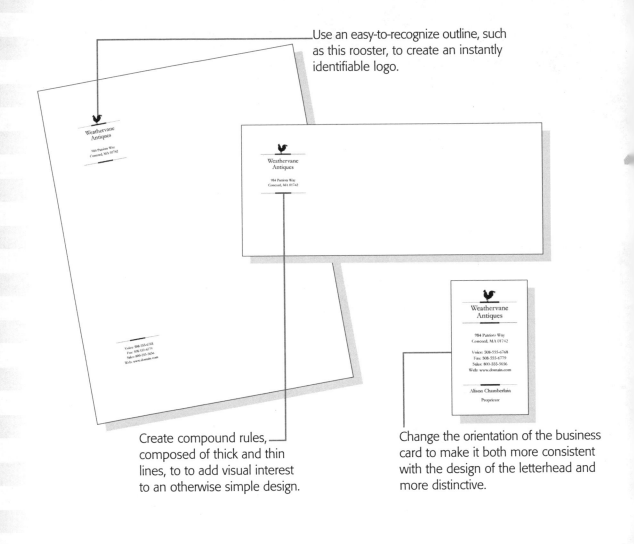

Use an easy-to-recognize outline, such as this rooster, to create an instantly identifiable logo.

Create compound rules, composed of thick and thin lines, to to add visual interest to an otherwise simple design.

Change the orientation of the business card to make it both more consistent with the design of the letterhead and more distinctive.

Letterhead, Business Card, Envelope

No matter how large or small your company, stationery is a necessity. With a strong logo design and an elegant typeface, this letterhead design makes a wonderful first impression on prospective customers. The matching envelope and business card complete the package.

Preparing the Letterhead Publication

You should set up page and column guides for this document as you would for any standard business document. Here, a narrow column on the left side of the page contains the logo and address information.

Set Up the Page

1. Start a new, blank, full-page publication.

2. Select the printer you will use. Confirm that the current paper size is 8.5-by-11 inches in Portrait orientation.

Set Up the Page *(continued)*

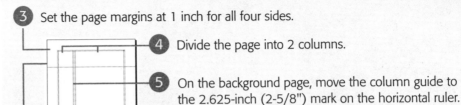

3 Set the page margins at 1 inch for all four sides.

4 Divide the page into 2 columns.

5 On the background page, move the column guide to the 2.625-inch (2-5/8") mark on the horizontal ruler.

6 On the foreground, create a horizontal ruler guide at the 2.625-inch (2-5/8") mark on the vertical ruler.

Finding conceptual or abstract art. In many cases, a simple abstract or geometric shape is the best choice for a logo design. You can find appropriate images quite easily in Publisher's Clip Art Gallery. In addition to literal descriptions, such as *cat* or *house*, images are identified by conceptual descriptions, such as *silhouette* or *symbol*. For example, you can find the two images shown below by searching for the keyword *geometric shapes*.

Creating the Logo

When you design a logo, you should first look for inspiration in the company name. Here, a picture of a rooster looks like a weathervane and so echoes the store's name. You should also develop a framing device to tie the picture and the company name together in a cohesive logo design.

Insert a Clip Art Image

1 Insert the picture An01044_.WMF from Publisher's clip art library. You can easily find the picture in the Clip Gallery by searching for the keyword *chicken*.

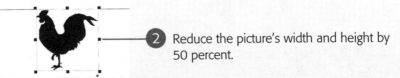

2 Reduce the picture's width and height by 50 percent.

3 Position the image in the center of the first column, aligned with the top row guide.

Use compound rules.
A simple design solution would use a single heavy rule across the width of the address column. The resulting design would be too dark for the font choice (Garamond) and visually boring. Instead of a single heavy rule, create a compound rule (composed of two overlapping and grouped lines) that lightens up the design and adds rhythm and variety to the logo.

Add a Compound Rule

1 Draw a 2.5-point, horizontal black line that measures 0.5 inch.

2 Draw a 0.25-point, horizontal black line that spans the width of the first column.

3 Center the two lines vertically and horizontally.

4 Group the lines.

5 Position the group in column 1 at the 2.625-inch (2-5/8") mark on the vertical ruler.

6 Place a duplicate of the compound rule at the base of the clip art picture.

7 Group the clip art picture and the compound rule.

8 Place another duplicate of the compound rule in column 1 at the 8.5-inch mark on the vertical ruler.

Will my primary business information appear in other documents? If you have previously created a document with Personal Information components for your primary business, you needn't worry. The documents continue to display the correct information.

However, when you insert a Primary Business Personal Information component into any subsequently created documents, Publisher displays the information for Weathervane Antiques. This is no cause for alarm. In a new document, simply open the Personal Information dialog box once again, and enter the correct information for your business.

Add Personal Information Components

1 Open the Personal Information dialog box from the Edit menu, and enter the following text into the appropriate text boxes for the Primary Business set:

Alison Chamberlain
Weathervane
Antiques
984 Patriots Way
Concord, MA 01742

Proprietor
Voice: 508-555-6768
Fax: 508-555-6779
Sales: 800-555-5656
Web: www.domain.com

2 Using the Insert command, insert a Personal Information component for your organization name.

3 Align the frame with the first column guide and with the 1.5-inch mark on the vertical ruler.

4 Resize the frame to the width of column 1 and to a height of 0.5 inch.

5 Insert the Personal Information component for your address.

6 Align the frame with the first column guide and with the 2-inch mark on the vertical ruler.

7 Resize the frame to the width of column 1 and to a height of 0.5 inch.

8 Format the text elements as indicated below.

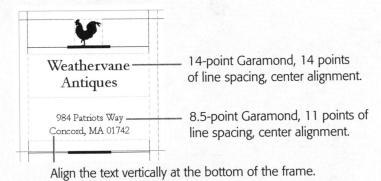

Weathervane Antiques —— 14-point Garamond, 14 points of line spacing, center alignment.

984 Patriots Way —— 8.5-point Garamond, 11 points of
Concord, MA 01742   line spacing, center alignment.

Align the text vertically at the bottom of the frame.

Accommodate multiple phone numbers and e-mail addresses.

Today's business climate requires most companies to have at least two phone numbers (one for voice communication and one for faxes) and a Web or e-mail address. Stores often add toll-free numbers for phone orders. When you design stationery, you must leave a sufficient amount of room to accommodate all of these numbers. In the current project, a separate column contains the current contact information and can easily accommodate more phone numbers as the business grows.

Add the Phone/Fax/E-mail Personal Information Component

1 Insert the Phone/Fax/E-mail component by selecting Phone/Fax/E-mail on the Personal Information submenu.

2 Align the frame with the first column guide and with the 8.625-inch (8-5/8") mark on the vertical ruler.

3 Format the text as indicated below.

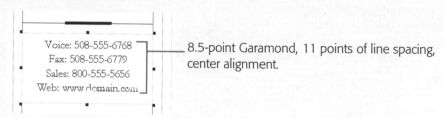

Voice: 508-555-6768
Fax: 508-555-6779
Sales: 800-555-5656
Web: www.domain.com

8.5-point Garamond, 11 points of line spacing, center alignment.

4 Resize the frame to the width of column 1. The frame should measure 0.75-inch deep.

Formatting the Body of the Letter

To ensure visual consistency, you should create text styles for the greeting and body of the letter that work with the logo design. You then can finalize the placement of the letter by drawing and formatting an empty text frame.

Letterhead Text Styles			
Text Style	**Font**	**Alignment**	**Line Spacing**
Address/Signature	Garamond, 11 points	Left alignment	14 points
Body/Date	Garamond, 11 points	Left alignment	14 points, 10 points of space after paragraphs
Greeting	Garamond, 11 points	Left alignment	14 points, 10 points of space before and after paragraphs
Closing	Garamond, 11 points	Left alignment	14 points, 30 points of space after paragraphs

Use descriptive text style names. Publisher allows you to type a lot of information in a text style name—up to 32 characters' worth. Take advantage of it by truly describing the purpose of each text style. In this project, the text style names identify the components to which they should be applied. For example, the Body/Date text style should be assigned to the dateline and the actual message of the letter.

Create an Empty Text Frame

1 Draw a text frame that spans column 2. The text frame should align with the horizontal ruler guide at the 2.625-inch (2-5/8") mark on the vertical ruler and the bottom row guide.

2 Select the text frame and turn off automatic hyphenation.

Save a Template

You should save the letterhead design as a template to protect the layout from inadvertent changes.

Save a Template

1 In the Save As dialog box, open the Save As Type drop-down list and choose Publisher Template.

2 Type an appropriate filename, such as "Letterhead," in the text box.

3 Click Save.

By default, Publisher stores the file in a specially designated templates folder. Each time you start a new publication based on this template, Publisher opens a copy of the file, leaving the original file intact.

Creating a Matching Business Card and Envelope

You can easily create a matching business card and envelope by copying essential elements of the Letterhead design to the Clipboard.

Create an Envelope

1. Open the Letterhead template, or start a new publication based on the Letterhead template.

2. Copy the clip art picture, the Organization and Address Personal Information components, and the surrounding compound rules to the Clipboard.

3. Start a new, blank publication.

4. Use the Page Setup dialog box to choose the Envelope #10 (4-1/8" x 9-1/2") layout.

5. Paste the elements into the document, group them, and align the group along the top and left margin guides.

6. Save the publication as a template with an appropriate name, such as "Envelope."

 Why can't I choose the Business Card page layout to create this publication? Publisher's Business Card page layout has a horizontal orientation; it measures 3.5 inches wide by 2 inches deep. You can't change the orientation of the layout. In order to create a vertically oriented card, you must enter custom values in the Width and Height text boxes in the Page Setup dialog box.

Create a Business Card

1. Open the Letterhead template, or start a new publication based on the Letterhead template.

2. Select all of the objects in the left column and copy them to the Clipboard.

3. Start a new, blank publication with a custom page size of 2 inches wide by 3.5 inches deep.

4. Create margins of 0.18 inch for the left and right sides of the page. Create margins of 0.15 inch for the top and bottom of the page.

Create a Business Card *(continued)*

5 The business card should contain only 1 column and 1 row.

6 Paste all of the elements from the Clipboard into the publication.

7 Reposition all of the objects as shown in the following illustration.

Align the group containing the clip art picture and the compound rule with the top row guide.

Snap this frame to the bottom of the previous rule (at the 0.592-inch mark on the vertical ruler).

Snap this compound rule to the previous frame at the 1.092-inch mark on the vertical ruler.

Snap this frame to the bottom of the previous frame at the 1.75-inch mark on the vertical ruler.

Align this compound rule to the 2.7-inch mark on the vertical ruler.

Align this frame at the 1.25-inch mark on the vertical ruler. Align the text vertically in the center of the frame.

8 Select all of the objects on the page, and center them left-to-right on the page.

9 Insert a Personal Information component for your job title. Align it at the bottom row guide, and resize the frame to the width of the business card. The frame should measure 0.25 inch deep.

10 Insert a Personal Information component for your name. Align the bottom of the frame with the top of the Job Title frame. Resize the frame to the width of the business card. The frame should measure 0.25 inch deep.

11 Format the text as shown in the following illustration.

Why do all of the objects overlap one another when I try to align them? If you want to align a group of selected objects horizontally without changing their vertical positions, you must choose the following options in the Align Objects dialog box.

- In the Left To Right area, select Centers.

- In the Top To Bottom area, select No Change.

- Select the Align Along Margins option.

Why does my printer prompt me to insert a #10 envelope? By default, Publisher is set up to print on envelope-sized paper whenever you choose an envelope page size in the Page Setup dialog box. In order to print a proof of your envelope design on letter-sized paper, you must turn this feature off. Open the Options dialog box (found on the Tools menu). Click the Print tab, and clear the check mark from the Automatically Use Envelope Paper Sizes item.

Proof on printer paper, but print on specialty papers. When you proof the stationery set you should use ordinary printer paper because it is inexpensive. You should use high quality specialty papers for the final printout, however. Specialty papers are typically colored, watermarked, or linen paper stocks, but they also include envelopes and perforated business cards that you can feed through your printer.

Create a Business Card *(continued)*

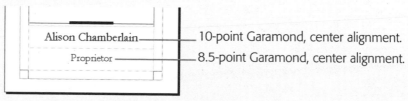

10-point Garamond, center alignment.

8.5-point Garamond, center alignment.

12 Save the file as a template with an appropriate name, such as "Business card."

Completing the Stationery Set

Though the stationery contains a minimal amount of text, you should still print the letterhead, envelope, and business card in order to proofread the copy.

Print a Proof of the Letterhead

1 Begin a new document based on the Letterhead template.

2 In the Print dialog box, click the Advanced Print Settings button, confirm that the Crop Marks option is checked, and then click OK.

3 Click OK.

4 Close the document without saving the publication.

5 Repeat steps 1 through 4 for the Envelope and Business Card templates.

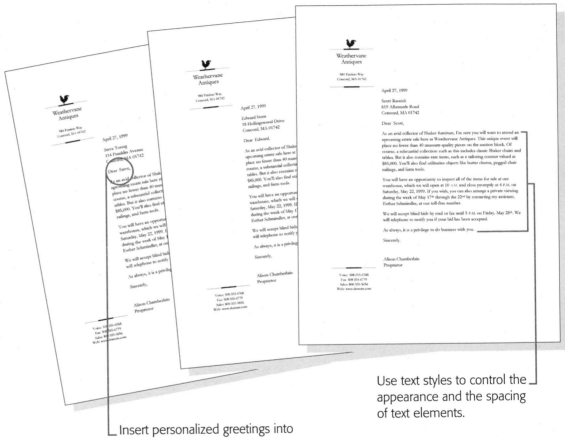

Use text styles to control the appearance and the spacing of text elements.

Insert personalized greetings into your direct mail project. Notice that each copy contains a different entry from the address list.

Mail Merge Letter

After you've designed a letterhead, use Microsoft Publisher 2000's mail merge functions to generate business correspondence efficiently. The following project employs the entire range of Publisher's mail merge functions, including personalizing a letter and using a filter to select only a portion of the Address List for the current mailing.

Preparing the Publication

Using a custom template can greatly simplify document setup.

Open a Template

Double-check the current printer settings. When you open a template, many document settings—including the choice of printer and paper—are loaded along with the publication. It's always a good idea to open the Print Setup dialog box and confirm that the printer and paper choices are correct. In this case, the printer is a PostScript device, and the paper is standard 8.5-by-11 inch letter-sized paper in Portrait orientation.

1. On the File menu, select New.

2. On the first page of the Catalog, click the Templates button.

3. Open the Letterhead template you created in Chapter 26.

Creating the Address List

Setting up a basic address list in Publisher is as easy as filling in the blanks, because the address list already contains fields for general information such as names, addresses, and phone numbers. You can make the address list even more powerful by creating custom fields for data that relate specifically to your business.

For the text of this mail merge project, see Appendix B.

Is it okay to misspell words when entering data in the address list?
No, you must be sure that you have spelled the information you enter into the address list correctly and consistently. Publisher's spelling checker doesn't work within dialog boxes—only within the actual publication file. In addition, when you create filters for your data, Publisher looks for exact spelling matches.

Is it okay to leave fields blank in the address list? Yes, it is perfectly okay to leave blank fields in the address list. The blank fields won't appear in your publication when you merge it with the address list. If you find the blank fields distracting, however, you can always delete them by clicking the Customize button in the address list dialog box.

Customize the Address List

1 On the Mail Merge menu, choose Create Publisher Address List.

2 In the Customize Address List dialog box, delete the following fields:

- Title
- Company Name
- Address Line 2
- Country
- Work Phone
- E-mail Address

3 Highlight the last item on the list—Home Phone.

4 Add a field called Period after the Home Phone field.

5 Return to the Address List dialog box.

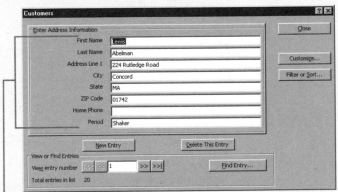

6 Enter the information for the address list, including names, addresses, and the period style that interests each customer.

7 When you have finished entering the names and addresses, save the address list to a file called Customers.mdb.

Why should I type general descriptions, such as "First" and "Last" instead of a person's name? You are typing dummy text to designate the position of a person's given name and surname. Later in this project, you'll replace this text with live field codes that link the letter to the address list. When you print the final version of the letter, actual names from the address list will replace the field codes.

Use typographic characters instead of typewriter characters. You can make your documents—even simple business letters—look much more professional by replacing typewriter characters with typographic characters. In this letter, for example, the days of the month—June 14th and June 21st—are followed by superscript characters. You must use the Font dialog box to apply the Superscript attribute to selected text. You should likewise format the letters A.M. and P.M. as small caps.

Creating the Letter

Because you created text styles and saved them as part of the letterhead template, generating this letter is basically a matter of inserting the text. You can even insert the date automatically using the Date And Time command on the Insert menu.

Type and Format Text

1. Select the blank text frame.

2. Type or import the text of the letter. Create separate paragraphs, but don't insert extra lines between paragraphs.

3. Assign text styles as indicated in the following illustration.

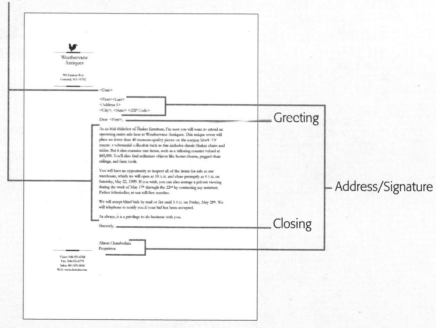

Body/Date

Greeting

Address/Signature

Closing

Insert the Date

1 Select Date And Time from the Insert menu.

2 In the Date And Time dialog box, select the appropriate (Month, Day, Year) format. Confirm that the Update Automatically check box is clear.

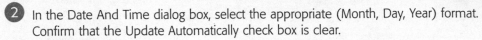

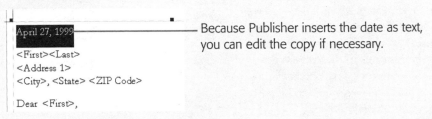

April 27, 1999 ———— Because Publisher inserts the date as text, you can edit the copy if necessary.

\<First>\<Last>
\<Address 1>
\<City>, \<State> \<ZIP Code>

Dear \<First>,

Inserting Field Codes into the Letter

Before you can take advantage of an address list, you must associate the current document with a data source. Once the connection is made, you can insert field codes that point to specific information in the address list.

Open a Data Source and Insert Field Codes

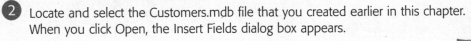

1 On the Mail Merge menu, choose Open Data Source.

2 Locate and select the Customers.mdb file that you created earlier in this chapter. When you click Open, the Insert Fields dialog box appears.

Use filters to find information in an address list. If you create an address list within Publisher (rather than connecting the publication to a data source created with another application), you can use filters to find information in the address list. In this letter project, for example, you can apply a filter to see how many people are interested in Mission furniture. Simply apply a filter where the Period field is equal to Mission. After you've viewed the results of the search, which show that only four people like Mission furniture, click the Remove Filter button.

Open a Data Source and Insert Field Codes *(continued)*

 Use the following table to replace dummy text in your document with live field codes that point to the address list.

Text to Be Replaced by Field Codes	
Highlight This Text	**Insert This Field Code**
<First>*	First Name
<Last>	Last Name
<Address 1>	Address Line 1
<City>	City
<State>	State
<ZIP Code>	ZIP Code

* Appears in the address and the greeting of the letter.

 When you have finished entering field codes, click the Close button. Your publication should resemble the following illustration.

Within the working view of a publication, field codes are identified with surrounding double angle brackets.

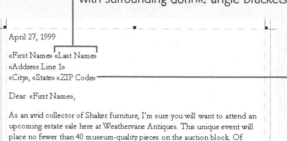

Field codes can be formatted with Publisher's full range of character and paragraph formats.

How should I sort the address list? Normally, you sort an address list alphabetically by last name in order to make entries easier to find. At print time, however, change the criteria and sort on the ZIP Code field. Mail that has been presorted in this way requires less handling by the post office and so qualifies for reduced postal rates.

Filtering and Sorting the Address List

Publisher allows you to manipulate an address list in two important ways. You can apply a filter, which uses the selection criteria you specify to create a subset of information from the address list. In this project, for example, you use a filter to select the entries of only those people who are interested in Shaker-style furniture.

You can also sort an address list to determine the order in which entries are viewed or printed. But you can't filter or sort an address list until you have merged it with the current publication.

Merge the Address List and the Publication

1 On the Mail Merge menu, choose Merge. The Preview Data dialog box appears, and the first entry in the address list appears in place of the field codes.

2 Use the controls in the Preview Data dialog box to see how each entry in the address list will appear when printed.

3 When you have finished viewing the entries, click Close.

Use Publisher's on-screen preview to check the results of filtering and sorting operations. If you have applied filtering or sorting criteria to an address list, you can see the results on-screen by selecting the Show Merge Results command on the Mail Merge menu. The Preview Data dialog box appears. Only those entries from the address list that meet your selection criteria appear on-screen, replacing the field codes in your text. In this mail merge project, for example, only eight entries from the address list meet the selection criteria you specified earlier.

Filter and Sort the Address List

1. Open the Filtering And Sorting dialog box.

2. On the Filter tab, apply a filter with the following selection criteria:

   - For Field, choose Period.

   - For Comparison, choose Is Equal To.

   - For Compare To, type "Shaker."

3. On the Sort tab in the Filtering And Sorting dialog box, create an ascending sort order based on the ZIP Code field.

Printing a Merged Document

Before you print the multiple copies that constitute a merged document, you should test the results of the filtering and sorting criteria you specified by using special mail merge options that appear in the Print Merge dialog box.

Print a Test of the Merged Document

1. On the File menu, choose Print Merge. The Print Merge dialog box appears.

2. Click the Test button to print a single instance of the mail merge letter.

Print the Merged Document

1. On the File menu, choose Print Merge. The Print Merge dialog box appears.

2. Select All Entries to print a copy of the publication for each entry in the address list that meets the selection criteria.

3. In the Advanced Print Settings dialog box, clear the Crop Marks check box.

4. Click OK.

Display a Web navigation bar
on every page in the Web site.

Use a font, such as Verdana, that is
legible when viewed on-screen.

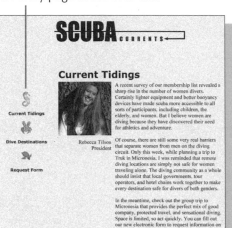

Collect customer
information and
reader feedback
with an electronic
response form.

Professional Web Site

Using Microsoft Publisher 2000's special Web publishing tools, you can design a multiple-page Web site complete with hyperlinks and multimedia events. Objects created using the Design Gallery or Publisher's Form Control tool can automate complex tasks, such as creating an interactive table of contents or programming an electronic reader response form.

Preparing the Web Publication

When you set up a Web publication, you must determine the general appearance of each page by specifying page size and background. However, you must also specify other, more sophisticated attributes. For example, you should choose the appropriate character set and HTML version for your target audience. In addition, you can associate searchable keywords with your publication to make your site easier to find on the World Wide Web. You can even play a sound file whenever a reader displays your Web page.

Set Up the Web Page

1. Start a new, blank Web Page publication.

2. In the Page Setup dialog box, choose the Standard option. Change the page height to 6 inches.

3. Set the page margins to 0 for all four sides.

4. Create a grid consisting of 4 columns and 1 row.

Determine the appropriate size for your Web pages. The width and height of your Web pages are determined by two different factors. Base the width on the display resolution most likely to be used by your readers. In this case, choosing the Standard option guarantees that even those readers with standard VGA 640 x 480 screens will be able to see the entire width of the page. Base the height on the amount of information you intend to place on each Web page. In this project, for example, the page height is reduced to only 6 inches, because each page contains a relatively small amount of information. Instead of scrolling down one long page, readers can click hyperlinks to move from page to page.

Choose Web-safe colors. Computer systems—notably Macs and PCs—use different color palettes to display Web pages. To be sure that the colors in your Web page display properly on a wide variety of computer systems, you should choose colors from a Web-safe palette. To specify a Web-safe color, use only values of 0, 51, 102, 153, 204 or 255 for the red, green, and blue components of the RGB color model.

Set Up the Web Page *(continued)*

5 On the background, create 4 horizontal ruler guides positioned as shown in the following illustration.

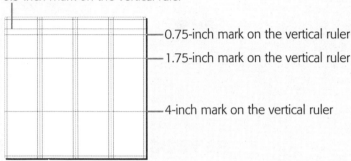

0.5-inch mark on the vertical ruler

—0.75-inch mark on the vertical ruler

—1.75-inch mark on the vertical ruler

—4-inch mark on the vertical ruler

6 Return to the foreground.

Create a Custom Background and Color Scheme

1 In the Color and Background Scheme dialog box, select the Custom tab.

2 Click the Texture check box (or the Browse button) and select the file Wb00760L.gif for the background.

3 Create a custom color scheme using the following RGB values, which are listed in order as red, green, blue:

- Main: 0, 0, 0
- Accent 1: 0, 0, 153
- Accent 2: 255, 0, 0
- Accent 3: 255, 255, 0
- Accent 4: 153, 204, 255
- Accent 5: 255, 255, 255
- Hyperlink: 0, 102, 51
- Followed hyperlink: 102, 0, 102

Confirm file naming conventions with your Internet Service Provider. When you generate the final HTML document, Publisher will create a separate file for each page in the publication using the file names and file extension you specify in the Web Properties dialog box. You should contact your Internet Service Provider (ISP) to determine the required file naming conventions and file extension. Once you have this information, enter it in the File Name text box and File Extension drop-down list on the Page tab of the Web Properties dialog box.

Should I use Verdana in my Web publications? Microsoft has approved the Verdana font and its variations (italic, bold, and bold italic) for use on the Web. However, there is always the chance that a reader with an older system or a Mac might not have the Verdana font available. If that should happen, Arial or Helvetica will most likely appear on-screen in place of Verdana. In this design, Verdana is used exclusively for display type. So even if font substitution should occur, it will not change the layout significantly.

Assign Web Site and Web Page Properties

1. In the Web Properties dialog box, click the Site tab. Then type appropriate keywords (such as "scuba," "diving," "water sports," "vacation," "travel") and a description (such as "Scuba Currents is a club for professional and amateur scuba divers"). Specify that the target audience will use HTML 3.0+ browsers and the Western European (Windows) character set.

2. Click the Page tab in the Web Properties dialog box. Then type an appropriate title for the page, such as "Current Tidings."

3. On the same tab, choose the file Ocean_01.mid in the Background Sound drop-down list box. Select the Loop Forever option.

4. Add two blank pages to the publication. In the Insert Page dialog box, be sure to click Add Hyperlink To Web Navigation Bar.

5. Making sure that page 2 is the currently displayed page, open the Web Properties dialog box, click the Page tab, and type an appropriate title for the page, such as "Dive Destinations."

6. Repeat step 5 for page 3, typing a different title, such as "Request Form."

Creating Text Styles

Publisher ships with several fonts that are appropriate for use on the Web. In this publication, Times New Roman (a serif font) and Verdana (a sans-serif font) are combined to provide visual variety.

HTML Text Styles			
Text Style	**Character Type and Size**	**Indents and Lists**	**Line Spacing**
Web Body	Times New Roman, 10 points	Left alignment	1 sp
Web Head	Verdana, bold, Accent 1 (blue), 18 points	Left alignment	1 sp
Web Contents	Verdana, bold, Accent 1 (blue), 8 points	Center alignment	1 sp
Web Form	Arial, 10 points	Right alignment	1 sp

Creating the Repeating Elements

Like traditional desktop publishing documents, Web documents contain repeating elements, such as a running head containing the company logo. Instead of a table of contents or footer that displays page numbers, however, Web documents contain hyperlinked navigation bars to move you forward or backward through a multiple-page document. Objects and hyperlinks placed on the background are duplicated and function identically on each page of the Web site.

 Use WordArt to incorporate unique fonts into a Web document. The logo in this sample Web site employs a nonstandard font, Impact. To be sure that the correct font appears on-screen when a reader views this document with a Web browser, create the object as a WordArt element. Publisher automatically converts WordArt elements to .gif pictures when it generates an HTML file.

Create a WordArt Logo

1 Go to the background.

2 Starting at the pink guide that divides columns 1 and 2, draw a WordArt frame measuring 1.7 inches wide by 0.65 inch high. The frame should align with the top row guide and the ruler guide at the 0.75-inch mark on the vertical ruler.

3 Type "SCUBA" into the WordArt text box, and format it as:

  @ Plain text shape

  @ Impact font

  @ Best Fit size

  @ Stretch

  @ Black text

4 Select the WordArt frame and create margins of 0.05 inch for all four sides.

5 Recolor the WordArt text with Accent 1 (blue).

Why should I use the Recolor Object command to choose colors for WordArt? Publisher's WordArt module allows you to choose colors from a limited palette. There is no guarantee that these are Web-safe colors or that they visually match the colors in your color scheme. In order to apply a Web-safe color from your color scheme to a WordArt object, you must use the Recolor Object command.

 Why should I use a box to connect the two horizontal lines in the logo? If you zoom in on the rules in the logo, you'll see that the box with the 3-sided border has perfectly sharp corners. Aligning the top and bottom (horizontal) edges of the box with the horizontal rules in the logo takes a small amount of effort. Although you certainly can create the same effect by connecting the two horizontal lines in the logo with a third (vertical) line, you'll find that it is much more difficult to achieve that same level of precision.

Add a Second WordArt Element

1 Starting at the blue guide for column 3, draw a WordArt frame measuring 1.4 inches wide by 0.25 inch high. Position the frame between the ruler guides at the 0.5- and 0.75-inch marks on the vertical ruler.

2 Type "CURRENTS" into the WordArt text box, and format it as:

- Plain text shape
- Impact font
- Best Fit size
- Letter Justify
- Black text

3 Select the WordArt frame and create margins of 0.1 inch for all four sides.

4 Recolor the WordArt text with Accent 2 (red).

Add Supporting Rules to the Logo

1 Starting at the 0.43-inch mark on the vertical ruler, draw a line that measures 3.45 inches wide. The left point of the line should align with the left edge of the "SCUBA" WordArt frame.

2 Format the rule with Accent 2 (red) and a line weight of 2 points.

3 Send the line to the bottom of the stack.

4 Draw a second rule at the 0.62-inch mark on the vertical ruler measuring 0.55 inch wide. The left point of the rule should align with the pink guide between columns 3 and 4.

5 Format the rule with Accent 2 (red), a 2-point line weight, and a left-pointing arrowhead.

Include pages in the Web navigation bar automatically. Publisher can automatically add pages, along with their titles and the appropriate hyperlinks, to a Web navigation bar. If you decide to delete a page from your Web site, Publisher can automatically delete the reference in the Web navigation bar. To take advantage of this feature, you must select the Add Hyperlink To Web Navigation Bar option in either the Web Properties dialog box (on the Page tab) or the Insert Pages dialog box. In this project when you inserted the Web navigation bar, Publisher automatically created three hyperlink buttons—one for each page in the publication.

Can I use the wizard to alter the Web navigation bar? Yes, you can click the wizard button, located at the lower right-hand corner of the Web navigation bar, in order to choose a different design from the Design Gallery. However, the wizard merely changes the layout. You must still select individual frames and use Publisher's standard tools to insert new pictures or to change the text.

For the text of this Web site, see Appendix B.

Add Supporting Rules to the Logo *(continued)*

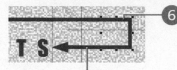

6 Zoom in to a 400 percent view and draw a box that measures 0.22-inch square. The box should align with the two red lines.

7 Format the box with a 2-point, Accent 2 (red) border on the top, right, and bottom sides. The left side should have no border.

8 Group all of these objects.

Insert a Web Navigation Bar

1 Insert the Summer navigation bar from the Design Gallery Objects.

2 Position the object in the first column at the 2-inch mark on the vertical ruler.

3 Reduce the width of the navigation bar to span column 1.

4 Select each text frame in the navigation bar, and format the text with the Web Contents text style.

5 Open the Clip Art collection. Insert the images shown in the following illustration by dragging them from the Clip Art window to each picture frame. You can easily find these images by searching for the keywords, "seahorse, shellfish, turtles."

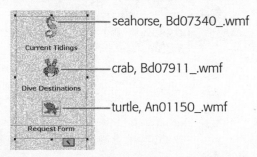

seahorse, Bd07340_.wmf

crab, Bd07911_.wmf

turtle, An01150_.wmf

6 Return to the foreground.

Create layouts with no overlapping objects to avoid graphic regions. When Publisher generates an HTML 3.0 document, it converts all overlapping objects into graphic regions, which are pictures that take longer to download. As you complete each procedure in this sample project, notice the precise placement of design elements and the use of column guides and ruler guides to prevent objects from overlapping. Frames are allowed to abut one another, but they never overlap.

Decrease download times by decreasing the size of pictures. The pictures in this sample Web publication are less than 2 inches square. Keeping the pictures (and their respective file sizes) small will allow your readers to download this page as quickly as possible.

Creating the Home Page

The first page of a Web site is often referred to as the home page. It's an opportunity to introduce the company to your readers and to inform them of the kinds of information they will find on subsequent pages of the Web site.

Insert a Photograph

1. Insert the portrait Ph01734j.jpg from Publisher's Clip Art collection. You can easily find this picture by searching on the keywords, "woman, leaning."

2. Align the top of the picture with the ruler guide at the 1.75-inch mark on the vertical ruler. Align the left edge of the picture with the blue guide for column 2.

3. Resize the picture. The width should span column 2 and extend to the pink column guide between columns 2 and 3.

4. Using the Crop Picture tool, hide the bottom of the picture until the image measures 1.4 inches wide by 1.4 inches deep.

Insert Text

1. First, change the default text frame attributes. Select the Text Frame tool, but don't draw a text frame. In the Text Frame Properties dialog box, set margins of 0 for all four sides.

2. Draw a text frame spanning columns 2, 3, and 4 that measures 0.35 inch high. Align the bottom of the text frame with the ruler guide at the 1.75-inch mark on the vertical ruler.

Current Tidings

Turn off automatic hyphenation. HTML doesn't support automatic hyphenation of any kind. You should therefore select each text frame in your Web publication and disable automatic hyphenation. This guarantees that the line breaks you see in your working version of the document will match the line breaks your readers see when they view the document using a Web browser.

Insert Text *(continued)*

③ Enter the text, "Current Tidings," and format it with the Web Head text style.

④ Draw a second text frame spanning columns 3 and 4 that measures 4.15 inches deep. The top of the text frame should align with the horizontal ruler guide at the 1.75-inch mark on the vertical ruler.

⑤ Draw a third text frame spanning column 2. The text frame should measure 1.4 inches wide and 0.5 inch deep. The top of the text frame should align with the 3.25-inch mark on the vertical ruler.

⑥ Enter the text and format it as shown in the following illustration.

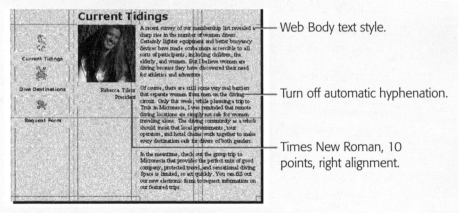

Web Body text style.

Turn off automatic hyphenation.

Times New Roman, 10 points, right alignment.

Creating the Second Web Page

In a traditional newsletter, you routinely jump stories from page to page because it's easy for readers to turn the page. In a Web document, however, it's important for each page to be a self-contained unit. The second page for this sample Web document contains short text blocks that are easy to read on-screen.

**The power of dupli-
cation.** When you dupli-
cate and reuse objects, you
work more efficiently. In this project, for
example, when you copy the Web Body
text frame from the first page to the second page, you duplicate a text frame
that is the correct width, is associated
with the correct text style, and has hyphenation already disabled.

Duplicate and Modify Text Frames

1 On page 1 of the publication, copy the Web Head and Web Body text frames to the Clipboard.

2 Paste the duplicates onto page 2. Position them exactly as they appear on page 1.

3 Replace the existing text with "Palau, Truk, and Yap." Make sure that Publisher retains the Web Head text style.

4 Replace the text in the larger text frame with the copy about Palau, Truk, and Yap.

Palau, Truk, and Yap

Sponsored by Scuba Currents, this trip makes
three stops on different islands known for their
rich marine life and stunning reef formations.
Imagine yourself snapping underwater photos of
the gray reef sharks at Blue Corner in Palau,
swimming with mantas in the Goofnuw channel
of Yap, or wreck diving among the Japanese
battleships sunk off the coast of Truk.
Experienced tour guides and scuba masters make
these adventures accessible and safe.

5 Format the copy with the Web Body text style.

6 Using the bottom selection handle, resize the frame to 1.75 inches deep.

7 Create a duplicate of the text frame containing the heading. Align the bottom of the text frame with the ruler guide at the 4-inch mark on the vertical ruler. Replace the existing text with "Saba Island."

8 Create a duplicate of the text frame containing the descriptive copy. Align the top of the text frame with the ruler guide at the 4-inch mark on the vertical ruler. Replace the text with the appropriate copy about Saba.

Insert Additional Photographs

1 Insert the photograph Ph0293j.jpg from Publisher's clip art collection. You can find the picture by searching on the keywords, "beach, photos."

2 Scale the image to 60 percent of its original size.

3 Using the cropping tool, crop the left and bottom edges of the picture until it measures 1.4 inches square.

Create text descriptions for Web pictures. When a reader accesses your Web site, he or she may not see the pictures you've inserted into the document. The reader might have chosen to view only text in order to speed up performance, or heavy Internet usage might slow down the transmission of graphics files.

You can assign a label to any picture in a Web publication by typing a phrase into the Alternate Text Representation text box in the Object Properties dialog box. If the picture itself doesn't appear on the reader's screen, the text label will appear. This feature is especially important if you've used pictures to create hyperlinks in your Web site, because it allows the reader to navigate the site without viewing the images.

Insert Additional Photographs *(continued)*

4 Position the picture in column 2. Align the top of the picture with the ruler guide at the 1.75-inch mark on the vertical ruler.

5 Insert the photograph Ph01390.jpg from Publisher's clip art collection. You can find the picture by searching on the keywords, "ocean, photos."

6 Scale the image to 50 percent of its original size.

7 Using the cropping tool, crop the top, left, and right edges of the picture until it measures 1.4 inches square.

8 Position the picture in column 2. Align the top of the picture with the ruler guide at the 4-inch mark on the vertical ruler.

Creating a Response Form

The third and final page of this Web site contains a response form. Using Publisher's Form Control objects, you can create a response form that includes text boxes, option buttons, check boxes, and drop-down lists. You should combine Form Control objects with standard text elements that explain the form's purpose and clearly identify each section.

Create Supporting Text Elements

1 Move to page 3.

2 Draw a text frame spanning columns 2, 3, and 4 and measuring 0.35 inch deep. Align the bottom of the text frame with the ruler guide at the 1.75-inch mark on the vertical ruler.

3 Enter the text, "Request For Information." Format it with the Web Head text style.

Why should I use the Arial font instead of the Verdana font for the response form? Certain objects in the response form, specifically the drop-down list and the Fax and E-mail text boxes, contain default text. Publisher automatically formats default text with the Arial font set at 10 points. You can't change these formats. Use the Arial font for the remainder of the form to produce a consistent document.

Create Supporting Text Elements *(continued)*

4. Draw a second text frame, measuring 3.5 inches wide by 0.5 inch deep. Align the top of the text frame with the ruler guide at the 1.75-inch mark on the vertical ruler, and align the left edge of the text frame with the column guide for column 2.

5. Select the text frame and turn off automatic hyphenation.

6. Type or insert the following text: "Fill out the following form to receive more information about our featured dive destinations."

7. Format the text with the Web Body text style.

8. Create three text frames that span columns 3 and 4. Each text frame should measure 0.25 inch deep.

9. Enter the text for each section of the form. Postion each frame and format the text as shown in the following illustration.

Arial font, bold, 10 points, left alignment, centered vertically

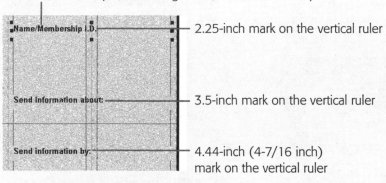

2.25-inch mark on the vertical ruler

3.5-inch mark on the vertical ruler

4.44-inch (4-7/16 inch) mark on the vertical ruler

Assign data processing properties to form control objects. Remember to assign useful data processing properties to each form control object in your response form. Form control properties can affect the way an object behaves in the reader's Web browser. In the current project, for example, the Membership I.D. item is a mandatory field, limits users to a total of 15 characters (the length of a legitimate I.D. number), and hides the membership number with asterisks. More important, form control properties allow you to structure and identify the information returned to you. In the dialog box below, the phrase Member_ID will be returned as the identifying label for the Membership I.D. text box.

Create Text Box Form Control Objects

① Draw a Single-Line Text Box that spans columns 3 and 4. A Single-Line Text Box is always 0.25 inch deep.

② Draw a text frame that spans column 2 and measures 0.25 inch deep.

③ Select both objects and align their bottom edges.

④ Group the objects and position them at the 2.55-inch mark on the vertical ruler (which is 0.063 inch below the bottom of the text frame containing the first section heading).

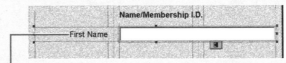

⑤ Type the phrase, "First Name," and format it with the Web Form text style.

⑥ Create two duplicates of the group and position them 0.063 inch (1/16 inch) apart.

⑦ Replace the existing text with the phrases, "Last Name" and "Membership I.D.," as shown below.

Create Check Box Form Control Objects

① Create two Check Box form control objects that span columns 3 and 4 and measure 0.25 inch deep.

② Position the objects beneath the second section heading, leaving 0.063 inch (1/16 inch) between each object.

Allow multiple selections. If you want the reader to choose more than one item in a group, you must create form control objects that permit multiple selections. Both the Check Box and the List Box form control objects are appropriate. In this project, for example, check boxes allow the reader to request information for both of the featured dive destinations.

Create mutually exclusive choices. Publisher can return only one value for each data processing label. When you assign the same data processing label to more than one option button, you create mutually exclusive items. In the current project, a reader can select only one delivery method—not both.

Create Check Box Form Control Objects *(continued)*

③ Enter the text as shown in the following illustration and format it as:

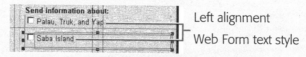

Left alignment

Web Form text style

Create Option Button Form Control Objects

① Create two Option Button form control objects that span column 3 and measure 0.25 inch deep.

② Position the objects beneath the third section head, leaving 0.063 inch (1/16 inch) of space between each object.

③ Type the words, "Fax" and "E-mail," and format the text as:

- Web Form text style
- Left alignment

④ Right-click the actual button (not the label text frame) for the Fax item and select the Option Button Properties command from the shortcut menu.

⑤ In the Option Button Properties dialog box, enter a data processing label, such as "Send_by," and a data processing value, such as "Fax."

⑥ Repeat steps 4 and 5 for the E-mail item, selecting the same data processing label ("Send_by") from the drop-down list and entering a data processing value of "E-mail."

⑦ Create two Single-Line Text Boxes that span column 4 and measure 0.25 inch deep.

⑧ Position the objects beneath the third section head, leaving 0.063 inch of space between each object. The text boxes should align with the option buttons in column 3.

Choose a data retrieval method. Before you publish your Web site, contact your Internet Service Provider (ISP) to determine the correct data retrieval method. If your ISP supports the Microsoft FrontPage Server Extensions, you can save the submitted form in an appropriate format (such as HTML) or have the responses delivered to your e-mail address.

For more information about form control objects and data retrieval methods, see Chapter 12.

Create Option Button Form Control Objects *(continued)*

9 Double-click each Single-Line Text Box and then enter the default text shown in the following illustration.

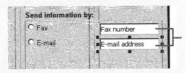

Publisher assigns the Arial, 10-point font to default text in a form control object. This text will be replaced by the text the reader types into the box.

Create Command Button Form Control Objects

1 Create a Command Button to submit the form.

2 Align the button at the left of column 3. Align the bottom of the button with the bottom row guide.

3 Create a Command Button to reset the form.

4 Align the button at the left of column 4. Align the bottom of the button with the bottom row guide.

Previewing and Producing the Web Site

A preview of this Web site allows you to confirm that the hyperlinks work, the multimedia objects play correctly, and the electronic response form can be completed.

Preview and Test the Web Site

1 On the File menu, choose the Web Page Preview command.

2 In the Web Page Preview dialog box that appears, click Web Site.

Test the functionality of form control objects.

When you fill out the reader response form, test the behind-the-scenes function of the objects. For example, in this project, you defined the Membership I.D. text item as a mandatory field with a maximum of 15 characters. Try entering an I.D. number that exceeds 15 characters to see whether the field is truly capped. Or try to submit the form without filling in an I.D. number. Your Web browser should display an appropriate error message, such as the one shown below.

For more information about publishing or posting a Web site, see Chapter 12.

Preview and Test the Web Site *(continued)*

③ Check the conversion to HTML. Confirm that the title you typed in the Web Properties dialog box appears in the browser's title bar, that the associated sound file plays continuously while page 1 is displayed, and that the text formatting in the browser matches the text formatting you created in Publisher.

④ Position the pointer over a hyperlink in the Web navigation bar. The hand pointer should appear. Click the hyperlink to move from page to page.

⑤ Move to page 3. Complete the response form.

⑥ When you are satisfied that the document appears and works as it should, close your Web browser.

Generate an HTML File

① On the File menu, choose Save As Web Page.

② In the Save As Web Page dialog box, specify or create a folder.

③ Click OK. Publisher creates an HTML document.

④ Contact your ISP for more information about posting your HTML document to its server.

Professional Web Site

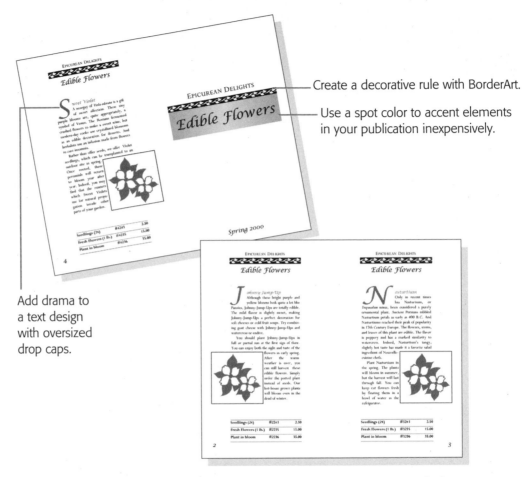

Create a decorative rule with BorderArt.

Use a spot color to accent elements in your publication inexpensively.

Add drama to a text design with oversized drop caps.

Use the Book Fold layout to produce a multiple-page catalog. Once assembled, the pages appear in the correct consecutive order.

Mail-Order Catalog

This project meets the basic criteria of good catalog design: the page layout is uncluttered, and the critical ordering information is easy to find and scan. The design reflects the nature of the products sold in its pages. The delicate text styles and the use of a spring-green spot color complement the copy about edible flowers.

Preparing the Publication

This project takes advantage of Microsoft Publisher 2000's spot color functions, which require you to set up the publication for a printing service.

For more information about creating a spot color document, see Chapter 16.

Select Commercial Printing Options

1 Create a new document with the following Custom Page options:

- ❦ Book Fold layout

- ❦ A custom page size of 4.5 inches wide by 7.5 inches high

- ❦ Landscape orientation

2 When Publisher asks whether you want to automatically insert additional pages, click No.

Spot color choices. You can select a spot color using either Publisher's standard palette of 35 hues or the Pantone color model. Pantone colors are an industry standard; they reference inks that have been mixed using an exact formula. This guarantees color consistency when the document is printed on a commercial printing press. Remember that the color you see on-screen is only an approximate preview. To judge the Pantone color accurately, you should use a printed Pantone swatch book, available from your printing service or an art supply store.

Select Commercial Printing Options *(continued)*

③ On the Tools menu, use the Commercial Printing Tools submenu to set up the document as follows:

- Pantone 569 CVU, Uncoated paper as Spot Color 1. Don't select a second spot color.

- Turn on Automatic Trapping; leave the default values for Width and Indeterminate at 0.25 inch.

- Embed TrueType fonts in the document, and create subsets of the fonts based on actual usage.

④ Select the local printer you will use and confirm that the current paper size is 8.5-by-11-inch letter size, in Landscape orientation.

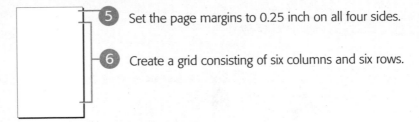

⑤ Set the page margins to 0.25 inch on all four sides.

⑥ Create a grid consisting of six columns and six rows.

⑦ Clear Create Two Backgrounds With Mirrored Guides.

Creating Text Styles

This document uses only two fonts: Lucida Calligraphy and Perpetua. Lucida Calligraphy serves a purely decorative function and is limited to display type. Perpetua is more legible and therefore is used for all the body copy. Use the table that follows to create the text styles that you will apply to the copy you type or import.

Catalog Text Styles			
Text Style	**Character Type and Size**	**Indents and Lists**	**Line Spacing**
Body Copy	Perpetua, 10.5 points	First line indent of 1 pica, justified alignment	12.5 points
Box Numbers	Perpetua, bold, 10 points	Right alignment	12.5 points
Box Text	Perpetua, bold, 10 points	Left alignment	12.5 points
First Paragraph	Perpetua, 10.5 points	Justified alignment	12.5 points
Subhead	Lucida Calligraphy, italic (default), 10 points, Spot Color 1 (Pantone 569 CVU)	Left alignment	12.5 points

Creating the Repeating Elements

You should place repeating elements, such as headers and page numbers, on the background page. Objects placed on the background are automatically duplicated on each page.

Create the Header

1. Move to the background.

2. Draw a text frame that spans columns 2, 3, 4, and 5. Align the top of the frame with the top of the first row. The frame should measure 0.25 inch high.

3. Type "Epicurean Delights" in the frame.

Alternative font choices. The design in this chapter uses the Perpetua and Lucida Calligraphy fonts, but other font combinations work equally well. You should experiment with alternative font choices, such as the Garamond and Edwardian Script ITC combination or the Calisto MT and Viner Hand ITC combination shown below.

EPICUREAN DELIGHTS

Edible Flowers

EPICUREAN DELIGHTS

Edible Flowers

Create the Header *(continued)*

4 Highlight the text and format it with the following attributes:

- ℯ Perpetua font
- ℯ Small capitals
- ℯ 12 points
- ℯ Center horizontal alignment
- ℯ Center vertical alignment

5 Select the text and assign Loose spacing between characters.

6 Starting at the 0.75-inch mark on the vertical ruler, draw a second text frame. The text frame should span columns 2, 3, 4, and 5 and should measure 0.567 inch high. It should align with the first row guide.

7 Type "Edible Flowers" in this second text frame.

8 Format the text as shown in the previous illustration.

- ℯ Lucida Calligraphy font
- ℯ 16 points
- ℯ Center horizontal alignment
- ℯ Center vertical alignment

Why can't I center the rule between the text lines? If you have difficulty centering the BorderArt rule between the two text boxes, clear Snap To Guides, Snap To Ruler Marks, and Snap To Objects.

 How can I be sure that the size of my text frame is correct? Publisher provides two different tools that can help you size a text frame. You can:

@ Keep your eye on the status line at the bottom of the screen to double-check the size of the text frame as you create it.

@ Use the Size And Position dialog box to enter explicit values for the width and height of the text frame.

Add a Decorative Rule

① Draw a box between the two text frames.

② Collapse the box to a single line by moving the top and bottom selection handles together until they overlap.

③ Format the collapsed box with the Vine BorderArt pattern at 15 points.

④ Center the rule between the text lines.

Insert a Page Number as a Footer

① Draw a text frame at the bottom of the background page. The frame should span the rightmost column and measure 0.25 inch high.

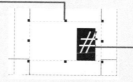

② Insert a page-number mark (#).

③ Highlight the page-number mark and format it with the following attributes:

@ Lucida Calligraphy font

@ 14 points

@ 15 points of line spacing

@ Right horizontal alignment, center vertical alignment

When you return to the foreground, Publisher replaces this symbol with the correct page number on each page.

When should I use the mirrored guides option?
When you created the layout guides at the beginning of this project, you cleared Create Two Backgrounds With Mirrored Guides because mirroring an empty background is inefficient. After you have added repeating elements (such as the page number and header), you should click this check box to reactivate it.

Copy Background Elements to the Left Facing Page

(1) Switch to Full Page view.

(2) In the Layout Guides dialog box, activate Create Two Backgrounds With Mirrored Guides.

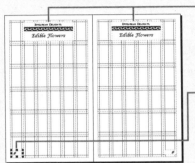

When you view the background, you see backgrounds for left and right facing pages.

The background for the left facing page now contains the same elements as the background for the right facing page, except that the page-number text frame has been moved to its mirror position at the outside of the page.

(3) Select the text frame containing the page number mark on the background for the left facing page.

(4) Click the Left alignment button on the Format toolbar.

(5) Return to the foreground.

Creating, Importing, and Formatting Catalog Text

Catalog copy doesn't have to be a hard sell. These sometimes historical, often whimsical descriptions of edible flowers create a mood that is supported by the delicate type treatment. Pricing information, on the other hand, should always be presented in a clear format that's easy to locate and read. Presenting the pricing information in a different format, such as a table, adds visual interest to a page.

For the text of this catalog, see Appendix B.

Clean up word processing files before you import your text. Before you insert the text into the Publisher document, use your word processing program to check for errors—run the spelling checker and the grammar checker. Proofread the copy for errors such as double words, dropped words, double spaces, and incorrect punctuation. But most important, read the text for sense.

Type the Text

1 In a word processing application, type the text for the body copy. Create three separate files.

2 Save the files as "Johnny," "Nasturtium," and "Violet."

Import and Format the Johnny-Jump-Up Article

1 Draw a text frame that spans columns 2, 3, 4, and 5. Vertically, the text frame should span rows 2, 3, 4, and 5.

2 Insert the file "Johnny."

> *Johnny-Jump-Up*
> Although these bright purple and yellow blooms look quite a lot like Pansies, Johnny-Jump-Ups are totally edible. The mild flavor is slightly sweet, making Johnny-Jump-Ups a perfect decoration for soft cheeses or cold fruit soups. Try combining goat cheese with Johnny-Jump-Ups and watercress or endive.
>   You should plant Johnny-Jump-Ups in full or partial sun at the first sign of thaw. You can enjoy both the sight and taste of the flowers in early spring. After the warm weather is over, you can still harvest these edible flowers. Simply order the potted plant instead of seeds. Our hot-house grown plants

3 Click in the first line (which is an entire paragraph) and format it with the Sub-head style.

4 Click in the next paragraph and format it with the First Paragraph style.

5 Click in the next paragraph and format it with the Body Copy style.

Create a Drop Cap

① Select the subhead by clicking anywhere in the paragraph.

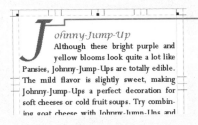

② Create a custom fancy first letter with the following attributes:

- Lucida Calligraphy font
- 4 lines high
- Combination letter position of 1 line above the paragraph and 3 dropped lines
- Spot color 1 (PMS 569 CVU)

Use tables instead of tabs. Price lists contain tabular material. However, you shouldn't structure tabular data with tabs, which can easily become misaligned. Instead, use Publisher's Table Frame tool. Tables automatically adjust row height to maintain the horizontal alignment of elements, even multiple-line elements.

Create the Pricing Table

① Draw a table frame that spans columns 2, 3, 4, and 5. The frame should measure 0.75 inch high. The top of the frame should align with the top of the last row.

② In the Create Table dialog box, create a table with three rows and three columns. Leave the Default table format selected.

③ Enter the text for Johnny-Jump-Up prices.

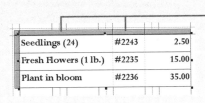

④ Using the Adjust pointer and the Shift key, widen the first column in the table until it spans columns 2 and 3 and stretches across the gutter between columns 3 and 4. Using the Shift-Adjust pointer combination, widen the second column of the table to span column 4.

⑤ Select the entire table. Format the top, center, and bottom of the table with a hairline black border.

Create the Pricing Table *(continued)*

6 Format columns 1 and 2 of the table with the Box Text style. Format column 3 with the Box Numbers style.

7 Select the entire table and assign margins of 0.02 inch to all four sides of each cell in the table.

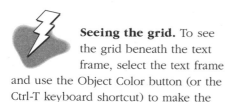

Seeing the grid. To see the grid beneath the text frame, select the text frame and use the Object Color button (or the Ctrl-T keyboard shortcut) to make the frame transparent.

Adding a Picture to the Catalog

In a mail-order catalog, pictures are a key sales tool. People rarely buy something they have never seen, and an attractive picture often convinces someone to make an impulse purchase.

Import and Modify a Picture

1 Starting at the guide for row 4, draw a square clip art frame that spans columns 4, 5, and 6.

2 Insert the clip art picture NA01141_.WMF from the Publisher CD. You can easily find this picture by searching on the keyword "dogwoods."

3 Recolor the picture using a 100 percent tint of the green spot color.

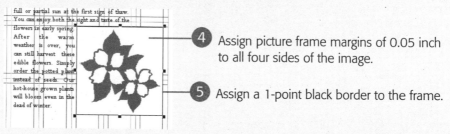

4 Assign picture frame margins of 0.05 inch to all four sides of the image.

5 Assign a 1-point black border to the frame.

6 If necessary, nudge the picture until it is positioned at the 2.35-inch mark on the horizontal ruler and the 3.85-inch mark on the vertical ruler.

When should I insert new pages into my design? If you wait until you have completed the layout for an entire page before inserting new pages, you can instantly duplicate the completed layout on each new page.

Can I add drop caps to a library of designs? When you customize a drop cap, Publisher automatically adds the design to the list box in the Drop Cap dialog box. This makes it easy for you to apply the effect to subsequent paragraphs in the current document. However, the custom drop cap is not available in other publications. If you want to use a custom drop cap in several publications, add the text frame containing the drop cap to the Design Gallery and save the file. You can then import the custom Design Gallery object into any other publication.

For more information about adding elements to the Design Gallery, see Chapter 14.

Completing the Catalog Pages

When you insert pages into a publication, you have the option of adding blank pages or duplicating an existing layout. In this sample project, you'll duplicate the objects on page 1 to quickly assemble the remaining catalog pages.

Insert Pages

1 Insert two pages. Be sure to add the pages after the current page and click Duplicate All Objects On Page Number 1.

2 When Publisher asks whether you want to automatically insert the correct number of pages for a booklet, click No.

Replace the Duplicated Text with New Text

1 Move to page 2.

2 Select the large text frame containing the duplicate text about Johnny-Jump-Ups, and highlight the entire story.

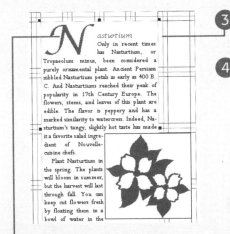

3 Insert the file "Nasturtium." The new text replaces the selected text.

4 When Publisher asks whether you want to use autoflow, click No.

5 Format the first line with the Subhead style and the drop cap you created earlier.

Replace the Duplicated Text with New Text *(continued)*

6 Format the first paragraph after the subhead with the First Paragraph style.

7 Format the final paragraph with the Body Copy style.

8 Move to page 3 and repeat steps 2 through 7 using the file "Violet."

Type New Table Text

1 Select the table containing the pricing information for Nasturtiums.

2 Enter the correct ID numbers.

3 Repeat steps 1 and 2 for Sweet Violets.

Creating the Cover Page

The exercises in this chapter have all stressed the importance of consistency in a publication, but every publication contains pages that are unique, such as the cover or title page.

Reuse design motifs.
One way to minimize your workload is to copy an element from another page and then reformat it. For example, in this project, the front cover mimics the header design. Instead of creating the individual elements again, copy the text frames from the background. Then resize and reformat them.

Insert a Cover Page

1 Move back to page 1 and insert a new blank page before the current page.

2 In the alert box that appears, click OK to insert the page.

3 Select Ignore Background. This command hides the header and page number on the cover. It affects only the displayed page.

Use gradients to enhance clip art. Many of the vector images in Publisher's clip art library have transparent backgrounds. You can fill a background with a gradient. In this catalog, for example, you could repeat the design motif of the front cover by adding a gradient background to the picture of the flower, as shown below.

Add and Format the Cover Text

1 Copy the three objects in the header design (found on the background) to the cover page (page 1).

2 Move and resize the "Edible Flowers" text frame to fill the entire third row. Increase the size to 32 points. Center the text vertically in the frame.

3 Fill the text frame with a symmetrical horizontal gradient. The base color is a 20 percent tint of the green spot color. The second color is a 50 percent tint of the green spot color.

4 Move the decorative rule to align with the top of the main text frame. Stretch it across all five columns.

5 Increase the height of the "Epicurean Delights" text frame to 0.44 inch. Stretch the frame across all five columns. Change the size of the text to 20 points. Center the text vertically in the frame.

6 Draw a text frame at the bottom of the page. The frame should span all five columns and measure 0.35 inch high.

7 Type "Spring 2000."

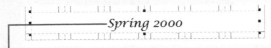

4 Format the text with the following attributes:

- ❧ Lucida Calligraphy font

- ❧ 14 points

- ❧ Center horizontal alignment, bottom vertical alignment

Viewing facing pages helps you to create a balanced design. Whenever you use the Book Fold layout, use the Two-Page Spread option (found on the View menu). As you work on your design, look at it the way the reader will—as a spread rather than as one page at a time. In the current project, thinking in terms of spreads will help you rearrange the elements in the spread so that facing pages form a mirror image of each other.

Use only true italics and boldface. You should apply italic and boldface formats only when you have the appropriate versions of a font installed on your system. In this project, the Perpetua font comes in four different versions: normal, bold, italic, and bold italic.

However, if you don't have the appropriate version of the font installed, Microsoft Windows simulates the effect by slanting a normal font at an oblique angle and by stretching a normal font (to simulate boldface). The results are often less than ideal.

Fine-Tuning the Layout and the Text

A careful proofreading of this publication reveals two problem areas:

- The picture on page 2 is not balanced with the layout on page 3.

- Typewriter-style text should be replaced with typographic-style text. For example, Latin names should be italicized and the abbreviation "B.C." should appear in small caps.

Balance the Pages

1 Move to pages 2 and 3.

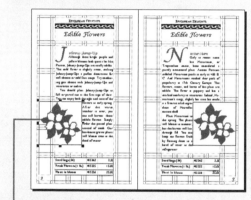

2 Select the picture frame on page 2 and move it to the outside of the page.

Adjust Text Formatting

1 In the Nasturtium story, italicize the Latin name "Tropaeolum minus."

*N*asturtium
Only in recent times has Nasturtium, or Tropaeolum minus, been considered a purely ornamental plant. Ancient Persians nibbled Nasturtium petals as early as 400 B.C. And Nasturtiums reached their peak of popu-

2 Change the letters "B.C." to small caps.

3 In the Sweet Violet story, italicize the Latin name "Viola odorata."

Printing a Proof and Producing the Catalog

When you print a publication created with the Book Fold layout, Publisher positions two pages of the publication on each sheet of paper.

What's a dummy? A dummy is a mock-up of the final printed, trimmed, folded, and bound publication. You can use the proofs you created on your local printer to collate, trim, and assemble a dummy catalog by hand.

Print a Proof of the Catalog and Assemble a Dummy

1 In the Print dialog box, select Print Composite.

2 Click the Advanced Print Settings button, choose the following Publication Options, and clear all other options:

- Print Full-Resolution Linked Graphics

- Use Only Publication Fonts

- Crop Marks

For more information about preparing files for a printing service, see Chapter 16.

What should I do if the printing service would prefer to receive Publisher's native format? Use the Pack And Go command on the File menu to collect and compress all of the necessary files. Publisher will create a file called Packed01.puz. Transfer this file along with the utility Unpack.exe (which Publisher copies to the same directory) to the commercial printing service. This approach requires the printing service to have a current copy of Publisher 2000.

Why does the file size increase so dramatically when I create a PostScript printer file? When you create a PostScript printer file, Publisher must produce a file with all of the information necessary to control the printer. As a result, the printer file can grow quite large. In this sample, the PostScript printer file requires 1.7 MB of disk space. Compare that to Publisher's format, which requires only 55 KB.

Print a Proof of the Catalog and Assemble a Dummy *(continued)*

3 Photocopy pages 2 and 3 right-side-up onto the back of the sheet with pages 4 and 1.

4 Fold the paper down the center to form the spine of the catalog.

5 Use the crop marks as a guide to trim away the excess paper.

Transfer a PostScript File to a Printing Service for Output

1 Check with the commercial printing service to determine their preferred settings for the following options:

- The paper or film size

- Composite or separated output

- Publication Options, such as Crop Marks, Registration Marks, Job Information, and Density Bars

- Device Options, such as Emulsion, Resolution, and Screens

2 Use the Save As Command on the File menu and select PostScript (*.ps) as the file type.

3 In the Save As PostScript File dialog box, choose MS Publisher Imagesetter as the output device.

4 Using the information you gathered in step 1, make the appropriate choices in the Properties, Print, and Advanced Print Settings dialog boxes.

5 Save the PostScript file to your hard disk.

6 Transfer the file to the commercial printing service, which will generate printing plates and reproduce the catalog on an offset press, using black and PMS 569 CVU inks.

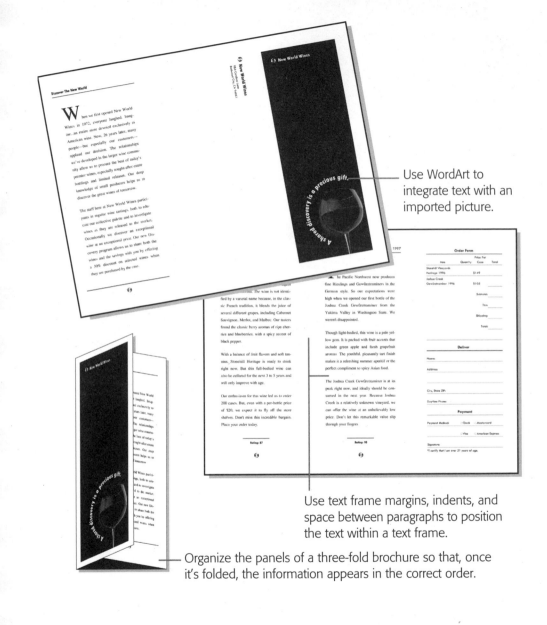

Use WordArt to integrate text with an imported picture.

Use text frame margins, indents, and space between paragraphs to position the text within a text frame.

Organize the panels of a three-fold brochure so that, once it's folded, the information appears in the correct order.

Three-Fold Brochure

Using Microsoft Publisher 2000 and a laser printer, you can produce a three-fold brochure entirely on the desktop. This self-mailing brochure is ideal as an inexpensive sales tool. You can avoid the cost of outside printing services—and the address area on the outside of the brochure eliminates the cost of envelopes!

Preparing the Publication

The layout of a three-fold brochure is determined by the two folds. It's important that you divide the page into three equal sections, called panels. You must also accommodate normal page margins for your printer's non-printing area. You can accomplish both goals using a combination of page guides and ruler guides.

Set Up the Page

1 Start a blank, full-page document. In the Catalog dialog box, click the Custom Page button on the bottom of the Blank Publications tab and change the orientation to Landscape.

2 Select the printer you'll use and confirm that the current paper size is 8.5-by-11 inches in Landscape orientation.

3 Set the page margins at 0 for all four sides.

4 Create a grid consisting of three columns and one row.

Can I really divide an 11-inch page into three equal sections? No. There is no easy way to divide a standard 11-inch page into three equal sections. Do the math and the result will be the infinite fraction of 3.6666666 inches. But if you have Publisher divide the page with column guides, the page divisions will be as accurate as possible.

 Why must I create separate text styles for the rules? When you assign the underline attribute in the Font dialog box, Publisher doesn't allow you to determine the position of the rule in relation to the text above it. The result is a rule that is simply too close to the text (shown below). As you can see, underlining can make text illegible by obscuring the descenders of the letters. When you create a separate text style for a rule, you can specify indents and line spacing to control the position of the underline.

<u>Stonehill Vineyards</u>

Set Up the Page *(continued)*

5 On the background, create ruler guides at the following positions:

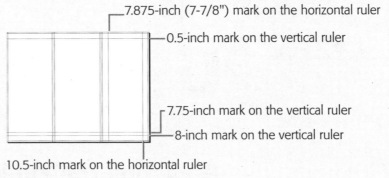

- 7.875-inch (7-7/8") mark on the horizontal ruler
- 0.5-inch mark on the vertical ruler
- 7.75-inch mark on the vertical ruler
- 8-inch mark on the vertical ruler
- 10.5-inch mark on the horizontal ruler

6 Return to the foreground.

Creating Text Styles

The following table specifies the formatting attributes of the text in this project. Notice how paragraph indents add white space around the text. You can also control the position of text by adjusting the spacing before or after a paragraph. For example, the Body Copy style includes left and right indents of 0.25 inch and 15 points of space after each paragraph.

In addition, there are three text styles that take advantage of Publisher's character underlining options. These text styles combine underlining, paragraph indents, and line spacing formats to position rules precisely between paragraphs.

Text Attributes for the Three-Fold Brochure

Text Style	Character Type and Size	Indents and Lists	Line Spacing	Tabs
Body Copy	Times New Roman, 10 points	Left indent of 0.25 inch, right indent of 0.25 inch, justified alignment	18 points between lines, 15 points after paragraphs	None
Heading	Tw Cent MT Condensed Extra Bold, 10 points	Left alignment	12 points between lines, 15 points before paragraphs	2.94 inches, right alignment
Rating	Tw Cent MT Condensed Extra Bold, 8 points	Center alignment	10 points between lines, 15 points after paragraphs	None
Rule Above Rating	Tw Cent MT Condensed Extra Bold, 4 points, thick underline	Left indent of 1 inch, right indent of 1 inch, left alignment	5 points between lines, 10 points before paragraphs, 5 points after paragraphs	1.94 inches, left alignment
Rule with Space After	Tw Cent MT Condensed Extra Bold, 4 points, thick underline	Left alignment	5 points between lines, 30 points after paragraphs	2.94 inches, left alignment
Rule with Space Before	Tw Cent MT Condensed Extra Bold, 4 points, thick underline	Left alignment	5 points between lines, 15 points before paragraphs	2.94 inches, left alignment
Order Form	Tw Cent MT, medium, 8 points	Left alignment	12 points between lines	None

Creating the Front Cover

The front cover sets the mood for the entire document. Publisher's WordArt tool is used to create a unique headline treatment.

Draw the Background

1 Draw a box on the right panel of the page. The box should measure 2.625 inches wide by 7.5 inches high. It should align with the ruler guides.

2 Assign a black fill.

Extend the background of a picture. By placing the photograph on a black box, you are merging its edges (which are also black) with the larger background. The result is a much more dramatic presentation, in which the single wineglass stands out against a stark backdrop.

Insert a Photograph

1. Insert the picture Ph02262j.jpg from Publisher's Clip Art Gallery. You can easily find the image by searching on the keywords, "wine, glasses, photos."

2. Scale both the width and the height of the picture to 53 percent.

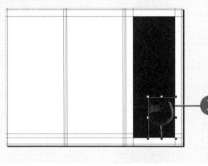

3. Align the picture with the right and bottom edges of the black box.

Add the Title

1. Draw a WordArt frame measuring 2.8 inches wide by 1.25 inches high.

2. Type the text, "A shared discovery is a precious gift."

3. Assign the following formats:

   - Arch Up (Curve)

   - Tw Cent Condensed Extra Bold font

   - Best Fit size

   - Letter Justify

   - White fill color

4. Close the WordArt dialog box. Select the WordArt frame.

Use WordArt to animate headlines. Instead of printing headlines as straight horizontal lines of text, consider using WordArt to flow the text into unique shapes. Here, placing the headline along a curve creates a sense of movement. And because the curve mimics the general shape of the wineglass, the WordArt effect also sets up an interesting visual interaction between the text and the picture.

Add the Title *(continued)*

5 Rotate the WordArt frame by 64 degrees and position it to surround the wineglass.

Add a Logo

1 Draw a text frame measuring 1.5 inches wide by 0.25 inch high.

2 Type the text, "New World Wines," and format the text and text frame as:

- Tw Cent Condensed Extra Bold, 12 point
- White
- Transparent fill

3 Draw a clip art frame measuring 0.25 inch wide by 0.25 inch high. It should align with the left edge of the text frame containing the store name.

Use picture frame margins to resize artwork. When creating the logo for New World Wines, it is best to draw the picture frame at 0.25 inches square. Doing so allows you to easily align the picture frame with the text frame. If you need to resize the picture further, just create picture frame margins. The larger the picture frame margin, the smaller the picture.

Add a Logo *(continued)*

④ Insert the image Dd00433_.wmf. You can easily find the symbol by searching on the keywords, "circles, geometric shapes."

⑤ Recolor the picture to make it white.

⑥ Create picture frame margins of 0.04 inch for all four sides.

⑦ Group the two elements and position them at the 0.75-inch mark on the vertical ruler and the 8.125-inch (8-1/8") mark on the horizontal ruler.

Creating the Return Address

The center panel on a three-fold brochure typically contains the address information. You'll leave most of the panel blank in reserve for the mailing address, but you should take this opportunity to create the return address. You can save time by editing a duplicate of the logo design you just created.

Copy and Reformat the Logo

① Copy the logo from the first panel.

② Restore the clip art image to its original color—black.

③ Change the font color to black.

Use Publisher's mail merge feature to address the brochures.

You can address these brochures using Publisher's mail merge feature. Simply create a text frame where a mailing label would normally be positioned, and then insert field codes from an address list you've created. When you print the document, Publisher prints multiple copies of the brochure, with each copy containing a different entry from the address list.

For more information on Publisher's mail merge functions, see Chapter 13.

Insert Address Information

1 Draw a text frame measuring 1.5 inches wide by 0.5 inch high. The top of this text frame should align with the bottom of the text frame containing the store name.

2 Enter the text shown in the following illustration and format it as:

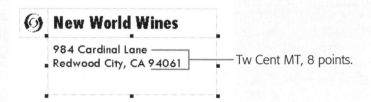

3 Group the text frame with the logo, and use the Rotate Right command to rotate the group 90 degrees to the right.

4 Position the group at the upper-right corner of the middle panel, aligned with the horizontal ruler guide and the blue column guide.

Creating the Second Panel

When the brochure is finished and folded, the left panel becomes the second panel, because it's the "page" that the reader will see immediately after the front cover. It is, therefore, the best position for general, introductory text.

For the text of this brochure, see Appendix B.

Why don't the rules appear in my publication? In order to have the rules appear, you must press the Tab key. This forces the current text insertion point to the right margin of the text frame and applies the underlining to the width of the text column.

Pick up formatting from the current paragraph. The Custom Drop Cap tab contains options that allow you to pick up formatting from the current paragraph. Specifically, you can choose to use the current font, the current font style, and the current color. Selecting these options guarantees that the drop cap matches the formatting of the remaining text in the paragraph.

Insert Introductory Text

① Draw a text frame on the left panel that measures 3.47 inches wide by 8.30 inches high. The text frame should align with the top and bottom blue row guides and the left and right blue column guides.

② In the Text Frame properties dialog box, create margins of 0.25 inch on all four sides. Turn off text wrap.

③ Insert the introductory text and format it as shown in the following illustration.

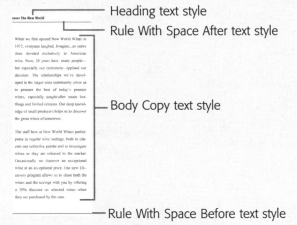

④ Place the text insertion point in the first Body Copy paragraph and add a custom drop cap with the following format:

Up position
2 lines high
1 letter

Insert Clip Art

1 Temporarily ungroup the logo on the first panel and make a copy of the clip art picture. (Be sure to regroup the logo.)

2 Restore the picture to its original colors.

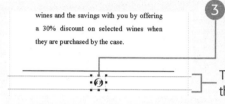

wines and the savings with you by offering a 30% discount on selected wines when they are purchased by the case.

3 Position the clip art picture in the center of the left panel at the 7.75-inch mark on the vertical ruler.

The clip art image should align perfectly with the two ruler guides on the background.

Use special typographic characters. When you create the text for this project in your word processing program, you should proofread the text carefully and insert the appropriate typographic characters. This project requires you to insert three different typographic characters.

- You should use a true em dash when separating phrases in a sentence—like this.

- You should insert a true ellipsis (which is different from three periods in a row).

- Finally, you should insert the letter "u" that includes a diacritical mark (called an umlaut) for the name of one of the wine varietals as shown below.

Gewürztraminer

Creating the Interior of the Brochure

The interior of the brochure contains descriptions of the wines for sale, as well as an order form. By duplicating the text frame from the left panel, you can insert the descriptive text quickly.

Insert Descriptive Text

1 Select the text frame and the clip art image on the left panel, group them, and copy them to the Clipboard.

2 Insert a new page.

3 Paste two copies of the group, and position them in the left and center panels.

4 Select all of the text in the left text frame, and insert the descriptive copy for Stonehill Vineyards.

Do I have to recreate the drop cap effect each time I apply it? No. Publisher stores the custom drop cap effect you created earlier in the Drop Cap Gallery. You can apply it as many times as you like within this publication only.

Insert Descriptive Text *(continued)*

⑤ Duplicate the formatting from the second panel as follows:

   ℓ Assign the Heading text style to the first paragraph.

   ℓ Assign the Rule With Space After text style to the following blank line. Remember to press the Tab key to have the rule appear.

   ℓ Assign the Body Copy text style to the next three paragraphs.

   ℓ Create a custom drop cap for the first Body Copy paragraph.

⑥ Assign the following text styles to the remaining text.

   Rating: 87 ————— Rule Above Rating text style
     ————— Rating text style

⑦ Repeat steps 4 through 6 with the text frame in the center panel, inserting the descriptive copy for Joshua Creek.

Fine-tuning Text Formats

① Place the text insertion point immediately before the word "Heritage" in the heading of the left panel.

② Insert a tab to align the text at the right edge of the frame.

③ Highlight the wine style and vintage and change the formatting as follows:

   Stonehill Vineyards   *Heritage 1996*——— Tw Cent MT, italic

④ Repeat steps 1 through 3 for the phrase, "Gewürztraminer 1996," in the center panel.

Creating the Order Form

You can create this complex order form within a single table frame. The custom borders organize the information into easily understood sections. Minor adjustments to the text formatting highlight section headings.

Insert Text into a Table

1 On the right panel, draw a table frame measuring 2.625 inches wide by 7.50 inches high. It should align with the green ruler guides.

2 Set up the table with 20 rows and 4 columns. Choose the None style.

3 Press and hold the Shift key to reposition the division between columns as indicated below.

The 9-inch mark on the horizontal ruler

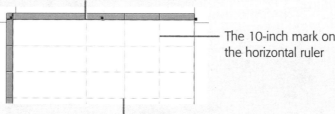

The 10-inch mark on the horizontal ruler

The 9.5-inch mark on the horizontal ruler

4 Select the entire table and assign the following formatting attributes:

- In the Cell Properties dialog box, set cell margins at 0 inches for the top, left, and right sides. Leave the bottom margin value at 0.04 inch.

- In the Border Style dialog box, choose a hairline rule for the bottom and center horizontal sides of each cell.

- Apply the Order Form text style.

- Align the text at the bottom of the text frame.

Create order forms that can be completed by hand. If you expect your readers to fill out an order form by hand, leave enough space for their entries. Check boxes, which need only a simple mark, require the least amount of space. But fill-in-the-blank items, such as name and street address, should accommodate the average person's handwriting and names of varying length. Ask yourself if someone named Alexander Rodchenko living in Worthington Springs, Florida, could fit his name and address into your order form. If you cram a complex order form into a tiny table frame, be prepared to have illegible answers returned to you.

Insert Text into a Table *(continued)*

 Enter the text as shown in the following illustration. Change the formatting as indicated:

Order Form

Item	Quantity	Price Per Case	Total
Stonehill Vineyards Heritage 1996		$149	
Joshua Creek Gewürztraminer 1996		$105	
		Subtotal:	
		Tax:	
		Shipping:	
		Total:	

Delivery

Name:

Address:

City, State ZIP:

Daytime Phone:

Payment

Payment Method: ☐ Check ☐ Mastercard

☐ Visa ⬭ American Express

Signature:

*I certify that I am over 21 years of age.

— Select the rows containing category headings. Merge the cells in each row. Increase the size to 10 points. Center each of the headings, and make them boldface. Change the custom border at the bottom of the cell to 1 point.

— Select the second row and the cells containing the actual prices, and center the text.

— Select the cells in the intersection of rows 5 through 8 and column 3; align the text at the right.

— Select the cells in the intersection of rows 5 through 8 and columns 1, 2, and 3. Remove their borders.

Select the cell containing the word "Mastercard," and merge it with the last cell in the row. Select the cell containing the phrase "American Express," and merge it with the last cell in the row.

Insert the open square bullet (from the Wingdings 2 font) immediately before each payment method.

— Select the last row and merge its cells. Italicize the text. Align the text at the top of the cell. Remove the border from the bottom of the cell.

Precision folds complete a quality brochure. Crooked, sloppy folds can ruin the appearance of a folded brochure. Use one of these methods to guarantee crisp, straight creases in your three-fold brochure:

@ Purchase special prescored paper from stationery stores or paper companies (such as Paper Direct). To fold your brochures, simply follow an existing crease in the paper.

@ Create a guide to help you fold the brochures manually. Draw a table frame that completely covers an 8.5-by-11 inch page in Landscape orientation. Divide the table into 3 columns and 1 row. Format the table grid with a 1-point rule. When printed, this document will show you the exact location of each fold.

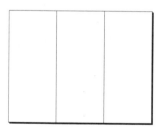

Printing and Folding the Brochure

The two different ways to fold a three-fold brochure are referred to by the shape that the edge of the paper makes. A Z-fold is an accordion fold, which is unsuitable for a self-mailer because the left and right edges of the folded document are open. A C-fold is the correct choice for a self-mailer because the second fold encloses the first fold so that only one edge has to be sealed for mailing.

 Z-fold   C-fold

Print the Brochure

1 In the Print dialog box, select All 2 Pages in the Print Range area.

2 Click the Advanced Print Settings button, and make the following choices:

@ Select Print Full Resolution Linked Graphics.

@ Select Use Only Publication Fonts.

@ Clear all check boxes in the Printer's Marks area.

@ Clear all check boxes in the Bleeds area.

3 Click OK twice. Publisher prints each side of the three-fold brochure on a separate sheet of paper.

Copy and Fold the Brochure

1 Copy page 2 of the publication on the back of page 1.

2 Fold the publication in a C-fold so that the brochure can be taped shut for mailing.

Use color or tints judiciously to emphasize important information, such as the name of the publication.

Develop a template to accommodate elements that repeat from issue to issue, such as the publication date and the table of contents.

A three-column grid gives you the flexibility to size stories according to their importance. Notice that the lead story spans all three columns, while the second story occupies only two columns.

Newsletter

Newsletters are a great promotional tool for small businesses. You can use newsletters to provide valuable information to customers, such as the impending release of a new product or a change in company strategy. In this project, you'll learn how to structure the first page of a full-color newsletter.

Preparing the Publication

Newsletters come in all shapes and sizes. This newsletter takes advantage of a letter sized page, which can easily be inserted into a standard mailing envelope or a marketing kit.

Set Up the Page

Consult your printer before choosing a page size. If you intend to send your publication to a commercial printing service, you should consult with the printer before you choose a page size for your publication. The printer will help you determine a page size that requires the least amount of trimming. In the long run, reducing the number of cuts and eliminating paper waste will save both time and money.

1 Start a new, blank full-page document.

2 Select the local printer you will use and confirm that the current paper size is 8.5 by 11 inches in Portrait orientation.

3 On the Tools menu, use the Commercial Printing Tools submenu to select Color Printing. Then select Process Colors (CMYK) for the publication.

Use line spacing consistently. In this project, many text elements are formatted with different point sizes, but all of the elements appearing in the body of a story—including body copy, captions, and bylines—are formatted with the same amount of line spacing. Consistent line spacing helps you align the baselines of text across columns for a professional look.

Set Up the Page *(continued)*

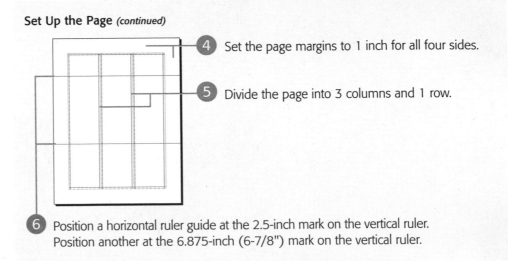

4 Set the page margins to 1 inch for all four sides.

5 Divide the page into 3 columns and 1 row.

6 Position a horizontal ruler guide at the 2.5-inch mark on the vertical ruler. Position another at the 6.875-inch (6-7/8") mark on the vertical ruler.

Creating a Custom Color Scheme

You should always choose—or develop—a color scheme for your documents. Doing so helps you to think about the function that color serves in your publication. For example, in this project the color scheme consists of only three colors: black for text, red for emphasis, and a neutral tan for use as a background color.

Define Custom Colors

1 In the Color Scheme dialog box, select the Custom tab.

Define Custom Colors *(continued)*

2 Create a custom color scheme using the following CMYK values, which are listed in order as cyan, magenta, yellow, and black.

- Main: 0, 0, 0, 100

- Accent 1: 0, 100, 90, 10

- Accent 2: 5, 5, 20, 0

3 Choose white (a value of 0, 0, 0, 0) for the remaining accent colors.

Creating Text Styles

Newsletters typically contain many different text styles for elements such as by-lines, headlines, photo captions, and table of contents entries. The following table summarizes the text styles you should create for this project.

Newsletter Text Styles				
Text Style	**Character Type and Size**	**Indents and Lists**	**Line Spacing**	**Tabs**
Body Copy	Bell MT, 10.5 points	First line indent of 1 pica, justified alignment	13 points	None
Byline	Franklin Gothic Book, 10 points	Left alignment	13 points	None
Caption	Franklin Gothic Book, italic, 8 points	Left alignment	13 points	None
First Paragraph	Bell MT, 10.5 points	Justified alignment (no first line indent)	13 points	None
Headline 1	Bell MT, bold, 32 points	Left alignment	32 points	None
Headline 2	Bell MT, bold, 22 points, Accent 1 (Red)	Left alignment	22 points	None
TOC Entry	Franklin Gothic Book, 9 points	Left alignment	13 points	None
TOC Number	Franklin Gothic Book, 9 points	Center alignment	13 points	None

Creating a Template

Magazines, newspapers, and newsletters are published in cycles; any publication issued on a regular basis (daily, weekly, monthly, bimonthly, or quarterly) is called a periodical. The structure of a periodical involves two kinds of repeating elements, which together should be saved as a template:

- Elements that repeat on every page, such as page numbers and running headers and footers, which are placed on the background of a publication.

- Elements that appear in every issue, such as the logo, the date, and the table of contents. The volume number, calendar date, and words in the table of contents change from issue to issue, but the placement and the style of these elements remain consistent.

Perfecting both the appearance and the placement of these elements in a template streamlines the production of subsequent issues of the publication.

Repeat elements of the masthead in the header and footer. Once you've created the masthead, you can easily generate a header and footer for subsequent pages in the publication. For example, to create a header, simply copy the Broadsides text frame to the background, resize it, and position it at the top of the page. Because you created this element using the Best Fit AutoFit Text option, Publisher automatically adjusts the text based on the size of the text frame. In the same way, you can generate a footer by copying the issue number and volume text frame to the background.

Create the Masthead

1. Draw a text frame that spans columns 1 and 2. The text frame should align with the top row guide and the horizontal ruler guide at the 2.5-inch mark on the vertical ruler.

2. Create left and top text frame margins of 0. Create a bottom text frame margin of 0.04 inch, and a right text frame margin of 0.07 inch.

3. In the Text Frame Properties dialog box, turn off text wrap.

4. Type the publication name, "Broadsides." Choose the following options:

    - The Best Fit AutoFit Text option.

    - Align the text vertically at the bottom of the frame.

5. Format the text as indicated in the illustration at the top of the next page.

Why should I be concerned about small margin values such as 0.07 inch? Type is normally measured in points. There are 72 points to an inch. What appears to be a small measurement, such as 0.07 inch, is actually a significant value when it influences the size or placement of text. In this project, increasing the left text frame margin to 0.07 inch correctly aligns the masthead's text elements along the left side.

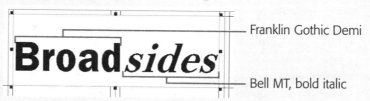

Franklin Gothic Demi

Bell MT, bold italic

6 Select all the text and format it with the Accent 1 (Red) color.

7 Starting at the top row guide, draw a second text frame overlapping the existing text frame. It should span column 1 and measure 0.4 inch deep.

8 Leave the top, bottom, and right text frame margins set to 0.04 inch. Change the left margin to 0.07 inch.

9 Type the text shown in the illustration below and format it as follows:

Franklin Gothic Demi, 8 points

10 Starting at the 2.25-inch mark on the vertical ruler, draw another text frame overlapping the main text frame. It should span columns 1 and 2 and measure 0.25 inch deep.

11 Leave the top, bottom, and right text frame margins set to 0.04 inch. Change the left margin to 0.07 inch.

12 Type the text shown in the illustration below and format it as follows:

Franklin Gothic Book, 8 points

Character spacing with expanded kerning of 0.5 point

Give the table of contents a prominent position. The table of contents is typically placed on the first page of a newsletter. Doing so gives you, the publisher, the opportunity to entice your readers with a list of special interest stories or favorite columns.

Create the Table of Contents

1 Starting at the top row guide, draw a table frame that spans column 3 and aligns with the horizontal ruler guide at the 2.5-inch mark on the vertical ruler.

2 Create a table with 2 columns, 5 rows, and a style of None.

3 While pressing and holding the Shift key, drag the column division in the table to the 7-inch mark on the horizontal ruler.

4 Enter the text shown in the illustration below and format it as follows:

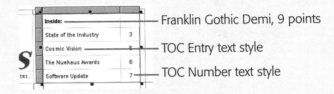

Franklin Gothic Demi, 9 points

TOC Entry text style

TOC Number text style

Create Rules for the Table of Contents and Masthead

1 Select rows 2 through 5 in the table containing the table of contents. In the Border Style dialog box, format the row divisions only with a hairline rule.

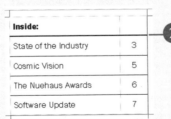

2 Select row 1 in the table. Format the bottom of the row with a 1-point rule.

3 Using the Line tool, draw a 2-point black line under the masthead that aligns with the horizontal ruler guide at the 2.5-inch mark on the vertical ruler and spans all 3 columns.

4 Draw a 1-point black line that aligns with the bottom pink page guide and spans all 3 columns.

For the text of this newsletter, see Appendix B.

Create word processing files. If you want to recreate the newsletter project, you must create two files—one for each story—using your favorite word processing application. Enter the text, and follow these guidelines.

- As you create the text, press Enter after each paragraph, but don't add extra line spaces. Don't press Tab to insert paragraph indents. The Body Copy text style creates indents.

- Type only one space after a period or colon.

- Run the spelling checker, and proofread the text before importing it.

- Save the files with names that will be easy to identify, such as Interior and Hometown.

Save the Newsletter as a Template

1. On the File menu, choose Save As. The Save As dialog box appears.

2. In the Save As Type drop-down list box, choose Publisher Template (*.pub).

3. Enter a descriptive filename, such as Newsletter, in the File Name text box.

Create a New Publication from the Template

1. Choose New on the File menu.

2. On the Publications By Wizard tab of the Catalog dialog box, click the Templates button.

3. Open the Newsletter template. The file that Publisher brings up is not the template, but a copy of it called "Unsaved Publication."

Importing the Newsletter Text

Microsoft Publisher 2000 automatically inserts white space, called a gutter, between column guides, which can make the default margins of a text frame unnecessary. As you create the text frames for this project, you should adjust the margins to avoid too much white space.

Insert the Lead Story

1. Draw a text frame that spans all 3 columns. The top of the frame should align with the horizontal ruler guide at the 2.5-inch mark on the vertical ruler and measure 1 inch deep.

2. Type or insert the text shown in the illustration on the next page and format it as follows:

Select text in the overflow area. When you use the Ctrl-A keyboard shortcut or the Highlight Entire Story command on the Edit menu, you are selecting all of the text in the story—even if it is temporarily stored in the overflow area. Doing so allows you to assign the correct text style to the entire story, even though the text in the overflow area remains hidden.

Insert the Lead Story *(continued)*

| An inside look at architecture and interior design at Broadside Associates | Software Update | 7 |

Broadside Associates
Acquires Integrated Space

❧ Text frame margins of 0 for all four sides.

❧ Headline 1 text style.

❧ Vertical alignment at the bottom of the text frame.

❧ Use Shift+Enter to force a line break after the word "Associates."

③ Starting at the 3.5-inch mark on the vertical ruler, draw a text frame that spans all three columns and measures 0.25 inch deep. This frame should abut the text frame containing the headline.

④ Type or insert the text in the illustration below and format it as follows:

❧ Text frame margins of 0 for all four sides

❧ Byline text style

❧ Vertical alignment in the center of the text frame

Acquires Ir

By Trisha Armstead

⑤ Starting at the 3.75-inch mark on the vertical ruler, draw a text frame that spans column 1 and extends to the bottom row guide.

⑥ Insert the lead story. When Publisher asks if you want to autoflow the text, click No.

⑦ Using the Ctrl-A keyboard shortcut, highlight all of the text and assign the Body Copy text style.

⑧ Place the insertion point in the first paragraph and change the text style to First Paragraph.

Draw a series of text frames. Clicking the Text tool while pressing and holding the Ctrl key keeps the Text tool active, allowing you to draw a series of text frames without having to choose the Text tool repeatedly. When you want to return to the normal work mode, select the Pointer tool.

Insert the Lead Story *(continued)*

9 Draw two more text frames in columns 2 and 3. Position the top of the text frames at the 3.75-inch mark on the vertical ruler. Align the bottom of each text frame with the ruler guide at the 6.875-inch (6-7/8") mark on the vertical ruler.

10 Connect the text frame in column 1 to the text frame in column 2. Then connect the text frame in column 2 to the text frame in column 3.

11 Select all three text frames, and change the left and right text frame margin to 0. Leave the top and bottom text frame margin at 0.04 inch.

Insert the Second Lead

1 Starting at the horizontal ruler guide located at the 6.875-inch (6-7/8") mark on the vertical ruler, draw a text frame that spans columns 2 and 3 and measures 0.48 inch deep.

2 Type or insert the text shown in the illustration below and format it as follows:

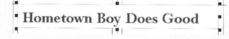

Hometown Boy Does Good

Newsletter (vertical tab, right side)

Why should I align headlines at the bottom of the text frame? Readers are sensitive to small amounts of white space. By aligning a headline at the bottom of a text frame, you create a strong visual relationship between the headline and the text that follows it.

Insert the Second Lead *(continued)*

- Left and right text frame margins of 0.1 inch, top text frame margin of 0, and bottom text frame margin of 0.04 inch.

- Headline 2 text style.

- Vertical alignment at the bottom of the frame.

3 Starting at the 7.36-inch mark on the vertical ruler, draw a text frame that spans columns 2 and 3 and extends down to the bottom row guide.

4 Change the left and right text frame margins to 0.1 inch. Leave the top and bottom text frame margins at 0.04 inch.

5 Format the text frame with 2 columns and column spacing of 0.17 inch.

6 Insert the second lead and format it as follows:

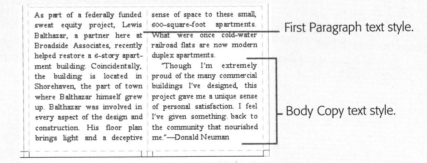

First Paragraph text style.

Body Copy text style.

Inserting and Editing a Photograph

Publisher's Clip Art Gallery contains a number of business-oriented portraits. You'll have to make a few minor adjustments to the size and position of the photo to integrate it into the layout.

Speed printing times by trimming portions of a picture in an image editing program. Publisher's cropping function doesn't actually trim away parts of the picture—it merely hides them. Although the hidden part of the picture won't print, your printer still has to process the information, which slows the print job. This performance hit can be significant if your document contains lots of scanned or bitmapped pictures. To speed up printing time, use your scanning or image editing software to cut away unwanted portions of a photograph before you import it into Publisher.

Insert, Position, and Crop the Picture

1 Without drawing a frame, insert or link to the picture Ph01617j.jpg from Publisher's Clip Art Gallery. You can easily find the picture by searching on the keywords, "businessman, photos."

2 Scale the height and width of the picture to 76 percent of its original size.

3 Position the picture in column 2 at the 3.75-inch mark on the vertical ruler. Align the right side of the picture with the right column guide for column 2.

4 Using the Crop Picture tool, select the left center handle and reduce the picture's width to the width of column 2.

5 Using the Crop Picture tool, select the bottom center handle and reduce the picture's height to 1.97 inches, making it a perfect square.

Fine-Tuning the Layout

Whenever you create a complex layout, you must take the time to review and adjust the various elements. At this stage of the project, there are two design problems:

- ❦ The photograph isn't identified with a caption.

- ❦ The second lead should be separated from the main story with a tinted box.

Use a color or tint to highlight a short story or sidebar. A small story or sidebar (supplemental information within a larger article) often needs a visual device to bring it to the reader's attention. In this sample newsletter, the second story is highlighted with both a color headline and a tinted color background.

Insert a Caption

1. Draw a text frame that spans column 2. The frame should abut the bottom of the picture frame and should measure 0.25 inch deep.

2. Type the text shown in the illustration below and format it as follows:

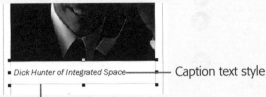

■ *Dick Hunter of Integrated Space* ———— Caption text style

Text frame margins of 0 for all four sides

Draw a Rectangle

1. Starting at the 6.875-inch (6-7/8") mark on the vertical ruler, draw a rectangle that spans columns 2 and 3. The bottom of the rectangle should align with the bottom row guide.

2. Fill the rectangle with the Accent 2 (Tan) color.

3. Send the rectangle to the bottom of the stack.

4. Select the two text frames that compose the second lead story and make the frames transparent.

Fix typographic problems like a pro.

Professional production editors always try to fix typographic problems that can occur in a complex layout, such as widows or orphans. In this story, a ladder (multiple consecutive hyphens) forms a distracting pattern. You can use the same basic techniques that they do:

@ Add or delete words.

@ Alter the character spacing, specifically the tracking values.

@ Use Shift+Enter to force a line break without starting a new paragraph.

@ Change the hyphenation zone.

Fine-Tuning the Text

Once you've finalized the layout, you can turn your attention to the particulars of the text. You should always use Publisher's spelling checker and carefully proofread the document for sense. In addition, you should make adjustments so that the copy fits the layout. At this point in the project, there are three noticeable problems:

@ Text remains in the overflow area of the Integrated Space lead story.

@ There are typographic problems in the lead story, including a widow and several consecutive hyphens.

@ There is too much white space beneath the photo caption where the body copy wraps around the caption frame.

Jump Text to Another Page

1 Insert a second page in the publication.

2 Draw a text frame anywhere on the page.

3 Return to page 1 and select the third text frame of the lead story.

4 In the Text Frame Properties dialog box, select the Include Continued On Page option.

5 Link this text frame to the text frame on page 2. Publisher automatically inserts a continued notice into the text frame on page 1.

Should I create a Continued On text style? No. Publisher automatically creates a Continued On text style when you assign the Continued On Page property to a text frame and link it to a text frame on a different page. Publisher always creates Continued On text with a default style: Times New Roman, 8 points, italic, right alignment.

Jump Text to Another Page *(continued)*

6 In the Text Style dialog box, change the font of the Continued On text style to Franklin Gothic Book.

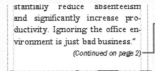

stantially reduce absenteeism and significantly increase productivity. Ignoring the office environment is just bad business."
(Continued on page 2)

Publisher updates the appearance of this continued notice (and any other continued notices in the publication) with the new text style format.

Adjust Line Breaks

1 Zoom in on the first paragraph in the lead story. You should see a widow at the end of the paragraph and a series of hyphens.

> The eight-year-old company grossed over $7 million in commissions last year and has projected billings of $11 million this year. That success is directly attributable to Dick Hunter—the firm's founder and current President.
>
> Hunter established his repu-

2 Place the text insertion point before the word "projected," and press Shift+Enter to force a line break without starting a new paragraph.

3 Check the entire story again for too many consecutive hyphens or other typographic problems.

Adjust Text Wrap

1 Select the second text frame in the chain containing the Integrated Space story.

2 Using the top selection handle, resize the text frame to 0.91 inch. The top of the frame should abut the bottom of the photo caption frame.

Use a photocopier as a replacement for a printing press. Because this newsletter was designed to fit on a standard 8.5-by-11-inch page, it can be reproduced at any copy shop or graphics service bureau that offers color copies. But be sure to check the price for color copies—you may find that traditional offset printing is actually less expensive on a per-copy basis. You should also ask if the copy shop can accept an electronic version of the file (in either Publisher's native format or in PostScript format). Printing directly to a color photocopier from an electronic file delivers the highest quality output.

To learn more about working with a commercial printing service, see Chapter 16.

Sending the Newsletter to a Commercial Printer

Many commercial printing services prefer to receive documents in Publisher's native format, because it allows them to easily correct potential printing problems. Publisher's Pack And Go command helps you to gather together all of the elements you need to produce your publication at a commercial printing service.

Pack the Publication

1. On the File menu, select Pack And Go. On the submenu, select Take To A Commercial Printing Service.

2. Respond to the wizard by choosing a location for the packed files.

3. When prompted, be sure that you are embedding TrueType fonts, including linked graphics, and creating links for embedded graphics.

4. Make sure the options to print a composite and a separated proof of the publication are selected.

5. Click Finish. Publisher packs all of the necessary files into a compressed format (with the .puz extension) to make them easy to transport. Publisher also copies a utility (called Unpack.exe) to the same location. The commercial printing service will need Unpack.exe to extract the Publisher files from the compressed .puz file.

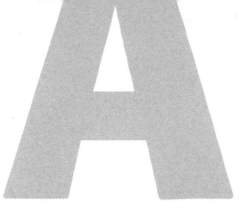

Microsoft Draw 98

Microsoft Draw 98 is a separate drawing program that is shipped with several Microsoft applications, including Microsoft Publisher 2000. Publisher's drawing tools and Draw's drawing tools work identically—meaning that you select a tool and drag to create an object. However, Draw employs a more intuitive interface. For example, most of the program's functions are available from conveniently accessible toolbars and submenus. In addition, Draw offers more advanced drawing functions, including:

@ AutoShapes: a wide variety of shapes and lines.

@ The ability to create and edit free-form shapes.

@ A sophisticated WordArt tool that includes a gallery of preformatted designs.

@ More robust formatting options including a wider choice of fill types, line attributes, custom shadows, and 3-D effects.

@ The ability to change the contents of an imported picture.

Although Draw isn't a part of Publisher, you can access it as though it were through a feature called OLE (Object Linking and Embedding). Any drawing you create in Draw is really an object embedded in a Publisher document. When you save the Publisher document, you also save the embedded object.

Accessing Draw as an OLE application. You can also insert a new drawing using the Object command (found on the Insert menu). In the Insert Object dialog box, choose Microsoft Draw 98 Drawing from the Object Type list box. The Object Type list box contains an index of all the OLE applications installed on your system.

For more information about OLE, see Chapter 11.

Why don't I see the New Drawing option on the Picture command's submenu? You didn't install Microsoft Draw 98 when you installed Publisher. Run the Publisher Setup program, choose Customize, and then select the Office Tools option.

Open Microsoft Draw 98

1 To predetermine the size of the Draw object, draw a picture frame. To create a new drawing at the default size, proceed to step 2.

2 On the Insert menu, choose Picture. On the submenu, select New Drawing. The Microsoft Draw 98 application appears, replacing Publisher's menu bar and toolbar. A gray frame appears around the Draw picture.

Draw uses Microsoft Office-style menus and formatting toolbars, which replace Publisher's menus and toolbars. You can dock toolbars (such as the Formatting toolbar shown here) at the top or bottom of the work area.

Resize handles indicate that an object or a group of objects is selected.

The gray frame indicates that the Microsoft Draw object is active and can be edited.

Draw also includes specialized toolbars, such as the AutoShapes toolbar.

The Drawing toolbar, docked at the bottom of the work area, contains standard functions, such as a Rotate tool and quick access to frequently used formatting commands such as Fill Color and Line Style. It also contains tools to create WordArt objects, custom shadows, and 3-D effects.

Use Publisher's Zoom functions. Microsoft Draw 98's Standard toolbar doesn't contain a zoom tool. If you want a magnified view of your drawing, close Draw. Then single-click the drawn object to select it, and use Publisher's Zoom tool to enlarge your view of the object. Double-click the object to open Draw and edit the image. Alternatively, you can use the F9 keyboard shortcut to switch between the current magnification level and the 100 percent view.

Invoke and Close Microsoft Draw 98

1 Double-click an existing Draw object. The Draw menu bar and toolbar appear.

2 Click anywhere outside the gray frame to close Draw and return to Publisher.

Creating AutoShapes

AutoShapes are drawn objects that *look* similar to Publisher's drawn objects. But AutoShapes have built-in functions that make them much more powerful than Publisher's drawn objects, as shown below.

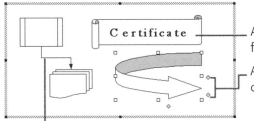

An AutoShape can function as a text frame. Simply select it and start typing.

Adjust handles (which appear as yellow diamonds) let you reshape objects.

You can draw special connectors between shapes that remain attached when you rearrange the shapes.

Microsoft Draw 98 AutoShapes		
Shape	**Description**	**Sample**
Lines	6 tools to create straight lines, lines with arrowheads, curved lines, freeform shapes, and scribbles.	— ↘ ⟲⟿
Connectors	9 tools to create straight, bent, or curved lines that connect two shapes. Connectors attach to special points on the outlines of shapes and remain attached when you move the shapes.	＼ ↳ ∿ ↖

Text frames in Draw. In addition to AutoShapes, you can use the Text Box tool (found on the Drawing toolbar) to draw text frames within a picture. Within a Draw picture, text frames look and function identically to an AutoShape rectangle.

Why aren't the curved lines and shapes in my drawing smooth when I print them? Draw simulates curves with small line segments. At larger sizes and with heavy line weights, the line segments become more noticeable. If you have drawn a curve or a freeform shape, you can add more points (creating smaller line segments) to smooth the curve.

For more information on adding points to an outline, see "Altering Imported Pictures," later in this chapter.

Microsoft Draw 98 AutoShapes *(continued)*		
Basic shapes	32 tools to draw geometric and picture shapes.	
Block Arrows	28 tools to draw arrow shapes.	
Flowchart	28 tools to draw standard flowchart symbols. Publisher identifies each tool with the function it normally represents, such as Predefined Process, Or, Collate, Stored Data, and Terminator.	
Stars and Banners	16 tools to draw scrolls, banners, simple stars, and starbursts.	
Callouts	20 tools to create speech and thought balloons and text frames with built-in pointers.	

Create an AutoShape

1 Open Draw.

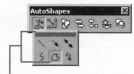

2 Select a category from the AutoShapes toolbar. On the submenu, select the shape you want to create.

3 Within the Microsoft Draw frame (not shown), drag to draw an AutoShape.

Use menu commands to create a WordArt object. You can also invoke the WordArt Gallery by selecting WordArt from Draw's Insert menu.

Combine multiple WordArt objects. As you can see in the following illustration, you can create multiple WordArt objects within a Draw picture frame. Each word or phrase is a separate object. However, when you exit Draw and return to your Publisher document, Publisher treats the collection of objects as a single drawing.

Creating a WordArt Object

Draw offers a WordArt tool that is similar to but more powerful than Publisher's WordArt tool. WordArt objects created in Draw are treated like any other shape, so the sophisticated formatting options available for AutoShapes are also available for WordArt objects.

Create and Format a WordArt Element in Draw

1 Open Draw.

2 On the Drawing toolbar, click the Insert WordArt tool (shown below). The WordArt Gallery appears.

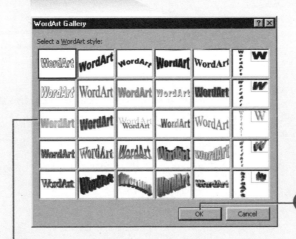

4 Click OK. The Edit WordArt Text dialog box appears.

3 Choose one of the 30 designs in the WordArt gallery. Don't worry if the effect isn't exactly what you want; you can easily change the formatting attributes later.

Can I enter a point size of my choosing into the Size box in the Edit WordArt Text dialog box? No, when you are working in the Edit WordArt Text dialog box, you must choose one of the predetermined point sizes from the Size drop-down list. You can't type a point size of your choosing. However, once you have clicked OK, you can use the resize handles on the WordArt object to adjust the size.

 Can I use a Special Effects dialog box to adjust the angle and arc of a Draw WordArt shape? No. Instead of using a separate dialog box to adjust the angle or arc of a WordArt shape, you drag the special Adjust handle that appears on the boundary of a Draw WordArt object.

Create and Format a WordArt Element in Draw *(continued)*

⑤ Type a word or phrase in the Text box.

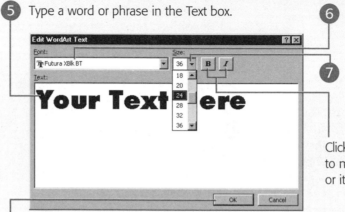

⑥ Open the Font drop-down list and choose a TrueType typeface.

⑦ Open the Size drop-down list and choose one of the predetermined point sizes.

Click the appropriate buttons to make the text boldface or italic.

⑧ When you are satisfied with the text, click OK. Draw inserts the WordArt object and formats it based upon the choice you made in the WordArt Gallery.

Resize or Reshape a WordArt Object in Microsoft Draw 98

① Select the WordArt element you want to change. Resize and Adjust handles appear around the WordArt element, and the WordArt toolbar appears.

To change the size of the WordArt object, drag a Resize handle.

To fine-tune the shape of the WordArt object, drag an Adjust handle.

Why can't I see the WordArt toolbar? You may have inadvertently closed the WordArt toolbar. To open it again, choose Toolbars on the View menu and select WordArt from the submenu. Alternatively, you may have docked the WordArt toolbar. Look for it at the top of the screen (next to the Formatting toolbar). Drag the toolbar's Move icon (the gray bar at the left) to create a floating palette.

Alternate access to formatting dialog boxes. You can also access all of Draw's formatting dialog boxes (for Colors And Lines, Size, Position, Shadow Settings, and 3-D Settings) by choosing the appropriate command on the Format menu.

Change the Format of a WordArt Object in Draw

1 Select the WordArt element you want to reformat. The WordArt toolbar appears.

2 Select tools on the WordArt toolbar to alter the appearance or content of the WordArt object, as shown here.

Click to insert a new WordArt object.

Click to open the WordArt Gallery where you can choose a new preformatted design.

Click to select a new WordArt shape from the submenu.

Click to make uppercase and lowercase letters the same height.

Click to stack letters vertically.

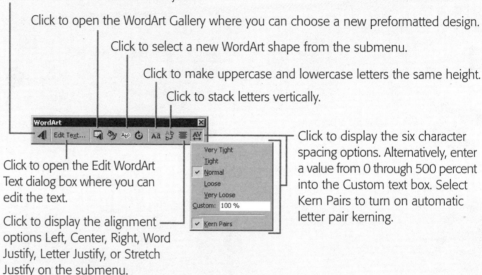

Click to open the Edit WordArt Text dialog box where you can edit the text.

Click to display the alignment options Left, Center, Right, Word Justify, Letter Justify, or Stretch Justify on the submenu.

Click to display the six character spacing options. Alternatively, enter a value from 0 through 500 percent into the Custom text box. Select Kern Pairs to turn on automatic letter pair kerning.

Formatting Options

The formatting options in Draw are much more powerful than the equivalent tools in Publisher. As an example, in Publisher you can fill an object with a two-color gradient. In Draw, you can fill an object with a one-color, two-color, or multi-color gradient. Draw also provides some unique capabilities, such as the ability to customize a shadow effect, extrude an object into the third dimension, or fill an object with a picture.

Choose colors in Draw that match the colors you use in Publisher.
There is only one way to guarantee that the colors you choose in Draw will match the colors you use in Publisher. You must use custom colors and specify exact RGB (or HSL) values.

Why can't I choose a scheme color for an object in a Draw picture? You can't access Publisher's color scheme within Draw. However, once you have closed the Draw application, you can use Publisher's Recolor Object command to assign a scheme color to the object.

To quickly assign a dash pattern or an arrowhead to a selected line, click the appropriate tool on the Drawing toolbar.

Choosing Colors in Draw

1 Select the AutoShape or WordArt object you want to color, or highlight the text phrase you want to color.

2 Select the Fill Color, the Line Color, or the Font Color tool, and choose one of 40 basic colors from the drop-down palette. Alternatively, click More Fill Colors to open the Colors dialog box.

3 Click the Custom tab to specify colors using the HSL or RGB color model.

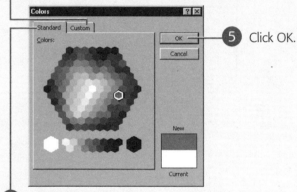

5 Click OK.

4 Alternatively, click the Standard tab, and choose one of 127 colors and 14 percentages of black.

Choose or Customize a Line or Outline in Draw

1 Create or select an AutoShape or WordArt element.

2 Click the Line Style button on the Drawing toolbar. Select one of 13 predefined line styles on the submenu, or click the More Lines command to customize the outline or line.

3 On the Colors And Lines tab (of the Format AutoShape dialog box), specify the color, dash pattern, arrowhead, and weight of the line.

4 Click OK.

What is the difference between a picture fill and a texture fill? Textures are small, seamless, bitmapped pictures that fill objects with a repeating pattern to simulate surfaces like marble or wood. Pictures are images stored in any graphics format that Publisher supports. When used as a fill, the picture is stretched and clipped to the outline of the shape.

Create Fill Effects in Draw

(1) Create or select the AutoShape or WordArt object you want to fill.

(2) With the object selected, click the Fill Color button on the Drawing toolbar. Select Fill Effects from the submenu. The Fill Effects dialog box appears.

(3) Click one of the four tabs.

Click the Gradient tab and choose a one-color gradient, a two-color gradient, or one of 24 predefined multicolor gradients.

Click the Texture tab and choose one of 24 predefined bitmapped textures, such as White Marble or Oak. Alternatively, you can import a bitmapped picture to use as a repeating texture pattern.

Click the Pattern tab and select one of 48 patterns.

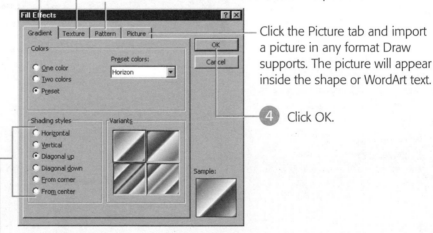

Click the Picture tab and import a picture in any format Draw supports. The picture will appear inside the shape or WordArt text.

(4) Click OK.

You can choose a variant for each gradient that includes both a shading style and a direction.

Choose or Customize a Shadow in Microsoft Draw 98

1 Create or select an AutoShape or WordArt element.

2 Click the Shadow button on the Drawing toolbar. Select one of 20 predefined shadows on the submenu or click the Shadow Settings button to customize the shadow. The Shadow Settings toolbar appears.

Click to toggle the shadow on or off.

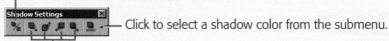

Click to select a shadow color from the submenu.

Click one of these four buttons to nudge the shadow up, down, left, or right.

Why doesn't the front of the 3-D object change color when I select a new color from the 3-D toolbar?
When you select a color from the 3-D Settings toolbar, you change the color of the 3-D extrusion—meaning the sides of the object. In order to change the color for the face of the object, use the Fill Color tool on the Drawing toolbar.

Choose or Customize a 3-D Extrusion in Draw

1 Create or select an AutoShape or WordArt element.

2 Click the 3-D button on the Drawing toolbar. On the submenu, select one of 20 predefined 3-D effects, or click the 3-D Settings button to customize the extrusion. The 3-D Settings toolbar appears.

Click to toggle the 3-D extrusion on or off.

Click to display six preset depths on the submenu or enter a value from −600 to 9600 points in the Custom text box.

Click to display nine directional views on the submenu. You can also toggle between Perspective and Parallel (isometric) views.

Click one of these four buttons to tilt the extrusion up, down, left, or right.

Click to display colors for the sides of the 3-D object.

Click to display four surfaces on the submenu: Wireframe (a 3-D outline), Matte (no shine), Plastic (slight shine), and Metal (very shiny).

Click to display eight lighting directions. You can also toggle between Bright, Normal, and Dim lighting.

Altering Imported Pictures

Just like Publisher, Draw lets you change the appearance of a picture by moving it, cropping it, resizing it, applying a border, or filling the background with a color. In addition, Draw offers tools to edit the individual elements within an imported picture. For example, you can reshape the outlines in a vector drawing or change the brightness and contrast of a bitmapped picture.

 For more information about vector and bitmapped picture file formats, inserting pictures, and using the Microsoft Clip Gallery, see Chapter 10.

Import a Picture into Draw

1. Open Draw.

2. On the Insert menu, select Clip Art to open the Microsoft Clip Gallery or select Picture From File to open the Insert Picture dialog box.

3. Using either the Clip Gallery dialog box or the Insert Picture dialog box, locate and import a picture in any format that Draw supports. The imported image appears in the document and is treated as a single object.

Edit an Imported Vector Drawing

1. Select an imported vector drawing.

2. Click the Ungroup button on the Standard toolbar, or select the Ungroup command from the Draw submenu on the Drawing toolbar.

3. Draw asks if you want to convert the imported object to a Draw object. Click Yes.

4. Click away from the image to cancel the selection of all the individual objects.

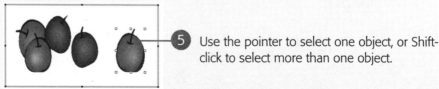

5. Use the pointer to select one object, or Shift-click to select more than one object.

6. Use any of Draw's tools to edit the object. You can move, delete, resize, or rotate the object. You can change any of the formatting attributes for the object's outline and fill.

Why can't I use Publisher's Crop Picture tool to delete part of an imported picture? You can use Publisher's Crop Picture tool (or Draw's Crop tool) to hide part of an imported picture. But you can adjust only the picture frame, which hides outside edges of the image, as seen below. You can't delete an element that overlaps another part of the picture without deleting the underlying element.

When you use Draw to delete part of an imported picture, the changes you make aren't limited to the straight edges of the picture. In fact, you can select and delete an individual object, like a single apple, even when it overlaps other elements in the picture (as shown below).

Alter the Outline of an Object in an Imported Vector Drawing

1 Select an imported vector drawing.

2 Click the Ungroup button on the Standard toolbar, or select the Ungroup command from the Draw submenu on the Drawing toolbar.

3 Publisher asks if you want to convert the imported object to a Draw object. Click Yes.

4 Click away from the image to cancel the selection of all the individual objects.

5 Use the pointer to select one object.

6 Open the Draw menu and choose Edit Points.

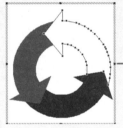

The object is now surrounded by control handles that appear at the vertex of each curve or line segment.

7 Use the pointer to grab a control handle and drag it to a new location, which changes the shape of the object.

Adding and deleting control handles. To add a control handle, press and hold the Ctrl key and click the outline of the object. To delete a control handle, press and hold the Ctrl key while you click the handle.

Why would I want to make a color in a bitmapped image transparent? You may want to create a silhouette effect with a bitmapped picture, where the irregular outlines of the picture's subject appear against the background texture you've chosen for your Web site. In order to create a silhouette, the color that surrounds the picture's subject must be transparent, like the globe shown below. Draw can make only one selected color transparent. This technique doesn't work well when multiple colors surround the photograph's subject.

A bitmapped picture silhouetted against a Web background texture

For more information about transparent .gif images, see Chapter 10.

Change the Picture Quality of an Imported Bitmapped Image

1️⃣ Select an imported bitmapped picture. The Picture toolbar appears.

2️⃣ Adjust the picture by clicking the appropriate tools on the Picture toolbar.

Click one of these two buttons to increase or decrease contrast (the difference between light and dark values) in the picture.

Click one of these two buttons to increase or decrease the brightness (the overall lightness or darkness) of a picture.

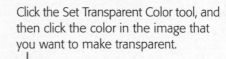

Click the Set Transparent Color tool, and then click the color in the image that you want to make transparent.

Click to reset the picture to its original colors and dimensions.

Click the Image Control button and select one of the four options on the submenu (see at right).

Automatic displays the picture's original colors.

Grayscale converts a color picture to shades of gray.

Black & White converts a color or grayscale image to a high contrast picture.

Watermark lightens the colors in a picture, making it a suitable background for text.

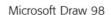

Text for Design Projects

The text that you will need in order to complete the design projects in Part 2 of this book appears below. For line spacing, indentation, and other formatting, refer to the design chapters.

You can also download this text from the Microsoft Press Web site at http://mspress.microsoft.com/mspress/products/1426.

Chapter 19: Postcard Announcement

JA ZZ
The Martin Krump Trio
At City Lights Café
Saturday and Sunday
July 24th and 25th

The
Martin Krump
Trio
Friday, July 24th and
Saturday, July 25th
At 10 p.m.
City Lights Café
449 Harrison Street
Cincinnati, Ohio
Call for Reservations
513-555-2222

Chapter 20: Phonebook Advertisement

Tournament Bikes
Sales, Custom Orders, Expert Repairs

Racing Bikes
Touring Bikes
Mountain Bikes
Children's Bikes
Jogging Strollers

Visit Our
Web Site
www.domain.com

215-555-8989
1653 Newfield Ave.
Norristown, PA 19401

Chapter 21: Résumé

Gregory Lanier
1987 Howe Avenue
Sacramento, CA 95826
916-555-1313
someone@microsoft.com

Objective
To obtain a position as the marketing director of a nationally known furniture and housewares manufacturer.

Experience
1994 to present
Vice President, Tamarind Designs, Inc., Sacramento, California.
Head up the marketing department at this furniture company with gross revenues in excess of $12,000,000 per year. Responsible for market research that drove the development of ecologically sensitive furniture featuring renewable materials, such as bamboo and hemp. Established the exclusivity of the Tamarind brand with to-the-trade-only sales.

1992 to 1994
Senior Marketing Associate, Coward's, LTD., Austin, Texas. Supervised a team of 6 research assistants, copywriters, and art directors at this innovative modern furniture design company. Developed international marketing campaigns for diverse product lines, including the popular Kidz Kraze™ line of children's furniture and the Zen signature collection by Yasuko Takashima.

1987 to 1992
Assistant Director, The James Foundation, Austin, Texas. Served as the second highest officer of the Research Department in this renowned design institution. Supervised an academic staff of 27 researchers and 10 administrative support personnel. Led efforts to document the work of seminal American designers, such as Gustav Stickley, Ray and Charles Eames, and Frank Gehry.

Apprenticeship
1981 to 1987
Assistant Designer, The Vermont Workshop, Manchester, Vermont.

Executed the concepts of senior staff members and guest artists at this crafts collective, well known for its traditional approach to furniture design. Duties included translating rough sketches into presentation-quality drawings and rendering final blueprints.

Education
1980
M.A., Industrial Design, Rhode Island School of Design
1977
B.F.A., Sculpture, summa cum laude, Brown University

Publications
"Marketing Persona Instead of Product," *The New York Marketing Association Newsletter*, Winter 1993
"A Tribute to Michael Thonet," *Collectible Furniture*, Vol. 15, No.2
"The Arts and Crafts Revival," *Collectible Furniture*, Vol. 14, No.10

Professional Associations
Sacramento Marketing Association, Board Member
International Interior Designer's Institute (IIDI), Member
The American Craft Council, Lifetime Member

Chapter 22: Flyer

The 5th Annual
Winter
Festival

Snowman Competition
Toboggan Rides
Snow Boarding
Ice Skating

Ridgewood High School Sports Field
Admission: Adults $5.00 Children $3.00
Sunday January 24, 1999
10 a.m. to 5 p.m.

Chapter 23: Family Web Page

The Clark Family Bulletin

Webmaster
Click here to contact Margaret Clark Russell.

Reunion Time
It's time to finalize the plans for our 4th biennial family reunion. Helen and George are lobbying for San Francisco in October. By October the fog has departed, leaving clear skies and warm temperatures. And there are lots of other things to do in San Francisco, like visit museums or take quick trips to the wine country.

Dave wants to go on a cruise. He has found a reasonably priced cruise that sails from Puerto Rico to Aruba. We'd have to change the date, because October is the rainy season in the Caribbean. But in Dave's words, "A cruise is perfect. You can sun or swim, go dancing after dinner, or indulge at the all-you-can-eat buffet!" Dave has agreed to keep track of everyone's vote. So please call him (not me!) with your opinions.

Becky Nunnelley (though she prefers Becca these days) is entering her junior year in high school. Like her Dad, she's a talented athlete. In fact, she's the youngest member of the varsity softball team.

Grandma Sylvia just got back from a visit with Lori and Mike's family in Minneapolis. Here's her summary of the trip: "The weather was simply spectacular. And all of my grandkids were a blast!"

Patrick Sean Clark II is about to turn 4. He's fascinated with computers, as you can see in this totally adorable picture taken by his Mom. If you're pondering a birthday present for Patrick, think computer games.

As we all know from the last family reunion, Diane is unusually camera shy. But her Dad captured this rare smile for the camera during a Sunday game of touch football. In case you're wondering, her team won.

Click here to contact Margaret Clark Russell.

Chapter 26: Letterhead, Business Card, and Envelope

Alison Chamberlain
Proprietor
Weathervane
Antiques
984 Patriots Way
Concord, MA 01742

Voice: 508-555-6768
Fax: 508-555-6779
Sales: 800-555-5656
Web: www.domain.com

Chapter 27: Mail Merge Letter

Address List

First	Last	Address	City	State	ZIP	Style
Lewis	Abelman	224 Rutledge Road	Concord	MA	01742	Shaker
Joan	Anderson	1440 Cactus Tree Road	Concord	MA	01742	Mission
Craig	Bishop	10 Sylvan Drive	Cambridge	MA	02139	Colonial
Jim	Brown	19 Kings Point Rd.	Concord	MA	01742	Shaker
Roscoe	Chandler	1850 Ingersoll Way	Cambridge	MA	02139	Mission
Sandra	Clark	2246 Boulevard East	Concord	MA	01742	Colonial
Ken	Diamond	159 Mulholland Drive	Cambridge	MA	02142	Art Deco
Margaret	Dumont	12 Rittenhouse Avenue	Cambridge	MA	02142	Shaker
Joe	Ehrlich	1625 Mesa Street	Concord	MA	01742	Mission
Howard	Friedman	200 Ocean Circle	Cambridge	MA	02139	Art Deco
Amy	Harte	36 Fortuna Avenue	Cambridge	MA	02142	Shaker
Dave	Howard	289 Olean Street	Concord	MA	01742	Colonial
Steven	Jackson	153 Palm Court	Cambridge	MA	02139	Shaker
Charles	Jones	19 Emerson Circle	Concord	MA	01742	Art Deco
Jackie	Prescott	1536 Windsor Circle	Cambridge	MA	02142	Colonial
Scott	Resnick	619 Albemarle Road	Concord	MA	01742	Shaker
Edward	Stern	18 Hollingswood Drive	Concord	MA	01742	Shaker
Bob	Taylor	4239 Cardinal Street	Cambridge	MA	02139	Colonial
Judy	Williams	7 Summer Street	Concord	MA	01742	Mission
Steve	Young	114 Franklin Avenue	Concord	MA	01742	Shaker

Letter

<Date>

<First><Last>

<Address 1>

<City>, <State> <ZIP Code>

Dear <First>,

As an avid collector of Shaker furniture, I'm sure you will want to attend an upcoming estate sale here at Weathervane Antiques. This unique event will place no fewer than 40 museum-quality pieces on the auction block. Of course, a substantial collection such as this includes classic Shaker chairs and tables. But it also contains rare items, such as a tailoring counter valued at $85,000. You'll also find utilitarian objects like butter churns, pegged chair railings, and farm tools.

You will have an opportunity to inspect all of the items for sale at our warehouse, which we will open at 10 A.M. and close promptly at 4 P.M. on Saturday, May 22, 1999. If you wish, you can also arrange a private viewing during the week of May 17th through the 22nd by contacting my assistant, Esther Schmindler, at our toll-free number.

We will accept blind bids by mail or fax until 5 P.M. on Friday, May 28th. We will telephone to notify you if your bid has been accepted.

As always, it is a privilege to do business with you.

Sincerely,
Alison Chamberlain
Proprietor

Chapter 28: Professional Web Site

Scuba Currents
Current Tidings
Dive Destinations
Request Form

Current Tidings
A recent survey of our membership list revealed a sharp rise in the number of women divers. Certainly lighter equipment and better buoyancy devices have made scuba more accessible to all sorts of participants, including children, the elderly, and women. But I believe women are diving because they have discovered their need for athletics and adventure.

Of course, there are still some very real barriers that separate women from men on the diving circuit. Only this week, while planning a trip to Truk in Micronesia, I was reminded that remote diving locations are simply not safe for women traveling alone. The diving community as a whole should insist that local governments, tour operators, and hotel chains work together to make every destination safe for divers of both genders.

In the meantime, check out the group trip to Micronesia that provides the perfect mix of good company, protected travel, and sensational diving. Space is limited, so act quickly. You can fill out our new electronic form to request information on our featured trips.

Rebecca Tilson
President

Palau, Truk, and Yap
Sponsored by Scuba Currents, this trip makes three stops on different islands known for their rich marine life and stunning reef formations. Imagine yourself snapping underwater photos of the gray reef sharks at Blue Corner in Palau, swimming with mantas in the Goofnuw channel of Yap, or wreck diving among the Japanese battleships sunk off the coast of Truk. Experienced tour guides and scuba masters make these adventures accessible and safe.

Saba Island
Scuba Currents is now booking a group excursion to Saba, the magical island in the Netherlands Antilles. The all-inclusive dive and travel package features low airfares, a rain forest trek, sea kayaking, and dive certification courses. Experienced dive masters and hiking guides with a personal knowledge of the island's flora and fauna make this an ideal trip for the entire family. The weeklong adventure is scheduled for the last week of November.

Request for Information
Fill out the following form to receive more information about our featured dive destinations.

Name/Membership I.D.
First Name
Last Name
Membership I.D.

Send information about:
Palau, Truk, and Yap
Saba Island

Send information by:
Fax
Your Fax Number
E-mail
E-mail Address

Chapter 29: Mail-Order Catalog

Johnny-Jump-Up
Although these bright purple and yellow blooms look quite a lot like Pansies, Johnny-Jump-Ups are totally edible. The mild flavor is slightly sweet, making Johnny-Jump-Ups a perfect decoration for soft cheeses or cold fruit soups. Try combining goat cheese with Johnny-Jump-Ups and watercress or endive.

You should plant Johnny-Jump-Ups in full or partial sun at the first sign of thaw. You can enjoy both the sight and taste of the flowers in early spring. After the warm weather is over, you can still harvest these edible flowers. Simply order the potted plant instead of seeds. Our hothouse-grown plants will bloom even in the dead of winter.

Johnny-Jump-Up Pricing Table Text

Seedlings (24)	#2243	2.50
Fresh Flowers (1 lb.)	#2235	15.00
Plant in bloom	#2236	35.00

Nasturtium
Only in recent times has Nasturtium, or Tropaeolum minus, been considered a purely ornamental plant. Ancient Persians nibbled Nasturtium petals as early as 400 B.C. And Nasturtiums reached their peak of popularity in 17th Century Europe. The flowers, stems, and leaves of this plant are edible. The flavor is peppery and has a marked similarity to watercress. Indeed, Nasturtium's tangy, slightly hot taste has made it a favorite salad ingredient of Nouvelle-cuisine chefs.

Plant Nasturtiums in the spring. The plants will bloom in summer, but the harvest will last through fall. You can keep cut flowers fresh by floating them in a bowl of water in the refrigerator.

Nasturtium Pricing Table Text

Seedlings (24)	#3243	2.50
Fresh Flowers (1 lb.)	#3235	15.00
Plant in bloom	#3236	35.00

Sweet Violet
A nosegay of Viola odorata is a gift of sweet affection. These tiny purple blooms are, quite appropriately, a symbol of Venus. The Romans fermented crushed flowers to make a sweet wine, but modern-day cooks use crystallized blossoms as an edible decoration for

desserts. And herbalists use an infusion made from flowers to cure insomnia.

Rather than offer seeds, we offer Violet seedlings, which can be transplanted to an outdoor site in spring. Once rooted, these perennials will return to bloom year after year. Indeed, you may find that the runners which Sweet Violets use for natural propagation invade other parts of your garden.

Sweet Violet Pricing Table Text

Seedlings (24)	#4243	2.50
Fresh Flowers (1 lb.)	#4235	15.00
Plant in bloom	#4236	35.00

Chapter 30: Three-Fold Brochure

New World Wines

A shared discovery is a precious gift.

New World Wines
984 Cardinal Lane
Redwood City, CA 94061

Discover the New World
When we first opened New World Wines in 1972, everyone laughed. Imagine...an entire store devoted exclusively to American wine. Now, 26 years later, many people—but especially our customers—applaud our decision. The relationships we've developed in the larger wine community allow us to procure the best of today's premier wines, especially sought-after estate bottlings and limited releases. Our deep knowledge of small producers helps us to discover the great wines of tomorrow.

The staff here at New World Wines participates in regular wine tastings, both to educate our collective palate and to investigate wines as they are released to the market. Occasionally we discover an exceptional wine at an exceptional price. Our new Discovery program allows us to share both the wines and the savings with you by offering a 30% discount on selected wines when they are purchased by the case.

Stonehill Vineyards Heritage 1996

Stonehill Vineyards Heritage is a Bordeaux-style red wine from the San Joaquin valley of California. The wine is not identified by a varietal name because, in the classic French tradition, it blends the juice of several different grapes, including Cabernet Sauvignon, Merlot, and Malbec. Our tasters found the classic berry aromas of ripe cherries and blueberries, with a spicy accent of black pepper.

With a balance of fruit flavors and soft tannins, Stonehill Heritage is ready to drink right now. But this full-bodied wine can also be cellared for the next 3 to 5 years and will only improve with age.

Our enthusiasm for this wine led us to order 200 cases. But, even with a per-bottle price of $20, we expect it to fly off the store shelves. Don't miss this incredible bargain. Place your order today.

Rating: 87

Joshua Creek Gewürztraminer 1997
The Pacific Northwest now produces fine Rieslings and Gewürztraminers in the German style. So our

expectations were high when we opened our first bottle of the Joshua Creek Gewürztraminer from the Yakima Valley in Washington State. We weren't disappointed.

Though light-bodied, this wine is a pale yellow gem. It is packed with fruit accents that include green apple and fresh grapefruit aromas. The youthful, pleasantly tart finish makes it a refreshing summer aperitif or the perfect compliment to spicy Asian food.

The Joshua Creek Gewürztraminer is at its peak right now and ideally should be consumed in the next year. Because Joshua Creek is a relatively unknown vineyard, we can offer the wine at an unbelievably low price. Don't let this remarkable value slip through your fingers.

Rating: 90

Order Form
Item
Quantity
Price Per Case
Total
Stonehill Vineyards Heritage 1996

$149

Joshua Creek Gewürztraminer 1996

$105

Subtotal:
Tax:
Shipping:
Total:
Delivery

Name:
Address:
City, State ZIP:
Daytime Phone:

Payment
Payment Method:
Check
Mastercard
Visa
American Express
Credit Card #:
Expiration Date:

Signature:
*I certify that I am over 21 years of age.

Chapter 31: Newsletter

Broadsides
An inside look at architecture and interior design at Broadside Associates.
March 6, 2000
Volume 8, Issue 3

Inside:

State of the Industry	3
Cosmic Vision	5
The Nuehaus Awards	6
Software Update	7

Broadside Associates Acquires Integrated Space
By Trisha Armstead

On January 30th of this year, Broadside Associates acquired Integrated Space, a cutting-edge interior design firm located here in Redwood City, California. The eight-year-old company grossed over $7 million in commissions last year and has projected billings of $11 million this year. That success is directly attributable to Dick Hunter—the firm's founder and current President.

Hunter established his reputation for innovation with a series of boardroom and executive-suite projects that go beyond utilitarian issues and use interior design to establish the client's corporate identity. He furnished an office with Frank Gehry cardboard chairs for the president of International Corrugated. And in what is perhaps his best known commission, the boardroom at Ridder Labs, Hunter created an eye-popping glass environment inspired by the retorts, condensation coils, and Erlenmeyer flasks found in a laboratory.

Known as something of a visionary in the industry, Hunter's most recent commissions transcend aesthetics and attempt to create a truly beneficial workplace for a company's employees. In recent years, Integrated Space has focused on creating healthier office environments for both new and existing buildings. When asked about this latest crusade, Hunter answered bluntly, "Research has proven that improved ventilation systems, natural light simulations, and ergonomic furniture can substantially reduce absenteeism and significantly increase productivity. Ignoring the office environment is just bad business."

CEO Logan Broadside summed up Broadside Associates' strategy in these words. "The merger with Integrated Space is just the beginning. We are already negotiating the purchase of a landscape architecture firm well known for designing public spaces. While I can't disclose the name of the company or the specifics of our timetable, I can say that Broadside Associates will be a full-service design firm by the end of the year."

Hometown Boy Does Good
As part of a federally funded sweat equity project, Lewis Balthazar, a partner here at Broadside Associates, recently helped restore a 6-story apartment building. Coincidentally, the building is located in Shorehaven, the part of town where Balthazar himself grew up. Balthazar was involved in every aspect of the design and construction. His floor plan brings light and a deceptive sense of space to these small, 600-square-foot apartments. What were once cold-water railroad flats are now modern duplex apartments.

"Though I'm extremely proud of the many commercial buildings I've designed, this project gave me a unique sense of personal satisfaction. I feel I've given something back to the community that nourished me."—Donald Neuman

Index

graphics, importing *(continued)*
  in professional Web site (sample project), 443, 445–46
  in three-fold brochure (sample project), 472
  trapping, 307
  linked, 187, 310–13
    embedding, 311–13
    exporting, 313
  modifying the size and appearance of, 176–78
  OLE objects treated like, 189
  positioning text and, 350–51
  printing hidden pictures, 163
  resizing, 177
  resolution of, 174, 175, 176
  vector, 157–61, 313
    resizing, 382
  in Web publications
    decreasing size of pictures, 443
    inline graphics (GIF and JPEG formats), 199–202
    professional Web site (sample project), 443–46
    text descriptions for, 446
  wrapping text around, 180–82
greeting cards, 25
gridlines, 121
grids
  drawing, 47
  making visible, 461
  setting up, 344
Group button, 49
Group Objects icon, 14

groups (grouped objects), 48–49, 357
  editing text within, 413
  moving, 50–51
  multiple selections compared to, 14
  stacking order of, 55
Group/Ungroup command, 49
Grow To Fit Text command, 122
guides. *See also* layout guides; ruler guides
  toggling the display of, 16
GUI (graphic user interface). *See* Interface, Publisher's
gutter, 45

Hanging indents, 103, 105
headers, in mail-order catalog (sample project), 455–56
headers and footers, 263
headlines
  aligning at the bottom of text frames, 492
  in flyer (sample project), 383–84
Help cursor, 5
Helpful pointers, turning off, 7
Help icon, 8
Help system, 8–9
  on dialog box items, 5
Hide Spelling Error option, 79
Highlight Entire Story command, 72
highlighting important information, 353
Highlight Text command, 120
History folder, 19
home page, in professional Web site (sample project), 443–46

horizontal axis, constraining the movement of an object to the, 147
hot spots (graphic hyperlinks), 212
  ALT text for, 204
  creating, 214
Hot Spot Tool, 215
Hot Spot tool, 212
HSL color model, 271, 272, 277, 280–81
HTML Code Fragment tool, 225–26
HTML (Hypertext Markup Language)
  automatic hyphenation not supported by, 397
  checking the conversion to, 399
HTML (Hypertext Markup Language; HTML documents), 191–93, 206–9. *See also* Web pages (Web publications); HTML documents
  design options for Web pages limited by, 193
  generating an HTML file, 399
  saving form data in, 224
  slow downloads of text, 206
hyperlinks, 191
  adding automatically, 196
  automatically updating, 264
  creating and managing, 211–16
  e-mail, 398
  in family Web Page (sample project), 398, 399
  graphic objects as. *See* hot spots
  removing, 216
  types of, 213
hyperlink text, 212
hyphenation zone, 90, 91, 92, 352

About the Author

Luisa Simone is a New York–based consultant, teacher, and journalist specializing in computer graphics. For the past ten years, she has been a contributing editor for *PC Magazine*, writing about desktop publishing applications, Web authoring tools, presentation graphics packages, illustration software, and multimedia computing. Her second book, *The Windows 95 Scanning Book* (John Wiley and Sons), provides tips and techniques for anyone using a scanner to generate images for desktop publishing, Web documents, on-screen presentations, or high-end film output.

The manuscript for this book was prepared and galleyed using Microsoft Word 97. Pages were composed by Helios Productions using Adobe PageMaker 6.52 for Windows, with text in Garamond and display type in Formata Bold. Composed pages were delivered to the printer as electronic prepress files.

Cover Designer:	Patrick Lanfear
Interior Graphic Designer:	designLab
Interior Graphic Artist:	Helios Productions
Principal Compositors:	Sybil Ihrig, Helios Productions / Ken Yaecker
Technical Editor	Greg L. Guntle
Copy Editor	Kathy Borg-Todd
Principal Proofreader:	Deborah O. Stockton
Indexer:	Maro Riofrancos

See clearly—now!

Here's the remarkable, *visual* way to quickly find answers about the powerfully integrated features of the Microsoft® Office 2000 applications. Microsoft Press AT A GLANCE books let you focus on particular tasks and show you, with clear, numbered steps, the easiest way to get them done right now. Put Office 2000 to work today, with AT A GLANCE learning solutions, made by Microsoft.

- MICROSOFT OFFICE 2000 PROFESSIONAL AT A GLANCE
- MICROSOFT WORD 2000 AT A GLANCE
- MICROSOFT EXCEL 2000 AT A GLANCE
- MICROSOFT POWERPOINT® 2000 AT A GLANCE
- MICROSOFT ACCESS 2000 AT A GLANCE
- MICROSOFT FRONTPAGE® 2000 AT A GLANCE
- MICROSOFT PUBLISHER 2000 AT A GLANCE
- MICROSOFT OFFICE 2000 SMALL BUSINESS AT A GLANCE
- MICROSOFT PHOTODRAW® 2000 AT A GLANCE
- MICROSOFT INTERNET EXPLORER 5 AT A GLANCE
- MICROSOFT OUTLOOK® 2000 AT A GLANCE

Microsoft Press products are available worldwide wherever quality computer books are sold. For more information, contact your book or computer retailer, software reseller, or local Microsoft Sales Office, or visit our Web site at mspress.microsoft.com. To locate your nearest source for Microsoft Press products, or to order directly, call 1-800-MSPRESS in the U.S. (in Canada, call 1-800-268-2222).

Prices and availability dates are subject to change.

mspress.microsoft.com

Stay in the *running*
for maximum *productivity.*

These are *the* answer books for business users of Microsoft® Office 2000. They are packed with everything from quick, clear instructions for new users to comprehensive answers for power users—the authoritative reference to keep by your computer and use every day. THE RUNNING SERIES—learning solutions made by Microsoft.

- RUNNING MICROSOFT EXCEL 2000
- RUNNING MICROSOFT OFFICE 2000 PREMIUM
- RUNNING MICROSOFT OFFICE 2000 PROFESSIONAL
- RUNNING MICROSOFT OFFICE 2000 SMALL BUSINESS
- RUNNING MICROSOFT WORD 2000
- RUNNING MICROSOFT POWERPOINT® 2000
- RUNNING MICROSOFT ACCESS 2000
- RUNNING MICROSOFT INTERNET EXPLORER 5
- RUNNING MICROSOFT FRONTPAGE® 2000
- RUNNING MICROSOFT OUTLOOK® 2000

Microsoft Press® products are available worldwide wherever quality computer books are sold. For more information, contact your book or computer retailer, software reseller, or local Microsoft Sales Office, or visit our Web site at mspress.microsoft.com. To locate your nearest source for Microsoft Press products, or to order directly, call 1-800-MSPRESS in the U.S. (in Canada, call 1-800-268-2222).

Prices and availability dates are subject to change.

mspress.microsoft.com

Register Today!

Return this
Microsoft® Publisher 2000 by Design
registration card today

Microsoft® Press
mspress.microsoft.com

OWNER REGISTRATION CARD   **1-57231-953-4**

Microsoft® Publisher 2000 by Design

_____ _____ _____
FIRST NAME   MIDDLE INITIAL   LAST NAME

_____
INSTITUTION OR COMPANY NAME

_____
ADDRESS

_____

_____ _____ _____
CITY   STATE   ZIP

                                          ( )
_____ _____
E-MAIL ADDRESS   PHONE NUMBER

U.S. and Canada addresses only. Fill in information above and mail postage-free.
Please mail only the bottom half of this page.

For information about Microsoft Press® products, visit our Web site at **mspress.microsoft.com**

Microsoft ® *Press*

BUSINESS REPLY MAIL
FIRST-CLASS MAIL   PERMIT NO. 108   REDMOND WA

POSTAGE WILL BE PAID BY ADDRESSEE

MICROSOFT PRESS
PO BOX 97017
REDMOND, WA 98073-9830

NO POSTAGE
NECESSARY
IF MAILED
IN THE
UNITED STATES